MODERN ITALY

Italy, 1939 boundaries

MODERN ITALY

A Topical History Since 1861

Edited by
EDWARD R. TANNENBAUM
and
EMILIANA P. NOETHER

NEW YORK: NEW YORK UNIVERSITY PRESS · 1974

Rosario Romeo's article has been translated from his *Momenti e problemi di storia contemporanea* (Assisi-Rome: Carucci, 1971) with the permission of the publisher.

A. William Salomone's article is adapted from his article published in *Italica*, 38, No. 3 (September 1961) with the permission of the pubilsher.

To Shepard B. Clough

PREFACE

Before the Second World War Italy was a terra incognita to most Americans. Only a few cognoscenti knew its rich heritage of art, music, and poetry. Others associated it with the *dolce far niente,* a hedonistic way of life by a people whose habits and mores were strangely exotic. A third group identified it with Fascism and saw little beyond this dictatorial oppressive regime. Thus the reality of modern Italy was obscured even further by these one-dimensional interpretations.

The Second World War forcibly brought thousands of young Americans to Italy. In the travail of battle and conquest, these Americans discovered the country and its people, and after the war many returned to study its past and present. Increasingly during the last twenty-five years, American historians, economists, sociologists, political scientists, and anthropologists have turned their attention to Italy. Numerous American universities and colleges now offer courses in Italian history, politics, and culture, and many have established junior-year-abroad programs in various Italian cities. Increased overseas tourism has enabled millions of Americans to acquire firsthand impressions. No longer can Italy be considered a terra incognita. Yet, despite this increased interaction between the two countries and their peoples, it remains difficult to become informed about specific problems and issues in Italian life.

This book aims to fill this lacuna. Arranged topically, it offers its readers a history of Italy since unification, organized around specific issues and problems, rather than narrated in chronological sequence. The diverse problems faced by modern Italy make such a topical treatment more appropriate than it would be for many other countries. Each chapter deals with some aspect of Italian history and is written by an expert who presents a distillation of the most recent scholarship in his or her field. The documentation is designed to provide an up-to-date guide to the literature on modern Italy, as it includes references to the major works on each particular topic. Most of the readily available books and articles in English are listed in the footnotes. Each chapter stands on its own, but cross-references enable the reader to see the relationship among the different chapters. Read sequentially, the book presents an integrated view of modern Italy.

We hope that the breadth and variety of this book will inform the reader about the Italian people—whose history goes back many centuries, but whose identity as a united nation is very recent—and give a broad understanding of their quest for a meaningful place in the modern world.

Numerous people have contributed time and effort to this volume. Unfortunately we cannot thank them individually, but we do want to express our gratitude to Miss Pauline M. Houle, of the Center for Italian Studies, the University of Connecticut, for her invaluable assistance in typing the manuscript.

CONTENTS

INTRODUCTION

Between 1860 and 1870 almost all of present-day Italy was brought under one government, but it took another hundred years for it to become a modern nation. Political backwardness, an antiquated social structure, regional and local differences, a stagnant economy, widespread illiteracy all contributed to the slow pace of modernization. By the turn of the century, parts of the north began to enjoy sustained economic growth, but regional and family attachments limited the ability of many Italians to adjust to the needs of modern industrial society well into the Fascist period. Since 1945 economic and social transformations have catapulted millions of ordinary Italians into the modern world and given them expectations beyond the wildest dreams of their parents. By the early 1970s Italy was approaching the most advanced countries of Western Europe in its levels of industrial efficiency, consumer spending, school attendance, health care, traffic congestion, and pollution. Even such archconservative institutions as the church and the universities have changed considerably during the past few years. Yet, as recent labor disputes and regional unrest have shown, the country's economic, social, and political structures have not been modified enough to make Italy a truly integrated modern nation. In fact, its political system has changed less than most other aspects of its national life.

This fact, along with the diverse but interrelated problems that Italy has faced and still must resolve, makes a topical treatment of its history particularly appropriate. Although each author develops his topic independently, they all address themselves to one or more of seven problems that explain why Italy's modernization was delayed. This delay cannot be attributed to a lack of scientific knowledge and technological and organizational competence, for by the nineteenth century these were readily available, and what Italians did not have, they borrowed from England, France, and Germany. The reasons for this delayed modernization must be sought in the mutually reinforcing handicaps inherited from the past.

The first major problem was Italy's political backwardness, based partly on centuries of foreign domination and disunity and partly on the continuing lags in other aspects of Italian life after independence and unity were achieved in 1861. Second, the limitations of Italy's ruling elites restricted their ability to function effectively and responsibly well into the twentieth century. Third, persistent social antagonisms delayed the integration of all Italians into the national society and the development of a civic culture. Fourth, Italy's economic growth was retarded by an antiquated agricultural system, meager natural resources, and the growing gap between the relatively prosperous north and the impoverished south. The fifth major problem has been an overemphasis on ideology, which has led to divisive factional conflicts, hampered effective political mobilization, and weakened the labor movement. Sixth, until its defeat in the Second World War, Italy frequently pursued a foreign policy beyond its means; efforts to achieve great-power status not only led to traumatic disappointments when they failed, but they also diverted resources and energies badly needed for improvements at home. Finally, despite its spiritual and social contributions, the church exerted a reactionary influence on many aspects of Italian life.

Perhaps the new nation needed greater and more sustained threats to its very existence to prod it into attacking its problems more vigorously. After 1870 the hostility of the Vatican presented no real danger, and during the first decade of the twentieth century it became negligible as the liberal state and the conservative church closed ranks against growing socialist strength. Until the First World War Italy's ruling elites reinforced their dominant position and managed to control the revolutionary impulses of the peasants and the emerging proletariat. When they were no longer able to do this in the crises of the immediate postwar years, the country offered no effective resistance to the Fascist take-over. Although the Fascists displaced the liberal politicians, they actually strengthened the rest of the power structure, particularly the state administration, the church, the army, and big business. The first threats to Italy's existence as an independent, unified nation were the humiliating military defeats in the Second World War and the division and occupation of the country by the Allies and Germany. In response to the turmoil and chaos of the last two years of that war, the Italian people seemed ready for fundamental changes in their way of life. The Armed Resistance in the north against the Nazis and their Fascist puppets was a spontaneous common effort, and many Italians hoped that the spirit of involvement and sacrifice generated in this struggle would carry over into peacetime. But by 1947 this hope was already fading.

Since the late 1940s no external threat or internal challenge has forced Italy's rulers to make needed changes in the country's political, economic, and social structures. Unlike Germany, Italy lost little territory in Europe and was not permanently divided into two rival states. Shorn of its colonies, Italy did not have to deal with the kinds of pressures that the Algerian crisis put on France to modernize its constitution. Italy's political elites certainly recognize the challenges of economic growth and social transformation, with all their implications for every sector of Italian life from education and family relations to urban survival; but, following the example of their pre-1914 predecessors, though somewhat different from them in political inspiration and social origin, they have lapsed into political byzantinism and immobilism. Only some new threat to the established order seems likely to force them out of this mold.

Political Backwardness

Modern Italy had its origins in Napoleon Bonaparte's military conquest in the late 1790s. From that time until 1814 most of the peninsula remained under French domination, and only the islands of Sicily and Sardinia escaped the overthrow of the old regime. Everywhere else, as the French extended their control, the modern system of unfettered private property replaced the traditional system of land tenure, with its common lands and feudal entail. Throughout Italy the lands of the church were sold to the highest bidder. Napoleonic rule also brought centralized institutions, uniformity in local administration, and the selection of government personnel on the basis of merit. It thus created a bourgeois class of functionaries, magistrates, and officials which became imbued with a national spirit and conscious of its new role in a changing political and social order. In the north, for the first time in modern history, an Italian Republic was created, and it soon became the Kingdom of Italy. As the capital of this large state, Napoleonic Milan increased in wealth and importance. It sought to have closer ties with the culture and the scientific and economic progress of the rest of Europe.

Despite a growing sense of national patriotism among many Italians during these years, Napoleonic despotism extinguished all hopes of unity and autonomy in the Italian peninsula. As in Germany, the liberal opposition to French rule was confined to cultural expressions and secret societies. Italy, however, had no independent state like Prussia to lead it in a war of liberation against the French, and in 1815 French power vanished from Italy without any concerted action on the part of the Italians. Moreover, the modernizing reforms of the state and the army that Prussia had instituted in the early 1800s became permanent, whereas the returning

Italian monarchs tried to restore as much of the old regime as possible
in their states.

From 1815 to 1848 Italy's political backwardness was reinforced in
several ways. Regionalism reasserted itself so vigorously that with the
exception of Giuseppe Mazzini, Italian patriots seemed to prefer a loose
federation rather than the unitary state. Many took this position because
federalism seemed the only way of including the Papal States, whose
sovereign was also head of the Catholic church and as such was unlikely
to subordinate himself to any other Italian prince. Austria represented
an even greater obstacle to a united, independent Italy. Not only did it
govern the key regions of Lombardy and Venetia directly, but it also
influenced the Hapsburg princes in Tuscany, Modena, and Parma and
stood ready to send troops anywhere in the peninsula to put down liberal
and nationalist uprisings. Regional and parochial antagonisms were perpetuated by the limited contacts Italians in one state had with those in
other states. Throughout the peninsula poor communication and transportation hampered economic as well as cultural exchanges, and Italy had
nothing comparable to the unifying effect of the Customs Union (*Zoll-
verein*), which Prussia induced most of the south German states to join
in 1834.

The years 1848 to 1861 were the heroic period in the Italian patriotic
movement for national unity and independence known as the Risorgimento, but even then the possibilities available to Italians for political
maneuvering were limited. Again, the parallel with Germany is instructive. The upheavals of 1848 and 1849 in the various Italian states did at
first promote a certain amount of cooperation against Austria, but no
national forum comparable to the Frankfurt Assembly brought Italians
together. After the revolutions of 1848 failed to unify Germany and Italy
under liberal and federal auspices, the leadership of the unification movements passed to Prussia and Piedmont respectively.

In Piedmont, during the 1850s, Count Camillo Benso di Cavour, the
liberal prime minister, did his best to stimulate economic growth and
reduce the influence of the reactionary clergy and nobility. He also
helped to organize an effective public administration, and under his leadership Piedmont became a model nineteenth-century constitutional state.
At the same time its moral prestige grew among Italians because it offered
political asylum to liberal patriots from other Italian states. Austria remained the main stumbling block to both German and Italian unification,
but Piedmont, unlike Prussia, lacked the military leadership and power
to remove the Austrian obstacle to political change. Cavour needed strong
allies, and he found one in Napoleon III. Skillfully he gained military aid
from the French emperor in Piedmont's war against Austria in 1859. As a
result of this war and revolts in Tuscany and other parts of central Italy,

the Kingdom of Northern Italy was formed in 1860. The invasion and annexation of the Kingdom of the Two Sicilies followed swiftly, and in March 1861 the Kingdom of Italy was proclaimed. Even though the French had withdrawn from the war before its goal of expelling Austria from Italy had been achieved, Cavour "paid" them with Nice and Savoy. Meanwhile Venetia remained under Austrian control, and Rome continued to be ruled by Pope Pius IX.

It is pointless to blame the leaders of the Risorgimento for not having accomplished more than they did. Cavour used the diplomatic and military resources available to him as brilliantly as Bismarck in achieving his political ends, but in comparison with Prussia, Piedmont's resources were indeed meager. The demand for an all-Italian democratic constitutional convention by the nationalist conspirator Giuseppe Mazzini was noble but unrealistic in view of the need to present Austria and France with a fait accompli as quickly as possible. Hence, Cavour hastily improvised plebiscites in Tuscany, Emilia, Romagna, and the Kingdom of the Two Sicilies in which the voters were in effect given no choice except annexation to an enlarged Piedmont. These "one shot" plebiscites were poor substitutes for the kind of mass political mobilization envisioned by Mazzini and the military hero Giuseppe Garibaldi. But Mazzini himself had little mass support in Italy, and Garibaldi, despite his spectacular conquest of the Kingdom of the Two Sicilies in the summer of 1860, quickly lost his initial popularity as a would-be political leader. Those critics who blame the absence of mass participation in the unification movement for the alleged ineffectiveness of the new liberal Kingdom of Italy overlook the fact that although the Prussian-led unification of Germany also lacked mass participation, this did not prevent the new, authoritarian German Empire from functioning quite effectively. And those patriots who lament the lack of great military victories probably exaggerate the permanent effect of such victories in rallying most citizens to any political regime.

To cope with the general political backwardness of the country, the liberal regime, which lasted from 1861 to 1922, adopted the French system of political and administrative centralization without the benefit of the French tradition of national loyalty on the part of the masses. Until 1913 it could not even bring itself to give them universal male suffrage. Thus, throughout its existence it was viewed by millions of Italians, particularly in the south, as a kind of institutionalized thief, taking their money in taxes and their young men for military service and seeming to give nothing in return. Its constitution, which was the Statuto promulgated in Piedmont in 1848, had been modeled on that of France under Louis Philippe. It allowed the ministers and deputies to carry out minor administrative decisions and the prefects to determine the outcome of elections and to enforce the law according to the momentary convenience of the politicians in power in Rome. Even more than in France under the July Monarchy, the independence of the judges in Italy was limited by pressures from the executive branch of the government. Italy's constitution also gave the king certain arbitrary powers, particularly in foreign policy, and King Victor Emanuel III has been blamed for using these powers to drag his country, against the will of parliament and the people, into the First World War in May 1915. Again, in October 1922 the king used his constitutional prerogatives to appoint Mussolini prime minister of Italy.

But Italy's old-fashioned liberal constitution was not the main cause of the nation's continuing political backwardness. (After all, the British and American constitutions, which are more old-fashioned in some ways, were adapted to new needs.) The heirs of Cavour, including Giovanni Giolitti, remained too wedded to their bourgeois liberal principles to provide effective leadership in an underdeveloped country that cried for innovative policies. It is true that in the early 1900s Giolitti tried to bring the more moderate socialist and labor leaders into the government, but his motive was not to introduce economic or social innovations and reforms. Rather, he wished to preserve the existing parliamentary system. In 1921 he tried to co-opt the Fascists for the same purpose. Giolitti epitomized the practice by liberal Italy's political leaders of managing Italians rather than leading them. These politicians could not conceive of an opposition party ruling without them. Between 1919 and 1922 their habit of discouraging responsible opposition parties brought about their own undoing when the Socialists and the Catholic Popular party refused to cooperate with them or among themselves in providing a viable alternative to Fascist rule.

From 1922 to 1943 Mussolini and his Fascist regime tried to regiment all classes in the interest of the state. After eliminating the political parties, leagues, and labor unions which had tried to mobilize the lower classes for a real revolution in the years 1919 and 1920, the new regime channeled these same classes into activities such as mass rallies and campaigns, sports, group singing, and the like. Although these activities were politically meaningless, the experience of this pseudomobilization was to have a major effect on Italian politics once freedom of political activity and trade unions became possible again after 1945. This experience was especially crucial for those people who had been brought up in the Fascist schools and youth organizations. Certainly it was the increasing modernization of Italy's economy and society that stimulated the mobilization of the masses in the post-Fascist period, but Fascist forms of regimentation and forced participation in group activities had conditioned people to vicarious participation in political life.

Under Christian Democratic leadership the Italian Republic, created in 1946, quickly evolved into an updated and more pious version of the liberal regime created by Cavour and crystallized by Giolitti. Just as that regime had been an imitation of France's July Monarchy, so the current one resembles France's Fourth Republic, with its game of governmental musical chairs and its immobilism regarding needed reforms. But governments whose main purpose seems to be the preservation of an expanding or contracting center are increasingly unacceptable in the second half of the twentieth century, when all sections of the population demand to be heard. Most of the parties and factions involved in these parliamentary maneuverings have been losing their differentiating characteristics. The resultant lack of real alternatives among the ruling groups has prompted almost 30 percent of the Italian electorate to support the Communists and almost 10 percent to vote for the antidemocratic parties of the extreme right. In a new crisis this kind of protest could turn to more radical alternatives than the ballot box. Modern Italy's political backwardness, though hardly unique, is particularly serious because of its function in preventing the solution of all the other problems that have retarded that nation's modernization.

Limitations of Italy's Elites

Modern societies tend to have four major types of elite rather than one ruling class. Political elites have as their primary purpose the achievement of certain goals in the national polity. To a society's military, economic, diplomatic, and scientific elites falls the task of mobilizing and adapting resources for the achievement of these goals. The third type of elite comprises high-ranking clergy, educators, certain intellectuals, and prominent families; one of their fundamental functions is to help integrate society by exerting their moral authority. Finally, there is a fourth type, which consciously or unconsciously helps keep society knit together emotionally, psychologically, and esthetically; these elites include outstanding figures in the arts, entertainment, and sports.

Italy has developed these four types of elite, but their effectiveness and their sense of responsibility have been limited by the country's other problems since unification. The relative lack of prestige of the political system discouraged many talented people from seeking careers in government; its narrow base and the hostility of the church excluded others. Persistent social antagonisms prevented cooperation and mutual understanding between the dominant classes and the masses. Furthermore, some of Italy's leading politicians and businessmen had a regional rather than a national outlook well into the twentieth century. Economic retardation in turn delayed the appearance of modern technological and managerial elites. Overemphasis on divisive ideologies hampered effective mobilization and collaboration by would-be leaders in many areas of Italian life, as did chronic disputes over foreign policy and the special role of the church in the society as a whole.

The liberal and radical elites of the Risorgimento were often rivals, but their respective heirs did not give the new nation dynamic leadership through coherent political parties. After 1876 the Cavourian right had too narrow a base in parliament to retain power, despite its achievements in dealing with rebellion in the south, foreign threats, an implacable papacy, and financial chaos. Thereafter many of its leading spokesmen adopted a "sour grapes" attitude toward national politics. A few, like Sidney Sonnino, did serve periodically as important ministers through the First World War, but without an effective conservative party behind them they could never give the country a workable alternative to the shifting coalitions of the self-styled left. The most notable Mazzinian-Garibaldian radical to serve as a national leader in the late nineteenth century was Francesco Crispi. By then, however, the leftist legacy of the Risorgimento had lost any inner coherence, and Crispi had become another manipulator of center-left coalitions. The true left was now socialist, and Crispi became its merciless opponent. Like the Communists since the Second World War, the Socialists before the First World War remained outside the national government. And they were much less effective in mobilizing the working classes and controlling local governments because of their interminable squabbles over ideology.

Rather than continuing to militate in politics, a number of those who had been youthful radicals during the Risorgimento became outstandingly successful businessmen in the late nineteenth century. The engineer Luigi Orlando, a former member of Mazzini's Young Italy movement, helped organize the Ansaldo shipping and armaments works. Vincenzo Florio, who had been active in Sicilian patriotic uprisings, was the most prominent figure in the new Italian Line. Giovanni Pirelli, who had fought with Garibaldi, was the founder of the Italian rubber industry. As in most capitalist countries, the first generation of Italy's leading industrialists and bankers had few ties with the nation's political leaders and took a generally negative view toward parliamentary politics. Their outlook was expressed by the conservative Milanese daily *Corriere della Sera*, founded, significantly, in 1876, the year in which the Cavourian liberals were definitively ousted from control of the national government. Until the rise of Fascism, the *Corriere* played an important role as opinion molder of Italy's middle class, and during the early 1920s Mussolini complained about its determination to make its outlook prevail. (Like all other Italian newspapers, it was brought under Fascist control.) Under the Fascists, Italy's second generation of leading industrialists and bankers generally remained aloof from politics and public service. In addition, they lacked the paternalistic tradition found in some of the older industrial countries, and they had particularly bad relations with the labor movement. Only after the Second World War did Italy's third-generation equivalents of the Rockefellers and Fords seek a more active role in promoting national goals, particularly in the Bank of Italy and the state-owned holding companies and utilities.

After 1922 the liberal and radical heirs of the Risorgimento were displaced by the Fascists. Mussolini was a shrewd politician, but his dictatorship failed to produce a new political elite. Part of the reason was that he downgraded the Fascist party to the role of "choreographer" of the regime by the early 1930s. Also, he could not reconcile his mania for making all political decisions himself with his growing indulgence toward the proliferation of rival administrative structures. Giuseppe Bottai, one of his most astute colleagues, compared him to "an electric power station that illuminated one small lamp bulb . . . an energy that dispersed itself and evaporated for want of collecting centers, of links that might articulate it."

By the eve of the Second World War the Christian Democratic political elite that succeeded Mussolini was already being molded by Pope Pius XI's pet lay organization, Catholic Action. During the late 1940s and early 1950s Pope Pius XII and Catholic Action vigorously backed Christian Democratic candidates in elections. At the same time they found themselves at odds with the Christian Democratic prime minister Alcide De Gasperi over the extent of clerical influence in Italian life. After De Gasperi's death, however, many Christian Democratic leaders have fulfilled Pius XI's hope that they would give top priority to the interests of the church, even when these interests clashed with those of the majority of Italians. Furthermore, despite the modernizing outlook of many Christian Democrats, domination by one party has been a serious limitation in recruiting political elites. The only other party with a comparable "cast" of modernizing leaders is the Communist party, and its talents are practically wasted as there is no real hope of gaining power.

During most of the liberal period Italy's ruling elites, outside of national politics and big business, were recruited predominantly from the inexperienced preindustrial bourgeoisie. Only the armed forces and the diplomatic corps remained partly under the influence of the Piedmontese aristocracy. By the late 1860s the government of the new kingdom had evolved an extensive bureaucracy with prefects and local representatives of national ministries, but the highest ranks of this new civil service did not have enough time to develop the degree of responsibility and esprit de corps found in the older bureaucracies in Prussia, France, or Austria. At first the prefects tended to attract dedicated men from the nobility and the upper middle classes, but by the 1880s most prefects had no independent livelihood and hence became increasingly subservient to the political demands of changing ministries in Rome. At the turn of the century Giolitti, who had spent twenty years in the civil service himself, trained a new generation of prefects and senior administrators while he was minister of the interior. The new administrative machine gained sufficient solidity to face and survive the First World War. But bureaucratic management was no substitute for forward-looking political leadership.

Well into the twentieth century the values of the preindustrial bourgeoisie dominated Italy's system of secondary and higher education, thus hampering the selection and training of the kinds of elites needed in a modern industrial society. The country had nothing comparable to the great professional schools (*grandes écoles*) in France or the advanced engineering colleges (*Technische Hochschulen*) in Germany. As in many underdeveloped countries, Italy's law schools attracted the most students, since legal training represented a stepping-stone to politics or the civil service. In its secondary schools the homeland of the Renaissance clung more doggedly to the classical curriculum than any other modern country. But unlike those in France, the secondary schools in Italy did not turn out finished products ready for professional careers. And unlike those in Britain, they did not (except for some of the Catholic colleges) emphasize building character or leadership qualities. From a democratic point of view all those European preparatory schools were detrimental because they perpetuated existing elites and conservative values. The point is that Italy's educational system was more conservative than most and did not produce a competent elite at a time when modernizing leaders were in short supply.

The third type of elite, which helps integrate society through its moral authority, was limited and divided by a number of factors. Italy's reactionary, high-ranking clergy were hostile to the national government during the liberal period and to some extent under Fascism. The nation's leading educators had little influence on or interest in national issues through the First World War. A few achieved prominence under Fascism, but the majority of them turned against that regime sooner or later. Since most leading Italian educators are anticlerical, the Christian Democratic political elite has not given them an important role under the present regime. As for Italy's intellectuals, they have been more consistently opposed to the established order, whatever it has been, than in almost any other European country. The one who came closest to exercising effective moral leadership was Benedetto Croce. But in a society where divisive ideologies were rampant, he was too anticlerical for the Catholics and too conservative for the Socialists and Communists. Italy's prominent families were also divided between Catholics and anticlericals and often limited by regional attachments. The most prominent family of all, the

House of Savoy, had neither the glamour nor the moral authority of the British, German, or Austrian royal dynasties.

In Italy (outside of clerical circles) glamour and moral authority seem to be reserved for stars in the arts, entertainment, and sports. During much of the nineteenth century Giuseppe Verdi tried to be a symbol of Italian patriotism, but his image hardly reached the masses. During the first two decades of the twentieth century Gabriele D'Annunzio used his glamour and questionable moral authority as a one-man elite for the regeneration of Italian society in *his* image and became the archetype of the poet who wore himself (and everybody else) out in politics. Italy has certainly produced its entertainment elite, but not even Vittorio De Sica or Sophia Loren can be said to have helped knit Italian society together in any significant way. Perhaps the most unifying elite has been in the world of sports, namely the national soccer team. But its effect is canceled out by the passionate rivalries between the fans of the local soccer teams contributing to regional divisiveness.

Social Antagonisms

Like the nation's ruling elites, Italian society has lacked cohesiveness since the country's political unification. Although the upper ranks of the bourgeoisie and the economic elite mingled relatively freely with the nobility in Piedmont, Lombardy, and Tuscany, these two classes never constituted a true national aristocracy. Furthermore, their interests and life styles differed markedly from those of their counterparts in the southern half of the peninsula and in Sicily. The patron-client relationship between local notables and poor people in the south fostered a certain degree of stability, but it also promoted gross abuses and exploitation. (So did the underworld arrangements of the *camorra* in Naples and the mafia in western Sicily, whose peculiar code of honor is familiar to many Americans.) In general, noblesse oblige among the higher classes and loyalty among the lower classes were less developed in Italy than in other countries. Instead, most Italians tended to show disdain for their inferiors and servility toward their superiors. They also viewed most relationships as personal ones and usually found it difficult to cooperate in small groups of strangers with common interests.

Class antagonisms were—and still are—compounded by a deep-rooted hostility between northerners and southerners. The north-south conflict remains one of the most divisive in Italian society. In 1860 Garibaldi and a small army of other northerners liberated the south from the Bourbons and turned it over to the House of Savoy. But in 1863 many southern peasants became bandits and for four years tied down another northern army, this time one hundred thousand strong, in a bitter guerrilla war against "Piedmontization." From then until the First World War, while educated southerners like the economist Francesco Saverio Nitti complained about the north's "colonial" exploitation of the south, several million poor southerners emigrated to the Americas in search of work and a better life. Northern leaders, in turn, complained about the lowering of standards in the bureaucracy by an influx of southerners during the liberal and Fascist periods. Most ordinary northerners feared and mistrusted southerners, especially Sicilians, whom they perceived as "Arabs." Since the 1950s these feelings have been heightened by the large-scale movement of southerners into the booming northern cities. Despite the lack of any language barrier, they are segregated and discriminated against in Milan and Turin like Puerto Ricans and Chicanos in New York and Los Angeles.

Cultural as well as social snobbery based on regional differences has delayed the integration of Italian society. While this phenomenon is not unique to Italy, it has added another dimension of conflict to Italian life. Educated Florentines looked down on all other Italians the way educated Bostonians once looked down on all other Americans. And in many underdeveloped regions of the world the inhabitants of a metropolis look down on the peasants in their hinterland in the same way that Neapolitans looked down on the *cafoni* in the rest of the south and Sicily. But the term *cafoni* is more derogatory than peasant or bumpkin, evoking almost subhuman creatures without brains or sensitivity. The Milanese, in turn, look down not only on the Neapolitans and Romans but on most other urban Italians as backward and inefficient.

In most modern European countries the popular culture of the urban middle classes has tended to spread to the masses and help integrate them into the national society, but until the Fascist period this did not happen in Italy. Like England in the nineteenth century, there existed "two Italys" side by side with few real contacts. The Fascist leisure-time organization (Dopolavoro) did introduce Italy's blue-collar workers to such lower-middle-class pastimes as community singing, roller skating, and tourism, particularly in the north. But neither these delights, nor films, nor radio broke down class antagonisms or regional hostilities. Since the mid-1960s the government-owned television network has reached a larger proportion of the population than any other medium, though much of its fare is Euro-American pap with an Italian accent. At least, all those who watch television, irrespective of social or regional origin, economic level, and educational background, watch the same pap. The more prosperous blue-collar workers have recently begun to imitate the white-collar employees in their tastes and buying habits. As Americans well know, however, mere consumerism (passive consumption of mass-produced goods and services) is not necessarily a force for national cohesion.

In Italy, as in other European countries, the nation's political and administrative elites tried to create feelings of national solidarity in more calculated ways beginning in the late nineteenth century. Compulsory elementary education and universal military service were the chief means at first. One argument for Italy's intervention in the First World War was that it would accelerate the process of integration. As it turned out, the very issue of intervention remained a divisive one and helped the rise of the Fascists to power. The Fascist regime tried harder than any other before or since to break down family and local loyalties and promote national patriotism. But its entry into the Second World War and its subservience to Nazi Germany again divided the country and eventually helped the growth of the Resistance movement. From 1944 to 1945 the struggle of the Armed Resistance came closer than any movement in modern Italian history to promoting patriotic solidarity among different sections of the population, at least in the north. As so often happens, however, once the common enemy was gone, the old domestic antagonisms reappeared.

The politicians who have been running Italy since the Second World War have also failed to integrate conflicting groups into the national society. Their anticommunism has alienated a large minority of the population, and their recent efforts to promote national solidarity by giving each region a greater voice in its own affairs have had mixed results at best. The inhabitants of Reggio Calabria deny any other center in their region the right to political or social parity, and their resistance may be repeated as each new region is assigned its capital. And so it goes. City against city, region against region, class against class, Communist against anti-Communist, Italy remains a divided society.

Economic Retardation

One of the greatest obstacles to the transformation of Italy into a modern, integrated nation has been economic retardation. Industrialization alone does not guarantee national cohesion, as Canada and Belgium have learned to their chagrin. This has been the case even when there are no language barriers, as in the British Isles. Nevertheless, traditional societies cannot be modernized until the majority of the population moves out of agriculture into industrial and service occupations. Only in these sectors can sustained economic growth take place. And Italy's economy did not begin to grow at a rate comparable to that of other industrial countries until the end of the nineteenth century.

On the eve of the First World War Italy remained primarily a land of peasants, illiterates, and emigrants. Fifty-eight percent of the work force were still peasants; 38 percent of the total population were still illiterates. The annual departure rate of emigrants reached a peak of 873,000 in 1913

—out of a total population of 37 million. Not until 1930 did the value of industrial production overtake that of agriculture. Not until the Second World War did the agricultural sector of the work force begin to drop drastically, from 48 percent in 1940 to 18 percent in 1973.

A basic cause of Italy's late economic development was the meagerness of its natural resources. Only half of the land is cultivable, thus limiting the amount of foodstuffs that can be produced. The country is even poorer in mineral deposits. It has practically no coal or iron, so crucial for industrialization in the nineteenth and early twentieth centuries. Natural gas, Italy's most important known mineral resource, did not play a role in economic development until after the Second World War. The one resource developed before the First World War was water power for electricity.

Difficulties in internal transportation also retarded Italy's economic growth. There has always been traffic between the major seaports, but only the Po River is partially navigable for small vessels, and all land routes extending the entire length or width of the peninsula are cut at least once by mountains. The railroad network, completed in the early twentieth century, could not entirely make up for the lack of canals and the isolation of many smaller communities, particularly in mountainous areas. Not until the late 1960s did new provincial highways make daily bus service possible for many remote southern villages and ease the problems of truck transport.

Although improvements in transportation and the exploitation of new energy resources have reduced the burden of a poor resource base, modern Italy has remained dependent on the vagaries of foreign trade and investments. For one thing, it has never had agricultural surpluses to export in return for imports of needed raw materials for industry. In fact, its agricultural productivity was so low that it had to *import* food beginning in the 1870s. During the late nineteenth century and periodically thereafter, foreign loans to industry and the state reduced the deficits in the balance of payments, but short-term capital movements in and out of the country frequently subjected the economy to severe financial strains. Beginning in the early 1950s Italian exports of manufactured goods skyrocketed, providing for the first time adequate foreign exchange for the purchase of needed raw materials. But in the early 1970s these exports began to lag owing to relative declines in production and productivity caused in part by labor unrest.

Another factor that partly delayed Italy's industrialization was a weak banking system. Not until the 1890s did ministers like Giolitti and Sonnino institute reforms that gave Italy a reasonably strong financial structure which provided monetary stability and a solid basis for industrial expansion. In addition, to develop its armaments and public utilities the government itself was a major customer of heavy industry at that time. In turn, the taxes it imposed in order to make these expenditures limited the ability of private industries to expand. This situation improved in the early twentieth century, but another crisis occurred during the depression of the 1930s. To save what remained of the existing economic system, the Fascist government reorganized the financial structure and assumed part of the role that the industrial-credit banks had played previously. Thus, it was able to coordinate government policy and industrial expansion more effectively. Only since the Second World War, however, have changes in the financial system and state-owned holding companies been used to preserve rapid growth and relatively stable prices.

Until the 1950s Italy's economic growth was retarded by the limited demand for its goods, both at home and abroad. In the early 1900s the blue-collar workers began to buy consumer goods with their slightly improved real wages, but they were still spending almost half of their income on food alone throughout the Fascist period. And the bulk of the nation's peasants were too poor to provide a mass market for anything. This was true in the north as well as the south.

After 1860 the contrast between growing poverty in the south and increasing prosperity in the north was also a persistent cause of the economic backwardness of the country as a whole. Conditions deteriorated in the south after unification for a simple and obvious reason: the local population grew at a faster rate than the economy. There were 6.7 million people in the south in 1861 and 12 million in 1901. Mass emigration until the First World War partially alleviated southern poverty, but during the interwar years the economic gap between the north and the south continued to grow. This problem is not limited to Italy, for other modern nations have had their backward regions and a dualistic economy, part modern and part traditional. But during the first half of the twentieth century these differences began to narrow in countries like the United States, Germany, and France. Only in the second half of the century has this begun to happen in Italy. This economic dichotomy has not only retarded the nation's overall economic growth, but it has also reinforced the political, social, and cultural antagonisms between the north and the south.

Ideological Movements

Liberalism, nationalism, socialism, communism, fascism, and Christian democracy have helped modernize many nations all over the world. Why, then, have they contributed so little to the modernization of Italy?

One reason is that except for the Fascists no regime has had the allegiance of the majority of politically aware Italians long enough to make them accept a new ideological course. We have already noted the failures of liberalism and its abject surrender to Fascism; yet even in its heyday under Giolitti, liberalism faced growing opposition from anarchists, revolutionary syndicalists, socialists, nationalists, and Catholic ideologies of both the right and the left. Even liberals could not agree among themselves. Giolitti rejected the argument of more conservative liberals like Sonnino and Antonio Salandra that Italy's intervention in the First World War would rally the opposition behind the liberal regime. This strategy of Sonnino and Salandra actually aggravated socialist and Catholic opposition without gaining the permanent backing of the nationalists.

Intervention and nonintervention themselves were converted into ideological issues, and they continued to divide the country during the immediate postwar crises. The Fascist regime certainly tried to give Italians a new ideology, but aside from nationalism, it offered contradictory goals to different classes and failed to live up to most of its promises. Since 1945 Christian democracy has been the dominant ideology of all Italian governments, but, like the liberals before them, its leaders have been divided among themselves and have devoted more effort to co-opting people from other parties into the system than to putting their principles into practice.

Within the ranks of the Christian Democratic party ideological differences have led to the formation of factions or currents whose leaders jockey for positions of control in the party apparatus. The result of this factional strife has been immobilism within the party for the past few years, and those Christian Democratic leaders who have wanted to put through positive, dynamic government programs have often been hamstrung. Fearful of losing the support and votes in parliament of one or more factions within their own party, they have brought its immobilism into the government itself.

Although Christian democracy has tried to promote modernization for thirty years, earlier Catholic ideologies had a preindustrial, antimodern bias. This was so even among the precursors of the Christian Democrats in the early years of this century. Romolo Murri, whose movement emerged at the turn of the century, was a kind of Catholic agrarian socialist. Like the Social Revolutionaries in Russia, he favored a brave new world based on agriculture rather than industry. The Popular party, led by Don Luigi Sturzo in the years 1919 to 1923, also concentrated much of its effort at mass mobilization among the rural workers. Other Catholic movements were more conservative and clerical. The Opera dei Congressi, which flourished between 1874 and 1904, was frankly paternalistic and had built its program of social action on regional ties that were of declining relevance to a national economy. In 1931, Pope Pius XI, in his encyclical *Quadragesimo anno*, exalted the type of corporativism developed by nineteenth-century reactionary Catholic thinkers. He also promoted clericalism by urging Catholic Action to train laymen to help expand the influence of the clergy in all aspects of public life. Between 1948 and 1952 Catholic Action tried to push Christian Democracy into an open alliance with the parties of the right and to make it adopt conservative solutions to pressing national problems. Catholic Action remains an effective force, but it no longer overtly attempts to dominate Christian democracy. The main conflicts are now among the factions within the party itself.

Until the Second World War the ideologies of the left—particularly revolutionary syndicalism, socialism, and communism—played a predominantly negative role in promoting the modernization of Italian society and the integration of the working masses into that society. At the turn of the century the revolutionary syndicalists and socialists vied with one another for control of the budding labor movement in the northern cities. Revolutionary syndicalism rejected political action through parliamentary parties and advocated working-class emancipation through organizations composed exclusively of workers. In Italy in the early 1900s it favored the Chamber of Labor over the trade union. The Chamber of Labor, organized on a territorial rather than occupational basis, represented the interests of all working people on the local level and appealed to their local loyalties. As a result, a metal worker in Milan felt closer to a carpenter, a printer, or even an office worker in his own city than to a metal worker in Naples or Bologna. Such feelings delayed the development both of a national working-class consciousness and of strong national trade unions until the end of the First World War.

The Socialists, on the other hand, concentrated on organizing the "aristocracy" of skilled workers from the top down in national federations of trade unions beginning in the early 1900s. Thus they too were remiss in promoting a working-class consciousness among all workers, despite their party rhetoric and interminable doctrinal disputes over how best to accomplish this Marxist task. From 1919 to 1920 most Socialist-party and trade-union leaders were swept along by the class-conscious aggressiveness of two million raw recruits driven by the material hardships and rising expectations of those years. The leaders of both the Socialist trade unions and the Socialist party were divided between revolutionaries who proclaimed the revolution without making it, and reformists who proclaimed the need for compromise without compromising. Furthermore, most Socialists failed to understand—as Lenin did—the demands of the peasants for land, thus missing the opportunity to rally the more radical peasants to the Socialist cause. And their doctrinaire anticlericalism prevented them from attracting radical Catholics.

The ideological battles within the Italian Socialist party and the breakaway of the Communists in January 1921 further weakened the ability of any Marxist party to mobilize the working classes against the counter-revolution, which was sparked partly by their own revolutionary rhetoric. Communist baiting of Socialists occurred everywhere in the 1920s in obedience to the international party line. But it had disastrous effects in Italy, for it helped the Fascists gain power. From 1924 to 1944 the Communist and Socialist parties ceased to have any influence in Italian life. It was the Armed Resistance in 1944 and 1945 which allowed them, along with the Christian Democrats, to reappear and compete once again for the leadership of the working classes.

Many critics argue that since 1945 the emancipation of the Italian workers has been hindered rather than helped by the subordination of the labor movement to ideologically oriented political parties. To be sure, the postwar Communist party has succeeded far more than its predecessors in mobilizing the working classes politically and even socially in its mass organizations. And where it has controlled municipal governments it has helped them considerably economically. But by the late 1960s its use of the trade unions under its control for political purposes—particularly in connection with the "cold war"—had little appeal to a new generation of workers who were primarily interested in their own economic and social improvement. These new, less ideologically oriented, workers included large numbers of former peasants, southern immigrants, young northern workers, and women. During 1968 and 1969 these "new workers" rejected the remote top leadership of the Communist party and the union bureaucracies and organized their own Unitary Base Committees in their factories for the purpose of forcing concessions directly from their employers through nationwide strikes. The success of their efforts marked the emergence of labor as a major power in Italian society. Whether or not the new labor militancy and power will sustain itself, it seems to have ended the traditional preoccupation with ideology in the Italian labor movement.

Foreign Policy

Preoccupation with ideology has also influenced Italian foreign policy since the national awakening during the Risorgimento. The Kingdom of Italy as constituted in 1861 had come into being with considerable foreign help, and it needed more such help to acquire Venetia and Rome during the next decade. Cavour's liberal heirs bided their time and thwarted the nationalist hero Garibaldi when he tried to liberate papal Rome in 1863 and again in 1867. Meanwhile, in 1866, Italy had joined Prussia in its war against Austria but had made such a miserable military showing that it had to accept the Austrian province of Venetia from

Prussia and France. Finally, in 1870, Prussia's defeat of France forced the French to remove their garrison from Rome. Regular Italian military forces were thus able to make the papal capital their own, and their "storming" of its eastern gate on September 20 was henceforth celebrated as a national holiday.

From 1870 onward many government leaders felt the need to follow a foreign policy that would establish Italy's great-power status in more than name only. In order to achieve this goal they had to associate their country with one or more of the other great powers. Here, too, the choice involved both ideological and practical considerations. On the one hand, the Cavourian right retained its affinity for France, not only out of loyalty for past services but also because it viewed France, even under the Third Republic, as more civilized than the brash new German Empire. On the other hand, a number of former Garibaldians, including Crispi, admired Germany's dynamism and power, despite its authoritarian political system. The deciding factor, however, was France's occupation of Tunisia, where Italy had its own colonial ambitions, in 1881. A year later Italy joined the alliance between Germany and Austria-Hungary, which henceforth was known as the Triple Alliance. Then, in 1896, Prime Minister Crispi launched the military conquest of Ethiopia, which ended in another humiliating defeat. In 1911 Prime Minister Giolitti took advantage of the Franco-German crisis over Morocco to begin the conquest of Libya, this time with some success. But, as we have seen, he opposed Italy's intervention in the First World War on the side of the Triple Entente, which the nationalists viewed as their biggest chance to get the "unredeemed" territories of Trieste and the Trentino from Austria and to gain a leading place in the new Europe that would emerge after the defeat of the Central Powers.

Despite the fact that these goals were largely achieved, disappointments over the "mutilated victory" persisted until the rise of Fascism. The Fascist regime continued to regard foreign policy as an expression of national power and pride, and when Italy finally conquered Ethiopia in 1936, it claimed to have reestablished the Roman Empire. The popularity of this achievement among the Italian people in the face of the opposition of Britain, France, and the other powers showed how important this conquest was in helping them overcome their feelings of inferiority after years of having been treated as a second-class power. Then Italy again allied itself with a brash, dynamic Germany, first by intervening in the Spanish Civil War, then by entering the Second World War as its junior partner. It was Italy's overwhelming defeat and occupation during that war that finally ended its efforts to gain international prestige by an aggressive foreign policy.

Social imperialism as well as nationalism influenced Italian foreign policy during the liberal and Fascist periods. Nowhere was this clearer than in the way Italy used colonial adventures in Ethiopia in 1896 and Libya in 1911 to divert attention from revolutionary unrest at home. This ploy was commonplace among all the major powers in the 1890s and 1900s and in part motivated the powers, including Italy, to enter the First World War. While there was no overt domestic unrest when Mussolini attacked Ethiopia in 1935 and brought Italy into the Second World War, there was much dissatisfaction over poor economic conditions. To bolster public support he used the pre-1914 nationalists' argument that Italy was a vigorous "proletarian" nation with a right to spoils from the decadent capitalist nations, principally Britain and France.

It is easy in retrospect to condemn Italy's overambitious foreign policy in view of its failures, but many Italians made more telling criticisms even before these failures occurred. They argued that the various manifestations of this policy wasted resources needed at home. During the 1880s and 1890s the large government expenditures on the army and navy, demanded by military leaders and King Humbert I, may well have delayed capital investments in industry. Italy's military effort during the First World War weakened the nation's economy far more than similar efforts weakened the economies of the wealthier powers and was in part responsible for the unrest of the postwar years. During the late 1930s Mussolini's aggressive foreign policy and his economic nationalism favored the armaments industry but caused shortages and unemployment in those branches of the economy that depended on foreign trade, once again subordinating domestic welfare to the demands of national pride.

Since 1945 Italy has become one of the staunchest supporters of European cooperation. Stripped of its colonies and committed to a relatively small military establishment, it has put economic growth at the top of its priorities. Its membership in the European Economic Community (Common Market) undoubtedly helped this growth. On the one hand, the EEC freed a much larger market for Italian goods from trade barriers. On the other hand, Italian manufacturers were forced to improve their productivity in order to meet competition from other European manufacturers. Also, the Common Market reduced restrictions on labor mobility, thus allowing large numbers of Italian workers to acquire technical training and find high-paying jobs in Germany, France, and Belgium. Their remittances helped Italy maintain a favorable balance of payments, and the newly acquired skills of those who returned home represented a costless rise in the value of the nation's human resources. No longer the poor relation, Italy has found its true international prestige within the European community. And along with Pepsi-Cola, Fiat was building plants in the Soviet Union in the early 1970s.

The Church

The fact that for centuries all popes have been Italians residing in Rome has given the church a special role in Italian life, but church backing for Italian government policies is a recent development. From the Risorgimento until the Lateran Accords in 1929 the Roman Question kept the church and the state permanently apart. Until the pontificate of John XXIII the church continued to resist change, and it partially revived its conservative stance under Pope Paul VI.

It all began with Cavour, who wanted "a free church in a free state," first in Piedmont, then in the new Kingdom of Italy. In 1864 Pope Pius IX vigorously asserted the opposite view in his *Syllabus of Errors.* This document not only opposed the separation of church and state but also condemned the whole liberal outlook. When the Italians occupied Rome in 1870, Pius IX declared himself a "prisoner in the Vatican" and refused to recognize Italian sovereignty over that city and its environs. In 1874 his *Non expedit* forbade Catholics to participate in parliamentary elections either as candidates or voters. It is still an open question whether Catholic abstentions (and not all abstained) helped or harmed the liberal regime. But the church's formal opposition to that regime certainly did nothing to help mobilize support for it among Italians with a traditionally negative attitude toward all governments. No Dreyfus case arose in Italy to unite half the nation in support of a liberal government. During the 1890s Italy's liberal leaders had to direct considerable attention and energy in defense of the secular state without much popular backing. Indeed one reason that they hesitated to extend the franchise for so long was fear that doing so would increase clerical influence in national politics (the *Non expedit* notwithstanding).

Although the Roman Question and church-state relations have posed major problems for successive Italian governments, they did not necessarily hinder the process of modernization. On the one hand, the church provided education and job training, networks of communication, and social relief, thus stimulating the process of change even when seeking to slow it. Lay activities sponsored by the church gave millions of Italians their first (and often their only) experience of how to combine and to act in their own interests. They taught the techniques of organization, propaganda, demonstration, and coercion necessary for influence in a complex, mass society. On the other hand, the church precociously exposed the weaknesses of modernization as an ideal and presented the process itself as an alien imposition, the result of foreign ideologies and special interests. In 1891 Pope Leo XIII recognized the need to cope with some of the adverse economic and social effects of modernization in his encyclical *Rerum novarum,* but the solutions he proposed were based on a backward-looking paternalism and corporativism. (We have already noted the reassertion of this view forty years later by Pope Pius XI.) Not until Pope John XXIII's encyclical *Mater et magistra* (1961) did the Vatican repudiate these solutions—still advocated by Catholic Action— and endorse modern means of achieving social justice and economic well-being. This encyclical also urged that the disinherited be finally integrated into the social and political order.

Since the Lateran Accords, in 1929, the church has regained much of its traditional influence in Italian life. Not only was Catholicism once more recognized as the official religion of the state, but religious instruction was restored to the schools, and the church regained some influence on censorship and public morals. In 1946, when the constitution of the present republic was being debated, even the Communists voted to preserve the Lateran Accords. Undoubtedly the church's influence has fostered, and has been aided by, the predominant position of the Christian Democrats in this republic. Yet, aside from this new rapport with Italy's political elite, the presence of the church has remained deeper, more varied, and more pervasive than is generally recognized. Despite the small percentage of practicing Catholics, Italian views of marriage, the family, and social justice, along with Italian cultural values and education, have remained very largely Catholic. In the end, this is what it means to say that Italy is a Catholic country.

Conclusion

The special role of the church in Italian life highlights the problems of transforming a traditional society into a modern one. As in Spain and France, the clergy consistently supported reactionary political elites until the Second World War. Although the church did not oppose the activities of Catholic trade unions, it clung to the outmoded ideologies of clericalism and corporativism, which did little to emancipate the workers as a class and integrate them into the national society. It also delayed the emancipation of women economically, socially, and sexually. The need to oppose clericalism not only divided the Italian people but may also have intensified many of their leaders' preoccupation with doctrinal and ideological disputes to the neglect of practical solutions. In recent times the doctrinaire anticommunism of the church and the ruling Christian Democrats delayed constitutional reforms such as those concerning regionalism out of fear of giving the Italian Communist party more power. It also perpetuated the alienation of those Italians who believed that communism could do a better job of transforming Italian society.

As the following chapters show, the Italians have often been their own worst enemies. The Risorgimento itself was not just a series of national wars against Austria but also a succession of civil wars in which there were Italians on both sides. Indeed, in 1866, Italians from the Austrian province of Venetia probably made up the bulk of the crews in the Austrian navy that defeated the Italian navy. The conquest and pacification of the south in the 1860s left scars that took almost a century to heal. And insofar as the Risorgimento was a revolution, it failed to remove important enclaves of counterrevolution, particularly the papacy and an outmoded system of land ownership. Other modern nations have been divided along regional, class, and religious lines, but few others have taken so long in eliminating or reconciling the opponents of progress. In the late 1960s and early 1970s Italy's wage earners were just beginning to confront their employers with demands that had been granted decades earlier elsewhere. The die-hard opposition of these employers—including the state—exacerbated the conflict and halted the steady economic gains of the preceding years. Increasing violence and crime in the streets made Italians more suspicious of one another than ever. Many people in all classes began to long for authoritarian leaders to tame troublemakers and make the public services function smoothly again. Others reasserted their cynicism about anything ever being done properly in the permissive, bumbling, and mildly corrupt "Italian-style."

Yet the chapters in this book also show that when sufficiently challenged, Italians can get things done in quite another style. From Garibaldi's Thousand to the Armed Resistance they have demonstrated their ability to fight bravely and effectively for a convincing cause. The same industrialists who took such a reactionary line with their workers were able to flood the European market with automobiles, refrigerators, and typewriters. Even the Southern Question has finally been tackled with a sustained effort by the government. The challenge of modernization once led Italy into Fascism, which repressed those sections of the population it could not win over. Today one can hope that the nation will cope with its problems by putting the interests of all its people into the balance.

PART I

POLITICS AND IDEOLOGY

Modern Italy has had an agitated political life, complicated by the persisting and disruptive role of ideology. Since the beginning of the past century, when liberals and nationalists began to plot and agitate for a constitution, independence, and unity (in that order), Italians have tried to achieve a viable and modern political system. But so far, it has eluded them, and political backwardness has continued to characterize Italian life. Not even during the Risorgimento, when the achievement of independence and unity should have imposed a common political effort, did Italians agree to set aside their ideological differences. From 1860 to 1922 one of the reasons for the failure of liberal Italy to carry out needed social and economic reforms was the regime's unwillingness to meet the demands of the masses. It preferred to rely on repression, bribery, and chicanery. Fascism, political Catholicism, and Marxism have all used ideology as the basis for political power. For twenty years Fascism mobilized the Italian people and forced them to march in step; at its end, it had altered the Italian way of life very little. Christian democracy, the political face of Catholicism, has evolved a modern party, but internal dissension inhibits action and leads to parliamentary immobilism. Marxism, its strongest rival, is split in various factions among which the Communists gather the largest popular vote, while the Socialists and Social Democrats struggle for the crumbs from the Christian Democratic government table.

The five chapters in this section trace the vicissitudes of Italian political life since 1815. A. William Salomone discusses the ideological conflicts among the leaders of the Risorgimento and brings out the pragmatic ability of Cavour to use the various ideological factions to serve the ends of Italian political unity. Salvatore Saladino traces the complicated course

1

of parliamentary politics in the liberal era from 1860 to 1914. For Saladino, the first decade of the twentieth century, when Giovanni Giolitti was in power, represented the high point in this period. Roland Sarti illustrates two possible interpretations that can be given to Fascism: Was it a revolutionary force working for the modernization of Italy, or was it the reaction of the old order to the challenges of the years after the First World War? He concludes that while many Fascists did initially see Fascism as a modernizing force, Fascism failed to achieve real changes in Italian life. Elisa Carrillo and Norman Kogan deal with Christian Democracy and the Marxist parties respectively. Today, these are the two major forces in Italian politics, and structurally the Christian Democrats and the Communists can be considered modern political parties. Both, however, have been involved in internal struggles that are ideological only in part. So far, neither party gives any evidence that it will be capable of resolving its problems and of providing effective political leadership for the country.

CHAPTER 1

STATECRAFT AND IDEOLOGY
IN THE RISORGIMENTO
THE ITALIAN NATIONAL REVOLUTION *

A. WILLIAM SALOMONE

The idea of the historic unity of Italy is an antinomy wrapped in a paradox. From the Renaissance to the Risorgimento Italian history unfolded in a manner that confounds the most flexible logic. Through four long centuries Italy was transformed from a unique center of European cultural and spiritual life into a geoeconomic frontier region, to reemerge at last as a political entity within a new complex of European international forces. By the end of the fifteenth century the particularistic politics of the Italian Renaissance had apparently struck at the roots of a universalist culture, just as the European culture of the mid-nineteenth century nourished the soil of the new national politics of Italy.[1] The myth of historic unity seemed strangely elusive even as it was always subtly and vitally at work trying to sustain the self-identity of a people. And yet the genuinely historical problem persists as to why Italy's forcible alienation from the European system of power in the sixteenth century took so long to be converted into a self conscious and full-fledged return within the European community of culture.

Nowhere else in the West had the promise of an early national-political unification been more apparent than in Italy. Again and again, however, the promise faded, the hope was lost. Despite (or perhaps because of) other, more glorious, cultural and spiritual achievements, "Italy" had remained a palpable shadow, a splendid mirage. Torn by local struggles for power and hegemony from the time of Dante to that of Machiavelli, Italy persisted as a lyrical vision of poets, the creature of the fantasy of dreamers, and then as the elusive prize of the demonic politicos of the Renaissance—Gian Galeazzo Visconti, Ladislaus of Naples, Cesare Borgia. Machiavelli, the most disingenuously passionate philosopher of politics in the history of modern Europe, grappled with a myth and lashed ferociously at an idea that would not become flesh. Blind to the signals of advancing disaster, Renaissance Italy was ground to pieces, mercilessly, before his very eyes, the victim of the conquering rapacity of upstart national states that had chosen other roads to power and cruder forms of domination.

It is easy to regret but still difficult to comprehend why Italy's historic tragedy was allowed to occur. Was there so grave a flaw, so obscure a defect, so congenital an imperfection in that fertile Italian intelligence of the Renaissance that it could more easily explore the mysteries of life, create wondrous new worlds of art, reconstruct philosophic systems than build necessary dikes against mundane civil disaster? Was it the fault of excessive individualism, nurtured as it was by the sterile and erosive particularism of political leaders and a premature overconsciousness of the disenchanting nature of politics? Or was perhaps a secret, narcissistic worship of intellectual *virtù* the inescapable price that Italian genius had to pay for its incomparable achievements in the luminous spheres of culture, art, and civilization? Whatever the answer, the historian can only acknowledge that the gates to catastrophe for Renaissance Italy were opened from within and from without: through them broke the flood of foreign arms and the contests of foreign masters.

At the close of the fifteenth century and during the early sixteenth century, Italians had found themselves confronted with a frightful dilemma: the choice of becoming real makers of politics, masters of their political fate, or of remaining pure children of culture and civilization. Unexpectedly faced with the alternatives of either power or culture, Italians had little time, found no opportunity, were given no other chance to break the chains of the historic dilemma. The glory of the Renaissance became fraught with the tragedy of Italian politics. While Europe was becoming more political and national, Italy turned more toward cultural, spiritual, and universalist preoccupations. Nino Valeri has beautifully formulated the tragic dilemma:

> The sentiment of belonging to a single republic of intelligence united the spirits of Italian artists throughout the world, united them in the name of the arts and of poetry, in the respect for the highest values of the spirit. . . . A wave of human sentiment of solidarity overflowed everywhere, carried by culture above political vicissitudes and wars for supremacy. . . . A new phase of the eternal conflict between civilization and power was opening in which the most spiritually refined nation of Europe ended by succumbing to the superiority of means and the politico-military organization of the great monarchies of the West.[2]

Undoubtedly, in choosing cultural universalism and spiritual imperialism over the political nationalism and dynastic expansionism of the Western states, Italy assured its permanent title to greatness within the civilization of the West. Was not the price disproportionately great? The Italian worlds within worlds of Pico della Mirandola, Machiavelli, and Michelangelo were pitilessly sucked into the dark vortex of the European power struggle waged for more than half a century upon the soil of Italy. Whatever the causal connection, the crisis of Italian political freedom became associated with the twilight of Renaissance civilization. Through a dreary time of trouble and conflict Italy was slowly crushed, body and spirit. From this tragic waning of the Italian Renaissance to the dawn of the Risorgimento not all the lights were put out in Italy, and some still shone brightly. But a great Italian day had ended.

In the age of Galileo the splendor of the Italian baroque became matched by the advancing decay of Italian society. Political servitude paved the way for religious conformity; economic decadence also brought moral passivity. The Italian political and social ruling classes of the late sixteenth and seventeenth centuries were on the whole content to live in peace in the shadow of a church they could no longer control and of states dominated by foreigners. Intellect and fantasy continued to flourish, and they alone survived as the last possible ramparts of pride for a defeated people. Indeed, the passionless marriage of intellect and fantasy brought forth the same trinity of culture-reason-beauty which had tragically failed Italy as tutelary spirits during the historic crisis of the Renaissance. Ironically, the post-Machiavellian generation of political thinkers lay bare the arcana of "reasons of state" even as their Italian mentors had dismally foundered as practitioners of constructive statecraft.

The Italian "heretics against all faiths"—who, with Castellion, the Socini, and Alberico Gentili, sought to transform rationality and the law of nature into norms for a religiosity beyond ritualism and into bases of a peaceful coexistence of contrasting creeds—found themselves uprooted and dispersed, prophets without honor on their Italian soil. The rebel Italian philosophers—who, with Bruno and Campanella, strove for a novel *pax philosophica* as the foundation for a human solidarity in serene utopias—became prisoners of their own visions without hope and then the tragic victims of the new Italian order founded upon civil and political quietism and authoritarian-philosophic conformism. And even Galileo, the incomparable architect of the new science of the universe, was momentarily broken by the iron discipline of a still-triumphant traditionalism. At the same time, however, the splendid examples of his master-method and his discoveries were eagerly accepted by the European mind, which, in Newtonian form, turned that new science into a channel of a revolutionary vision of nature, the foundation of an organic secular alternative to an ancient system of philosophy, and, if with violence to its essential character, into a premise of those rationalistic ideologies that kept European societies in ferment through the age of the Enlightenment.

During the seventeenth and eighteenth centuries Italy had indeed survived as an active element of Western civilization. Even through the "crisis of the European consciousness," so keenly dissected by the historian Paul Hazard, the Italian "republic of intelligence" thrived as it was transformed. But at the same time Italy had become more and more estranged from the center of Europe's newer social, civil, and political order.

In the European world of struggles for power and ideas, clashes of dynastic ambitions and economic interests, wars for self-preservation or hegemony, Italy was a marginal frontier region. In a "Europe without heroes" Italy had the appearance of a land without history. As the European Leviathans—the modern states, monarchies, and empires—rose and fell, clashed and grew, political Italy sought refuge and repose in that long, dreamlike sojourn in Arcadia from which it was tentatively shaken by the enlightened despots of the eighteenth century and then suddenly roused by revolution in France. From Machiavelli to Alfieri many a prophet and poet had espied Italy's tragedy in all its frightful range, and with fierce passion had tried to sweep away the shadows and tear off the veils with which Italians obstructed their vision of the world. But theirs were voices crying in the wilderness, unheeded, misunderstood, and rejected.

The stirrings of a new life in Italy nevertheless preceded and were then precipitated by the French Revolution. Those historians who still insist on viewing the French Revolution and Napoleon as the first or sole agents of the beginning of political redemption for Italy are, at best, guilty of factual inaccuracy and, at worst, the victims of an ideological illusion. During the second half of the eighteenth century, Italian thinkers were already participating in the general European Enlightenment, with its search for rational solutions to social, political, and economic problems, while farsighted statesmen, reformers, and experimenters were trying to introduce the principles of enlightened despotism. But it was only the coming of the Revolution and of Napoleon to Italy which changed the direction, accelerated the tempo, enlarged the scope, defined the goals, and laid new foundations of the Risorgimento. Undoubtedly, the French invasions and the Napoleonic conquests of Italy could be, and frequently were, viewed as little more than the exchange of one domination for another. But under the old regime Hapsburg and Bourbon domination had not altered the traditional structure of Italian society, whereas the revolutionary and Napoleonic upheavals, for all the exploitation and civil dissension they brought, gave Italy a legacy of experiences and ideas which marked the point of no return to a past without promise.

If at first this legacy seemed only to expose the failings of Italy's ruling classes, it also pointed the way to a new idea of Italy. This new idea was born of the clash of intelligence with necessity, of the war waged by desire upon reality, and of the irrepressible conflict between history and myth. Now the master-ideas of Italian philosophers living and dead—Machiavelli, Vico, Romagnosi—were vivified and fused with the great currents of European thought; soon they were adopted as secular guides toward an historic transformation, the "redemption," the "reawakening" of Italy. By themselves, however, the discovery of Italy and the dream of redemption might have remained indefinitely separate elements in a scheme without threads, counterpoints and variations without theme, a vision without hope, had not a third discovery been made—of the harder stuff that molds peoples into nations.

Faintly at first and then more and more clearly, Italians began to perceive some of the deepest secrets at the heart of modern politics. Thus they gradually learned that culture was in fact a function of life. They at last understood that thought and action are moments, inseparable aspects of a single vital process. They sensed that ideology had become a subtle instrument of statecraft and glimpsed the most mysterious secret of all, the great secret of Machiavelli: power was indeed demonic, but it was also bifrontal, stamped on one side with the signs of human corruption but bearing on the other the symbols of freedom's shield.

Thus, despite the diversity of interpretation and emphasis which each of these three discoveries was eventually given, together they constituted the true ideal foundations of the Italian Risorgimento. A variety of vicissitudes was inevitably connected with the attempts at their application. A series of violent contrasts among new ideological creeds, political means, and institutional objectives subsequently broke out in Italy, each claiming exclusive rights toward the realization of the Risorgimento. Moderatism, liberalism, radicalism, republicanism, neo-Guelphism, socialism, federalism—all sought to lead the Italian revolution. Ultimately, therefore, those discoveries alone persisted as common master-doctrines, the new spiritual bonds of a nascent Italian community, the bedrock of a moral consensus toward the making of a national revolution.

Not fatality but the subtle historic logic of the deep crisis of the Italian consciousness guaranteed the ultimate failure of the Restoration in Italy. With the fall of Napoleon in 1814, the old order returned to Italy in its most repressive and uninspiring forms. Metternich's Austria, the requirements of the European balance of power, the fear of revolutionary subversion, all reinforced reactionary rule in Italy. The old rulers—the pope, the dynasts, the princes, the generals, the hierarchs—came back to their citadels of power and privilege in Milan, Florence, Rome, Venice, Bologna, Naples, and a dozen other cities and regions of Italy, lulled by bittersweet remembrances of things past and protected by barrages of soldiers, informers, and spies. Gripped by fear, weariness, and despondency, the people witnessed their return but did not applaud.

The men of the post-Napoleonic Italian generation were indeed tired of wars and adventurers and liberating demigods who had come to impose new taxes and to send their children to die in distant battlefields. A convulsive age had taken its toll of Italian energies, and, for the moment at least, it seemed that peace, any peace, was preferable even to the most fertile innovation that called for strife and sacrifice. The restoration of ancient law and order offered the illusion to the Italian people that the throne and the altar, hierarch and dynast, priest and policeman were the sole true pillars of the peace of Italy.

Yet not all men, not all classes of Italian society, were so oblivious to the history of Italy as to deny the lessons of the recent revolutionary experience. To be sure, the peasantry—and it was the vast majority throughout Italy—had not understood the revolutionary ideas, except perhaps as these ideas masked familiar tyrannies, new forms of old oppressions. But there were groups of men throughout Italy, particularly in the more urban north, who quickly espied in the return of the old order the end of all Italian hopes and of their efforts toward moral renovation and material progress, the death of their dream of a free, independent, and perhaps united Italy. Limited in numbers and resources as they were, the emerging Italian middle classes, the younger intelligentsia, and members of a liberal aristocracy saw themselves overwhelmed by the reimposition of the old political and moral order, reduced to inferior positions or impotence in society, and excluded from any active participation in government by the restored princely aristocracy, both native and foreign. It was thus chiefly through their persistent discontent and then through their tenacious labor and open or secret agitation that the Italian revolution and the larger Risorgimento of Italy, which was its ideal historic context, assumed the form of an epic movement of liberation.

Undoubtedly the drawing up of a standard honor roll of the leaders of the Risorgimento would only elaborate the obvious fact that almost all of them came from the Italian liberal middle classes, intellectual and professional groups, and the lower aristocratic orders. On the other hand, to understand the social and ideological dynamics of the politics of the Risorgimento, the student must penetrate somehow beneath the surface of the chronology and choreography of that epic movement to its basic historical meaning. But this meaning should not be reduced to a phenomenon of social and economic dynamics, a sort of precapitalistic revolution of the Italian bourgeoisie, or nothing but a civil war between the old and new ruling classes. Few serious students would now be so obtuse as to deny the great part played by the social struggle and economic conflict in the Italian national revolution. Nevertheless, an absolute equation between the Risorgimento and any one of its aspects through any monolithic interpretation of its historical actualities cannot but prove to be either an absurdity or historiographical politics. Such equations have frequently been attempted, but only on the level of ideological bias, of conscious purpose or unconscious desire.

For over a decade after the end of the Second World War both the Italian and non-Italian historiography of the Risorgimento were astir with challenging, often enlightening, revaluations and reinterpretations of Italian unification, with special emphasis on the economic and social problems it involved or raised. The publication of Antonio Gramsci's *Prison Notebooks*, containing his vast and acute reflections and his Marxist interpretations of Italian history and culture in general and of the Risorgimento and united Italy in particular, brought a strong gust of fresh historiographical winds, but also controversy, polemics, and new ideological problems. The Gramscian exegesis contributed in exceptional fashion toward drawing the Risorgimento once again within the greyish zone that lies between politics and history. Apparently the most genial, certainly the most seductive, of Gramsci's historical interpretations was that which led him to see the Risorgimento as "a complex and contradictory historical movement" that ultimately amounted to a new, perhaps decisive, historic defection of the Italian ruling classes: a sort of great betrayal of the cause of the agrarian masses by the Italian "Jacobins"—radical leaders and Party of Action of the Italian revolution. For Gramsci the Risorgimento was essentially an agrarian-proletarian revolution that failed.

In the extensive exegetical and polemical literature on the Gramscian interpretation of the Risorgimento, an interesting connection has not so far received sufficient attention. Gramsci's reflections on the Risorgimento were indeed serious and impressive, based as they were upon a vast and often profound reading of Italian history and guided by a disingenuous Marxist methodological and ideological inspiration. But they were not as original in form as they at first appeared. The fact is that stripped of its economic-dialectical-ideological trappings, the Gramscian interpretation reveals at its core a forceful variation on a kind of model concept frequently adopted by unorthodox interpreters of Italian history. This is the recurrent idea that Italian history at its critical, crucial moments "failed" to realize the potentialities, the promise, intrinsic to the historic situation. Each moment of crisis in Italian history—be it identified with the Renaissance, the Reformation, the Jacobin Revolution, the Risorgimento, the

Democratic Revolution, the Industrial Revolution—is seen as resulting in essential, organic "failure."

In this manner, the history of Italy becomes subsumed under the negative concept of the *rivoluzione mancata*—the failed revolution.[3] The link with the past, this pessimistic vision of the Italian historic development maintains, is recurrently deviated but not broken, the channels to the future obscurely but forcibly obstructed. From Machiavelli to Mazzini, from Edgar Quinet to Francesco De Sanctis, from Carlo Cattaneo and Giuseppe Ferrari to Piero Gobetti and Mario Missiroli, and from Gramsci to the neo-Marxist ideologues as well as to a few non-Italian contemporary interpreters, the history of Italy appears, *mutatis mutandis,* as a series of *rivoluzioni mancate,* a chain of revolutions that failed or missed, that never really occurred or were betrayed, or that at any rate were all eventually "transformed," Italian style, into defections or reactions. *Trasformismo* is thus raised to the unenviable dignity of an exclusively Italian historical paradigm. The reductio ad absurdum of this position is that the history of Italy is so uniquely antihistorical that the student's chief concern should be to analyze and document that which did not actually occur in Italian history.

Certainly more serious is the argument that the Risorgimento was not and perhaps could not be altogether divorced from the open or unconscious pursuit of some self-interest on the part of its leaders, whether as individuals or as members of economic, social, and political classes. According to Denis Mack Smith, "The making of Italy was to prove a victory for the intellectuals, the liberals, the middle classes; *not* for the uneducated . . . *not* for the poor . . . *not* for those who lost a paternal, protective ordering of society . . . *not* for the Catholic masses. . . ." "—*not*, in a word, for the ordinary people" of Italy.[4] But, legitimate as such assessments of the success and failure, of the victory and defeat in the Risorgimento might be judged on a subjective, personal basis, they risk a reduction of the history of the Italian national revolution to something it was *not* and perhaps could not be. Highly suggestive of an admirable moral sense, a fine democratic *forma mentis,* a sort of liberalizing tendency in the revaluation of modern Italian history, such judgments also imply a view of the Risorgimento as a simplified arithmetic problem, a ledger of assets and liabilities, the tallying of the score at the end of a fairly uncomplicated game. And such judgments are also problematical in reference to the fundamental point as to what the Risorgimento really was, what it intended, attempted, and achieved.

Occurring within a particular context of European developments and within a special set of Italian realities and possibilities, the Risorgimento was not a bloc. Ends and means in its history must be carefully assessed; conscious purpose, desirable results, and unpredictable consequences must be distinguished. Thus the Risorgimento need not be put on trial and visited with even the most praiseworthy biases of a later generation in order to receive historical justice. Perhaps a paraphrase of a great historian's exhortation to polemicists might not be inappropriate in this connection: Risorgimentalists and anti-Risorgimentalists, we beg of you, for pity's sake, please tell us simply what *was* the Risorgimento.

Far above the fantastically contradictory series of episodes—revolutions, conspiracies, battles—and above the complicated succession of programs and alternatives, the clash of interests, and the persistent conflict of ends and means which are associated with the Risorgimento through its classic phases, three fundamental characteristics emerge clearly: its multiplicity, continuity, and universality. Contrary to those who would petrify it into a monolith, a static and particularistic historical bloc, the Risorgimento sprang from many sources, thrived through many elements. It rose, evolved, moved almost ceaselessly in many directions—conservative and radical, republican and monarchial, federalist and socialist, utopian and realist. It expressed its objectives in many ways, for different people, for Italy and for Europe, in fact and in promise. The Risorgimento revealed multiplicity in its expressions, continuity in its development, universality in its significance.

Unique as an experience of the Italian people, the Risorgimento was nevertheless a function of the evolution of modern Europe. Extraordinary as an episode in the history of the nineteenth century, the Risorgimento and the creation of the unitary state were positive achievements, despite the series of failures with which they were punctuated in their origins, in their development, and in some of their consequences. On all three of *these* levels there were indeed shadows aplenty about them: dark moments of error and defeat, examples of chicanery and deceit from many quarters, strange touches of blood and iron, wild fits of anger and rancor, fearful individual suffering and collective violences, terrible repressions and outbursts of dangerous self-righteousness, matchless blunders and unspeakable tortures, acts of barbaric injustice, hatred, and recrimination, and often terrible calamities for the defeated of party and class. Yet these things, many of which also appeared in the unification and national liberation of other European countries, were far surpassed by the tenacity and courage of two generations of modernizing "new" Italians of almost every social class, political persuasion, and ideological creed.

Above and beyond the dark side of the Italian national revolution there were acts of incredible valor and heroic resistance to oppression, to persecution and ostracism; and the self-sacrifice of the flower of Italian youth from the cities, the shops, the schools, the universities—an essential rectitude, a consistent devotion to a cause by the angry young men who incorrigibly defied Austrian whip, Bourbon prison, Papal anathema, bloody barricades, uneven battle, and bitter exile. Strange but true, catastrophe found a sort of mysterious way of being converted into challenge and into a springboard toward renewed effort. In a larger sense, therefore, the multiplicity of the Risorgimento may be said to have been a function of a new unity of Italian purpose, seeking, beyond political and ideological antagonism, to reassert Italy's right to freedom in the context of its cultural heritage and its newer vital needs.

Recurrently, the contrasting hopes of national liberation and those multiple forces at work in Italy were smashed in the teeth of disaster. Failure could easily give the impression of having been a built-in feature of the Italian national revolution. In fact, it would seem almost natural to believe, on the basis of the recurring disparity between revolutionary effort and immediate result, that the Risorgimento can be equated only with the achievements of its apparently conclusive phase during the *biennium mirabile* of 1859 to 1861. If this were really, completely true, the heroic trinity of the Risorgimento, Cavour-Garibaldi-Mazzini, would have to be canonized as the greatest miracle workers in the secular history of modern Italy, perhaps of modern Europe. Yet nothing would have been more alien to their nature, expectations, or desires; nothing would perhaps have been further from their self-appraisal of their work, life, and missions; nothing certainly would have been more contrary to their differing but acute sense of the background and realities of the Italian national revolution.

The sentiment of an ideal continuity in the Risorgimento, once its historic necessity and novelty had been assumed, was keen, even when not always openly admitted, in all its major leaders. Cavour himself, in what proved to be the swan song of his amazing career, in a speech delivered in the first parliament of newly united Italy on March 27, 1861, testified to that sentiment. Pricked to the quick by the forbidden word "conspirator" hurled at him by Giuseppe Ferrari, one of his most persistent and loquacious opponents sitting on the left of the Chamber, Cavour calmly replied:

> Using a rhetorical expression and referring to a noun that it seemed this Chamber did not wish to hear, the Hon. Ferrari added that he had no love for conspirators, not even when they sit on the bench of the prime minister. The Hon. Ferrari has thus done me the honor of considering me among the conspirators. For this I should like to thank him and to take this occasion for declaring to the Chamber that I was indeed a conspirator for twelve years. Yes, gentlemen, for twelve years I devoted all my strength to being a conspirator: I conspired in order to achieve and realize my Country's independence.

But I conspired in my fashion, a singular fashion, by proclaiming in the press, before the entire Parliament, in the Councils of Europe, the very purpose of my conspiracy. I then continued my activity by searching for fellow-conspirators and I discovered that they were all or almost all members of this Subalpine Parliament. I then found brother-conspirators in practically all the provinces of Italy. In recent years very nearly the whole *Società Nazionale* has taken up with me. And today I conspire in the company of twenty-six million Italians.

In 1846, not twelve but fifteen years before Cavour's proud assertion of his participation in and leadership of that open Italian conspiracy, Massimo D'Azeglio, another member of the Piedmontese group of liberal-moderate *notables,* had exhorted "all good Italians" to join with him in an "open protest against the injustices from which we suffer" and had invited them all to conspire with him in this barefaced conspiracy completely out in the open. But still further back, in 1831, fifteen years before D'Azeglio's own bold challenge to Italian and European public opinion, Giuseppe Mazzini had openly issued an ardent, fruitless appeal to an Italian dynast, Charles-Albert of Piedmont, inviting him to place himself at the head of the Italian national revolution:

Sire! . . . Place yourself at the head of the Nation and write upon your banner: *Union, Freedom, Independence!* . . . Declare yourself the vindicator, the interpreter of popular rights, the redeemer of all Italy. Liberate the Motherland from the barbarians! . . . Be the Napoleon of Italian freedom! . . . Let posterity say of you: *He was the first among the new Italians, the last of the tyrants of Italy.*—Choose!

Mazzini's appeal of course proved preposterously premature. In a sense which he could not and did not suspect, that Mazzinian appeal, its very ineffectuality in that form and at that moment, and through its almost immediate conversion into a genuinely revolutionary master-idea, may be taken as the well-nigh perfect, the ideal document of the paradoxical continuity in the apparently episodic "progress" of the Risorgimento. Just as at an almost equally desperate moment in his own life and in the affairs of Italy, Machiavelli had quickly returned to his primordial idea of a people defending its own freedom, so now had Mazzini, the self-conscious anti-Machiavelli of the Risorgimento, founded the *Giovine Italia* as a means of stimulating popular action. For he was the irremovably antidynastic demiurge, symbol, and instrument of a republican, democratic, and popular Italian national revolution.

And the ways of the Risorgimento were to prove indeed mysterious, the irony of Italian history exquisitely resourceful. In March 1861 a Machiavellian statesman, Cavour, crowned his cautious dynastic work with the investiture of a prince, son of Charles-Albert, as first king of united Italy. But beyond all antinomies, it was Mazzini who constituted, represented, cemented the ideal continuity of the Risorgimento. Risorgimento Italy was Mazzinian before it became anything else. Mazzini's "failure" lifted the Risorgimento to a sphere that reduced all the successes of his opponents to momentary victories. For he had envisaged and struggled for a free and democratic Italy as part of a new order of spontaneously constituted national states which would be the foundation of a United States of Europe. To create this Europe became his self-appointed task through a lifetime of devotion to an ideal. But ultimately he went much further and engaged in desperate pursuit of his last magnificent illusion: the truly anti-Machiavellian mission of rejoining politics to a new morality. In this, his true "failure," Mazzini joined the ranks of the tragic protagonists of universal history who have failed in Promethean missions.

During the less than forty years that passed between the fall of Napoleon in Italy and the rise of Cavour in Piedmont, there appeared a new generation of active, hard-working, middle-class Italians. Their cohesion and strength varied within each of the more than half a dozen separate Italian states. Yet by the eve of the Italian revolutions of 1848, the organization of their resources and energies, the tentative fusion of their ingenuity and ambitions had brought about startling changes in Italian economic, social, and moral life. The fact was that a new, unofficial political class, a potential ruling elite, had slowly emerged from their midst. The bulk of mid-nineteenth century Italian liberals, however shaded or divided in their ideological outlooks and political program, stemmed from this new class which, for practical reasons, ranged from a Count Cavour on the liberal right to a Carlo Cattaneo on the radical left. Mazzinian ideology cut both vertically and horizontally within and across this class, but it was not the only one to do so.

Bound as they were by similar economic interest in land, commerce, and, partially, industry, related by common intellectual preparation and an awakening European outlook, and drawn together by a common anti-feudalistic, increasingly bourgeois social consciousness, the liberal middle classes of the various Italian states came to possess one fundamental common denominator: a reformist, constitutional, limited political objective. But their generous illusions had not prepared them for the Bacchanalia of demonstrations in the wake of the election of the reforming Pope Pius IX in 1846 or, less than two years later, the outbreak of real revolutionary activity in the cities and even in the countryside of both the north and the south. The dilemma of Italy's liberal leaders involved the alternatives of either quickly assuming the direction of the "hot" revolutions or of being overwhelmed by them and then seeing their hopes for Italy smashed between democratic radicalism on the left and military reaction on the right. Fearing war, they wanted to avoid the revolution; dreading the revolution, they thought of avoiding war. They assumed the direction of the revolution and they were overwhelmed.[5]

In 1848 Italian liberalism had to drop the last veil to reveal its glowing national soul—but too much and too early. All of the problems of Italian and international politics which the moderate liberals had tried to wish away during their own experiment at a "cold revolution" now at last came to enmesh them and brought them down to defeat. The Pandora's box of the Italian national revolution broke open with cruel violence in 1848. From within it there burst forth in the face of the liberal leaders the nightmarish visions of a sorcerer's apprentice: the figures of faith-breaking princes who, with one exception, would not be Italian and of the pope who could not be an Italian patriot; hesitations and equivoca-tions in the international policy of liberal England and republican France; threats or at least suggestion of possible reprisals by not so distant tsarist Russia; the military might of Austria in the Lombard plains and then the smashing defeats on the battlefields of Custoza and Novara; barricades and blood and terror and the anger of the people in the streets of Milan, on the hills of Rome, on the lagoons of Venice; peasants' revolts, violent seizures of land, and heavy-handed repressions in the Kingdom of Naples; and then the cries of betrayal and treachery mixed with the calls for democracy, the Republic, socialism, and the dreaded convocation of an Italian Constituent Assembly.

The years 1848 and 1849 were indeed full of wrath, great hopes, and tragic defeat for Italy. No political class, not even one tested in the fire of a longer experience than the Italian liberals possessed, could have leashed all the contradictory forces and elements at work in the Italian revolution. A total and irreversible failure appeared to have overtaken the Italian Risorgimento. For now, it seemed, all efforts, however heroic, all programs, however carefully planned, all ideals, however sacred, lay shattered on the barricades and the battlefields of Italy. The disastrous defeat of the Italian revolution of 1848 brought a second Restoration upon Italy. Soon it called for a reexamination of the whole set of alterna-tives that had been tried and found wanting for a realization of the Risorgimento.

A self-probing by the Italian national conscience made some things quite clear while others remained obscure. Most obscure was the fate of Italian democracy, which had been allowed to fall at the barricades by its friends and enemies at home and abroad. Quite clear was the fact that the pope had finally retracted his impossible Italian patriotism; that Piedmont had been beaten in the field and its Hamletic king Charles-Albert had left for self-imposed exile; that the Bourbon king of the Two Sicilies had forgotten nothing and learned nothing but was somehow back in power; that the French troops of the Second Republic and Louis Napoleon had generously "liberated" Rome—from Mazzini, Garibaldi, and Pisacane; that Austria had put down in blood the Milanese and Venetian revolutions and was back in force on the plains of Lombardy and in the formidable Quadrilateral. Anger and despondency gripped Italy, as did fear and repression, which led to the dispersion of the best among her new leaders. Exile was once again a familiar Italian road: in 1849 and 1850 it led to London, Paris, Zurich, Lugano, and New York. From these asylums Italian patriots of many political faiths and shades of opinion—with Mazzini, Cattaneo, Montanelli, Pisacane, Garibaldi, and Gioberti towering among them—planned, dreamed again, and worked for a return to the unfinished business of the Italian revolution.

In the meantime, at home in Italy, Italians learned to extract small but life-giving fires from the ashes of their disaster. Soon these fires lighted their way to unsentimental revaluations of their recent calamities. And thus many came to see the essential problems of the new day in sharper focus. The realm of the realizable became more distinct from that of the desirable. The all-or-nothing atmosphere of 1848 and 1849 was perhaps tragically but necessarily dispersed. In the grey aftermath of defeat, the Italian vanquished turned their faces toward the future.

Pure ideas were too much, force alone would not be enough. The Italian liberal middle classes learned slowly and painfully that in such a world as Italy lived in, a shield of statecraft might be an absolute, if costly, requirement for the realization of their ideals. Political force, warfare itself, if necessary, would not betray their dream of an Italian bloodless revolution if realistic leadership kept liberty on its banner and was ready to impose the right of a people to live in freedom. After mid-century, Piedmont came to supply that force, and Cavour assumed the mantle of leadership which Italian liberals had sought in vain for so long within their own divided ranks or in creatures of their own imaginations.

In less than a decade Cavour beat, molded, and transformed a tiny state on the territorial and cultural periphery of Italy into a magnetic and central element of the newer liberal Italian politics, into a factor of international diplomacy which the greater European powers could no longer ignore. More significantly, Cavour soon began "usurping" for himself, for his king, and for Piedmont the "scandalous" privilege of speaking for all Italy. In 1852 Cavour began his meteoric career as a minister of the Piedmontese state in a divided Italy; he was to end that amazing career as prime minister of united Italy in 1861. Through economic liberalism and cautious secularism, by subtle diplomatic activity and participation in the Crimean War against faraway Russia on the side of liberal England and Napoleonic France, he won for Piedmont a primacy in Italian politics and a place at the summit in European diplomacy.[6]

At the Paris Peace Congress of 1856, Cavour somehow—for it is still the kind of mystery historians find hard to solve—managed to make the Italian question a responsibility of big-power relations as well as a disturbing element in the guilt-ridden conscience of the European, and particularly of the British, *notables*. Napoleon III was fascinated and then captivated by Cavour. Cavour was ever careful to repay the useful homage of the Emperor of the French: he took every occasion, as long as it was necessary, to let the former Carbonaro, now ruler of France, believe that he, Cavour, believed him to be the sole master of European politics and the true arbiter of the fate of Italy. They concocted an alliance at Plombières, and in 1859 they struck together against the Austrian enemy in the plains of Lombardy. And then Napoleon III and Francis Joseph abruptly ended the fighting behind Cavour's back!

Their "private" meeting at Villafranca brought the Cavourian war of liberation of the north to a premature halt. It had stopped short: it had been frozen by something worse than defeat, or so it seemed, by a negotiated "peace," a half-victory. Cavour fumed and cursed at his guiltless king—and then resigned. He gained six precious, refreshing months of vacation and fertile meditation in his beautiful estates at Leri and in Switzerland and the chance to take stock of his own affairs and those of Italy. Before long he was heard to exclaim "Viva Villafranca!" It seemed incredible but typical: what he had cursed as a catastrophe only a short time before, Cavour now called a blessing in disguise. Those who had real political eyes to see would understand such a strange conversion. At Villafranca, he apparently came to believe, the French and Austrian emperors had unmasked their respective fears and ambitions and found them of a similar color.

Villafranca, according to Cavour, might therefore serve to open Italian eyes to the new European diplomatic facts of life: Austria was still the hereditary enemy, but France was not quite the full-fledged friend of Italy. At Plombières Cavour had struck a contract with the master of France. The young Piedmontese princess given to Napoleon's rowdy cousin could not come home again; Savoy and Nice would have to go; Venice was still Austrian. Was Lombardy alone fair price for all that could have been gained? Cavour mused and rediscovered revolution. Revolution, too, like diplomacy, religion, and economics, was nothing but an instrument of statecraft for Cavour. Liberty alone, but cautiously gained, guarded, and granted, was not a means but an end of his political art. In the spring of 1860, having lost more than half the prize through war and peace, Cavour had recourse to revolutionary tactics to win a full victory. His faithful agents in Tuscany, Romagna, and Emilia guaranteed those provinces to Cavour and Piedmont through revolutionary-plebiscitary politics. A Cavourian, a Piedmontese-Italian quadrilateral of Turin-Milan-Bologna-Florence stood guard now against the ancient Austrian fortresses. But it was less than half of Italy.

Venice and Rome had been placed out of bounds for Italy even by liberal England; the roads to Rome and Venice, the greater European powers clearly intimated, lay only through a general European war. Cavour quickly understood that Venice and Rome were beyond reach. In the spring of 1860, the newly formed Kingdom of Northern Italy seemed destined to be frozen into an uneasy balance of divided and opposing forces held in the grip of a larger, if no less precarious, balance of European power. Cavour had to wait upon time and hold in leash the irrepressible populist leader Garibaldi, who perhaps would never really understand why Rome and Venice could not be touched, and meanwhile keep at bay Mazzini, the dangerous prophet of pan-Italian revolution, who certainly understood it too well. Yet it was Mazzini who came to offer the key to the Italian enigma and Garibaldi who seized it to shatter the Cavourian-European idyll of caution and quiet diplomacy.

Mazzini, the anti-Cavourian antagonist par excellence, the ineffectual democratic "sectarian," the lonely, ostracized idealist of the Italian revolution, calmly whispered into the proper ears a realistic secret that stirred his former disciple Garibaldi as a siren call and sent shivers through the spine of Cavour. Mazzini offered a magnificent, if dangerous, solution to the Italian problem through a simple formula for realistic revolutionary-military action, a genial strategic-political plan which the old soldier and brilliant tactician Garibaldi eventually made his own. "Al Centro, mirando al Sud! [To the center by aiming at the south]," Mazzini said simply. That center, of course, was Rome. Rome alone, Mazzini had consistently preached, would consecrate the Risorgimento of Italy. The idea of Rome, the myth of Rome, the liberation of Rome had sustained him before and after the tragic fall of "his" republic there in 1849. Rome alone aroused to high pitch the pulsating universalist core of the messianic Mazzinian vision.

Cavourian statecraft, Mazzini felt, had led Italy only to a military-diplomatic compromise, a bureaucratic-centralist blind alley. The Italian democratic revolution of the years 1848 and 1849 had been deflected by conservative Italian liberalism and then had been defeated by the concerted forces of European reaction. Now, in 1859 and 1860 Cavourian politics and Napoleonic ambitions were repeating the old, tragic trick and threatened to institutionalize the counterrevolution in a resurgent Italy.

Now or never the Gordian knot of the Risorgimento had to be cut. For it was no longer true, Mazzini insisted, that all roads led to Rome. The only Italian road to Rome—and thence also to Venice—now started at Palermo and passed through a liberated Naples. The destinies of the Bourbons in the south, of the pope in the center, and of the Austrians in Venice were indissolubly linked, and they could and would be unloosened together by an organic revolutionary strategy for the fulfillment of the Risorgimento. Only Garibaldi, even if he denied his master Mazzini, could be the general of the Italian democratic revolution.

Giuseppe Mazzini had once again revised and fused the elements of his revolutionary thought and action into a concrete alternative strategic implementation of the Cavourian model of Machiavellian statecraft and liberal ideology. This was to prove Mazzini's last, bold, desperate gamble with the radical initiative of the national revolution. The very simplicity of the last Mazzinian formula could not and did not hide the frightful risks that its total application by Garibaldi might involve. Perhaps only the two archantagonists Mazzini and Cavour, each in his fashion, fully understood this.

Garibaldi's conquest and liberation of the south from May to September 1860 was indeed the most dramatic but also the most decisive moment of the post-1848 course of the national revolution. For that brief, magnificent, expectant moment, Garibaldi held the fate of Italy and perhaps of European peace in his soldier's hands. An Italian civil war, a religious war, a new war against Austria, and, possibly, a wider European conflict seemed to be his to precipitate or prevent. But for the sake of the Italy they were so desperately, if so differently, fighting for, Garibaldi "gave" the Kingdom of the Two Sicilies to his sovereign, Victor Emmanuel II. Thus he denied again his ancient master Mazzini and permitted their common antagonist Cavour once again in his subtle way to bring statecraft to bear upon the Italian national revolution. Cavour deflected the revolution in the south, appropriated it in the center minus Rome, agitated the democratic ideology to neutralize a fearful Rome, and hastened to destroy the radical-republican organizations in the south, in the center, and in the north of Italy. The last, crucial, historic confrontation of all the fundamental alternatives within the Risorgimento and of the major protagonists of the Italian national revolution had apparently occurred. Only Cavour, it seemed, had gained the final victory in a conflict of giants.[7]

Cavour: a name, an event in Italian and European history. This shrewd Piedmontese statesman looked like the incarnation of the prosaic and acted like a passionate visionary. A master of politics, steeped in economics, he rattled off statistics as if he were reciting poetry. A former aristocratic playboy turned journalist, he molded himself into an incomparable practitioner of international diplomacy. An authoritarian politico, he was indeed "a son of liberty," to which, as he consistently avowed, he "owed all" that he was. Cavour was to combine a genuine Machiavellian realism with a patriotic fervor that left Europe sometimes in fear, often in wonder, and practically always in admiration. Aided and abetted by Victor Emmanuel II, a sovereign who was neither Hamlet nor Caesar but a real master in his own house and mind; assisted by a few faithful colleagues, with Costantino Nigra later towering among them; loyally served by some personal friends; and applauded or cursed all the way, from extreme right and left in parliament and out, in Turin, throughout Europe and in Italy, Cavour seemed to turn the mysterious wheels of politics and diplomacy slowly but never in a vacuum. Some intimate collaborators gained a glimpse from the threshold of Cavourian statecraft. Very few penetrated into the arcana of his art in his day, and it is still a source of fascination—admired, condemned, analyzed by biographers, historians, and political scientists. In his day and later, Cavour was seen by some as a demonic exponent of the awesome formula of "a free church in a free state," an upstart subverter of an ancient social order, the despotic manipulator of Italian consciences. For still others, Cavour's methods and objectives became immediately suffused with sacrosanctity, even when they seemed to bespeak nothing but uncertainty and contradiction, violent wrath and calculated fury.

Cavour's was the métier of the real politico, of the genuine statesman, of a maker of states. Perennially on the job, restlessly ready to begin again after every bad turn, he was keen-eyed enough to learn the secret of extracting the potential of success from almost every failure. He occasionally enjoyed the self-dramatizing privileges of the political demiurges, but he always generously paid for them with the hard coin of realistic work and action, never with the cheap counterfeit of empty rhetoric and facile histrionics. Though he knew how to lead, there was no *duce* complex in him; though he knew how to manipulate political allegiances and men and self-interest, he never lost the sense of the permanent values involved in all political action.[8] Thus, on both the Italian and the European stage, at some moment or other, he had nearly everyone, particularly his enemies, working for him. He acquired and exquisitely exploited an incredible proficiency at reconciling impossible contradictions in Italian politics and European affairs. Victor Emmanuel II, the pope, and "King Bomba" of the Two Sicilies, Leopold of Tuscany and the miniature tyrants of north central Italy, Mazzini and Garibaldi, La Farina and Crispi, Depretis and Visconti-Venosta, Nigra and Ricasoli, Massari and Sir James Hudson, the bomb-thrower Felice Orsini and the seductress Countess Castiglione, the Emperor of the French and the

Austrian emperor, the British foreign office and the Tsar of All the Russians—all, at one moment or another, were subtly turned into instruments of Cavourian politics. Directly or reluctantly, gladly or unwittingly, they all played a part in the complex Cavourian job of making Italy.

There was much in the complicated Italian and European worlds of his day that Cavour did not, perhaps would not even try to, understand. But he knew that he was neither philosopher nor philanthropist, neither prophet nor moralist, neither priest nor reformer. His real world was circumscribed by many things: tradition, interest, and time. But in that world Cavour was a genuine Machiavellian prince in action. He loved his vocation, his work, but not as a game; he knew that politics is also of the stuff of men's lives. Until his finest hour in March, indeed to the eve of his premature death in June of that incredible Italian year 1861, Cavour had dreamed with his eyes wide open, fixed upon the realities of Italy but also upon the potentialities of a new European era.

Thus Cavourian realist-Machiavellian statecraft and the Piedmontese liberal initiative had sought to steer and lead toward a special form of Italian state-making and unity. Giobertian neo-Guelphism, Mazzinian republicanism, Pisacane's social-revolutionary activism, Garibaldian populism, and Cattaneo's radical federalism lay strewn in defeat amid the debris of impossible dreams along the road that had made for success in the Piedmontese initiative and in that Cavourian statecraft. As it was, both of these, whatever defects and defections they did possess, had helped to bring Italy once again, promisingly, within the active circle of the European political order, back to a Europe astir with new ferments of life and work and culture through what proved to be the last great phase of a European age.

Europe and Italy, Italy-in-Europe: these were the terms of reference of all the great figures of the Risorgimento. However they had differed on means and objectives in their vision of the Italian national revolution, Romagnosi and Confalonieri, Cattaneo and Mazzini, Pisacane and Garibaldi would have agreed with Cavour on this larger mission of the Risorgimento. If, therefore, Cavour empirically succeeded *against* most of them, he also fundamentally succeeded *for* them. In the passage from a conservative to a liberal Europe in mid-nineteenth century, from romantic to realist Europe, from the merging extremes of a lingering cosmopolitan-parochial Europe to the new national Europe, Cavour the man and the statesman proved to be the most effective, the sturdiest, perhaps the safest link between Italy's political past and his day's tough, new requirements for survival and advance. Expert navigator that he was, Cavour finally brought his ship of state safely into port by steering cannily with, and frequently against, the currents and countercurrents of his times.

Cavour's final victory was as amazing as it had seemed necessary. Italy had to be made, he felt, and there was little time to lose. There were other possible solutions to the "Italian question," and not a few had been tried during 1848 and 1849. But thereafter no other had seemed or was made feasible. The European powers of his day—post-Metternichian Austria, Napoleonic France, tsarist Russia, liberal England itself—could not be expected to possess an inexhaustible fund of patience with "little upstarts" who went around playing with fire—diplomatic, political, ideological, psychological, and military fire. Whatever the cost, he led many to believe Italy had to be made—half of it if absolutely necessary; all of it if possible. "Jolly fellow" and "fine gentleman" though he was, as his British friends thought of him, Cavour could not risk also appearing a *mauvais coucheur* and a rascally disturber of the European peace for nothing. In the Machiavellian game of European politics he learned to play as fine a hand as any player and ultimately won against great odds. He helped decisively to make Italy in the image of a Europe he admired —an Anglo-French Europe at its best and at its worst—but not a Prussian Europe.

Cavour had reinserted Italy into the European state system. He would have needed time, the time he did not have, to plunge that Italy again fully into the mainstream of European civilization. To this task he undoubtedly would have applied the resources of his genuine political genius. His sometimes hard, authoritarian ways were not necessarily functions of a crypto-Caesarism: he always stood equidistantly away from the imperial dreams of a Napoleon and the blood-and-iron arrogance of power of a Bismarck. As it was, he had to leave the harder, larger work of reconstruction defective and unfinished. The accidents of Italy's historic heritage and the twists of his personal fate conspired cruelly toward a postponement and unpredictable deviations in the work of reconstruction.

Today Cavour's own work, such as it was, seems inflexibly rooted to the national politics and liberal ethos of an Italian and European moment that he himself helped to create. Perhaps this might not have been the case had fate accorded him the eighty-four years it so generously allotted Otto von Bismarck through war and peace. But Cavour had worn himself out by the age of fifty-one. He survived for less than a hundred days his great hour of triumph. Therefore, the stress and strain of war and revolution, of actual or potential civil war, of international intrigue and national conflicts, of authoritarian means to liberal ends rather than the product of serene and fruitful days of peace are stamped deeply upon the Cavourian historic features. He lives, fascinatingly but also somewhat remotely, at once a hero and a victim of an age that gave him no time to refashion the Italy he had made and to bring it still closer to the Europe he had loved.

Cavourian state-making was one result of the Italian national revolution, just as this had become an aspect of the Risorgimento. A re-creation of Italian life, a great spiritual-cultural revolution, an organic transvaluation of Italian historic values had been cemented in the foundations of the Risorgimento. Like all great, ideal revolutions, the Risorgimento failed to realize a total transformation of the Italian people. In this sense, perhaps no more and no less than all the historic European revolutions, the Risorgimento may indeed be judged a *rivoluzione mancata.* Certainly, neither in the years 1848 to 1849 nor 1859 to 1861 could the practical results be equated to the ideal sum envisaged in some quarters. "We willed ten," Mazzini wrote, "and produced two," and, as the historian Gaetano Salvemini later remarked, "to produce that 'two,' other forces, foreign to his thought and action, contributed powerfully."

Legitimately standing on the mountaintops of their contrasting incorruptible faith in a larger regeneration of Italy, Giuseppe Mazzini, the unique ascetic of the Risorgimento, and Carlo Cattaneo, the unbending federalist thinker, made self-confessions of "defeat," of utter "failure," for their visions of the Italian world and for their efforts to change it. In a way that the professional "total" revolutionist Karl Marx never suspected, Mazzini and Cattaneo had indeed not been content merely to reinterpret the world but had spent a lifetime to change it. Now they felt like disarmed prophets, broken and defeated. In the midst of the Garibaldian movement of liberation in the south, which was his own as well as Mazzini's last chance, Cattaneo wrote: "My life is without pleasure and without hope. Only continual work puts my sad thoughts to flight, but inside me I am dead." [9] The year before his death, in 1871, Mazzini confessed: "I attempt to do the little I can for an ideal Italy and for men who are not yet. And if this religious sentiment had not fortunately remained in me, I would have killed myself." [10]

Ironically, the slow, often redeeming, labor of history has at last transmuted the cruel sentiment of failure and death of these tragic figures of the Risorgimento and of their brother spiritual master-guides of the national revolution into a new inspiration, a sense of an ideal fulfillment of their broken lives and visions. A century after their "failures," they too live again in that realm of thought and spirit and passion for European values and human freedom which they had so preeminently made their own. Mazzini and Cattaneo and their disciples, however otherwise in disagreement, had *not* regarded politics as a game or an instrument of power. Politics had been for them *not* statecraft alone, but a truly noble dedication, an activity of the intellect and of the spirit, an instrument of the Promethean act of human liberation. Whether they had spoken, as Mazzini had, of a holy alliance of the European peoples or, as Cattaneo had, of the United States of Europe, whether of the necessity of national freedom as a prerequisite of an international order or of well-protected federal pacts as the links of a world community, they had raised freedom to the status of an imperative of the Italian and European conscience.

The unity of Europe, they had taught in their different ways, was not in its system of states, but it was rather imbedded in the conscience of its peoples: the unity of Europe sprang from a moral and spiritual sphere. Divided by power, Europe was destined to be united by culture. The European political system, they believed, had been a mask for the legalized violence of states. The United States of Europe was the sole hope for a Risorgimento of the European peoples. They had thus seen Italy as a function of a continuing European revolution, not merely of politics but of culture and of conscience. They had at last envisioned a European Risorgimento in which the big necessities of life—politics, economics, diplomacy, social change, scientific achievement, technical progress, material well-being—would prove empty prizes if they did not minister *in freedom* to the potentialities of European civilization. Mazzini and Cattaneo, these defeated, these failures and disarmed prophets, had indeed helped to make an Italy that "was not yet" when Cavour, the great victor of the Italian national revolution, died. But this is not their sole title to the veneration of their spiritual heirs. For if they had shaped the Risorgimento into a rich legacy to future generations of Italians, they had also stamped it with their passionate vision of freedom into a unique, a truly ideal, moment in the history of all the European peoples.

NOTES

* This article was originally published in *Italica*, 38, No. 3 (September 1961), 163–194. Slightly revised and with the addition of select footnote references, up-dated wherever possible, it is reprinted with the permission of the publisher.

1. Four works in English on the Risorgimento are A. William Salomone, ed., *Italy from the Risorgimento to Fascism* (New York: Doubleday, 1970); Edgar Holt, *The Making of Italy* (New York: Atheneum, 1971); the popularized account by George Martin, *The Red Shirt and the Cross of Savoy: the Story of Italy's Risorgimento (1748–1871)* (New York: Dodd, Mead, 1969); and Luigi Salvatorelli, *The Risorgimento: Thought and Action*, trans. Mario Domandi (New York: Harper & Row, 1970). An indispensable analytical guide to the literature of the Risorgimento is Walter Maturi, *Interpretazioni del Risorgimento*, 2nd ed. (Turin: Einaudi, 1962). The following are important for an understanding of the various aspects of the Risorgimento: Piero Gobetti, *Risorgimento senza eroi* (Turin: Baretti, 1926); Adolfo Omodeo, *Età del Risorgimento italiano* (Messina: Principato, 1931); Kent R. Greenfield, *Eco-*

nomics and Liberalism in the Risorgimento: A Study of Nationalism in Lombardy, 1814–1848 (Baltimore: Johns Hopkins Press, 1934; 1965); Antonio Gramsci, *Il Risorgimento* (Turin: Einaudi, 1949); Adolfo Omodeo, *Difesa del Risorgimento* (Turin: Einaudi, 1951); Giorgio Spini, *Risorgimento e Protestanti* (Naples: ESI, 1956); Franco Della Peruta, *I democratici e la rivoluzione italiana: Dibattiti ideali e contrasti politici all'indomani del 1848* (Milan: Feltrinelli, 1958); Giorgio Candeloro, *Storia dell'Italia moderna*, first 5 vols. (Milan: Feltrinelli, 1956–1968), covering the period 1700 to 1871; Rosario Romeo, *Risorgimento e capitalismo* (Bari: Laterza, 1959).

Major up-to-date works on the leaders of the Risorgimento are Denis Mack Smith, *Garibaldi: A Great Life in Brief* (New York: Knopf, 1956), *Cavour and Garibaldi in 1860: A Study in Political Conflict* (Cambridge, Eng.: Cambridge University Press, 1964), and *Victor Emanuel, Cavour, and the Risorgimento* (New York: Oxford University Press, 1972); Rosario Romeo, *Cavour e il suo tempo*, Vol. I, *1810–1842* (Bari: Laterza, 1969). See also the following older works on Mazzini: Gwilym O. Griffith, *Mazzini: Prophet of Modern Europe* (London: Hodder and Stoughton, 1932); Gaetano Salvemini, *Mazzini* (Stanford: Stanford University Press, 1957), originally published in 1905.

The following are useful bibliographical guides: Ettore Rota, ed., *Questioni di storia del Risorgimento e dell'unità d'Italia* (Milan: Marzorati, 1951), *Nuove questioni di storia del Risorgimento e dell'unità d'Italia*, 2 vols. (Milan: Marzorati, 1961), and *La storiografia italiana negli ultimi vent'anni*, 2 vols. (Milan: Marzorati, 1970); Kent R. Greenfield, "The Historiography of the *Risorgimento* Since 1920," *Journal of Modern History*, 7 (March 1935), 49–67; Charles F. Delzell, "Italian Historical Scholarship: a Decade of Recovery and Development, 1945–1955," *Journal of Modern History*, 28 (December 1956), 374–88.

2. Nino Valeri, *L'Italia nell'età dei Principati dal 1343 al 1516* (Milan: Mondadori, 1949), p. 715.

3. On the historiographical problems connected with the adoption of this concept, see A. William Salomone, "The Risorgimento Between Ideology and History: The Political Myth of *Rivoluzione Mancata*," *American Historical Review*, 68, No. 1 (October 1962), 38–56.

4. Denis Mack Smith, *Garibaldi: A Great Life in Brief* (New York: Knopf, 1956), pp. 67–68 (italics added).

5. For a more particularized analysis of Italy's 1848 revolution, see A. William Salomone, "The Liberal Experiment and the Italian Revolution of 1848—A Revaluation," *Journal of Central European Affairs*, 10 (October 1949), 267–288.

6. On the rise of Cavour in Piedmontese politics and then in European diplomacy through the Crimean War, see Adolfo Omodeo, *L'opera*

politica del Conte di Cavour (1848–1857), 2 vols. (Florence: La Nuova Italia, 1945) and Franco Valsecchi, *L'Europa e il Risorgimento: L'Alleanza di Crimea* (Milan: Mondadori, 1948).

7. For a reinterpretation of Garibaldi's personality at the height of his political and military activity, see A. William Salomone, "The Great Fear of 1860: Garibaldi and the Risorgimento," *Italian Quarterly*, 14, No. 56 (Spring 1971), 77–127.

8. See the fine essays on Cavour's political action in Ettore Passerin d'Entrèves, *L'ultima battaglia politica di Cavour. I problemi dell'unificazione italiana* (Turin: ILTE, 1965); see also Raymond Grew, *A Sterner Plan for Italian Unity: The Italian National Society in the Risorgimento* (Princeton: Princeton University Press, 1963) for the use Cavour made of the society as a curb on the "revolutionaries."

9. Quoted in Gaetano Salvemini, ed., *Le più belle pagine di Carlo Cattaneo* (Milan: Garzanti, 1922), pp. xxvii.

10. Quoted in Nello Rosselli, *Mazzini e Bakunin. Dodici anni di movimento operaio in Italia (1860–1872)*, rev. ed. (Turin: Einaudi, 1967), p. 348; see also Alessandro Levi, *Mazzini* (Florence: Barbèra, 1955), p. 269.

CHAPTER 2

PARLIAMENTARY POLITICS
IN THE LIBERAL ERA
1861 TO 1914

SALVATORE SALADINO

United Italy was born in March 1861 as a liberal state in the image of its founding father Cavour, who died three months later. The erstwhile republican Garibaldi was at best a disgruntled and unwelcome relative at the baptismal rite; Mazzini, forever republican, remained absent from the festivities by his own choice and governmental edict. The birth certificate was signed by a parliamentary assembly, stamping on the new nation an imprint that marked its origin and nature from the very first. It was parliament that proclaimed Victor Emmanuel II King of Italy, joining monarchy and national assembly in a union not indissoluble but so intimate that the end of the parliamentary regime under Fascism was also to mean the end of the monarchy as a meaningful organ of government.

Thus, at the time of unification the Piedmontese monarchy, revitalized in the preceding decade by Cavour, had become the ruling dynasty of Italy by an act of parliament. By accepting the crown under these conditions, Victor Emmanuel II had recognized the preeminence of parliament and his role in a responsible monarchy, which remained, however, conservative in its emphasis on continuity. Responsible monarchy meant that the dynasty accepted a fundamental political dependency on parliament. In the absence of monarchy, parliament could still survive in Italy, perhaps less securely; but a national monarchy could not stand without the popular warrant given it by a parliament, the only truly, though imperfect, national institution the country possessed. To remain vital, Italy's monarchy had to prove itself liberal, at least in its acceptance of a limitation of its powers.

Cavour's preference for parliamentary rule had stemmed largely from his belief that this form of government was the most progressive, that it was part of an inevitable march of history, and that for Piedmont and

Italy to remain illiberal meant sinking to the status of a Spain or a South American republic. To be sure, Cavour was not a democrat, nor did he envisage that the Italy he helped make would soon become a democracy. But he neither foreclosed nor dreaded its eventual evolution toward more democratic forms. When material progress, education, and general enlightenment produced among the mass of Italians that minimum requisite of civic responsibility without which democracy can easily become the road to new despotisms, on such a day Cavour would approve bequeathing the people control of their destinies.

In 1861 Italy's constitution, its electoral laws, and its parliament reflected Cavour's thought that a limited constitutional monarchy was best for the country.[1] The Statuto, granted by King Charles Albert to Piedmont in 1848 and extended to united Italy in 1861, was a constitution characteristic of its day: liberal in political provisions, conservative on socioeconomic matters, but flexible in the latitude it allowed for its eventual transformation by the tests of experience. The Statuto gave the king complete control of the executive power, exercised through ministers of his own choosing (Articles 5, 6, 65); the magistracy was instituted not as a separate branch of government but as a judicial order, with justice emanating from the king and administered in his name by judges he appointed (Article 68); the legislative power was shared by the king and two chambers (Article 3), an elective Chamber of Deputies, and a Senate consisting of members appointed for life by the king, who retained the right to veto acts of the two houses (Articles 7, 56).

In its original form the Statuto established, therefore, a monarchical government then styled as constitutional rather than parliamentary; but the primacy, if not supremacy, of parliament was a reality from the very beginning. During the Piedmontese or preunification period, from 1848 to 1860, this primacy resulted more from the force of Cavour's personality than from established precedent. After unification, the weight of accumulating precedents, the proclaimed fact that Victor Emmanuel II was King of Italy by "the will of the people" as well as by the grace of God, and the more significant fact that the various parts of Italy were joined into a united state by popular plebiscites—carefully manipulated but nonetheless important for their explicit recognition of the need for popular consent—all pointed to the growing importance of parliament, especially its elected chamber.

But all this did not make united Italy a democracy. Apart from several minor provisions, the Piedmontese electoral edict-law of March 17, 1848, accorded suffrage only to literate male citizens twenty-five years of age or older who paid direct taxes of at least forty lire (a minimum of twenty lire in some provinces) or who tenanted a building for purposes of domicile or business with a rental value ranging from 200 to 400 lire, again depending on geographical location. The country was divided into 204 single-member constituencies, and provision was made for secret ballot. The 1848 law was modified during the next two decades to take into account the accession of new territories, but the breadth of the suffrage was changed only slightly. A scant 1.9 percent of the population was eligible to vote in the general elections of January and February 1861 (418,696 from about 22 million inhabitants), and 2 percent in November 1870. In the latter year 240,974, or about 45.5 percent of the eligible voters, participated in the general elections. Of the votes cast, 177,339 were declared valid. Thus a mere seven-tenths of 1 percent of the total population elected the deputies who sat in parliament and legislated for all Italians.

So restricted a suffrage was disconcerting to those democrats who argued that inasmuch as the unity of Italy had been ratified by universal manhood suffrage plebiscites, a similarly wide popular mandate should ratify all the country's subsequent political acts. But the moderate liberals who created Italian unity shaped it according to their own biases: monarchical yet liberal, even progressive in Cavour's fashion, but not democratic and certainly not revolutionary. This was the political position favored by that assemblage of leaders called the liberal right; their opponents on the left, inspired principally but not exclusively by Mazzini, continued to follow him in his democratic principles even when they abandoned his republicanism. Some few others on the left followed the lead of Carlo Cattaneo and Giuseppe Ferrari, who while sharing Mazzini's faith in the republican form of government rejected his demand for a unitary state and advocated an Italian federation. After unification these various elements on the left continued to demand the institution of a wider suffrage.

During the first decade of unity Italy faced problems more pressing than suffrage reform and more indicative of the differences dividing right from left. Rome and Venice remained outside the new kingdom. The south was so troubled by banditry and open rebellion that Massimo d'Azeglio—Piedmontese nobleman, writer, artist, prime minister from 1849 to 1852, and possibly the only Italian political leader of any note who knew the various regions of Italy through his travels—wondered whether it had not been a mistake to have annexed it to the rest of Italy. Influencing all political considerations was the state of the country's finances, weighed by mounting deficits and verging toward total collapse. The right, in power until 1876, struggled to achieve a balanced budget. To do so, it had to levy high and predominantly indirect taxes, opposition to which was one of the factors that helped maintain some sort of unity among the heterogeneous groups comprising the left.

The most abiding element uniting the factions constituting the right was fear of social revolution. Cavour had successfully exploited this fear by arguing that unless a liberal monarchy effected reforms in Piedmont and led the movement for Italian unification, the standard would fall to the revolutionaries of Mazzinian or other persuasion. To be sure, the bulk of the left had no revolutionary objectives: its program of extended suffrage, tax reform, compulsory public-supported education, and a measure of decentralization in administration was progressive and democratic but hardly revolutionary.

Actually the left did not differ fundamentally from the right, despite the virulence of the polemical exchanges between them. But it served the left well to point to the danger of revolution in order to emphasize the urgency of the reforms it espoused. Basically the two political factions represented the same social and economic class interests. With a limited suffrage that allowed only 2 percent of Italy's population to vote in 1870, control of parliament remained in the hands of the upper classes. Men of property and substance, active in the professions or in the world of finance, commerce, and trade, most of the representatives of the left and right and their supporters shared the same ideological outlook. Only toward the end of the century did the emergence of the socialists change this situation.

Both the left and the right harbored centralists and autonomists, proponents of universal and of restricted suffrage, economic liberals and interventionists, anticlerical champions of the laic state and proponents of compromise and reconciliation between church and state. Stefano Jacini's famous dictum ("The right acted, the left incited to action: that is the difference") is certainly an incomplete judgment, but it does identify a significant feature in the left's political complexion. If Rome continued to be denied to Italy by the protective screen of French arms, the left argued that it was the fault of the government's timidity. If the government finally moved into Rome when the French withdrew in 1870, the left alleged that its popular agitation had spurred the government to action. If the government refused to accede to Victor Emmanuel's wishes to side with France in the war against Prussia, again, according to the left, it was popular agitation that held the government back from a disastrous step.

True, the Giovanni Lanza government (December 1869 to July 1873) did argue with the king that the nation did not want, and was not ready for, a war on behalf of imperial France. By threatening to resign, Lanza and his finance minister Quintino Sella succeeded in negating Victor Emmanuel's personal diplomacy, which was motivated in part by the aim of securing French acquiescence to Italy's seizure of Rome and in part by the king's chivalric sense of obligation to Napoleon III. Vindicated by France's subsequent defeat, the Lanza government helped to establish the precedent that, contrary to Article 5 of the Statuto, the conduct of

foreign policy was not the king's exclusive prerogative.[2] This same government of the right had already forced the king to dismiss three of the more conservative ministers of the Royal Household after having come to power contrary to Victor Emmanuel's preferences, thus compromising another constitutional royal privilege. Obviously the men of the right were not slavishly monarchical, as their more bitter opponents alleged. Whatever republicanism survived could find refuge only on the left; still, until the crisis at the end of the century the more prominent leaders of the right did not envisage the strengthening of royal authority.

By curtailing the king's independence of action, the Lanza-Sella government had strengthened parliament and belied the left's allegations that the right was susceptible to monarchical control. These charges had been more plausible under the governments led by General Alfonso La Marmora (1864 to 1866) and General Luigi Federico Menabrea (1867 to 1869). As army officers close to Victor Emmanuel, they could be swayed by royal pressure. But the left's criticisms lost validity after Victor Emmanuel reluctantly dismissed Menabrea and appointed Lanza as his successor. By the end of the 1860s it became clear that so long as the king accepted the progressive diminution of his constitutional prerogatives in favor of parliament's primacy and eventual supremacy, republicanism would lose its appeal.

The seizure of Rome in 1870 removed another cause of conflict between the left and right, but differences remained over church-state relations, tax, electoral, and educational reforms, and the perennial Southern Question. On almost all these problems the left's position assured it the greatest possible popularity.

No one denied that the country's tax structure, based primarily on indirect levies, was grossly unfair. Sella, the right's remarkable minister of finance, was obsessed by the need to reduce the budget deficits and to maintain the solvency of the new state. But he did not reject in principle the left's proposals for heavier direct taxes based on ability to pay. Unfortunately the yield from such reforms would have to await a general assessment of property values and the creation of an adequate machinery for the collection of the new taxes, whereas the budget's needs were immediate and could not wait for the reforms to become effective. For this reason, during his tenure of office (1869 to 1873) Sella refused to reduce even the grist tax, the most hated levy on consumer goods. Crispi and others on the left called it a tax on the food of the poor. Symbolizing all that was hateful in Sella's fiscal policies, the grist tax made the right seem insensitive to the needs of millions of Italians. In rebuttal Sella insisted that in saving the country's finances he served the interests of all citizens. Even so, his reputation as the most hated minister in the country's short history made him unpopular among members of his own party,

many of whom were not as indifferent as Sella to popular support. It was the defection of some of these dissidents on the right which led to the fall of the Lanza-Sella government in 1873, bringing to power Marco Minghetti, the Bolognese who had been an influential supporter of Cavour in the crucial years, 1860 to 1861. From 1873 to 1876 Minghetti headed the last long-term government of the right until the First World War.

Although Minghetti's manner was more accommodating than Sella's, the past policies of the right burdened the new prime minister with a heritage not easily disowned. Furthermore, the crisis that had brought down the Lanza-Sella ministry pointed up the fact that the right was no longer a compact grouping. Originally the determination by the moderate liberal leadership of the middle classes to unite Italy under the banner of monarchy had joined together diverse elements in its ranks. With unification accomplished and with the growing abandonment by the left of its former "revolutionary" program, the distinctions between left and right faded, and the right lost its appeal for many of its followers. For a time, the desire to remain in power and the network of personal interests and ties could serve to keep these elements sufficiently united to resist opposition from the left. Increasingly, Minghetti came to understand that the more the left moderated its program, the more difficult it would be for the right and left to remain politically distinct. Once this distinction became sufficiently blurred, the right could no longer claim the exclusive privilege of governing because of its past role as the party that had "made" Italy while saving it from revolution.

The left no longer spoke the language of revolution. Even Francesco Crispi, the former Mazzinian, Garibaldian, and most prominent leader of the democratic or radical wing on the left in the early 1870s, presented a program of moderation. Minghetti acknowledged this in April 1874, in reply to a speech by Crispi outlining his reform program. Rejecting none of Crispi's proposals in principle, Minghetti found manhood suffrage, administrative decentralization, an elective Senate, and tax reform unacceptable only because he deemed them untimely or impractical. Moreover, Minghetti knew that the right was not alone in its factional fragmentation. He pointed out that Crispi spoke for only a part of the left, and turning to the other and more moderate faction in the Chamber of Deputies, Minghetti said, "The time of great political questions being ended (I mean the great questions regarding independence and unity), it should be possible to come to an understanding on other matters and thus to form a great parliamentary majority. . . . Although faithful to their principles, [parties] nevertheless do become transformed in the face of new problems."

Minghetti's transformist invitation was directed primarily to Agostino

Depretis, who, although nominal leader of the whole left, in fact commanded only its moderate wing. Crispi was not then inclined to be "transformed." He continued his attacks on the government, especially for its sponsorship of a public safety law providing for preventive arrest and internment by administrative ruling. Crispi chose to view the proposed law as aimed especially against the south. In a speech of June 10, 1875, he aired all the south's grievances against fifteen years of "misrule" by the right. Although Crispi's indictment of the right on the Southern Question was too sweeping, it emphasized one of the government's major domestic failures. Many of the south's problems—disparity of economic development vis-à-vis the north, a stagnant social order, apathy in the discharge of civic responsibility, and rule by corrupt local cliques—were hardly the fault of the central government and of northerners in particular. But the government could be held accountable for a grist tax that weighed more heavily on the south, and for tariff policies that worked to the benefit of the north and against the south.[3] Simply because it was the national government, in power for fifteen years, it could not escape the south's centuries-old distrust of all public authority.

Clearly, a change in government could not redress all the south's grievances; but there was the expectation that if the left, traditionally the champion of the south, were to come to power, a more understanding and benevolent administration would follow. In October 1875 Depretis announced his "Program of Hope"; in March 1876 Minghetti's forced resignation offered him and the left the opportunity to translate their hopes into reality.

The left that came into power in 1876 was led by men who during the period of unification had been revolutionaries only in their opposition to the regimes they helped to overthrow or to the moderates' program for Italian unity. Having reconciled themselves to constitutional monarchy and, except for some isolated figures, never envisaging a radical reordering of society, the only revolution the leaders of the left could effect in 1876 was a parliamentary one. Their success in forming a government strictly from the ranks of the left, excluding any collaboration with those dissidents of the right whose opposition to Minghetti had caused his fall, represented the only truly new fact. Thus, even after the overwhelming electoral victory recorded by the left in November 1876, its leaders presented no radically innovative government and program.

The reality thus never matched the hopes. The so-called parliamentary revolution heralded by the left's advent to power could not be the revolution awaited by those whose agitation for radical changes characterized them as extreme. Yet only such changes could fulfill the hopes engendered by the left during its years of opposition.

Indeed, the very quality and magnitude of the left's electoral victory worked against the realization of a truly revolutionary program. Conducted under the aegis of the left's minister of the interior Baron Giovanni Nicotera, the elections of 1876, which were a veritable referendum on the right's fifteen years of rule, reduced the right's representation in the Chamber to less than a hundred seats out of a total of 508, with only four candidates being elected in the south. The composition of the new parliamentary majority, whose numbers owed much to Nicotera's less than scrupulous conduct of the elections, was most varied. It included moderates such as Depretis, progressives led by Benedetto Cairoli and Giuseppe Zanardelli, old Jacobins like Crispi and his fellow-Sicilian Nicotera, other former republicans and Garibaldians, and assorted regionalists, especially the southerners. The unity of this heterogeneous coalition derived more from the desire to acquire and retain power than from agreement on a common program. As a result, Depretis's famous program of hope had to be reduced to the lowest common denominator able to attract a majority in the Chamber.

Depretis, the new prime minister, knew all too well the political and personal divisions within his nominally massive majority. These divisions persuaded him that it was not possible to govern Italy with a ministry recruited exclusively from one party and with a program too advanced to be acceptable to the fundamentally moderate outlook of parliament. Even Cairoli, the former Garibaldian who broke with Depretis over the latter's slowness in carrying out the program of hope, acknowledged this fact by including some men of the right in his government when he succeeded Depretis in 1878. Party government having proved impossible for the fragmented left, the only alternative appeared to be government by a majority gathered from all quarters of the Chamber, rallied around a man more than around a program. This was the conclusion reached by Depretis; he translated it into systematic practice during his long tenure of power in the 1880s and thus bequeathed Italy that transformism forever associated with his name.[4]

The transformation effected by Depretis stemmed from many sources and acquired many forms. In coming to power, the left put an end to its republican and Mazzinian past, which had exposed it to suspicions about its loyalty to monarchical institutions and had strengthened the right's claim to continue in office. Proclaiming themselves liberal, progressive, but monarchist, the major leaders of the left showed a special fondness for the new king, Humbert I, whom the old Garibaldian Cairoli shielded with his own body during an assassination attempt in 1878. But their leaders' devotion to the monarchy seemed like moral treason to those extreme members of the left who would not overcome their original distrust of the house of Savoy and who remained convinced that political unity was but one of the Risorgimento's goals. Suspicious of the moderate trend emerging in the left, as early as 1874 they had gathered their parliamentary forces into a bloc whose generic name, extreme left (*Estrema sinistra*), indicated more an expression of discontent than a precise program. As the parliamentary transformist trend within the left became more pronounced after 1878, the extreme wing's assorted coalition of republicans, radical democrats, irredentists, and various social reformers sought to offset the moderate left's preponderance in parliament by appealing to the country at large. Moreover, they attempted to organize a viable opposition to the government forces. In 1879 the *Estrema* formed the Garibaldi-sponsored democratic league (*Lega della democrazia*) and in 1883 the democratic *fascio*, or bloc (*Fascio della democrazia*), led by the radical democrat Felice Cavallotti, the republican Giovanni Bovio, and the socialist Andrea Costa.

By 1883 the left and the right, led by Depretis and Minghetti respectively, had once again buried the issues that had divided the two parties during unification and had announced their willingness to collaborate in forming a stable majority to support a program of cautious reforms within the framework of existing institutions. This collaboration by the moderates in the two wings of Italian liberalism made it possible for the left to remain in power until the early 1890s. It also spurred the determination of elements on the extreme left to continue their common efforts to function as critics and opponents of the government coalitions.

Nevertheless, the collaboration between right and left was not merely a tactic to defend the established order, as the extreme left charged. Although in a campaign speech in October 1882 Depretis exaggerated by claiming that the left's program of hope had been realized almost in its entirety, the suffrage had been more than tripled by the electoral reform law of 1882, the hated grist tax had been repealed, and elementary education had been made compulsory. Yet, critics could and did point out the limited scope of Depretis's legislation: the education law of 1877 remained a fiction in those poorer communities, especially in the south, where local tax resources could not cover the expenditures required by the new law. The electoral law hardly fulfilled the democratic reform championed by much of the left before it came to power. The repeal of the grist tax was not the same as a general reordering of the fiscal structure. Little had been done in the way of administrative decentralization, and now that they were in power the men of the left ignored their former proposals to reform the Senate and otherwise amend the Statuto. Finally, the left's foreign policy of alliance with Germany and Austria and hostility toward France convinced the *Estrema* that the left had altogether abandoned its traditional outlook (see Chapter 14). In 1882 collaboration by much of the right had facilitated both Italy's participation in the Triple Alliance and the moderate domestic reforms accomplished by that year. The formation of the democratic *fascio* by discontented elements in the traditional left who joined with the emerging socialists in 1883 was in part an attempt to force the left to return to its traditions as champions of radical reforms. Had the democratic *fascio* been able to come to an agreement with other dissidents from the left, such as Crispi, Zanardelli, Cairoli, Nicotera, and Alfredo Baccarini, who had organized yet another faction, the "pentarchy," Depretis's position in parliament would have been compromised. Then his only salvation would have been either to veer more openly toward the right or to make common cause with the dissidents in his own party. In either case, the result could have been a major realignment of political forces into two compact groupings of conservatives and progressives, which in turn could have led to the formation of a two-party system and put an end to transformism.

For years, many on both right and left had invoked such a political "clarification." Ruggero Bonghi and Silvio Spaventa, two of Italy's most respected leaders whose views of transformism differed from Minghetti, spoke for the right. Crispi represented the dissident left. As late as 1886, the year before he resolved his differences with Depretis, Crispi called for the formation of distinct parties around concrete programs rather than around personalities. He characterized the then prevailing transformism as making a lie of the parliamentary system because it substituted "the despotism of a minister for the despotism of a king." But Crispi and his fellow dissidents were too divided among themselves to offer effective opposition to the system they decried. Even greater differences separated them from the men of the extreme left bloc whose residual republicanism, sympathy for socialism, and foreign-policy outlook made anything more than transient collaboration against a common opponent impossible.

In April 1887, Crispi made his peace with Depretis and became his minister of the interior. Four months later at Depretis's death he succeeded him as prime minister and announced that his was a national, not a party, government. Although this first Crispian ministry was decidedly of the left and, at first, not unwelcome even to the extreme left bloc, Crispi's announced intention of governing for the nation and not for a party presaged his subsequent lapse into the very transformist practices he had condemned in his predecessor.

When not in office, Crispi's customary place in the Chamber was at the extreme left, where as a former republican, Mazzinian, and Garibaldian he sat next to men who did not share his conversion to monarchy and special devotion to King Humbert. Never indifferent to the misery of the lower classes, Crispi nevertheless could not accept the socialists' solution for this misery. Class struggle, social revolution, and internationalism he rejected as subverting the integrity of the state for whose creation he had sacrificed the better part of his life. The pronounced dislike for the Triple Alliance by the extreme left bloc, its benevolence toward republican France, and its espousal of irredentism all irritated Crispi. He saw in the alliance Italy's assurance of great-power status. Loyalty to it made it difficult for him to improve relations with France, whose intentions he distrusted partly because of personal aversion for French leaders and partly because their actions were not always devoid of provocation, as in the case of the tariff war that began in 1888.[5] Although mindful of the ideal to free all Italians from foreign rule, he could not give encouragement or even tacit tolerance to irredentist demonstrations, fearful for Italy's relations with Austria and ever suspicious that the irredentists' open favor for France was proof that the two were in league against him. Finally, the extreme left bloc's opposition to Crispi's policy of colonial expansion increased the gap separating him from men with whom he had had much in common in the past but whose present political orientation created unsurmountable differences between them. Crispi remains a controversial figure, yet his motives and conduct in office become clearer if we remember that he remained loyal to his dream of a united, strong Italy.

During 1888 and 1889, Crispi's forceful personality and the merits of his program persuaded parliament to approve a number of reforms, long promised and delayed. These included a reform of the judiciary, the completion of a unified penal code, the reordering of local administration, an extension of the electorate eligible to vote in local contests, and measures for more effective supervision of public health and emigration. But these important accomplishments were tarnished by mounting budgetary imbalance, in large measure the result of Crispi's determination that domestic reform should not compromise the country's military posture as a great and expansive power. This emphasis on military strength and colonial greatness was opposed by the extreme left bloc, which in 1890 indicted Crispi's policies and his personal "megalomania." A growing number of conservatives, especially Lombard industrialists, found themselves united with the extreme left bloc in opposition to increased military expenditures.[6] In fact, it was the right, restive under Crispi's aggressive manner and distressed by the tariff war with France as well as by his excessive dependency on Germany, which opened the crisis leading to his fall in 1891. Inasmuch as dissidents from the left, especially the followers of Crispi's personal enemy Nicotera, had joined with the right against Crispi, the Marquis Antonio di Rudinì, who succeeded Crispi as prime minister, reverted to the practice of transformism by offering the ministry of the interior to the old Jacobin Nicotera in his right-wing government. Crispi at least had ruled with a government predominantly of the left.

The foreign policies followed by Di Rudinì and by Giovanni Giolitti, who succeeded him as prime minister in 1892, aimed at a measure of reconciliation with France and a corresponding attenuation of dependency on Germany. Efforts were made at relaxing tensions with the church, especially strained under Crispi, who suspected France and the papacy of being in league against Italy. Domestically, proposals were advanced to alleviate the tax burden borne by the poorer classes by reducing military and colonial expenditures. But neither Di Rudinì nor Giolitti could implement this program of general economic retrenchment aimed at bringing Italy's foreign and domestic policies within the means available to the country. Di Rudinì's parliamentary base was too insecure—as was his position at court—for him to last more than a year in office. Giolitti appeared surer of royal favor. His parliamentary position was precarious at first, but he remedied this weakness in the elections of November 1892, when he secured a majority by methods that earned him the lasting reputation of a manipulator of votes. But a scandal involving a Roman bank (Banca Romana), a veritable massacre of Italian emigrant workers in southern France, and disturbances in Sicily so compromised Giolitti's first ministry that he had to resign, and his subsequent political career appeared seriously impaired.

One of Giolitti's basic goals in his first government had been to rally the more flexible members of the extreme left bloc around a program stressing more reforms at home and fewer foreign involvements. Inasmuch as Giolitti's fall had resulted more from his personal involvement in the bank scandal than from a rejection of his program, this program could have been continued by his designated successor Giuseppe Zanardelli (one of the pillars of the progressive left and wholly free of any suspicion of personal or political corruption). Faced with the king's refusal to accept the appointment of Trentino-born General Oreste Baratieri as minister of war (out of concern over Austria's reaction), Zanardelli preferred to relinquish his mandate, thus opening the door to a return of Crispi to power at the end of 1893.

Nothing could have been more disastrous for Italy at that time. In spite of some revolutionary rhetoric, the bulk of the extreme left in the 1890s had proved its willingness to operate within the confines of existing parliamentary institutions, even though its avowed purpose was to change these institutions. One of the results of this course of action during the 1880s was an effective if unwitting collaboration with the government in neutralizing the popular unrest. Contrary to Crispi's growing fears for the integrity of the state, there is no convincing evidence that the extreme left was any more revolutionary in the 1890s than in former decades. However, it was then that the various groups loosely associated in the extreme left sought to assert their independent identity.

The most numerous among them at this time was the Radical party, whose parliamentary representation rose to forty-seven seats in the elections of 1895. Ably led by Cavallotti until his death in a duel in 1898, it consisted largely of former republicans reconciled to the monarchy but still devoted to the democratic principles of the old Party of Action. The Radical party had firm ties with Freemasonry and remained strongly anticlerical. Its principal strength was in Lombardy; its members were predominantly professional people and state employees; and its most vital parliamentary function was that of providing a link between the extreme left and liberal majority in the Chamber. It lacked a large and coherent organization in the country at large, where it hoped to play the role of preparing the middle classes for their leadership of the masses. The Radicals' chief rival for this leadership was the Marxist Socialist party, formed at the Genoa congress in 1892, and whose progressive differentiation from anarchism, radical democracy, and republicanism is fully described in Chapter 5.

Fearful of being absorbed or overshadowed by the Radicals and Socialists, the various republican organizations joined in April 1895 to form the Italian Republican party to represent an uncontaminated republicanism. At the end of the year the new party formulated a program that sought to distinguish traditional republicanism from both socialism and radical democracy: from the Socialists because they appeared indifferent to the institutional question of monarchy or republic; from the Radicals because they were committed to collaboration with monarchy in order to "transform" it.[7] That republicanism retained some of its old attractive force is revealed by the elections of 1900, when the Republican party won 29 seats, as compared to 33 for the Socialists and 34 for the Radicals. But the Republican popular vote of 79,000 (less than half the Socialist vote of 165,000) presaged its steady decline during the next two decades. Among the reasons for this decline, examined with candor by the Republican deputy Napoleone Colajanni in 1912, was the Republicans' failure to wean the masses and the lower middle classes away from Socialist and Catholic organizations.

As early as the 1890s there were signs that the ban on participation in national politics imposed on Italian Catholics by the unreconciled Pius IX in the *Non expedit* of 1874 was faltering. The prohibitions in the *Non expedit* were the political corollary of the church's refusal to recognize the existence of the Italian state and of its rejection of the modus vivendi offered by the state to the church in the Law of Papal Guarantees of 1871. The gradual change in the papacy's attitude toward the Italian state and the growth of numerous Catholic economic and social organizations are examined in Chapters 4 and 11 respectively.

The strength of politically oriented Catholic groups and the vigor revealed by the extreme left gravely concerned Crispi during his last ministry. In his mind Crispi hardly distinguished between them. He labeled both subversive because of their doubtful loyalty to the Italian state and its institutions. Both were strong in the north; both exhibited pro-French sympathies and ties; both opposed his grandiose dreams of expansion and power; and both centered their activity among those masses who still remained alien if not hostile to the Italian state in whose making they had played little or no role. Perhaps most alienated were Crispi's own fellow Sicilians.

In 1893 and 1894 Sicilian discontent erupted in a series of upheavals by local groups loosely organized under the name of *Fasci siciliani*. Crispi reacted to this outburst of socioeconomic grievances among the Sicilians by concluding that it was the work of the Socialists, who supplied many of the leaders of the *Fasci siciliani*,[8] and that it represented a revolutionary plot to overthrow the government. Fearing a revolution and even the separation of the island from Italy, in January 1894 he reacted by imposing martial law on Sicily. As the unrest spread to Lunigiana on the mainland, Crispi extended martial law. At first the parliamentary majority supported Crispi's methods and shared his fears that the state was in danger. Late in 1894 he ordered mass arrests of Socialists and other "subversives." But this time parliament's support failed him, for at the end of 1894, Giolitti revealed Crispi's and his wife's financial dealings with the discredited Banca Romana, thus questioning Crispi's integrity and honesty. Crispi reacted with a royal decree suspending parliament on December 15, whereupon Cavallotti of the extreme left joined with Zanardelli of the progressive left and with Di Rudinì of the right in an extraparliamentary demonstration against the suspension.

Crispi campaigned in the elections of May 1895 on the issue of "monarchy or anarchy." The "ministerial" candidates won 334 seats out of 508, but the popular vote of about seven hundred thousand for the government and nearly five hundred thousand for the opposition indicated a high degree of dissatisfaction in the country. During the elections the opposition made much of the "moral question" involved in Crispi's relations with the Banca Romana. Crispi's prestige suffered further when after the elections Cavallotti accused him of having contracted a bigamous second marriage in 1878 and again emphasized the "moral question." In March 1896 Italy's defeat at Aduwa by the Ethiopians completed the process of Crispi's political disintegration and ended not only his career but also the colonial ambitions he had come to personify.

For two years Crispi's successor Di Rudinì sought to liquidate Crispi's legacy in foreign and domestic policies. Abroad, in response to the national cry of "Away from Africa," Di Rudinì limited Italy's colonial activity to holding Eritrea. He also resumed with some success his old policy of reconciliation with France. At home, he sought to pacify the country with amnesties for political offenses and special reforms for Sicily. But his inability to reduce military expenditures and to effect a thorough reform of the tax structure lost him the benevolence originally accorded him by the extreme left bloc. In 1898 when Italy was hit by a wave of popular agitation, the first in which peasants and urban workers joined to express their dissatisfaction, Di Rudinì's policies lost him whatever support he may have had in parliament, and his repression of the May disturbances, especially heavy-handed in Milan, aroused the opposition of the extreme left bloc and much of the left as well. Even the right, led principally by Sonnino, abandoned Di Rudinì, holding him responsible for the disturbances because of his earlier mildness toward the parties of the extreme left.

Di Rudinì's successor was General Luigi Pelloux, but the "grey eminence" behind the government was Sidney Sonnino. His theories on the restoration of constitutional—as distinguished from parliamentary—government interpreted events during the preceding several years as the result of a grave institutional crisis. According to Sonnino's famous article of 1897, "Torniamo allo Statuto [Let us return to the constitution]," the then much-publicized degeneration of parliament stemmed primarily from the legislature's usurpation of the king's constitutional prerogatives. But parliament in turn had lost its independence to prime ministers who, adept at manipulating transient majorities, had made themselves independent of both king and parliament, behaving toward the kings as "mayors of the palace." Sonnino's solution was a "return to the constitution" with a restoration of the king's full executive power, a solution he thought especially urgent because of the dangers that the liberal state was facing from what he considered the tyranny of egalitarian socialism and the intolerance of obscurantist clericalism.

In the light of Sonnino's views, the crisis of the Pelloux period appears to be less an attempt at blind reaction and more properly a systematic effort to erase fifty years of Piedmontese and Italian parliamentary precedents by going back to the strict letter of the 1848 Constitution. Royal assent was implicit in the choice of Pelloux, who, although originally of the moderate left, was the first general to head the government since General Luigi Menabrea (1867 to 1869). After six months of comparative mildness, early in 1899 Pelloux introduced a number of bills designed to curb alleged excesses in the exercise of public freedoms. The character of this legislation was made more repressive when a committee of the Chamber revised the government's original proposals by giving the government, rather than the judiciary, the power to dissolve allegedly subversive organizations. Zanardelli and Giolitti led the liberals of the left in opposing this significant change and joined the opposition, which was still in the minority. Certain that the majority would sustain Pelloux, the extreme left bloc adopted the tactic of obstructionism. On June 22, 1899, Pelloux retaliated by promulgating the pending bills through a royal decree, which he presented to parliament for approval. Obstructionism was resumed, and when fistfights broke out in the Chamber, the government adjourned the legislative session.

For the rest of the year the ministry moved with caution in using its decree powers and even amnestied all political prisoners detained for involvement in the disturbances of 1898. But in January 1900 the Supreme Court of Appeal, ruling only on the procedural propriety of the legislation, decided that the decree of June 22, 1899, had no legal validity. The government once again was obliged to present the decree for parliamentary approval. When the opposition resumed its obstructionist tactics in March 1900, the government, aided by the somewhat arbitrary rulings of the president of the Chamber, sought to amend the rules of debate in the Chamber. Zanardelli and the liberal left rebelled and walked out of the Chamber on April 3, followed by the extreme left, including the Socialist leader Leonida Bissolati, who shouted "Down with the king!"

That the government did not aim at a coup d'etat or any other extralegal approach was confirmed by its decision to consult the country. But the elections of June 1900 gave it a slender majority in the Chamber and a problematic one in the country. Whatever intentions the government may have harbored, these could no longer be executed as the clear will of the electorate and of parliament. Pelloux's decision to resign after the elections and the king's acceptance of his resignation seem to prove that neither king nor government had determined to follow an extraconstitutional course. But the whole crisis had engendered much fear for the country's parliamentary institutions. Rightly or not, the monarchy's prestige had become impaired among those who wished to safeguard these institutions. Fortuitously, King Humbert's death at the hands of an assassin in July 1900 eliminated from politics the issue of the king's responsibility in the crisis. The accession of his son Victor Emmanuel III and the subsequent rise of Zanardelli and Giolitti to power seemed to augur the beginning of a new era.

Small in stature and reserved in manner, Victor Emmanuel III was the antithesis of his father in outward attributes. The new king did not share Humbert's predilection for Crispi and the Triple Alliance. His sympathies were anticlerical, and in domestic politics he appeared to be inclined toward the popular parties [9] whose obstructionist defense of parliament's prerogatives and opposition to the Pelloux laws foreshadowed a new alignment in the country's political life. The architect of this transformation—his critics called it a new and worsened transformism—was Giovanni Giolitti, returned to power as Zanardelli's minister of the interior in February 1901.

For the preceding eight months, Italy had been governed by Giuseppe Saracco, formerly president of the Senate, whose ministry had included representatives of all parliamentary factions except the extreme left. It discharged well its task of pacifying the country after the Pelloux episode and the king's assassination. But it was clearly a stopgap government, and it fell when the protagonists of the victory against Pelloux decided that their day had come. On February 4, 1901, Giolitti made his celebrated speech to the Chamber, in which he accused the current and past governments of pursuing a policy hostile toward the organization of labor, and announced a new era for the country: "The rising movement of the lower classes becomes ever more rapid every day. It is an irresistible movement. . . . The supporters of existing institutions have one duty above all, and that is of persuading the lower classes, by means of acts, that they have much more to hope for from existing institutions than from dreams of the future."

Piedmontese by birth, bureaucrat by training, Giolitti seemed to personify the new Italy for which the Risorgimento was past history. Unlike his predecessors, he had not participated in the struggle to form a united Italy. Thus, when compared with Crispi, the last of the old conspirators, he appeared lusterless and bland. But he recognized the new forces at work, not only in Italy but throughout Europe. Hence his appeal first to Filippo Turati and then to Bissolati to enter his cabinets, for Giolitti realized that the Socialists spoke for the masses and that the masses could no longer be ignored. Rebuffed by the Socialist leaders, he turned to the Catholics who had considerable influence among the peasantry and the middle classes. Giolitti effectively dominated Italian political life from 1901 to 1914 and left on it his own stamp.

Giolitti had read the signs of the elections of June 1900 and concluded that the country was assuming a new political orientation, opposed to that represented by Crispi and Pelloux. The extreme left as a whole had won 96 seats and gained more than 100,000 votes in comparison with the elections of 1895. Most of the gains had gone to the Socialists, whose popular vote of about 165,000 was double the vote received in 1895 and constituted nearly half the votes cast for the extreme left. Socialist parliamentary representation also doubled, from 16 to 33. Had the election been based on proportional representation, the Socialist total would have been 66 seats, and that of the entire extreme left 133, larger than the 116 seats won by the constitutional opposition. Accordingly, the leaders of this opposition, Giolitti and Zanardelli, concluded that they could come to office only with the support of the extreme left, and particularly of the rising Socialist party, whose evolution since 1892 indicated that it was prepared to abandon its traditional noncollaboration with bourgeois governments.

The attitude of "intransigence" adopted by the Socialist party congress at Reggio Emilia (1893) had been restated at the congresses of 1895 and 1896, but the substantive collaboration of Socialists, Radicals, and Republicans in a common resistance against the repressions of the later Crispian period led the Bologna Socialist party congress of 1897 to agree to collaborate in local elections with the other two parties of the extreme left. The experience of the last three years of the century strengthened the hand of those Socialists who favored collaboration. The thesis of these "reformists" gained formal recognition at the Rome congress of September 1900 with the adoption of the "maximum" and "minimum" programs.

The results of the Rome congress were an open admission of the divided spirit of Italian socialism. Was the minimum program (the germ of which had been stated at the Genoa congress of 1892 as the "struggle for the immediate improvement of the conditions of the workingman") to become an end in itself, or was it to be only the avenue to the "wider struggle aiming at the conquest of the power of the state"? And if it was to be but an avenue, was the journey to the ultimate goal to be pacific, parliamentary, constitutional, or was it to be accomplished by revolutionary means? In 1904 Filippo Turati, one of the founders of the party and spokesman for a double reformism that championed both the intrinsic merits of the minimum program and the peaceful, evolutionary transition to the ultimate goal, described the ambivalence or dualism in the Socialist party in these terms: "One road travels straight to socialism by means of arduous steps [study, propaganda, conquest of offices, laws, and practice]; the other road [contempt for voters, for parliament, and for legislative reforms; the mirage of proletarian dictatorships; unrestrained and savage class struggle; the entrusting of revolution to the thaumaturgical efficacy of miracles] meanders through a worsened status quo and ends up in reaction. It is impossible to find a way out through an intermediate path." [10]

For twelve years after 1900, the Socialist party oscillated between the two approaches, and this oscillation had a direct effect on Giolitti's policies. However one judges the motives behind Giolitti's program (political opportunism, love of power, promotion of a grand design) or the results of this program (political fragmentation, a pernicious and unnecessary transformism, or the last effort at saving the liberal regime), the program failed as much because of the divisions in the socialist movement as because of the mistakes made by Giolitti.

Between 1901 and 1903 the Socialists and most of the extreme left supported the Giolittian program of promoting the organization of labor in order to channel its force for constructive purposes. Wittingly or not, they also furthered Giolitti's plan of achieving a measure of control over the masses through the parties of the extreme left. Giolitti made his purpose clear in the speech to the Chamber on February 4, 1901: "I never fear organized forces; rather I fear much more those that are unorganized . . . because the government may exercise legitimate and useful influence on the former, but with the latter only force will do."

The aim of "domesticating" the popular parties of the extreme left was too transparent not to arouse those who viewed Giolitti's success as the undoing of their revolutionary expectations. But Giolitti's policies produced some promising results. Most of the Radicals did not resist domestication. From the time of Cavallotti's leadership, they had begun to prepare themselves for a role in the government. Although they refused Giolitti's invitation to join his government when he succeeded the ailing Zanardelli as prime minister in 1903, one of their leaders agreed to become president of the Chamber in 1904 with Giolitti's support. Eventually the Radicals accepted posts in the cabinets of Sonnino in 1906, Luigi Luzzatti in 1910, and finally Giolitti in 1911. The "pure" Republicans proved less docile. But their days were numbered under a Giolittian regime which, albeit monarchal, was prepared to become more representative of the country and more truly democratic. The Republicans found it difficult to rebut the famous reply Giolitti gave in 1903 to the Republican deputy Napoleone Colajanni, who had interrupted Giolitti's argument that inasmuch as the French socialists had rallied to the bourgeois government of René Waldeck-Rousseau, socialists could do the same in Italy. When Colajanni noted that France was a republic, Giolitti replied: "Now I ask you, what laws and what social measures approved in France could not be approved under the liberal Italian monarchy?"

The conviction expressed in this rhetorical question had led Giolitti to invite Turati to enter the government in 1903. The reformist Socialist leader's reply (similar to one given later by Bissolati in 1911 when Giolitti made the same offer to him) was that the mass of the Socialist party was not ready to assume the responsibilities of power. This judgment by the two moderate Socialist leaders was confirmed on both occasions. Bissolati's "Giolittian" stance in 1911 eventually brought his expulsion from the party in 1912, and Turati's diagnosis of the ferment in the party in 1903 was more than validated by the extremists' decision to engage in the "experiment" of a general strike in September 1904.

During the strike Giolitti showed his customary restraint in using force and waited for the disturbance to wear itself out. After the strike he decided to teach the Socialists a lesson by calling general elections to offer the voters the opportunity of judging between his position and that of the revolutionaries. But the lesson was misdirected. The revolutionaries in the Socialist party refused to be cowed by the party's electoral defeat. On the other hand, the Socialist moderates, who had not needed a lesson on the absurdity of the strike, felt betrayed by Giolitti's electoral manipulation of the strike and his exposure of their weakness. Nor could they be pleased by the fact that the elections provided the occasion for the Catholics' open entry into national politics.

In 1904 Pope Pius X suspended the prohibitions in the *Non expedit* of 1874 sufficiently to allow Catholics to vote in constituencies where their participation would help defeat candidates of the extreme left or secure the election of an avowed Catholic. The injunction that there were to be "no Catholic deputies, only deputies who were Catholics" made it clear that the object of the partial suspension was not the creation of a Catholic party but the defeat of the church's more extreme opponents. Nevertheless, two candidates with explicitly Catholic views did enter parliament in 1904; their number grew to about twenty in the elections of 1909, and to over thirty by 1913, forming if not a party at least the nucleus of one in the making.[11]

Inasmuch as Giolitti conducted all three elections, he was accused of corrupt bargains with the Catholics, particularly in 1913 when the so-called Gentiloni Pact between Count Ottorino Gentiloni, leader of the Catholic organizations, and government representatives assured Catholic support to liberal candidates who pledged to defend the church's views on free (Catholic) education, religious instruction in public schools, and divorce. The controversy on the extent of Giolitti's alleged complicity in this pact still continues.[12] At the time it was widely believed that the allegations were true, and in 1913, as in 1904 after the relaxation of the *Non expedit* had allowed Catholics to participate openly in the national elections, these allegations contributed to the disaffection of Giolitti's allies on the extreme left.

On both occasions the defection of the extreme left eventually led to governments of the right. Giolitti's resignation in 1905 produced the Alessandro Fortis transitional ministry which lasted a difficult year, to be followed by Sonnino's first "ministry of a hundred days." For four years after the fall of Pelloux in 1900, Sonnino had remained adamant in his opposition to the Giolittian approach. Sympathy for labor organizations, tolerance of strikes, and a wide latitude on questions of public order had seemed to Sonnino to be an open invitation to social revolution. But the apparent successes of the Giolittian program and the initiation of a policy of extensive socioeconomic reforms finally convinced Sonnino that what was wrong with Giolittism was not the program but the manner and spirit of its implementation. In 1906, Sonnino formulated an even grander program of reforms and managed to secure the participation of the Radicals in his government as well as the Socialists' benevolent neutrality.

That the extreme left should support Sonnino after abandoning Giolitti seemed an extraordinary event.

In fact, Sonnino had never been indifferent to social and political grievances, as his advocacy of suffrage, tax, and social reforms as early as 1880 attests. Having lost his fear of social revolution, he returned to his old thesis that eventual revolution could be averted by timely reforms. The extreme left, moved by the desire to free itself from total dependency on Giolitti, opted for Sonnino, of whom at least it could be said that he was unmarked by the taint of those electoral expediencies and manipulations associated with Giolitti's rule.

But the majority in the Chamber remained essentially Giolittian in 1906; and when later in the year Giolitti decided to end his vacation from office, this loyal majority ended Sonnino's experiment. For the next eight years, until his resignation in March 1914, Giolitti exercised so thorough a sway over Italy's political life that it became customary to speak of his long tenure as a parliamentary dictatorship. Even when not formally in office (as in 1910), the substance of power remained in his hands. In 1912 his old antagonist Colajanni spoke for all of Giolitti's opponents when he said that since the same majority had supported all the governments from 1904 to 1910 (Giolitti, Fortis, Sonnino, Luzzatti), it was a joke to speak of parties: "There is only one true party. More precisely, there is only one man, who has supplanted all parties: Giolitti." [13]

But the Giolittian era was nearing its end. The decision to embark on the Libyan War in 1911 (see Chapter 14) was the prelude to the great political transformation—a veritable revolution—to be accomplished by the First World War. The colonial enterprise led not only to the first electoral success of the newly formed Nationalist party, it is also produced a general schism among the parties of the extreme left. Bissolati's support of the war alienated him permanently from Turati. Separated by their differences over the Libyan episode, the two wings of Italian reformist socialism met defeat at the hands of the revolutionaries, who, in expelling Bissolati and his followers in 1912, served notice to the Turatians as well that their day was ended. This was implicit in the sudden ascendancy of young Benito Mussolini at the party congress of that year.

The Libyan War also divided the Republicans and the Radicals. The anticlerical and anti-Giolittian elements among the Radicals came to the fore during and after the general elections of 1913, the first ones conducted under a new system of virtual universal manhood suffrage and contested in November primarily on the issue of opposition to or support of the campaign in Libya. Incensed by Giolitti's alleged involvement in the Gentiloni Pact, the dissident Radicals and his other opponents on the extreme left argued that Giolitti's collusion with the Catholics had falsified

the results of Italy's first experiment with popular suffrage and had
denied the popular parties their political due. The Radicals' disaffection
was particularly dangerous to the stability of Giolitti's government,
which had included three Radical ministers when formed in 1911. Pressed
by a resolution of their party's congress, these ministers decided to resign
in March 1914, whereupon Giolitti abandoned his office in obedience to
the dictum that no government could long survive the concentrated
opposition of the extreme left.

The Giolittian era had come to an end. Its demise was confirmed by
the advent and survival until 1916 of Antonio Salandra's government of
the right, one of whose ambitions was to revitalize the right by reversing
what Salandra considered the inauspicious policies of the Giolittian
decade. The same Salandra government also decided on intervention in
the First World War, whose domestic consequences were to bring about
the demise of Italy's parliamentary institutions.

It would be simplistic to attribute parliament's failure to cope successfully with the myriad of postwar economic and social problems exclusively to Giolitti for his alleged obstruction of the development of a
sound party system during his decade of personal rule before the First
World War. Admittedly, this so-called parliamentary dictatorship did
not facilitate the formation of the much-idealized two-party system.
In addition, the fragmentation of political forces characteristic of the
postwar years and the resulting parliamentary paralysis do in some measure derive from the "Giolittian system." But there is also the fact that
the war itself—with the destructive effects of nine months of virulent
debate during 1914 and 1915 on the wisdom of intervention in the conflict, the three and a half years of exhausting war effort, and the disillusionment with the peace treaties—does not result from the real and
alleged failures of the Giolittian decade. After all, Giolitti *opposed* Italy's
intervention in the war. Furthermore, the appearance of a new party—
the Catholic Partito Popolare Italiano—coincided with the splintering of
the old Socialist party, which in 1919 was the largest in parliament. The
failure of these two mass parties to collaborate in defending the parliamentary system against old and new enemies had more to do with the end
of representative government at the hands of Fascism than any prewar
failures of commission or omission.

This is not to say that the postwar crisis preceding Fascism's rise to
power was unrelated to the imperfections revealed in Italy's preceding
sixty years of parliamentary life. In leaving too many political and social
problems unsolved before 1914, the liberal regime bequeathed them to
the men and the times of the postwar era. Enmeshed after 1919 in the
polarization between those who would change everything and those who
would change nothing, the middle path represented by Cavourian and

Giolittian liberalism was replaced by an extremism—Fascism—which promised the instant cures that are the almost irresistible lures of a dictatorial regime.[14]

NOTES

1. The following works on Italy during the liberal era are particularly useful: Denis Mack Smith, *Italy: A Modern History*, new ed. (Ann Arbor: University of Michigan Press, 1969); Christopher Seton-Watson, *Italy from Liberalism to Fascism, 1870–1925* (London: Methuen, 1967); H. Stuart Hughes, *The United States and Italy*, rev. ed. (Cambridge: Harvard University Press, 1965); John Alden Thayer, *Italy and the Great War: Politics and Culture, 1870–1914* (Madison: University of Wisconsin Press, 1964); A. William Salomone, *Italy in the Giolittian Era: Italian Democracy in the Making*, 2nd ed. (Philadelphia: University of Pennsylvania Press, 1960).

2. See Federico Chabod, *Storia della politica estera italiana dal 1870 al 1896*, 2nd ed. (Bari: Laterza, 1962), pp. 120, 654–657, for Victor Emmanuel II's attempts at personal diplomacy and the successful resistance by his ministers. See also Renato Mori, *Il tramonto del potere temporale, 1866–1870* (Roma: Edizioni di storia e letteratura, 1967) on Victor Emmanuel's personal diplomacy regarding the Roman Question.

3. See the brief but excellent synthesis of the Southern Question in Bruno Caizzi, "La questione meridionale," in *Nuove questioni di storia del Risorgimento e dell'unità d'Italia*, 2 vols. (Milan: Marzorati, 1961), II, 573–619.

4. The most thorough work on Depretis's domestic politics is by Giampiero Carocci, *Agostino Depretis e la politica interna italiana dal 1876 al 1887* (Turin: Einaudi, 1956). See also Christopher Seton-Watson, *op. cit.*, p. 92, who observes that in his methods Depretis had little choice but to work with what was available.

5. For the effects of the tariff war on Italy, see Shepard B. Clough, *The Economic History of Modern Italy* (New York: Columbia University Press, 1964), pp. 114–118, 120–121, 126, 145. For a variety of appreciations of Crispi's political career see Gualterio Castellini, *Crispi* (Florence: Barbera, 1924); Nicolò Inglese, *Crispi* (Milan: Dall'Oglio, 1961); Arturo Carlo Jemolo, *Crispi* (Florence: Vallecchi, 1922); Margot Hentze, "A Dictator of Modern Italy, F. Crispi," *Politica* (London) (March 1938), pp. 54–67; and Crispi's *Memoirs*, ed. Tommaso Palamenghi-Crispi, 3 vols. (London: Hodder and Stoughton, 1912–1914).

6. Fausto Fonzi, *Crispi e lo "Stato di Milano"* (Milan: A. Giuffrè, 1965) develops the theme of the hostility between Crispi and the Lombard business community with a wealth of detail.

7. Giovanni Spadolini, *I repubblicani dopo l'unità* (Florence: Le Monnier, 1960), pp. 74–75.

8. See Salvatore Francesco Romano, *Storia dei Fasci siciliani* (Bari: Laterza, 1959), especially pp. 1–11 as an introduction to the problem.

9. For accounts of Victor Emmanuel III, see Alberto Bergamini, *Il Rè Vittorio Emanuele III di fronte alla storia* (Rome: Tipografia del Senato, 1949) and Alberto Consiglio, *Vita di Vittorio Emanuele III* (Milan: Rizzoli, 1950).

10. Filippo Turati, "L'ora delle responsabilità," *Critica Sociale* (September 16–October 1, 1904), p. 277.

11. A. William Salomone, *Italy in the Giolittian Era*, pp. 36–41. More extensive treatments are in Ernesto Vercesi, *Il movimento cattolico in Italia, 1870–1922* (Florence: La Voce, 1923) and Gabriele de Rosa, *Storia del movimento cattolico in Italia*, Vol. I, *Dalla restaurazione all'età giolittiana*, Vol. II, *Il partito popolare italiano* (Bari: Laterza, 1966).

12. See Frank J. Coppa, "Giolitti and the Gentiloni Pact Between Myth and Reality," *Catholic Historical Review*, 53 (July 1967).

13. Napoleone Colajanni, *I Partiti politici in Italia* (Rome: Libreria Politica Moderna, 1912), p. 25.

14. There is already a vast literature on the immediate postwar years and the subsequent advent of Fascism. Only a sampling of works is noted here. A very useful guide is Emiliana P. Noether, "Italy Reviews Its Fascist Past," *American Historical Review*, 61 (1956), 877–99, which examines Italian works published between 1943 and 1956. Some recommended studies are: Paolo Alatri, *Le origini del fascismo*, 4th ed. (Rome: Editori Riuniti, 1963) and by the same author, *Nitti, D'Annunzio e la questione adriatica, 1919–1920* (Milan: Feltrinelli, 1959), René Albrecht-Carrié, *Italy at the Paris Peace Conference* (New York: Columbia University Press, 1938); Ivanoe Bonomi, *La politica italiana dopo Vittorio Veneto* (Milan: Einaudi, 1953); John M. Cammett, *Antonio Gramsci and the Origins of Italian Communism* (Stanford: Stanford University Press, 1967); the early chapters in Federico Chabod, *A History of Italian Fascism* (London: Weidenfeld and Nicolson, 1963); Guido Dorso, *Mussolini alla conquista del potere* (Milan: Mondadori, 1961); Giacomo Perticone, *La politica italiana nell'ultimo trentennio*, 3 vols. (Rome: Edizioni Leonardo, 1945–47), Vol. II; Antonino Rèpaci, *Marcia su Roma: Mito e realtà*, 2 vols. (Rome: Canesi, 1963); A. Rossi (pseud. for Angelo Tasca), *The Rise of Italian Fascism, 1918–1922* (London: Methuen, 1938), issued in a revised edition in Italian, *Nascita e avvento del fascismo: L'Italia dal 1918 al 1922*, 2 vols. (Bari: Laterza, 1965); the early chapters in Luigi Salvatorelli and Giovanni Mira, *Storia d'Italia nel periodo fascista*, 4th ed. (Turin: Einaudi, 1962); the concluding chapters in Christopher Seton-Watson, *Italy from Liberalism to Fascism* (London: Methuen,

1967); the early chapters in Luigi Sturzo, *Italy and Fascism* (1926; reprint ed., New York: Fertig, 1967); Roberto Vivarelli, *Il dopoguerra in Italia e l'avvento del fascismo, 1918–1922*, Vol. I, *Dalla fine della guerra all'impresa di Fiume* (Naples: Istituto Italiano per gli Studi Storici, 1967). Among the many biographies of Mussolini, the following are recommended for an understanding of his role in the postwar years: Renzo de Felice, *Mussolini il rivoluzionario, 1883–1920* (Turin: Einaudi, 1956), and by the same author, *Mussolini il fascista*, Vol. I, *La conquista del potere, 1921–1925* (Turin: Einaudi, 1966); Ivone Kirkpatrick, *Mussolini: A Study in Power* (New York: Hawthorn, 1964); and the pioneer work by Gaudens Megaro, *Mussolini in the Making* (London: G. Allen, 1938).

CHAPTER 3

POLITICS AND IDEOLOGY
IN FASCIST ITALY

Roland Sarti

Political movements associated with a revolutionary ideology always invite comparison between their stated objectives and their actual accomplishments after they have gained power. Italian Fascism is a case in point. At the root of the long controversy over the nature of Fascism lies the generally recognized gap between its promises and its achievements. The promises were as grandiose as the results seemed disastrous. Fascism began with a promise to renovate Italian society by adopting and combining the most workable parts of available political models regardless of their ideological provenance. This promise of synthesis in turn became the basis for its subsequent and more ambitious aspiration to rescue humanity from the opposite evils of communism and liberal-capitalist democracy. When these ambitious plans foundered in the physical and moral devastation of the Second World War, it was easy to conclude that Fascism had been a colossal and tragic hoax perpetrated on a gullible people by corrupt and self-seeking politicians. The failure of Italian Fascism to carry out its promises of social renewal is a fact of history. The question remains whether the failure is attributable to the inevitable compromises that are forced upon all revolutionary movements when they are confronted by the realities and responsibilities of power or whether it is due to the intrinsically sham quality of Fascist thought and politics. To answer this question, we must consider Fascism as a system of government rather than as an abstract doctrine.

Italians, who are often their own most severe critics, have diligently searched their national history for the precedents that would account for the glaring inadequacies of Fascism as a principle of social organization or for the "sinfulness" of its values. The search has not been confined to academic circles. The debate over the nature of Fascism was a burning

52

public issue after the Second World War. Nevertheless, the public debate revolved around two classic interpretations already worked out by scholars and political analysts: on the one hand was the Crocean argument that Fascism marked an unforeseeable and temporary departure from the progressive policies pursued by liberal governments from Cavour to Giolitti; on the other the more damning view that Fascism was the revelation of hidden but crippling defects of public life in Italy since the unification. The elements that allegedly made for continuity between liberal and Fascist Italy were identified variously with the political immaturity of the masses, the domination of political life by a series of "strong men," the prevalence of political *trasformismo*, or the presence of unrealistic dreams of national grandeur and great-power status.

To study the emergence of Italian Fascism is to be immediately confronted by the problem of continuity in history. Scholars are increasingly approaching this problem by asking specific questions about how, and by whom, power was actually exercised in Fascist Italy. There seems to be a general tendency in recent scholarly literature to turn away from the "choreographic" innovations of Fascism which captured the imagination of contemporary observers (the mass rallies, party ceremonials, nationalistic rituals, the glorification of the Duce and so on) and to study instead the behavior of competing interest groups both within and outside the party.

In following this approach, we have no intention of minimizing the importance of imagery and ritual as elements of popularity for the regime or as social bonds. It seems evident, however, that the public image and the inner reality of the regime were at considerable variance. This study of the links between thought and action in Fascist Italy hopes to throw some light on the inner reality hiding behind the rhetoric of Fascist totalitarianism. The questions that concern us here relate to the nature of the decision-making process in Fascist Italy. Did Fascist leaders govern in a manner significantly different from that of the older liberal leadership which they replaced? Were they guided by a systematic, ideological view of society or were they merely manipulators of power? Was Fascist ideology, however defined, an operative, directive element in the formulation and implementation of public policies, or was it merely a rationalization for decisions made on the basis of traditional pressure politics? They are questions which, in the words of a recent historiographical study, seek "on the one hand, to avoid separating Fascism from the context of Italian reality. . . [and] on the other, to go beyond the external image of Fascism, seeking rather to reveal its complex nature by emphasizing the interaction of its component elements." [1]

A study of Fascist ideology reveals the complexity of this interaction of component elements. Unlike other contemporary political movements

that have sought to preserve the semblance of doctrinal coherence even
when the responsibilities of power were forcing them to compromise and
dilute their original principles, Fascism always took pride in its rejection
of permanent doctrinal guidelines. This rejection of doctrinal coherence
is perhaps the fundamental theme of Fascist thought. Giovanni Gentile,
often considered the official philosopher of the Fascist period, stressed
that the essence of Fascism was "spirit" rather than "creed," and reiter-
ated on many occasions its activist, pragmatic nature:

> The truth, the significance of Fascism, is not measured in the spe-
> cial theses that it assumes from time to time, in theory or in prac-
> tice. . . . Often, having set up a target to be reached, a concept to
> realize, a way to follow, it has not hesitated to change its course
> when put to the proof, and to reject that aim or that concept as in-
> adequate or repugnant to its own principle. It has never wished to
> bind itself by pledging the future.[2]

Gentile's words remind us that Fascism could incorporate many ideologies. What really counts is not what may have been said from time to
time by particular leaders, currents, or interest groups operating within
the regime but, rather, what emerges from their competition for power.
The role played by ideology in this contest for power remains to be
determined. In one recent attempt to vindicate an independent role of
Fascist ideology in shaping Fascist society, we read that "by knowing
the ideals to which knowledgeable Fascists were committed we are in a
better position to reconstruct their influence in the 'logic' of historical
events. The implied assumption is, of course, that *some* identifiable
Fascist precepts and convictions exercised *some* influence over overt behavior." [3] It remains unclear, however, just what degree of influence was
exercised by specific "knowledgeable Fascists" in the course of the
many political arrangements worked out under the regime. It is a question that can be answered only by comparing what was said with what
was actually done. In the words of the maverick Marxist historian Angelo
Tasca, "to define fascism is, above all, to write its history." [4]

The slightest familiarity with the history of Italian Fascism reveals a
wide assortment of competing ideologies present within it. No single
ideological label will fit them all. Nationalism was unquestionably the
most pervasive of the Fascist "isms." There was also the temperamental
anarchism of many early *squadristi;* the names of Italo Balbo and Dino
Grandi immediately come to mind for the early years, while for the
period after the March on Rome, Roberto Farinacci best exemplified
this rebellious mood. Other "isms" included the confused radicalism of a
labor leader like Edmondo Rossoni, the libertarian "revisionism" of an
intellectual like Giuseppe Bottai, the statism and corporativism of a na-

tionalist theoretician like Alfredo Rocco, and in the 1930s, the mock militarism of Party Secretary Achille Starace.

Nationalism and, to a lesser degree, the cult of leadership were virtually the only axioms shared by all these leaders and groups. Nationalism was the ideological matrix in which these diverse, often antagonistic, groups sought to reconcile their differences. The unity, however, was more impressive from the outside than from within. When it came to shaping public policy, these groups were essentially rivals. The principle of leadership, on the other hand, plays a more central but unexpected role in this discussion. Mussolini was the logical leader of Fascism because he knew how to deal with and hold together the most disparate political elements. It was his talents as an accomplished compromiser and temporizer which served him best behind the scenes, the iron-willed *Duce* of textbook and newsreel having been manufactured essentially for public consumption. Largely because of the heterogeneity of the Fascist following and of the type of leadership provided by Mussolini, the history of the Fascist regime is essentially a history of compromise and flexibility.

The internal heterogeneity of Fascism and Mussolini's style of leadership indicate that the totalitarian slant of Fascist thought and the monolithic structure of the Fascist party are the least reliable clues to the social realities of the regime. To understand these realities we must study the mutual interaction of currents within the Fascist party and with outside vested interests such as the monarchy, the church, the government bureaucracy, and organized business. The development of Fascist syndicalist and corporativist doctrines reflected that complicated give and take.

In the process of studying these internal contrasts, current historians are rediscovering the revolutionary components of Fascism. In addition to the traditional and for many years prevalent identification of Fascism with capitalist reaction, we now have studies that attempt to classify Fascism as a movement of the political center, or to draw our attention to the revolutionary aspirations of Fascist regimes, or even to point to striking similarities between Fascism and the new left.[5] We are reminded that Fascism was, among other things, the revolt of an idealistic younger generation against the conventional wisdom, gross materialism, and alleged timidity of the old order. Fascism did indeed glorify the *Ardito*, that youthful activist hardened on the battlefields of the First World War. The *Ardito* was, above all, a man of action unencumbered by allegedly outdated moral prejudices or by excessive knowledge, intolerant of organizational restraints, and a heroic figure who lived according to the maxim *me ne frego* (I don't give a damn).

These reminders of the novelty that was Fascism after Mussolini began to organize his *Fasci di combattimento* in March 1919 are extremely useful. They help us to recreate the historical image of Fascism and to see it with the eyes of contemporary observers who could not anticipate its subsequent development. It was a movement to which traditional political or ideological labels did not easily apply. Originally, Fascism was essentially an urban phenomenon with a minority following in a few industrial centers of northern Italy (the agrarian Fascists did not materialize in force until 1921). Beyond these urban bases, Fascism did not have a clear social profile: it was not identified with any particular social class, and its program expressed conservative, reformist, and revolutionary aspirations. It was essentially the brainchild of one man, Benito Mussolini, who was born and bred to political agitation. His break with the Italian Socialist party in the fall of 1914 was due to his decision to embrace the interventionist cause and did not alienate him, at least in his own eyes, from his revolutionary past. The slogan with which he urged intervention in the war, "War Today, Revolution Tomorrow," denoted disagreement with the Socialist party's revolutionary strategy rather than a rejection of the principle of revolution.[6]

But while Mussolini remained a revolutionary after 1914 in the sense of wanting to subvert the liberal state, it is clear that he also began to reject many axioms of socialist doctrine.[7] Capitalism seemed less heinous to him when, after the military defeat of Caporetto in October 1917, he concluded that military victory required the expansion of production above all and that considerations of redistribution of wealth ought to be postponed. This productivist outlook implied a recognition of the social usefulness of capital, a theme soon to be incorporated into Fascist propaganda. Productivism eventually enabled Mussolini to establish a working relationship with business interests who remained otherwise suspicious of Fascism.

The war alienated Mussolini from socialism in still another and more immediately significant way. The controversy between neutralists and interventionists (see Chapter 14, pages 325–326), somewhat muted during the war, flared up once again with renewed vehemence after the armistice. Mussolini, who was completely identified with the interventionist cause, discovered that on that particular issue there was little room to maneuver. Not that he didn't try. Unlike most intransigent nationalists, Mussolini endorsed the Treaty of Rapallo of November 1920, which formally ceded most of the Dalmatian coast to Yugoslavia and provided that the city of Fiume, still occupied by D'Annunzio's legionnaires, should become a free state. Ultimately, however, Mussolini could not escape the legacy of his interventionism, which made any dialogue with the left impossible. Like productivism, Mussolini's nationalism opened up many possibilities for a dialogue with the right. The connection between productivism and the nationalist mystique of war was dramatized when on August 1, 1918, Mussolini dropped the old subtitle "A Socialist

Daily" from the masthead of his newspaper *Il Popolo d'Italia,* replacing it with a new description as "A Soldiers' and Producers' Daily."

For the time being, however, Mussolini would not commit himself to the right. The political situation in Italy after the armistice was too fluid for him to seek complete identification with either conservatives or revolutionaries. He did not hide his bias against the monarchy or his anticlericalism. The Fascist program of June 1919 called for such radical innovations as the participation of workers in factory management by means of factory councils, adoption of a confiscatory progressive tax on capital and war profits, and land reform. It also featured a number of typically reformist demands such as the introduction of the eight-hour day, minimum wages, old-age and disability pensions. In fact, the program provided something for everyone. Conservatives could admire its nationalist tone, social malcontents its more radical demands, while the program's bread-and-butter clauses could be expected to appeal to organized labor and the working masses in general.

This varied and unconventional program gave Mussolini an enviable and unique political latitude. The ability and open-mindedness with which he exploited this freedom of action gave him a lasting reputation for unprincipled opportunism in some quarters and for supreme political realism in others. He did not stress the radical aspects of his program until Fascist candidates were totally defeated in the national elections of November 1919. His subsequent radicalism in turn proved to be only a temporary expedient to gain favor with the masses. The decisive turning point in Mussolini's political tactics occurred after the failure of the workers' occupation of the factories in September 1920. When the workers failed in their attempt to wrest control of production from management, the poor organization and indecisive leadership of the so-called revolutionary forces became evident. Public opinion was growing tired of continual and inconclusive agitations. Businessmen and landowners, disappointed in the government's failure to back them in their dispute with labor, began to look around for new political allies. Mussolini sensed the imminence of a backlash reaction and conducted himself accordingly.

Fascism became increasingly more conservative after 1920. Landowners and industrialists increased their financial contributions, with the landowners being particularly generous. Fascist *squadre* organized by Italo Balbo and Dino Grandi roamed through the Romagna countryside pillaging and burning Socialist headquarters, chambers of labor, workers' cooperatives, and the headquarters of agricultural workers' leagues. Rural Fascism thus imparted a narrow classist image to the entire movement. Mussolini's flirtation with conservative groups was more subtle. He continued to make friendly gestures in the direction of the reformist General Confederation of Labor (the labor union affiliated with the Socialist party) and reserved his barbs for the leadership of the Socialist party. He did not want to destroy the possibility of future cooperation with organized labor. His major concession to business interests before the March on Rome on October 30, 1922, brought him to power was his endorsement of economic laissez faire. Although that was as much as most business leaders expected of him, some of them remained suspicious of Fascism because of the continuing presence of radical elements within its ranks. As one industrial leader put it shortly before the March on Rome, "How can we, men of the right, admit without hesitations that Fascism is a party of the right and not, perhaps, actually a party politically on the left?" [8]

The perceptive political observer Mario Missiroli described Fascism in 1921 as "the heresy of all other political parties." Fascist activists and sympathizers did indeed come from nearly all shadings of the political spectrum. They did not submit readily to discipline and direction. The *ras* (local chieftains) were notoriously unmanageable and scarcely acknowledged the authority of Mussolini's Fascist Central Committee in Milan. Mussolini's role was often that of mediator between his turbulent followers and the outside world, not an easy task given the nature of his following. Fearful perhaps that Fascism was becoming too closely identified with blind reaction and wanting to leave himself room to reach an understanding with the moderate left, he decided in August 1921 to commit his followers to a formal treaty of pacification with the Socialists. But Grandi and Farinacci led a revolt that forced Mussolini to abandon the pact and brought about his temporary resignation as party leader.

Mussolini's desire to give Fascism a minimum of political coherence and organization, thereby bringing it more effectively under his personal direction, found expression in other ways. In November 1921 he finally prevailed upon his followers to agree to the transformation of the movement into a full-fledged political party. At the same time, he called upon his followers to clothe themselves in a respectable ideological garb. On August 27, 1921, *Il Popolo d'Italia* greeted the appearance of the first school of Fascist culture and propaganda with the comment that unless Fascism developed its own body of doctrine, it would perish slowly but surely.

Fascism never did create its own doctrines, but it did borrow and synthesize widely. For a doctrine to be incorporated into the body of Fascist thought, it had to meet certain requirements. Since doctrines were to serve Fascism in an instrumental way, they had to be somewhat ambiguous and flexible. Revolutionary syndicalism, as represented by Edmondo Rossoni's labor organizations, met this requirement only in part. Rossoni's usefulness to Mussolini was based on the fact that he proposed to further the interests of labor by promoting the expansion of production, cooperating with management to increase productivity, and fostering a sense of patriotism among the workers. Rossoni, who suspected that Mussolini might give in too readily to the demands of management, agreed nevertheless to associate his labor organizations with the Fascist party in January 1922 because he wanted the party's support in his drive to recruit followers from the Socialist organizations being wrecked by Balbo's *squadristi*.

Mussolini discovered, however, that the alliance with Rossoni also had its political drawbacks. Although Rossoni professed a belief in class collaboration, his behavior suggested that he wanted it on his own terms. His efforts to organize mixed syndicates of workers and employers (integral syndicalism, also described in the early 1920s as corporativism) aroused the hostility of the powerful General Confederation of Italian Industry, better known in Italy as Confindustria, which spoke for the industrialists. The leaders of Confindustria (who eventually forced Rossoni to abandon his plans) feared that if the employers lost their organizational autonomy they would be forced to do most of the cooperating. Rossoni's revolutionary past and his rabble-rousing rhetoric made him persona non grata among the industrialists and landowners.

Mussolini felt more secure when in March 1923 Fascism finally incorporated its old ally, the Nationalist party. The numerically small Nationalist party owed much of its influence to the brilliant intellectuals who were active within it. Men like Enrico Corradini, Filippo Carli, Luigi Federzoni, and, most of all, the jurist Alfredo Rocco had begun to develop the ideological foundations of what eventually came to be known as Fascist corporativism long before the appearance of the Fascist movement. Their ideas bore some resemblance to those of the revolutionary syndicalists. Both spoke in terms of class collaboration and argued that the legitimate aspirations of the workers were best satisfied in the framework of the national state. But the similarities were essentially superficial. Unlike the syndicalists, who did not shrink from the idea of violence and revolution, the nationalists were committed to gradual change by legal means. Their evolutionist view of society gave Mussolini the time he needed to reconcile differences within the Fascist party, neutralize the irreconcilables, and convince vested interests that they ought to go along with institutional innovations.

Nationalist theoreticians wanted institutional reforms that would strengthen the authority of the state. Their ideal was an authoritarian society based on the recognition that the interests of competing social groups and classes ought to be reconciled for the sake of national unity. In other words, they rejected the classist premises of both socialism and classical capitalism, which were to be superseded by the integrated society of the corporative state. The corporative state would institutionalize the representation of labor and capital, thereby recognizing their legitimate functions. Corporativism provided something for everyone. Its appeal was broad enough to accommodate both the conservative and revolutionary elements that were attracted to Fascism. It gave Fascism the universal dimension that had long been sought by Mussolini without in any way restricting his political freedom of action. Intrinsically, corporativism was neither conservative nor revolutionary: it could be either, depending on the structure of its institutions, the relative power of the interests it represented, and the intentions of its leaders. It was the perfect doctrine for a movement as undefined and fluctuating as Fascism.

Although Mussolini certainly appreciated social doctrines as a means of raising Fascism above the political contingencies of the moment, he was at his best only when operating precisely within these contingencies. The success of the March on Rome was certainly not due to the ideological appeal of Fascism. The Fascist bid for power succeeded because Mussolini was able to convince the monarchy and most of the old liberal guard that they had much to gain by appointing him prime minister.

To those liberals who were willing to dismiss Fascist violence as a peripheral phenomenon, it seemed as if Mussolini was coming to power as the latest champion of the liberal tradition. This misreading of Fascism probably accounts for the fact that parliament gave Mussolini's government the authority to rule by decree on Mussolini's promise to enact urgently needed administrative and fiscal reforms. He promised to restore a sense of fiscal responsibility in government, reduce public expenditures, balance the budget, and rationalize bureaucratic procedures. Conservative Fascist activists and sympathizers welcomed these reforms as necessary corrective steps to the drift to the left, which they attributed to Giolitti's politics. They did not see them as the beginning of a new social order.

The "liberal phase" of Fascism lasted until the end of 1924. Its most noticeable feature was probably Alberto De Stefani's valiant effort to enact the promised administrative and fiscal reforms. As minister of finance, De Stefani ran afoul of the complicated politics of Fascism. His straightforward policies, inspired by the purest laissez faire philosophy, earned him powerful enemies. Some of his most insidious critics turned out to be businessmen who repeated all the catchwords of economic liberalism but who were far more interested in securing high protective tariffs, public subsidies, and government contracts. Nor did De Stefani find much support within the Fascist party. Mussolini finally dismissed him as a "budgetary maniac."

In these initial years of Fascist government, radical Fascists felt frustrated in their efforts to launch the famous "second wave" of the Fascist revolution. Rossoni had to abandon his plans to set up mixed syndicates of workers and employers. The industrialists prevailed because Rossoni found little support in Fascist circles and because Mussolini and other party leaders, who now found Rossoni an embarrassing rival, were mostly interested in curbing the power of the Fascist trade unions. The government-sponsored Acerbo electoral law of November 1923, which assigned two-thirds of the seats in the Chamber to the party or coalition of parties receiving at least 25 percent of the popular vote, seemed to indicate that Mussolini now wanted to assure Fascism and its allies a dominant but not necessarily exclusive role within a restricted parliamentary system.

At the same time, Mussolini could not afford to discard the idea of the continuing Fascist revolution because it was the myth that held the party together. As long as that myth prevailed, discontented Fascists could still hope to obtain satisfaction by supporting Mussolini. Thus, to preserve his credibility as a revolutionary leader in the eyes of his followers, Mussolini encouraged Fascist revisionists like Giuseppe Bottai and Massimo Rocca to explore alternatives for social development. Bottai urged the adoption of democratic procedures within the party and supported Rocca's plans to encourage the formation of managerial and technocratic elites which would put their special skills at the service of government. Mussolini backed the revisionists as long as he needed them to keep the intransigents in line and dropped them after they had served that purpose; his behavior reflected his indifference to the ideas germinating within Fascism in the early 1920s.

The radicals in the party found the "liberal phase" of Fascism a frustrating experience. The only new institutions created during this period were the Fascist Militia and the Grand Council. Despite appearances, the Grand Council had a purely advisory role within the party. The establishment of the Militia was an effort on Mussolini's part to bring the *squadre* under central control, not to give the party an independent basis of power. With the electoral landslide scored by the Fascist party and its allies in the national elections of April 1924, it seemed as if Fascism would soon settle down to peaceful coexistence with the country's traditional political institutions and vested interests. Parliament had been chastened but not disbanded. The reform of the bureaucracy was being pursued discreetly with minor reshufflings of personnel. The business leadership had supported the Fascist electoral list without reservations. Secret negotiations were already under way to bring about a settlement of the old dispute between church and state. The king saw no reason to doubt Mussolini's loyalty to the monarchy. It looked as if the expectations of the old-guard liberals that the responsibilities of power would lead Fascism to shed its revolutionary aspirations were about to be realized. But this outcome was thwarted by the assassination of the Socialist deputy Giacomo Matteotti by a group of Fascist thugs in June 1924.

The Matteotti crisis brought Fascism to a political crossroads. The opposition reasserted itself within and outside parliament in the hope of bringing down Mussolini's government. There seemed to be a genuine fear within the Fascist party that the entire Fascist experiment might soon be liquidated. Dissension flared up among party leaders, with some actually suggesting that Mussolini step down as prime minister. Provincial party bosses, Farinacci foremost among them, lashed out against what they considered to be political indecisiveness in the higher echelons. The political ties with outside interests which Mussolini had been cultivating carefully since 1921 were seriously impaired. Mussolini, now virtually isolated in the silent, deserted halls of Palazzo Chigi, vacillated between discouragement and bluster. He overcame his hesitation only when confronted by the Fascist intransigents who threatened to take matters into their own hands. His response to that threat was his famous speech to the Chamber of Deputies on January 3, 1925, in which he assumed personal responsibility for the misbehavior of his followers and promised a speedy solution of the crisis: "When two irreducible elements are locked in combat, the solution is force. In history there has never been any other solution, and there never will be."

The speech of January 3 is often taken to mark the end of "liberal" and the beginning of "totalitarian" Fascism. In reality, there was no such sharp break. The speech did, however, register the important fact that the political frame of reference had changed. Conservative Fascists could no longer pretend that Fascism had exhausted its political mission with the reform of the parliamentary system and the defeat of socialism. The vehement political opposition that had been mobilized in the course of the Matteotti crisis could be overcome only by forging ahead to the next phase of the Fascist revolution. Mussolini also had his own tactical reasons for wanting to do so. Since his previously friendly relations with outside groups had been impaired during the crisis, he now had to rely more heavily on the Fascist party. To keep its various factions united, he naturally fell back on the idea of the continuing revolution. Already, in September 1924 the government had appointed a Commission of Fifteen (recast in January 1925 into a Commission of Eighteen, better known as the Commission of Solons) to investigate possible guidelines for reform. Action was delayed until the end of 1925 when the powers of the head of government (Mussolini's new title) were expanded, the role of parliament curtailed, and civil liberties practically eliminated.

The new system could almost be described as a "presidential regime" were it not for the fact that the head of government could not be removed by electoral means.

Former nationalists like Minister of the Interior Luigi Federzoni and Minister of Justice Alfredo Rocco were now in control, and the reforms conformed to their authoritarian, centralizing mentality. The centralizing intent of the new laws was perhaps most evident in the expansion of the power of the prefects, who represented the state in the provinces and were appointed by the minister of the interior. Although the functions of the prefects continued to overlap in many instances with those of other local agencies, at least in principle their authority exceeded that of elected and party officials.[9]

An authoritarian and dictatorial regime clearly emerged in Italy in 1925 to 1926. Mussolini created its slogan: "Everything in the state, nothing against the state, nothing outside the state." It is debatable, however, whether his regime can properly be called totalitarian. A fundamental goal of totalitarian regimes, the desire to create a new type of personality, was already clearly evident. During these years the party reorganized its youth organizations, where, in the words of the Fascist anthem *Giovinezza*, future generations of Italians were to be trained "for the wars of tomorrow." The government established a systematic control over the means of mass communications. But the chain of command, the social institutions, and the economic policies of the regime were not what one expects to find in a totalitarian society. The regime's institutional arrangements often worked at cross purposes with its totalitarian aspirations.

The machinery developed to deal with labor controversies is a good case in point. According to the Labor Law of April 3, 1926, workers and employers were to be organized in separate, state-controlled associations, or unions. Thirteen such national associations were promptly established, six for labor and six corresponding ones for employers, with an additional union for artists and intellectuals. While the six employer unions were each fully autonomous, their labor counterparts were the constituent sections of a national association of workers, the Confederation of Fascist Trade Unions, led by Rossoni. The employers, particularly the industrialists, insisted that this arrangement gave Rossoni's group an undesirable monopoly over the representation of labor. Partly in response to their demands, and partly because Mussolini and the party secretary Augusto Turati did not want to see so much power concentrated in Rossoni's hands, the Confederation of Fascist Trade Unions was dissolved in December 1928.

Labor and capital were now theoretically on an equal footing. Employers and workers in all trades, geographical districts, and sectors

of the economy were organized in separate, parallel associations authorized to negotiate and conclude collective labor contracts. Everyone was
theoretically subject to the same degree of public regulation. It was not
that way in practice. Whereas the labor organizations were indeed run
like appendages of the public administration and expected to conform
to government and party directives, the employers, particularly the
industrialists who continued to be represented by Confindustria, remained
masters in their own house. The totalitarian aspirations of Fascist leaders
always found an obstacle in the employers' stubborn insistence on
managing their own affairs.

Fascist labor leaders were handicapped in several ways. Tullio Cianetti,
who headed the industrial unions in the 1930s, complained repeatedly
about the lack of support for labor in high party echelons. Relations
between the old timers of revolutionary syndicalism and the younger
organizers were often strained, the former proud of their activist,
colorful past, the latter boasting diplomas and a general education that
few of the older members possessed. Few of the younger labor organizers were of working-class origin. Pietro Capoferri, who headed the
industrial unions after 1939, was a former employer. Furthermore, as
Bottai sometimes complained, the practice of having labor leaders
appointed by the party and the total absence of elections in the Fascist
labor organizations meant that workers could not easily identify with
their representatives.

The leaders of the Fascist unions were often subject to outside
pressures seeking to influence the course of labor negotiations. As party
appointees they could not disregard the Fascist principle that national
or party interests ought to take precedence over those of their working-
class constituency. Thus, Fascist labor leaders who revealed a classist
mentality exposed themselves to the charge of ideological heresy. When
business leaders argued that wage reductions were in the national interest
(as they always did), labor leaders could not dismiss their arguments
as mere rhetoric. The usual technique was for the employers to ask a
very substantial wage cut, for the workers' representatives to accept a
much smaller one, and for the government to settle on an intermediate
figure. Final decisions thus reflected political as much as economic
considerations.

Labor leaders thus had to know how to argue their cases on grounds
of political expediency. On such grounds, they were often able to
obtain partial compensations for wage cuts in the form of such fringe
benefits as government subsidies for workers with large families, sickness
insurance, end-of-the-year bonuses, paid holidays, and severance allowances. Employers could be persuaded to go along with such measures
because they knew that they would be sharing their cost with govern-

ment and labor. It was in the government's interest to close the traditional gap between the country's political leaders and the masses by sponsoring social programs. Particularly successful in this respect was the "after work" organization Opera Nazionale Dopolavoro, which, with its group excursions at popular prices, sports activities, theatrical performances, courses in technical subjects and general education, made the government visible even in the most isolated communities. Political considerations were not extraneous to the wage increases introduced after 1935, when the country was mobilized for war. However, these gains do not alter the fact that the labor organizations were designed more to control than to represent the workers. Fascist leaders always suspected that Italy's industrial workers were not entirely loyal to the regime and had no intention of providing the workers with independent organizations that would reflect the wishes of the rank-and-file membership.

Employers, on the other hand, were far better organized and protected under a leadership that was largely of their own choice. They continued to be represented after 1926 by their old organizations, now operating under slightly different names. They thus enjoyed a continuity of representation which labor could have had only if the old Socialist and Catholic labor unions had been allowed to function freely. The minor changes the employer associations experienced as a result of the Labor Law of April 3 actually made them more cohesive. For the most part, they continued to choose their own officials, whose powers were considerably broader than they had been before the reform. Firms that had refused to join business associations were now required to do so by law. The result was greater unity and a more effective chain of command, enhanced by the fact that Confindustria consolidated its dominant position among business associations and successfully defended its organizational autonomy against the Fascist party. Many employer associations were now in the enviable position of enjoying the autonomy of private pressure groups and the authority of public associations.

One of the ironies of the situation is that the regime had to pressure the industrialists into accepting this rather favorable arrangement. Mussolini used both threats and reassurances to overcome their initial opposition. A series of Fascist-sponsored strikes in late 1924 and early 1925 served to remind them that they should not take the regime's benevolence for granted and that the threat from the old Socialist labor unions, which sometimes joined these strikes, was not to be discounted in spite of the reverses they had suffered since 1920. At the same time, Mussolini promised substantial concessions if the industrialists would cooperate. These clever tactics convinced Antonio Stefano Benni, the president of Confindustria, that the industrialists ought to perform "an act of courage" that would give business organizations official status in the institutions of the "syndical state."

The "act of courage" was the Vidoni Palace Agreement of October 1925 by which Confindustria and Rossoni's Confederation of Fascist Unions agreed to recognize each other as the sole bargaining agents for industrial employers and workers respectively. The Labor Law of April 3, 1926, simply extended that provision to the other national associations of workers and employers. Since only those associations approved by the government now had the right to conclude collective labor contracts that were legally enforceable, non-Fascist labor unions were forced out of existence without making it necessary for the government to actually disband them. Socialist and Catholic labor unions were driven from the scene, much to the advantage of Fascist labor organizations, which no longer had any rivals to contend with.

Several prominent industrialists, most notably Gino Olivetti, the secretary of Confindustria, and Giovanni Agnelli of Fiat, were reluctant to grant a monopoly of representation to the Fascist trade unions. They feared that due to their still small following among industrial workers, the Fascists would be unable to guarantee observance of labor contracts and order within the factories. In order to avoid possible disturbances within the factories, the industrialists actually spoke out in favor of retaining the Socialist and Communist factory councils which were elected by the workers. In the past the employers had opposed the councils on the ground that they challenged the authority of management, but at that particular moment they saw them as useful allies against Rossoni's syndicalists and as a means of keeping the labor movement divided. A primary reason that the industrialists did not want to strengthen Rossoni's position was his insistence that the factory councils be replaced by Fascist *fiduciari di fabbrica* (workers' trustees), who would have made the Fascist trade unions a living presence within the factories. It was only after they received Mussolini's reassurances that the government would not countenance easy recourse to strikes and that the *fiduciari* would not be introduced that the industrialists agreed to sign the Vidoni Agreement. The *fiduciari* appeared only in October 1939, and because of the war, they never played a meaningful role in labor relations. With the disappearance of the factory councils and the failure to introduce the *fiduciari*, management gained uncontested authority at the factory level. Starting in 1927, management used that authority to introduce new labor techniques that required additional exertions from the workers without extending proportionate compensation.

Although the labor reform grew out of the need to justify the revolutionary image of Fascism, it fell far short of the initial goals of

Fascist revolutionaries. It strengthened the authority of management within the factories and of business associations over individual firms. In their new capacity as official agencies of the syndical state, employers' associations were guaranteed representation in many government councils from which they might otherwise have been excluded. Most important, the reform sanctioned the defeat of more radical alternatives. What emerged in 1926 was a syndical state where workers and employers were organized separately, rather than a corporative state in which workers and employers were supposed to be organized side by side in the same associations.

Nevertheless corporativism became the official label of the next phase of the Fascist revolution, in spite of the fact that Fascist theoreticians disagreed on what was to be expected of the corporations—which seemed like modern versions of medieval guilds. It was by no means clear, for instance, whether the corporations would replace the unions and what role they would play in the regulation of production. These persisting ambiguities developed a special political usefulness of their own because they kept the intellectuals busy, discontented Fascists hopeful, and public opinion expectant. In other words, the concept of corporativism prolonged the myth of the continuing revolution while giving conservative groups the opportunity to prepare for the next confrontation. The twenty-two corporations that were eventually set up in 1934 thus represented still another compromise between the innovators and the conservatives. Fascist theoreticians found themselves saddled with the unenviable task of providing ideological respectability for arrangements that were the results of power politics.

The inability of Fascism to pursue an ideologically coherent course is evident from the regime's failure to implement in society at large the one doctrine that was accepted by all Fascists: the cult of leadership and rigid hierarchy. To be sure, the chain of command that ran from the ministries to their representatives in the provinces was strengthened, particularly between the Ministry of the Interior and the prefects. Through these agencies, individuals were subjected to an unprecedented degree of centralized control. But in other important sectors, such as the party, business, labor, and youth organizations, the lines of jurisdiction and responsibility were by no means well defined. In this vast administrative quagmire we sometimes encounter duce-like figures who in theory were fully responsible to the real Duce but in reality enjoyed broad discretionary power. Power, instead of being concentrated at the top according to the principle of leadership, was often dispersed into separate and uncoordinated pockets. This lack of coordination is one reason that it is misleading to describe Fascist Italy as a totalitarian society. Contrary to the emphatic assertion of one authoritative and popular study of totalitarian societies, the documentary evidence does not show that Mussolini's views were "decisive" and his power "absolute." [10]

What the evidence indicates is that in certain areas Mussolini and his immediate collaborators were indeed able to impose their will, while in others they had to bargain for support in a manner hardly compatible with Mussolini's image as an all-powerful dictator. He did have at his disposal a chain of command in the police and a basis of power in the Fascist party and the militia which he could use effectively in many circumstances. There can be little doubt, for instance, that the conduct of foreign affairs rested ultimately in Mussolini's hands. The *Diaries* of Galeazzo Ciano, Mussolini's son-in-law and foreign minister from 1936 to 1943, make it clear that even the Duce's closest collaborators remained essentially subservient to the dictator in the area of foreign affairs. Parliament also discovered that the Fascist leaders could be harsh taskmasters. The electoral reform of May 1928 completely changed the character of the Chamber of Deputies. The membership of the new Chamber was regulated by the Grand Council and originated from various associations approved by the party. After this reform, parliament resembled a cheering squad before which the leaders appeared to have their decisions ratified by acclamation.

Fascist leaders behaved differently, however, when dealing with groups or institutions that could be useful as political allies and had an independent base of power. The monarchy survived during the Fascist period partly because Victor Emmanuel III was able to convince Mussolini that he could count on its support in times of crisis and partly because of its continuing popularity in many parts of the country and among conservative elites. Nevertheless, Victor Emmanuel had to accept various infringements on the monarchy's traditional prerogatives, such as the Grand Council's assertion of December 1928 that it could intervene in determining the succession to the throne and Mussolini's announcement of March 1938 that in case of war he would assume complete command of the armed forces. As his prestige increased, Mussolini became more and more resentful of having to share his honors with a *roi fainéant*. The army, whose officers continued to take an oath of allegiance to the king, had to accept the presence of a rival military organization, the Fascist Militia. The Militia, however, never gained a military importance comparable to that of the *Waffen-SS* in Nazi Germany. Although Italian generals professed complete loyalty to the regime, the army maintained an image of formal aloofness from the regime. Army generals who were completely identified with Fascism, like Emilio De Bono, were the exception rather than the rule.

Mussolini's desire to bargain with powerful groups that were willing to accept the Fascist regime is also evident in his dealings with the church. The Lateran Accords of February 1929, which put an end to the long conflict between church and state, took the form of an agreement between two sovereign powers. The Accords were the result of long negotiations that tried to reconcile real conflicts of interest. Mussolini's personal prestige increased enormously as a result of the settlement, while the church gained by having Catholicism designated as the religion of state. Furthermore, the financial claims of the papacy against the state were settled, the territorial independence of the Holy See was guaranteed, and the legal status and financial prerogatives of the holy orders were defined. But the Concordat was vague on the controversial issue of who was to educate the young. The regime recognized that Catholic schools had a right to function freely, but Mussolini also made it clear that Fascism could not renounce its claim on the ultimate allegiance of the individual. Fascist leaders and religious authorities continued to bicker over the role of religious youth associations, particularly Catholic Action and its affiliates, until Mussolini more or less acknowledged their legitimacy in September 1931. Such ad hoc understandings, however, could not settle the basic issue of whether church doctrine or Fascist ideology were to have prior claims on individual conscience. In dealing with the one institution whose universal claims resembled those of Fascism, the regime displayed its characteristic tendency to temporize and compromise. Mussolini was usually reluctant to turn a potential supporter into an opponent by acting out the totalitarian premises of Fascist thought.

There is one Fascist document, the Charter of Labor of April 1927, which fully reflects the web of compromises and the precarious balance of forces sustaining the regime. The text of the Charter reflects, above all, Mussolini's desire to reconcile such contrasting social views as those of Benni, Bottai, Rocco, and Rossoni. In its final form, it was a document that could be accepted by Fascists of virtually all descriptions because of its built-in ambiguities.[11] Advocates of private initiative often invoked those provisions of the charter which acknowledged the social usefulness of private property. Fascist radicals quoted other passages affirming the priority of public over private interest. To the extent that the charter revealed the equivocal character of Fascist social policy, it can truly be called the "Magna Charta" of the regime. Eventually, Mussolini proved to be the most severe critic of the social system he had labored so hard to create. Reacting against his government's lack of vigor in waging war in the summer of 1940, he commented bitterly: "It is not possible to remain between the semipublic and the semiprivate; undefined responsibilities can only create this atmosphere of general irresponsibility."

Mussolini thus acknowledged that his regime had been unable to achieve the primary goal of Fascism: the efficient mobilization of the country's natural and human resources for the pursuit of nationalistic objectives. In trying to exculpate himself and his collaborators, he ascribed this failure to lack of cooperation from those same vested interests whose support he had courted assiduously in previous years. His diatribes against the supposedly corrupt and self-seeking bourgeoisie mounted in intensity as disaster piled upon disaster during the Second World War. He could not bring himself to admit that the failures of his regime in wartime were perhaps implicit in the way he and his associates had exercised power during eighteen years of peace.

The Fascist government certainly tried to assert itself in the conduct of economic affairs. De Stefani's laissez faire policies had given way after July 1925 to a new interventionist phase that continued with minor interruptions right through the 1930s. (For a discussion of these economic policies, see Chapter 8, pages 181–186.) But Fascist economic interventionism aimed primarily at achieving a consensus for politically motivated objectives.

Political motivations were evident in a number of Mussolini's economic policies beginning in 1926 with his drive to overvalue the lira. In this instance, Mussolini was convinced that a strong currency was required to assure the political prestige of his regime. To compensate business interests for the losses they sustained in foreign trade as a result of the revaluation, the government increased protective tariffs, gave domestic producers almost absolute preference in awarding government contracts, carried through the Battle for Wheat to make the country agriculturally self-sufficient, encouraged major firms to monopolize production and distribution in the various sectors of production, and legislated compulsory wage reductions. Most business groups did support Mussolini's monetary policy on these terms, but the result was to launch the economy in the direction of autarchy, a policy of national self-sufficiency which ultimately proved to be economically self-defeating. Furthermore, these concessions strengthened the bargaining power of established business groups, thus helping them resist subsequent government efforts to revamp the national economy.

The increased power of resistance of established business groups became evident in the 1930s when the Fascist leadership decided that the time had come to fully implement the principles of corporativism, which had suffered a setback during the syndical reform of 1925 to 1926. The economic depression of the 1930s goaded the government into resuming the course of the Fascist revolution. After having insisted for many years that Fascism was a revolutionary alternative to capitalism and socialism, Fascist leaders felt compelled to propose far-reaching innovations in dealing with the economic crisis. Controversy ranged far and wide during the early 1930s over the nature and functions of the corporations envisaged by the Labor Law of 1926 but not yet established.

The problems of the corporative state were discussed with unusual seriousness and intellectual commitment at a colloquium held in Ferrara in May 1932. There the two most incompatible views of the role of the corporations were voiced by Gino Olivetti, the secretary of Confindustria, and Ugo Spirito, a young professor of philosophy at the University of Rome. Olivetti, expressing apprehensions still widely shared in business circles, argued that the corporations ought to be purely advisory bodies and not restrict the role of private initiative. Spirito, on the other hand, argued that the corporations ought to be invested with title of ownership over the means of production and be endowed with economic decision-making powers. Bottai, who as minister of corporations spoke in an official capacity (the ministry of corporations had been set up in July 1926, without the corporations), took a moderate stand between Olivetti and Spirito, probably because he did not share Spirito's notion that the corporations ought to absorb the unions. Bottai was convinced that the separation of workers and employers in parallel associations reflected a real social division that Fascism eventually ought to transcend but could not afford to ignore while it still existed. Bottai's words in effect reassured the industrialists that the corporative reform would not be a leap in the dark.

The twenty-two corporations described by the Corporative Law of February 5, 1934, were far closer to Olivetti's than to Spirito's model. Still, the employers took no chances. To indicate how seriously they viewed the corporations they appointed their most prestigious representatives to sit on their councils. The corporations actually made it easier for the employers to practice self-regulation; they also gave big business an official place in the Fascist state and may have helped ward off more stringent forms of public control. Other vested interests accepted the corporations without reservations. Church authorities welcomed the institutionalization of the concept of class cooperation, which Catholic social theoreticians had been proposing since the 1890s. The bureaucracy eagerly anticipated the proliferation of corporative agencies, which nearly doubled the size of the civil administration and provided new opportunities for careers, rewards, and prestige. Although the corporative reform was not formally completed until the old Chamber of Deputies was abolished in December 1938 and replaced by the Chamber of Fasces and Corporations, the appearance of the corporations in 1934 indicated that the myth of the continuing social revolution had run its course. Conservative supporters of the regime also took comfort in the fact that the Fascist party had ceased to be the breeding ground of radical ideologies. The party's loss of political autonomy was barely disguised by the proliferation of colorful uniforms and by the rallies and parades that were the special concern of Party-Secretary Achille Starace in the 1930s. Party membership had swollen into the millions by indiscriminate enrollment of new recruits who were Fascists in name only. Mussolini, always distrustful of independent-minded collaborators, surrounded himself with docile lieutenants. His success in strengthening the state and weakening the party made businessmen, bureaucrats, members of the royal household, and military and religious leaders enthusiastic "Mussolinians." In the final analysis, Mussolini's prestige rested on his ability to empty Fascism of its revolutionary content. Ironically, the social consensus demanded by Fascist ideologists was achieved by sacrificing their formulas to the politics of procrastination and compromise.

After 1934 Mussolini could preserve the dynamic image of Fascism only by pursuing an aggressive foreign policy. In his speech of November 10, 1934, to the representatives of the corporations he explicitly tied the advent of the corporations to the international mission of Fascism:

> In our relations with the outside world, the corporation aims at steadily increasing the power of the nation in order to facilitate its expansion abroad. It is worth asserting the international significance of our system because relations between races and nations will soon be tested as Europe approaches another fateful crossroads in spite of our desire for collaboration and peace.

Fascist leaders cannot be held solely responsible for the fact that international relations deteriorated rapidly in the 1930s, but their actions certainly aggravated an already tense and dangerous situation. Italy's attack against Ethiopia, intervention in the Spanish Civil War, its alliance with Nazi Germany, the emergence of political racism and anti-Semitism in Italy, and, finally, intervention in the Second World War all reflected the imperialistic goals of Fascism. But Mussolini was far less successful than Hitler in minimizing the international repercussions of his aggressive moves.

Aggression abroad provoked noticeable strains at home. Vested interests, particularly big business, had rallied to Fascism with the tacit understanding that they would be allowed to manage their own affairs. Indeed the corporations had embodied the principle of self-regulation in the various sectors of production. But the demands of war from 1935 on made government officials more assertive in their efforts to mobilize the nation's resources and manpower. And the unilateral way in which Mussolini forced aggressive nationalism on the country undermined the social consensus that had sustained the regime. After 1935 businessmen became apprehensive as the government imposed a ceiling on distributed dividends, raised taxes on profits and corporate assets, strengthened price controls, raised wages, and expanded social security benefits. Relations with Victor Emmanuel III were subjected to new strains in March 1938, when Mussolini claimed for himself the king's traditional right to be commander in chief of the armed forces in case of war. After 1938 Vatican authorities openly expressed their disapproval of the regime's racial policies.

Another important development during this period was the unanticipated expansion and consolidation of government initiative in production. The state had gained a controlling interest in major sectors of the economy through the Industrial Reconstruction Institute (IRI), which had been set up in January 1933 as a stopgap means of aiding industrial and financial concerns on the verge of bankruptcy. In return for the massive subsidies granted by the government to private concerns, IRI took over large holdings of devaluated securities in such unprofitable industries as steel, shipbuilding, and machinery. Industrialists and bankers hoped that IRI would fade away after having rescued private industry from its financial predicaments, but their expectations were proved unfounded. A government decree of June 1937 transformed IRI into a permanent state agency authorized to expand its domain wherever public initiative might be in the interest of "national defense, the policy of autarchy, and the development of the Empire."

Political considerations were thus responsible for making state intervention a permanent feature of Italian life. Yet IRI's operations reveal once again how the Fascist government was torn between conflicting demands. In this case, the government had to balance political needs against the demands of business leaders who welcomed public subsidies but not public regulation of production. The results left no one completely satisfied. Supporters of private initiative have pointed to IRI as an example of bureaucratic inefficiency and the economic wastefulness of public initiative. Others have criticized IRI for the indecisiveness of its efforts at economic planning and have argued that Fascist economic interventionism was a gimmick to collectivize losses and "privatize" profits.

Regardless of how one feels about IRI's role in the economy (and the controversy still goes on), it cannot be denied that IRI represented a novel solution to the problem of how private and public initiative can coexist within the same economic system. And it makes sense to argue that the particular mix achieved by IRI has facilitated economic growth in the long run.[12] In fact, with IRI Fascism came closest to creating its promised postcapitalist economic order. The general reluctance to acknowledge the significance of IRI in this respect is probably due to the way IRI grew and operated. IRI simply was not the brainchild of Fascist social theoreticians; it was born of economic necessity in the depth of the depression and survived because of the government's commitment to war. It was run by technocrats who professed indifference to politics and ideology. Nevertheless, it is possible that without Fascist political expansionism public enterprise might have come to Italy in a very different form. In any case, it was Fascism's nationalist and expansionist policies, not its social doctrines, that changed Italian society. Of the two major components of Fascist ideology—nationalism and corporativism—nationalism was by far the most important. Aggressive nationalism, however, could not develop without significant social change. And it was this connection between war and social change that ultimately undermined the internal stability of the regime.

Mussolini's conservative supporters miscalculated in assuming that a nationalist regime was also bound to be a socially conservative one. This assumption was valid only in the context of liberal politics, where the choice was between pacifist-revolutionary socialism and aggressive-conservative nationalism. With the demise of liberal politics, it was quite possible for a government to combine aggression abroad and revolution at home. Fascism never went this far in the sense that it did not become explicitly revolutionary. Nevertheless, there were clear indications in the late 1930s of Mussolini's mounting irritation over what he considered to be lack of enthusiasm for his foreign policy from his conservative supporters at home. He vented his irritation in his speech of October 25, 1938 to party leaders, accusing the *borghesia* (bourgeoisie) of being pacifist, egalitarian, humanitarian, reluctant to raise large families, averse to danger, adventure, sports, and to the recently adopted *passo romano* (the Fascist version of the Prussian goose step).

Mussolini's outburst expressed his increasing intolerance of even the most cautious forms of dissent. This reaction was unforeseen and alarming in a man who had risen to power largely on his ability to be all things to all men. His talent as a political manipulator had gained powerful outside support for Fascism because many vested interests had expected a Fascist victory to give them freedom of action in their respective spheres of interest. Although those expectations had been largely realized, the new assertiveness of the Fascist leadership indicated that there might yet be unpredictable changes in the future.

These vague apprehensions about the future were not strong enough to create outright opposition to Fascism. On the contrary, they seemed to generate a defensive mentality that expressed itself in declarations of unswerving loyalty to constituted power. No one was willing to criticize openly the regime's political policies for fear that such criticism might provoke Mussolini into impulsive retaliation. The period of Italian neutrality from September 1939 to June 1940 evoked no public debate such as had developed in 1914 and 1915. The silence can be ascribed simply to the suppression of political freedoms. However, a general reluctance on the part of vested interests that could have expressed their views to the government was also traceable to their fears of jeopardizing their acquired privileges. The regime's accommodating economic and social policies thus gave the Fascist leadership a freedom from criticism in the sphere of international diplomacy, which they exploited to their ultimate undoing.

The Fascist principle of leadership was fully implemented only in the area of political decision-making. Although this was extremely significant for the future of the Italian people, it did not justify calling Fascist Italy a totalitarian society. Beyond the realm of "pure politics," the institutions and the social arrangements of the regime created numerous pockets of power where the authority of the government and the party was felt only indirectly. Indeed Fascism spawned a whole new generation of little Mussolinis who in their various capacities as employers, political bosses, labor leaders, magistrates, and civil servants invoked the principle of leadership only to concentrate greater power in their own hands. They were probably the most typical social product of Fascism, a far cry from the *Homo fascistus* of Fascist ideology. Their presence at all levels of public and private life did nothing to increase people's confidence in the political leadership or in the ability of the political process to solve basic social problems.

The most harmful legacy of Fascism was the way it widened the gap between the masses and their political leaders, thereby aggravating the great unsolved problem of the Risorgimento. The Fascist regime unquestionably gained wide popular support by catering to the suppressed desire for national glory and international respectability, by waging a successful struggle against illiteracy, and by its policies of bread and circuses. But this popular support faded rapidly when the regime failed to enact far-reaching social reforms and ineptly committed the country to total war. A party that after nearly twenty years in power could boast of nothing more than having strengthened the authority of the state, created a new privileged elite, and left old vested interests only vaguely apprehensive about the future was anything but revolutionary. Fascism did not always conform to the expectations of its conservative supporters, but neither did it follow any of its own prescriptions for social renewal. In Fascist Italy, ideology could only be the handmaid of manipulative politics. The failure in performance ultimately reinforced the popular suspicion that politics responds far more readily to the pressure of powerful vested interests than to demands for social justice. A disenchanted public opinion, suspicious of all ideologies and all politicians, remains a serious obstacle to effective political action in post-Fascist Italy.

NOTES

1. Renzo De Felice, *Le interpretazioni del fascismo* (Bari: Laterza, 1969), p. 210.

2. Quoted in H. S. Harris, *The Social Philosophy of Giovanni Gentile* (Urbana: University of Illinois Press, 1960), p. 190.

3. A. James Gregor, *The Ideology of Fascism* (New York: The Free Press, 1969), pp. 13–14.

4. Angelo Tasca, *Nascita e avvento del fascismo* (Bari: Laterza, 1965), II, 553.

5. Recent Marxist writings are taking into account the complexity of Fascism, as evidenced in Vittorio Foa's "Le strutture economiche e la politica economica del regime fascista," in *Fascismo e antifascismo (1918–1936)* (Milan: Feltrinelli, 1963), I, 266–286. Fascism is presented as a center movement in Seymour M. Lipset, *Political Man: The Social Bases of Politics* (Garden City: Doubleday, 1960), pp. 130–176. The revolutionary aspects of Fascist ideology are discussed in Eugen Weber, *Varieties of Fascism* (Princeton: Van Nostrand, 1964). Some similarities between early Fascism and the new left are outlined in Edward R. Tannenbaum, "The Goals of Italian Fascism," *American Historical Review*, 74 (April 1969), 1183–1204.

6. Mussolini's continued commitment to revolution after 1914 is the theme of Renzo De Felice's *Mussolini il rivoluzionario, 1883–1920* (Turin: Einaudi, 1965).

7. Roberto Vivarelli, in his admirable book *Il dopoguerra in Italia e l'avvento del fascismo (1918–1922)*, Vol. I, *Dalla fine della guerra all'impresa di Fiume* (Naples: Istituto Italiano per gli Studi Storici, 1967) calls Mussolini a "subversive" rather than a revolutionary (p. 220). Vivarelli bases his argument on the undeniable fact that Mussolini strayed from Socialist ideological orthodoxy; he thereby rejects De Felice's and Gregor's thesis that Mussolini's intolerance of ideological constraints did not make him less of a revolutionary.

8. Quoted in Roland Sarti, *Fascism and the Industrial Leadership in Italy, 1919–1940* (Berkeley: University of California Press, 1971), p. 35.

9. On the expansion of prefectoral power, see the excellent study by Robert C. Fried, *The Italian Prefects: A Study in Administrative Politics* (New Haven: Yale University Press, 1963), pp. 186–211.

10. Carl J. Friedrich and Zbigniew K. Brzezinski, *Totalitarian Dictatorship and Autocracy* (New York: Praeger, 1965), p. 31. Contrast this view with Alberto Aquarone, *L'organizzazione dello Stato totalitario* (Turin: Einaudi, 1965).

11. The most complete description of the politics behind the charter appears in Renzo De Felice, *Mussolini il fascista*, Vol. II, *L'organizzazione dello Stato fascista, 1925–1929* (Turin: Einaudi, 1968), pp. 286–296.

12. IRI's contribution to Italian economic growth since the Second World War is the theme of M. V. Posner and S. J. Woolf, *Italian Public Enterprise* (Cambridge: Harvard University Press, 1967).

CHAPTER 4

CHRISTIAN DEMOCRACY

Elisa A. Carrillo

Three powerful ideologies have competed for the allegiance of the Italian people during the twentieth century: Marxism, Fascism, and Christian Democracy. Though differing widely in origins, tactics, and historical evolution, all three have held out the attractive prospect of modernization and a more equitable social order. This chapter will attempt to analyze the impact of Christian Democracy—both as an ideology and as a party—on Italian political and socioeconomic development during the past seven decades. Just as Marxism and Fascism lend themselves to varied interpretations and definitions, depending on the individual and the times, so too does Christian Democracy. Most Christian Democrats would probably agree, however, that their ideology stresses personalism, pluralism, and reformism. They would see the goal of Christian Democracy as a just social order, inspired by Christian values and achieved by democratic, constitutional means.[1]

Christian Democracy had its immediate origins in the church-state quarrel that accompanied Italian political unification. Pope Pius IX encouraged the formation of Catholic organizations under direct episcopal jurisdiction for the purpose of defending the church from further encroachments on the part of the Kingdom of Italy. The Opera dei Congressi, which guided most Catholic societies and activity until 1904, was under the control of "intransigent Catholics," that is, Catholics wholly unreconciled to Italian unification and determined to restore the political, cultural, and economic position of the church. They viewed the masses as victims of the same liberal bourgeoisie that had despoiled the church. In 1891 Leo XIII's encyclical *Rerum novarum* further stimulated interest in socioeconomic problems, and soon Catholic study groups, cooperatives, savings banks, and benevolent associations were interlacing the Italian peninsula.

By the end of the nineteenth century, however, a basic division had emerged within the congress movement: some members still regarded Catholic organization primarily as a papal weapon against the Italian state, while others, more positive in outlook, envisaged a Catholic mass party that would effect a renovation of Italian society. But the proponents of a mass party were not united among themselves. The moderates, led by the young Milanese lawyer Filippo Meda, saw no essential incompatibility between the existing political regime and the goals of social Catholicism. Having "baptized" the Italian state, they were prepared to work within the system. The other group, the Christian Democrats, headed by Romolo Murri, a young priest from central Italy, was bitterly hostile to the established order and sought structural change. Publishing their own program in 1899, the Murri adherents demanded (1) the democratization of political life through the enactment of proportional representation, the initiative, and the referendum, (2) the formation of corporative bodies for the various professions and trades, (3) social legislation to improve working conditions and provide greater security in sickness and old age, (4) protection of small landowners and agricultural workers, (5) reform of the tax structure, (6) development of religious education, and (7) general and progressive disarmament. Within the context of the times, these Christian Democrats could be considered almost as radical as the Socialists, because instead of allowing economic forces free play, they would compel the state to assume a greater role in protecting the masses and in striving for socioeconomic democracy.

Murri was active in organizing leagues of Catholic workers, but unlike many of his coreligionists he did not view Socialists with apocalyptic horror. Through his periodical *Cultura sociale* and his *Lega democratica nazionale*, he attracted a substantial number of young people, much to the dismay of the older and more conservative Catholics. Murri inevitably came into conflict with the Vatican during the latter's war on modernism, and he was excommunicated. His disenchantment with the representatives of Catholicism led him to reexamine the relationship of the individual with the church and to conclude that the individual had to answer to his own conscience rather than to the church.[2] We should note here that Murri, who was to make his peace with the church in 1943, was the spiritual ancestor of the postwar Christian Democratic party, especially of its leftist currents.

Both the Murri and Meda factions of the early twentieth century drew their inspiration from Giuseppe Toniolo, the Venetian-born professor of political economy at the University of Pisa. Toniolo saw the goal of

Christian Democracy in industry as the participation of labor in management and profits through stock ownership; in agriculture the objective was the extension of land ownership through agrarian reform. Though Toniolo's conception of the socioeconomic order failed to take into sufficient account the dynamism of the times, and was moreover excessively colored by his studies of the guild system of medieval Tuscany, his ideas enjoyed a tremendous vogue among socially minded Catholics, particularly among those of the Meda school.[3]

Even before Murri's break with the church, dissension within the congress movement had become so pervasive that in 1904 Pope Pius X dissolved the Opera dei Congressi, subsequently replacing it with three national unions: the Unione popolare, the Unione economico-sociale, and the Unione elettorale. About the same time that he terminated the congress movement, Pius X authorized the suspension of the *Non expedit* in those electoral districts in which anticlerical candidates might win in the absence of Catholic voters. In a few cases Catholics were even permitted to run for seats, though it was understood that if elected they would sit as deputies who happened to be Catholics, not as official Catholic deputies. The church was not prepared to acquiesce in the formation of a Catholic party, but the advance of socialism was making it cognizant of the need for some Catholic electoral intervention. In 1913, after parliamentary elections had taken place under popular suffrage for the first time, Count Ottorino Gentiloni, president of the Unione elettorale, revealed the existence of a pact between himself and Giolitti, whereby Catholics were permitted to vote for those Giolittian candidates who agreed to respect the rights of the church. Under the pact 228 majority deputies had been elected with Catholic support. The conclusion was inescapable that the Catholic vote was no negligible factor in Italian politics.

At the beginning of the First World War most Italian Catholics, like most Italian Socialists, favored neutrality, but once the Salandra government decided on intervention, the church associated itself with the nation's patriotic goals in the war effort. The war increased the prestige of Italian Catholics, and Filippo Meda, minister of finance in the governments of 1916 to 1919, was regarded by some people as the unofficial representative of Italian Catholicism. The war also accelerated those forces that were undermining Italy's preindustrial society, producing unrest and riots both in rural areas and urban centers. Catholics had to become activists if they hoped to eradicate or at least mitigate the evils in Italian society. After the Vatican had indicated that it was prepared to rescind completely the *Non expedit*, forty Christian Democrats assembled in Rome late in November 1918 and decided to organize the Partito Popolare Italiano. On January 18, 1919, the Executive Committee launched its now-famous appeal, "A tutti gli uomini liberi e forti [To all free and strong men]."

Reflecting its historical evolution, the platform of the new party called for proportional representation, the widest decentralization, female suffrage, an elective senate (to represent national academic, administrative, and trade-union organizations), extension of land ownership, social legislation, and liberty and independence for the church. The platform also demanded that the League of Nations recognize national aspirations, hasten the advent of universal disarmament, abolish secret treaties, effect freedom of the seas, and promote social legislation. The Roman Question was not mentioned, for the founders of the party did not think that it should entangle itself in strictly ecclesiastical matters.

Primary credit for the organization of the party and the formulation of its platform belonged to Don Luigi Sturzo, the Sicilian priest who had made his entry into the Catholic movement as an associate of Murri. In 1918, while head of Italian Catholic Action, Sturzo had promoted the organization of two unions that were to become strong supporters of the Popular party, the Confederation of Cooperatives and Rural Banks and the Italian Confederation of Laborers. After the entry of the Popular party into the Italian political arena, Sturzo severed his connection with Catholic Action. He firmly believed that the new party should be non-confessional, open to anyone who would accept its platform. He considered it dangerous to make Catholicism the point of differentiation, for this might embroil the church in issues that were not inherently religious or moral. Confessionalism might also bring into the party Catholics who were actually hostile to its political, economic, and social objectives.

Sturzo was unable to prevent the almost immediate development of right and left wings in the party. The right wing, favoring gradual change and emphasizing political and administrative reform, was led by Stefano Cavazzoni, Count Grosoli, and Fathers Agostino and Francesco Olgiati. The two priests also advocated a repudiation of the Popular party's aconfessionality, its "negative Christianity," as they termed it. The left wing, whose exponents included Guido Miglioli and Francesco Luigi Ferrari, both active in organizing peasant unions, favored immediate and drastic socioeconomic reform in the name of "Christian proletarianism." Both wings, however, failed to modify the platform substantially when the first national congress convened in Bologna in June 1919.

The presidency of the first congress was conferred on Austrian-born Alcide De Gasperi, who had headed the Partito Popolare Trentino when the Trentino was still part of the Hapsburg Empire. The choice of De Gasperi as presiding officer served a dual function: a recognition of the man's political acumen as leader of the Trentine Christian Democratic party, and a recognition of the "redemption" of the Trentino by the Kingdom of Italy. With respect to the forthcoming (November 1919) parliamentary elections, the Bologna congress decided that the party should refrain from making any alliance or entente with other parties and should fight instead for its own program and candidates with "absolute intransigence." The national leadership of the Popular party eagerly looked forward to testing its strength at the polls. A law passed by parliament in the summer of 1919 provided for modified proportional representation, an electoral change that gave the mass parties an edge over the caucus groups of Liberal politicians. The Popular party was clearly a mass party; it was interclass in structure, its membership embracing trade unionists, middle-class intellectuals, clergymen, landless peasants, and large and small landowners. Geographically the greatest strength of the party lay in the north, where study clubs and workers' associations helped to publicize its program. To many conservatives the new party with its advanced socioeconomic platform was simply "Black Bolshevism."

The election returns in November 1919 were among the most extraordinary in the history of the Italian kingdom. For the Liberals they constituted an "electoral Caporetto," while the Fascists, who had appeared to be making considerable progress since the formation of the *Fascio di combattimento* in March 1919, failed to elect a single candidate. For the Popularists, on the other hand, the results were a stupendous triumph: 100 seats out of 508. The unexpected magnitude of their victory owed much to the support of the clergy, who saw in popularism an acceptable alternative to socialism and liberalism and therefore allowed their parish churches to become unofficial party headquarters. Unfortunately the Popularists did not win a sufficient number of seats to enable them to form their own government. The strongest single party to emerge from the elections was the Socialist party, but, true to their doctrinaire opposition to collaboration with bourgeois parties, the Socialists refused to assume their mandate to lead a coalition government.

The Popularists decided to support a Nitti government, but it not only failed to enact any Popularist measure but also openly favored the Socialists. When Socialist unions called strikes of postal, telegraph, and railroad workers at the beginning of 1920, the Catholic, or "White" unions, backed by the Popular party, kept the public services in operation. They were rewarded by being abandoned to the reprisals of their Socialist companions, with whom the Nitti government negotiated. When the Popular party's second national congress convened in Naples in 1921, the membership served notice that they would no longer support a government that showed itself incapable of upholding the rights of Catholic unions.

Upon the fall of the Nitti government, the king offered the premiership to Filippo Meda, but the Popularist leader declined it, alleging that his party did not have a sufficiently strong base in the nation at large to warrant assumption of the responsibility of government. The veteran politician Giolitti then returned to form his fifth (and last) ministry. Accepting Popularist support, he agreed to combine their demands for agrarian reform and freedom for Catholic schools with his own program for fiscal and administrative reform. Meanwhile Fascist squads were attacking Socialist and Catholic unions and cooperatives in northern and central Italy on the pretext of saving the nation from a Bolshevik revolution. The Italian middle classes had a genuine fear of Bolshevism, and in the expectation that the reaction against the left (whether Socialist or Popularist) would enable him to enlarge the center majority, Giolitti called for new elections. His strategy failed: the Socialist party was weakened, but not as much as Giolitti had hoped, while the Popularists improved their position. His National Bloc captured a majority of the seats, but thirty-five Fascists now entered the Chamber of Deputies, joined by ten Nationalists. After the new Chamber assembled in June 1921, Giolitti was succeeded as prime minister by Ivanoe Bonomi.

Among the five Popularists returned by the Trentino was De Gasperi, who was elected president of the Popularist parliamentary group. In his first speech to the Chamber of Deputies, he sought to illustrate the need to reform the bureaucracy by pointing out that certain postal operations in the Trentino which had required only two hours under Austrian rule now required eight and a half hours under the new Italian administration.[4] It was not a speech to win friends and influence people, particularly in view of his birth and upbringing in Austrian territory, and it helped to ensure the Lombard conservative Stefano Cavazzoni the effective leadership of the Popularist parliamentary group. The Popularist legislative program continued to be ambitious, but the chaotic state of the country and the inertia of the government were insuperable obstacles to its realization. The foreign policy objectives of the party, which were predicated upon the establishment of a Popularist International (to rival the Communist Third International) were also difficult if not impossible to achieve at this time.[5]

A sense of frustration understandably permeated the third national congress when it convened in Venice in October 1921. Some of the delegates suggested Popularist-Socialist collaboration to work for essential reforms and to impede the march of Fascism. However, the influential and experienced labor leader Giovanni Gronchi was sceptical regarding collaboration. At the conclusion of the congress the principles that the party considered indispensable for collaboration with "responsible political groupings" were enumerated: (1) liberty and respect for the Christian conscience, (2) restoration of the national economy and finances, (3) recognition of labor unions and the equality of those supported by the Popular party with other unions, (4) restoration of the authority and functions of the state, and (5) a foreign policy capable of forging inter-

national ties based on justice and solidarity with all nations. Though not
so designed, it was a program that effectively precluded collaboration
with any political party.

In January 1922 the Bonomi government fell when Fascists and Giolittian Liberals withdrew their support, hoping to bring Giolitti back to
power. The Popularists, however, refused to accept Giolitti, distrusting
his ability to oppose Fascist violence. The king then offered the premiership to Meda, who, fearful as always of responsibility, declined it without
even consulting Sturzo or De Gasperi. In February Luigi Facta, one of
Giolitti's lieutenants, formed a government that was accepted by the
Popularists more out of weariness brought on by the prolonged crisis than
out of confidence in the new premier. A few months later the leftwing
Popularist Guido Miglioli gave parliament a highly dramatic account of
Fascist outrages in his native Cremona. The speech touched off a demonstration among the Popularist and Socialist deputies which toppled the
Facta ministry and precipitated another ministerial crisis. For the third
time the king approached Meda, but in spite of Sturzo's plea that he
"sacrifice himself," the cautious Popularist again refused the premiership,
alleging that an official position would interfere with his legal practice.
Facta was called once again to form a government, the last one in the
liberal period.

Although talk of a Popularist-Socialist coalition was renewed as Fascist
Blackshirts expanded their operations, none could emerge. The ideological
differences between Popularists and Socialists were too great to be reconciled, and the protest strike called by the Socialists in August 1922
alienated whatever support the reformist Socialist element might have had
among the Popularists. The prospect of an accord had always horrified
conservative Popularists, and in September, eight Popularist senators sent
Sturzo a letter denouncing any attempt on the part of Popularist deputies
to reach an understanding with Socialists. The leftwing Socialists were
equally adamant concerning any collaboration with Popularists.

At the end of October, as alarming reports reached Rome of Fascist
concentrations in many provincial cities, a royal telephone call summoned
Benito Mussolini to Rome. Christian Democracy had not been strong and
experienced enough to prevent a Fascist triumph. Yet in retrospect one
can see its positive contributions to Italian political life from 1919 to 1922.
The Popularist party had helped to mobilize the rural masses, and it supported policies that have since proven their validity. Many reforms that
are now being enacted or implemented in Italy, such as regionalism, a more
relevant educational experience, and a more equitable social order, were
advocated by the Popular party in the early twenties.

The first government formed by Mussolini was a coalition that included
Fascists, Nationalists, Liberals, and Popularists. Not wishing to overplay

his hand, and recognizing the need for men experienced in public affairs, Mussolini was willing to accept the collaboration of non-Fascists in this initial stage. A dilemma had confronted the non-Fascists: if they worked with Mussolini, they might become responsible for policies inconsistent with their own; if they refused collaboration, Fascist violence might be intensified. Perhaps too hastily and without due regard for the implications of such a move, the Popularists, led by Cavazzoni and De Gasperi, decided in favor of participation in Mussolini's government. Like many of their contemporaries, they believed that Fascism could be inserted into the constitutional framework once violence and disorder came to an end.

During the early months of 1923 there was a heated intraparty controversy among the Popularists concerning collaboration. The right wing, led by Cavazzoni, took the position that the party should make no demands on Mussolini; it should pose no conditions for collaboration; rather it should suspend its own life and program to advance Mussolini's projects for national reconstruction. The left wing, represented by Miglioli, Ferrari, and Gerolamo and Luigi Meda (sons of Filippo Meda), opposed collaboration, convinced that Fascism could never be reconciled with the political and ethical principles of Popularism. The party secretariat assumed a center position. Although he had initially opposed participation in Mussolini's government, Don Sturzo, the party secretary, did not want a sudden break with it, for fear of provoking a crisis not only in the government but in the Popular party as well. He argued that just as the party had cooperated with Liberals and Freemasons in the past, so it could now cooperate with the Fascist government for the purpose of solving national problems: "Today, to deny collaboration to the government would be absurd, since it would lead the country to civil war. Since the Popular party has always subordinated its desires to the collective well-being, there is no road other than that of sustaining the government, always, however, preserving intact the essential features of our party." [6] De Gasperi supported this position, arguing that Popularist membership in Mussolini's government was a "collaboration of emergency, a collaboration without collaborationism," undertaken as the lesser of two evils. The intraparty debate ended, however, when Mussolini, angered by the anti-Fascism of some Popularists and the demand for autonomy by others, forced the resignation of his Popularist ministers on April 24, 1923.

The Popular party had trouble not only with the Fascists but also with the church hierarchy. The Catholic press gave wide publicity to Mussolini's conciliatory gestures toward the Holy See, and many bishops who condemned individual acts of Fascist violence against Catholic laymen and priests officially dissociated themselves from Sturzo's party. Achille Cardinal Ratti, who became Pope Pius XI in early 1922, opposed the political and socioeconomic aspirations of the party, a predictable response from this Lombard reactionary. His first concern was the settlement of the

Roman Question, and he viewed an autonomous Catholic party as a possible hindrance to such a settlement.

After the Vatican forced Don Sturzo's resignation as political secretary in July 1923, Fascist pressures further fragmented the Popular party. Its growing disunity came out into the open during the debate in the Chamber of Deputies on the Fascist bill proposing radical changes in the way elections should be conducted (see Chapter 3, page 61, on the Acerbo Law). When Cavazzoni and eight other Popularist deputies broke party discipline and voted for this bill, the party's parliamentary leader De Gasperi ousted them. In 1924 these rightist deputies, together with some Popularist senators, formed the Centro Nazionale Italiano and supported the Fascist list of candidates in the parliamentary elections in April of that year.

Because of basic differences in principles and tactics the opposition parties could not present a united front against the Fascist electoral list. With *Libertas* as its motto, the Popular party offered its own list and called upon Italians to resist the "centralizing and pantheistic" state. When the results of the elections were tallied, the Fascists had rolled up four and a half million votes to three million for the opposition parties. The Popular party elected only thirty-nine deputies, but, in view of ecclesiastical antagonism and Fascist violence and intimidation, even this modest achievement is surprising. Shortly after the elections, the National Council of the Popular party elected De Gasperi as its political secretary, thus uniting in one mandate the presidency of the parliamentary group and the party secretaryship. Under De Gasperi the party continued along the line of moderate, legal opposition. The influence of Don Sturzo on the party remained strong, even after he was forced to go into exile at the end of 1924.

Fascist violence did not abate after the April electoral triumph. Catholic clubs and cooperatives continued to be sacked, and the editorial presses of anti-Fascist Catholic papers were invaded by Fascist thugs. After the shocking murder of Giacomo Matteotti in June 1924, Popularists joined Republicans, Socialists, and a number of liberals and withdrew from the Chamber in the so-called Aventine Secession, which was both a moral protest and an attempt to oust Mussolini by provoking a government crisis. The reformist Socialist Filippo Turati called upon the Unitary Socialist party and the Popular party to cooperate against Fascism, and through the columns of *Il Nuovo Trentino* De Gasperi expressed his willingness to participate in a government that included Socialists.

A Socialist-Popularist combination, proposed by Turati and De Gasperi as an alternative to Fascism, evoked a hostile response from the church. The influential Jesuit review *La Civiltà Cattolica* was sharply critical of the proposed collaboration, characterizing it as "neither convenient, nor opportune, nor licit." The Popular party had been founded to effect a Christian restoration of society, and this objective, asserted the review, could not be achieved in union with Socialists.[7] Pius XI was similarly disturbed by the prospect of collaboration, and in a speech to university students he expressed his strong disapproval.[8] Once again a Popularist-Socialist entente failed to emerge, but even if it had, it is doubtful that it would have appreciably weakened Mussolini's hold on the country. By the beginning of 1925 both the Matteotti murder and the Aventine Secession had become matters of public indifference, and in 1926 a parliamentary resolution depriving the Aventine deputies of their seats was scarcely noticed. Hindsight leads us to the conclusion that the Aventine Secession was a serious tactical error; by withdrawing from Parliament the opposition enabled the Fascists to monopolize the public forum.

In June 1925 the Popular party convened in Rome for its fifth and last national congress. It was here that De Gasperi consolidated his hold on the party; he controlled the congress, and having obtained a vote of confidence, he urged the party to hold firm to its principles. A realist, he recognized that the battle for Popularism had to be abandoned temporarily, but he wished to leave guidelines for the resumption of the war at a more propitious time. At the end of 1925 he resigned as party secretary but refused to make his peace with Fascism, as many of his former associates had done or were to do in the succeeding years. In March 1927, while en route from Rome to Trieste, De Gasperi was arrested and charged with trying to leave the country illegally. Whether this charge was true or not is a moot point, but the evidence on which he was convicted and sentenced to imprisonment was certainly flimsy.[9]

The release of De Gasperi from prison in July 1928 (thanks to a royal pardon) coincided with the drafting of the Lateran Accords, which settled the Roman Question. Although De Gasperi believed that the settlement involved a sacrifice of the Popularists, he rejoiced in the reconciliation of church and state. The only part of the Lateran Accords that caused him misgivings was the Concordat, for its terms could lead to an identification of Catholicism with Fascism. His fears were warranted, but in the meantime he personally benefited from the signing of the pacts. In April 1929 he joined a few other former Popularists in finding employment at the Vatican. Prior to the signing of the pacts, such an act of charity on the part of the pontiff might have been interpreted in Fascist circles as a rebuke to Mussolini. From his "exile" in the Vatican Library, which was to last fourteen years, De Gasperi helped to keep alive the message of Christian Democracy through his publications. Forced to use pseudonyms and veiled language, he fought Fascism as best he could in this way. Except during the controversy over Catholic Action in 1931, when Mussolini unsuccessfully sought to have De Gasperi dismissed from his

Vatican post, the Fascist world appeared to have forgotten the former leader of the Popular party. His relative obscurity enabled him to re-establish contacts with Popularist and other anti-Fascist friends both at home and abroad.

Catholicism and Fascism proved to be essentially incompatible, and after 1938 the forging of closer ties between Italy and Nazi Germany and the adoption of a racist program in Italy prompted the Vatican to move farther away from Fascism. When Italy entered the Second World War as the ally of Hitler, various Catholic groups and movements organized to form a Christian Democratic party. These included Catholic Action (especially the Giorgio La Pira circle in Florence), the Guelf movement in Lombardy, the FUCI-Movimento Laureati groups (composed of university students and graduates), and former members of the Popular party. Within three years a fusion had been achieved of these different groups and individuals, and on July 25, 1943, the same day that Mussolini fell from power, the new (or revived) party adopted the name Democrazia Cristiana. As Anglo-American forces landed at Salerno, the Central Committee of the Christian Democratic party was organized, with De Gasperi as its president. During these same years, other anti-Fascist parties (Socialist, Actionist, Labor Democratic, Communist, and Liberal) were formed or revived, and these joined the Christian Democratic party in setting up the Comitato di Liberazione Nazionale (CLN). The institutional question was capable of arousing strong differences of opinion, but all parties were agreed on the need to rid Italy of Fascism, end the war as soon as possible, and press for a democratized and modernized postwar Italy.

By the time the Allies entered Rome in June 1944, the Christian Democrats had a well-formulated platform of ideas for reconstructing their party.[10] Drawing its basic inspiration from Popularism and its phraseology from De Gasperi, who drafted the final copy, the program postulated political liberty as the indispensable foundation for human rights. It envisioned the regime of the future as a representative democracy, with a bicameral legislature, one chamber elected by universal suffrage and the other by professional associations. Regions would be established as autonomous entities to represent and administer local and professional interests. The greatest social effort of the state would be directed toward the acquisition of property for all. In industry, workers would participate in the management, capitalization, and profits of their companies. Monopolies that derived from the nature of the business would be removed from private control and placed under associated (that is, private and public) management. In agriculture the objective of Christian Democracy would be the gradual transformation of day laborers into tenant farmers and proprietors, or when technical reasons so dictated, into associates in the management of agricultural enterprises. A better distribution of wealth would also be achieved through a reform of the tax system, which would be preceded by the confiscation of profits derived from war or the Fascist regime. In the international order Christian Democracy would uphold the right of national self-determination but at the same time urge limitations upon national sovereignty in the interest of a wider solidarity. It would support the creation of confederations having continental and intercontinental ties and would view the progressive and controlled disarmament of all nations, victorious and vanquished, as one of the tasks of the international community.

Under the pseudonym of Demofilo, De Gasperi elaborated upon this program in a series of articles published in the revived party journal *Il Popolo*. In one such article De Gasperi took care to point out the autonomous character of the party and to disclaim any intent of having it act as the "officially delegated" representative of Italian Catholics.[11] In defining and clarifying the role of the party in the postwar political order, De Gasperi was probably anticipating and seeking to prevent Vatican or other ecclesiastical interference with the Christian Democratic party.

With its appealing blend of tradition and modernity, the credo of the Christian Democrats found ready acceptance among the Italian people as the war came to a close. Once again Italy had a mass party that was interclass in composition as peasants, trade unionists, industrialists, large and small landowners, fervent Catholics, and nominal Catholics flocked to the standard of Christian Democracy. This heterogeneity was to constitute both the strength and weakness of the party to a far greater degree than was the case with its predecessor the Popular party, which never had to assume the responsibility of government.

The Christian Democrats participated in the Resistance-sponsored cabinet that governed Italy in 1945, but not until December did the head of the Christian Democratic party become prime minister. Confounding friend and foe alike, De Gasperi was to preside over eight consecutive ministries, lasting eight and a half years. Centrism, pragmatism, and personal integrity were his most noteworthy characteristics. Like the Popular party of the twenties, the Christian Democratic party developed right and left groupings ("tendencies" or "currents"), and it required all of De Gasperi's political skill and personal stamina to hold these together. Though the enactment or implementation of many promised reforms had to await a later date—partly because of the intraparty strife—the De Gasperi era was on the whole an auspicious beginning for post-Fascist Italy.

In June 1946 there were elections for a Constituent Assembly and a referendum on what kind of political regime Italy should have. The Christian Democratic party declared itself in favor of a republic but wisely left to its members and supporters the choice of voting for or against the monarchy, which was associated with war and Fascism. By not attaching an overriding importance to this question, the party could concentrate on winning seats in the Constituent Assembly. The results of the elections confirmed the voting pattern of the administrative elections held earlier in the spring: victory for the mass parties—Christian Democratic, Socialist, and Communist. The Christian Democrats won a plurality (35 percent) of the votes; and in forming his second government, De Gasperi established the tripartite coalition (Christian Democrats, Socialists, and Communists) which was to last until May 1947.

With the onset of the "cold war" the tripartite coalition became more formal than real, and in May 1947 De Gasperi expelled the Communists and their leftwing Socialist allies from the government, accusing them of fomenting strikes and riots in the nation and thus working against the very government in which they were participating. In December 1947 he formed the quadripartite coalition, which was composed of parties more congenial to each other: Christian Democratic, Republican, Liberal, and Giuseppe Saragat's rightwing Socialists. By this time Italy's internal and external position had vastly improved. Inflation had largely been brought under control and the economy was reviving appreciably. A peace treaty had been signed and ratified, and though the nation expressed disappointment, its terms could hardly be considered vindictive by objective standards. Another stabilizing factor was the republican constitution, which went into effect at the beginning of 1948. Excessively long and the product of too many compromises, it nevertheless provided the framework for a modernized and democratic Italy.

In April 1948 the nation, in the first parliamentary elections held under the new constitution, endorsed the quadripartite formula. But the elections also involved massive ecclesiastical intervention, with momentous implications for the future of the party and of the nation. When the campaign got under way, Pope Pius XII was determined to use Catholic organizations to help insure victory for the Christian Democratic party. Catholic Action, whose members numbered about three million, probably played the major role in lining up support for Christian Democratic candidates, and it did so through its Civic Committees, organized on both a national and diocesan level. The leftist parties accused the Vatican of intervening in politics, and they were especially incensed by Cardinal Schuster's pastoral letter to the clergy of Milan, instructing them to deny absolution to members of the "Communist party or to members of other movements contrary to the Catholic religion." Vatican spokesmen took the position that the church was merely defending its legitimate interests; the Concordat was not being violated inasmuch as neither priests nor Catholic Action had entered a political party.[12] In his Easter address Pope

Pius XII maintained that "the great hour of Christian conscience has struck."

By this time the electoral campaign had assumed the character of finality, and the sole issue appeared to be communism versus anticommunism. Piero Calamandrei, editor of *Il Ponte*, might deplore the oversimplification, but with the example of the Communist coup in Czechoslovakia before the eyes of Italian voters, such oversimplification is understandable. The accomplishments of the De Gasperi governments up to that time, the American promises of more material aid for Italy, the Western pledge of diplomatic support in recovering Trieste for Italy—these were also major considerations in the minds of the more thoughtful voters.

The election returns gave the Christian Democrats 48 percent of the votes and the leftist Popular Democratic Front (mostly Communists and Pietro Nenni Socialists) only 31 percent. Vatican circles hailed the victory of the Christian Democrats as a victory for Christian civilization and a rejection of "Communist atheism and tyranny." In the Communist camp, Palmiro Togliatti (see Chapter 5, page 113) complained—and not without some justification—that the vote had not been a free one: the church had utilized weapons of spiritual coercion, the United States, weapons of material coercion.

Although the pope would have preferred a government composed entirely of Christian Democrats, De Gasperi's own preference was for the continuation of the quadripartite coalition of Christian Democrats, Republicans, Liberals, and Social Democrats (Saragat's rightwing Socialists). De Gasperi thus hoped to restrain the exclusiveness (called "integralism") of some members of his party and also to preserve his own liberty of action. On the other hand, De Gasperi failed to oppose the development of close ties between Catholic Action and the party; the explanation probably lies in the fact that the Christian Democrats still lacked a strong machine that could deliver the vote at election time. The power of Catholic Action, which retained its Civic Committees after the 1948 elections, extended to the selection of party candidates and even to the appointment of ministers.

The most serious crisis in the relations between the Christian Democratic party and the leaders of Catholic Action was the so-called Sturzo Operation (actually a misnomer, because Sturzo, confined to a hospital bed, played the least important role) in 1952, when Rome was due to elect a new municipal government. In view of the possibility that the Communists might win the elections, Luigi Gedda, then national president of Catholic Action, proposed a "sacred union" between the Christian Democrats and the parties of the right, including the Neo-Fascist Italian Social Movement. On behalf of Catholic Action and at the request of Pius XII, Father Riccardo Lombardi, a well-known Jesuit, visited Signora

Francesca De Gasperi in an effort to secure her husband's acquiescence in the project. But the plan for a "sacred union" was utterly repugnant to De Gasperi, not only because of his anti-Fascist past but also because he rejected the right of Catholic Action to issue political directives to the party. In the end the "sacred union" did not materialize, and even without it, the Christian Democrats and their allies (Republicans, Social Democrats, and Liberals) won the elections.[13] The episode was instructive, however, in that it clearly pointed up the dangers of a close association with Catholic Action.

In spite of Catholic Action's intervention in the affairs of the Christian Democratic party—an intervention that usually favored conservative candidates and conservative solutions to pressing problems—much was accomplished during the early 1950s. Having decided on a Western orientation for Italy through acceptance of Marshall Plan aid, it was a logical development for the ruling coalition to make Italy a part of NATO and of the European communities that were coming into being. In retrospect, participation in NATO may have been a mistake (De Gasperi privately protested that the United States expected too much of Italy in the way of military expenditures), but at that time both internal and external exigencies seemed to warrant Italy's adhesion to the pact.

Socioeconomic reform was another major undertaking of the early Christian Democratic governments. In 1950 a two-pronged attack was launched against the age-old *miseria* of the Mezzogiorno, involving agrarian reform and a long-range plan for southern development and industrialization. The immediate incentive was in part political—to counter Communist advances in the south—but the long-term goal was to establish a better balance between the economies of north and south. The land reform project was designed to provide landless peasants with plots of their own from expropriated large estates (the state indemnifying the owners) and to improve southern agriculture by crop diversification. The program was to be administered by special organizations set up in each region, thereby fulfilling the old Popularist pledge of agrarian reform on a regional level. Complementing the land reform project, and often operative in the same area, was the Cassa per il Mezzogiorno (Southern Development Fund), a ten-year plan (later extended to fifteen years) to industrialize the south. Its first task was to provide the infrastructure for the development of industry, a monumental job in itself.

The Cassa proved to be the more successful of the two plans to bring a better life to southern Italians. The land reform program was adversely affected by the ingrained individualism of the Italian peasant and the availability of industrial jobs in the north. But it must be remembered that both schemes involved a break with traditions that were centuries old, and in the case of the land reform program, a political price was paid, for many a southern landowner who had supported the Christian Democratic party from its inception turned away from it in the 1950s.

The reforms of the early fifties, modest though they may seem to a later generation, helped to solidify the tendencies or currents that existed in the Christian Democratic party, and these must now be surveyed, for they significantly affected the subsequent evolution of Christian Democracy, both as an ideology and as a political party. Neither the Christian Democratic left nor the right constituted a single homogeneous bloc but rather was composed of a number of groups that had little in common with one another except their aversion to the centrism of De Gasperi.

The most important of the leftist currents was led by Giuseppe Dossetti, Amintore Fanfani, and Giorgio La Pira and had *Cronache Sociali* as its mouthpiece from 1947 to 1951, when the review ceased publication.[14] The most influential and articulate member of the group was Dossetti, professor of church law at the Catholic University of Milan. According to Dossetti, Italy's problems stemmed from three sources: the country's position vis-à-vis the two great world imperialisms, Russian and American; the inability of the Christian Democratic party, because of the myopia of its conservative members, to come to terms with the Communist party, a party rooted in the socioeconomic reality of Italian life; and a church weighed down by the errors of the past and a theologically illiterate laity. He saw the revitalization of the Christian Democratic party as a task to be executed by a young and educated Catholic laity conscious of a "theology of earthly reality." In foreign affairs Dossetti and his followers favored a policy of neutrality for Italy and opposed Italy's membership in the North Atlantic Pact. In the domestic sphere the Dossettiani stood for the rapid achievement of far-reaching socioeconomic reform, and they regarded De Gasperi's reformist measures as inadequate. They opposed the quadripartite coalition so dear to De Gasperi because they regarded it as an evasion of Christian Democratic responsibility. They also criticized the failure of the government to implement regionalism (De Gasperi was convinced that regional governments would be captured by the Communist party), as pledged in the wartime platform *Idee ricostruttive*. Dossettism reached its peak at the party congress in Venice in 1949 and was on the decline thereafter, at least in the governing circles of the party. Discouraged by the lack of progress and subject to persistent pressures from the right, Dossetti retired from politics in 1951, thereby removing a thorn in the side of De Gasperi, who had long resented the professor's criticisms of his policies. But the withdrawal of Dossetti from politics by no means marked the end of Dossettism; the movement was continued, if modified, by the more pragmatic and realistic Amintore Fanfani in the *Iniziativa democratica* current.

Two other currents in the Christian Democratic left represented labor.

The earlier of these was grouped around Giovanni Gronchi, militant organizer of Catholic trade unions in the pre-Fascist era and a founder of the Popular party. These Christian Democratic leftists proclaimed the "preeminence of labor" and called for a radical reform of capitalist society. In foreign affairs they tended toward nationalism, eschewing alliances with either the United States or European states and bemoaning the loss of Trieste and the colonial empire. During the last years of De Gasperi's domination of the party, the trade-union branch of Gronchi's faction broke away under Giulio Pastore, head of the Confederazione Italiana dei Sindacati Lavoratori (CISL; see Chapter 9). This syndicalist left opposed the party's emphasis on class harmony, seeing it as an obstacle to the realization of a more equitable social order. The Pastore program included the democratization of industry, with nationalization of key enterprises, a larger role for unions in the determination of national priorities, and greater cooperation between labor and government in combatting unemployment and in increasing production.[15]

The last leftist current to emerge during the De Gasperi era was the so-called Base.[16] Under former leaders of the Catholic Resistance, notably Enrico Mattei, head of the state-controlled Ente Nazionale Idrocarburi (National Hydrocarbons Agency), the Basists sought substantive social reforms in cooperation with the leftist parties. In foreign affairs, they resisted European integration (seeing it as another weapon in the "cold war") and favored a weakening of Italy's ties with the United States.

The Christian Democratic right was more amorphous than the left and is therefore more difficult to isolate and describe. Some members of the right looked back nostalgically to the monarchy and even to Mussolini, regretting the seeming inability of republican Italy to uphold morality and law and order as effectively as past regimes. They were haunted by the spectre of communism, and castigated De Gasperi for not taking more energetic measures against the Red peril. The conservatism of other rightists was principally in the economic sphere; upholding the principles of classical liberalism, they opposed government intervention in the economy. For them, agrarian reform, for example, was little better than communist collectivism. Generally speaking, the Christian Democratic right was close to Vatican spokesmen and usually formed part of Catholic Action. Though as opposed to Fascism or Neo-Fascism as De Gasperi, Giulio Andreotti and Guido Gonella may be said to be representative of the Christian Democratic right.

Holding together a party with so many currents was a time-consuming and emotionally and physically draining task for De Gasperi, who frequently voiced his preference for a more unified party. Particularly helpful in rallying the party around him were the friends and associates from the Popular party era; these included Mario Scelba, minister of the interior from 1947 to 1952, and Antonio Segni, minister of agriculture from 1946 to 1951 and architect of the agrarian-reform program. De Gasperi's own sympathies were more with the moderate left than the extreme right. He too believed that democracy had a social content and that more fundamental reforms were necessary to make democracy meaningful; however, he also believed that they had to be achieved gradually, without doctrinaire approaches, and with respect for the "method of liberty." He was not opposed to collaboration with the Nenni Socialists to achieve reform, but he made Nenni's severance of ties with the Communist party a precondition for collaboration.

At the fourth National Congress of the Christian Democratic Party (1952), De Gasperi's policies won the endorsement of the *Iniziativa democratica* current. Perhaps it was a combination of physical and psychological exhaustion that led De Gasperi to commit at this time the most serious error of his political career, namely his support of the Electoral Law of 1953 (the so-called swindle law). This law recalled the Acerbo Law that had been passed thirty years earlier insofar as it provided that any alliance of parties receiving one vote more than 50 percent of all votes cast in a parliamentary election would receive two-thirds of the seats in the Chamber of Deputies. The bill had encountered strenuous opposition within and without the party, and privately De Gasperi himself expressed reservations about it. In public, however, he supported it as the only alternative to the ministerial instability threatened by the strength shown by Monarchists and Neo-Fascists in the local elections of 1951 and 1952.

The elections held in June 1953 justified the misgivings of those in the governing coalition who had opposed the new electoral law. De Gasperi's political death was an outcome of the elections: on July 28, 1953, his one-party government was voted down. His physical death occurred a year later, and the two events are not unrelated. The last year of De Gasperi's life was filled with more spiritual than physical anguish as he watched both the general public and party associates turn their backs on him. To many conservatives in the party, his policies had caused the ruination of the party and nation; to many of the younger generation, he had simply become irrelevant.

Between 1953 and 1958 immobilism became the dominant feature of Italy's Christian Democratic governments, but the election of Fanfani as party secretary in 1954 seemed to confirm De Gasperi's prediction that "The Christian Democratic party is a party of the center which moves to the left." Such a new orientation was essential for the enactment of more basic reforms. Fanfani was realistic enough to see that such reforms would require the support of new forces outside the party, as well as the weakening of conservative and clerical forces within it, and these changes came slowly. Meanwhile, foreign policy remained tied to that of the United States, and domestic reforms remained minimal. The outstanding new development of this period was Italy's entry into the European Common Market in 1957. Under Fanfani's leadership the Christian Democratic party seemed to be marking time in anticipation of a rapprochement with the Socialists.

By 1958 new trends in Nenni's Socialist party, after the brutal suppression of the Hungarian Revolution in 1956, gave Fanfani reason to be optimistic about a possible government coalition with the leftwing Socialists. By this time, moreover, Fanfani had succeeded in reducing the control of Catholic Action over party nominations, and a party apparatus began to develop which was less dependent for electoral support on the church and its agencies. The accession to the papal throne of Angelo Cardinal Roncalli in October 1958 was also of great assistance in the declericalization of the party. In dealing with Catholic Action, the policies of Pope John XXIII marked a new departure. Addressing its leaders, the pontiff stressed their spiritual mission, and refrained from giving any encouragement to their political activities. In the words of one prominent Catholic Action leader, Pope John put the Civic Committees "on ice." [17]

After the May 1958 parliamentary elections, Fanfani formed a government composed of Christian Democrats and rightwing Socialists to replace the exclusively Christian Democratic government. Though planned as a transition to one of center-left, Fanfani's new coalition government turned out to be brief and troubled. A financial scandal (the so-called Giuffrè case) involving fantastic speculation that enriched Catholic societies and parish priests created great tension between Christian Democrats and Social Democrats. But it was dissension within the ranks of the Christian Democratic party that was primarily responsible for bringing down the Fanfani government. The "Snipers"—Christian Democrats opposed to both the *apertura a sinistra* (opening to the left) and the enormous political power wielded by Fanfani—refused to support the government's program. Hence, early in 1959 Fanfani submitted his resignation both as head of the government and secretary of the party. His withdrawal was merely a tactical expedient designed to allow the ultraconservative elements in the party to exhaust themselves.

As Fanfani had foreseen, the right wing of the party was unable to hold onto the reins of power. Under the government of Ferdinando Tambroni (April to July 1960), which had Neo-Fascist support, serious riots and strikes occurred which were symptomatic of widespread dissatisfaction with the rightist orientation of the ruling Christian Democrats. Upon Tambroni's resignation, Fanfani once again formed a government, but not until eighteen months later could it be said to represent a center-left program. In the meantime Fanfani encouraged the formation of local center-left governments. Cardinal Siri of Genoa protested against the collaboration of Christian Democrats with Socialists, but Pope John remained silent. He had apparently decided that the church should not involve itself in politics. Taking a cue from the pontiff, the Italian bishops issued a statement in 1961 which was noteworthy for the absence of the usual anathemas and admonitions.

At the Christian Democratic congress held in Naples in January 1962, an overwhelming majority was persuaded by the report of the political secretary Aldo Moro (a former *Dossettiano* and now representative of the moderate left current known as the *Dorotei*) to support an agreement between Christian Democrats and Socialists. Fanfani soon formed a government made up of Christian Democrats, Republicans, and Social Democrats which was supported in parliament by the Nenni Socialists. The center-left program called for an ever-increasing participation of the masses in the exercise of political power, the nationalization of the electrical industry, the expansion of regional governments, the democratization of the educational system, and the enactment of the "Green Plan" for agriculture. In foreign affairs, the program reaffirmed Italy's participation in European and Atlantic integration, and it also pledged Italy, together with its allies, to work for an easing of East-West tensions.[18]

The "opening to the left" was inaugurated at a time when demands for profound social changes were being voiced more stridently than at any time since the early postwar years. Although the center-left program did not threaten the fundamental structure of Italian society, the conservative classes were alarmed, and the rightwing members of the Christian Democratic party made no secret of their distaste for their new allies.

A bizarre campaign preceded the parliamentary elections of April 1963. Conservative parties sought to capitalize on the Italian workers' dissatisfaction with inflation and on middle-class opposition to nationalization, while the leftist parties stressed the inadequacy of the center-left in promoting any fundamental reforms. The official leadership of the Christian Democratic party, with Aldo Moro as political secretary and Fanfani as premier, was hard put to retain the party's usual sources of electoral strength. Those who had previously voted the Christian Democratic ticket but were now disaffected for one reason or another found themselves being wooed or cajoled on all sides. As the weekly *L'Espresso* so well put it on March 24, 1963, the campaign resolved itself into a "race to corner the Catholic vote."

In *L'Unità*, its official daily, the Communist party spoke of a basic split between the pope and the Christian Democratic party. It heaped praise on John XXIII, who had received Nikita Khrushchev's son-in-law in a private audience and whose encyclical *Pacem in terris* (1963) called for a dialogue between Catholics and nonbelievers. According to *L'Unità*, the pontiff differentiated the religious terrain from the political, thereby freeing Catholics to vote for Communist candidates. Saragat's rightwing Socialists sought to present themselves as a movement essentially Christian in origin, while Nenni's leftwing Socialists appealed to young Catholics to join the Socialist party, *Pacem in terris* having endorsed cooperation between those of diverse ideologies. Under the able leadership of Giovanni Malagodi, the traditionally anticlerical Liberal party also solicited Catholic votes, promising to do a better job than the Social Democrats in safeguarding Catholic rights.

The results of the 1963 elections were startling and contrary to the forecasts made on the eve of the balloting. As compared with the 1958 elections, the Christian Democrats lost over seven hundred thousand votes, while the Liberal party and the Communist party each gained about a million, and the Social Democrats half a million. The votes of the Socialist and Republican parties differed only slightly from the previous tallies. The Christian Democrats unquestionably sustained the greatest losses, even though they again emerged with a plurality of the total vote. The lost votes appear to have been those of conservative electors who feared that the center-left policy and the alleged radicalism of the pope might engender radical change in Italian society.

The Christian Democrats could not rule alone, and by the end of 1963, under the more prudent Moro as premier, they succeeded in hammering out a program for a new center-left coalition, one that brought Socialists back into the government for the first time since 1947. This program provided for the creation of regions, the enactment of fiscal and administrative reforms, the allocation of additional funds to the south, urban planning, and modernization of the school system. Definition of foreign policy objectives, a matter capable of sundering the delicate alliance, received short shrift.

Under Moro and his successors Mariano Rumor and Emilio Colombo the center-left coalition lasted eight years. Despite a lagging economy, labor unrest, and continuing factionalism in the ranks of both the Christian Democrats and the Socialists, the center-left formula brought substantial benefits to the nation as a whole. Regional parliaments with broad legislative and administrative powers were finally established, thereby carrying out a constitutional provision and redeeming with Socialist assistance a Christian Democratic pledge dating back to the turn of the century. Regionalism may have increased bureaucracy, as its critics charged, but it also enhanced the individual voter's sense of participation in government. Other center-left measures long overdue were the enactment of divorce legislation (over stiff Vatican opposition) and the democratization and decentralization of the school system. In foreign affairs Italy adopted a more flexible and independent posture. The People's Republic of China was recognized, and more cordial relations were inaugurated with the countries of Eastern Europe. A modification of the special statute of the Trentino-Alto Adige region to guarantee the rights of the German-speaking communities in that area improved relations with Austria. The expulsion in 1970 of 13,000 Italians from Libya, together with confiscation of their property and the freezing of their assets, was met with admirable restraint on the part of the Italian government, much to the dismay of ultranationalist elements.

Unfortunately the gains seemed inconsequential as compared with expectations, and stresses and strains in the governing coalition reached a breaking point in 1971. In June the Neo-Fascists, profiting from a law-and-order backlash against persistent social turbulence, student protests, and anarchistic bomb-throwing, scored gains in local and regional elections at the expense of the Christian Democrats. In December the election of Giovanni Leone as president of the Italian Republic, after the longest election deadlock in postwar Italian history, signaled the fall of the center-left coalition. Emilio Colombo resigned the premiership in January 1972, to be succeeded by Giulio Andreotti, long identified with rightist elements in the party. His government was composed only of Christian Democrats and therefore lacked a majority in parliament. A coalition could not be forged with Socialists, Social Democrats, and Republicans because of conflicting views on ways to stimulate the economy, widen social reform, and settle the dispute arising from the controversial divorce law (the opponents of divorce demanded a national referendum). Another important issue concerned relations with the Communist party, which was now under the able and moderate leadership of Enrico Berlinguer. The Socialists favored closer cooperation with the Communists, while the other parties adamantly opposed any moves that might bring the Communists into a governing coalition.

The parliamentary paralysis compelled Leone to dissolve parliament fourteen months before the expiration of its term of office. It was the first time in the twenty-five-year history of the Italian Republic that such a measure had been deemed necessary. Elections were set for May 7–8, 1972, and in the meantime Andreotti continued his minority Christian Democratic government in a caretaker capacity. During the ensuing campaign both Christian Democrats and Communists took more conservative positions than in previous contests. National and international interest tended to focus on two questions in particular: the viability of another center-left coalition and the strength of the Neo-Fascist Italian Social Movement. But the election results did not provide clear-cut answers to either question. Although the Christian Democrats showed resilience, recouping losses in local and regional elections incurred during the preceding two years, their strength in the new parliament was almost unchanged. The Italian Social Movement and its ally the Monarchist party registered only slight gains. The strength of the Communist, Social Democratic, and Socialist parties remained substantially the same as in the previous legislatures. Paradoxically, the greatest losses were sustained by the conservative Liberal party.

The tentative conclusion to be drawn from the 1972 elections was that the Italian government would continue to be plagued by political instability, resulting in abortive or halfhearted measures in the social arena. As Italy prepared to move into the final quarter of the twentieth century, the electorate seemed to be saying that it would prefer to wait until another day to decide crucial questions. But procrastination may erode and eventually destroy Italy's essentially democratic and forward-looking constitution. The solution to Italy's malaise would seem to lie in an honest self-appraisal on the part of the Christian Democratic party, still the largest in the nation. Organizationally speaking, it should adopt effective measures to minimize factionalism; philosophically speaking, it should shake off its status quo mentality and recognize the reality of evolution, not only for individual men, but also for men organized in political parties.

NOTES

1. For the role of the Catholic church in Italian life, see Chapter 11 of this book. The most important works on Christian Democracy in Italy include the following: Francesco Malgeri, ed., *Gli Atti dei congressi del Partito Popolare Italiano* (Brescia: Morcelliana, 1969); Gabriele De Rosa, *Storia politica dell'azione cattolica in Italia*, 2 vols. (Bari: Laterza, 1953–1954) and *Storia del Partito Popolare* (Bari: Laterza, 1958); Mario Einaudi and François Goguel, *Christian Democracy in Italy and France* (Notre Dame: University of Notre Dame Press, 1952); Fausto Fonzi, *I Cattolici e la società italiana dopo l'unità* (Rome: Studium, 1960); Angelo Martini, *Studi sulla questione romana e la conciliazione* (Rome: Cinque Lune, 1963); Giorgio Tupini, *I Democratici cristiani* (Milan: Garzanti, 1954); Leicester C. Webb, *Church and State in Italy 1947–1957* (New York: Cambridge University Press, 1958); Richard A. Webster, *The Cross and the Fasces* (Stanford: Stanford University Press, 1960).

2. Romolo Murri, *Della Religione, della Chiesa e dello Stato* (Milan: Treves, 1910). For two sympathetic accounts of Murri, see Sergio Zoppi, *Romolo Murri e la prima Democrazia cristiana* (Florence: Vallecchi, 1968) and Maurilio Guasco, *Romolo Murri e il modernismo* (Rome: Cinque Lune, 1968). For Toniolo's antagonism toward Murri, see *Lettere di Giuseppe Toniolo,* ed. Nello Vian, 3 vols. (Rome: Studium, 1953), II, 134–135, 282–283, 291, 294–295, 334–335.

3. The essence of Toniolo's thought may be found in his *Democrazia cristiana*, ed. Comitato Opera Omnia di G. Toniolo, 2 vols. (Rome: Studium, 1949).

4. "Atti parlamentari, Camera dei deputati," 26th Legislatura, Discussione 1, June 24, 1921 (Rome: Tipografia della Camera dei Deputati, 1921), pp. 206–210. For De Gasperi's Austrian years, see Elisa A. Carrillo, *Alcide De Gasperi, the Long Apprenticeship* (Notre Dame: University of Notre Dame Press, 1965), pp. 1–44; for his role in the Italian Popular party, *ibid.*, pp. 45–97.

5. For the plan for a Christian International, see Igino Giordani, *La Politica estera del Partito Popolare Italiano* (Rome: Francesco Ferrari, 1924); Giorgio Gualeri, *La Politica estera dei Popolari* (Rome: Cinque Lune, 1959).

6. Bertini to Ministero dell'Interno, March 24, 1923, Protoc. 8836, Archivio Centrale dello Stato (Rome), Ministero dell'Interno, Direzione Generale della Pubblica Sicurezza, Divisione Affari Generale e Riservati (1919–1926), 1923, pacco 70.

7. "La Parte dei cattolici nelle presenti lotte dei partiti politici in Italia," *La Civiltà Cattolica*, 75 (1924), 297–306.

8. *L'Osservatore Romano*, Sept. 10, 1924.

9. Archivio Centrale dello Stato, Ministero dell'Interno, Pubblica Sicurezza, Casellario Politico Centrale, Busta 55, Fascicolo 2, No. 6775.

10. Franco Salvi et al., eds., *Atti e documenti della Democrazia Cristiana 1943–1959* (Rome: Cinque Lune, 1959), pp. 1–12.

11. Alcide De Gasperi, *I Cattolici dall'opposizione al governo* (Bari: Laterza, 1955), pp. 487–488.

12. *L'Osservatore Romano*, Feb. 25, April 16, 1949; *La Civiltà Cattolica*, 94 (1948), 572.

13. Description of the Sturzo Operation is based on interviews with Signora Francesca De Gasperi and Father Lombardi, as well as on the unpublished diary of De Gasperi's close friend Emilio Bonomelli, who very kindly gave this writer a photostat of the diary.

14. *Cronache Sociali 1947–1951*, ed. Marcella Glisenti and Leopoldo Elia, 2 vols. (Rome: Luciano Landi, 1961).

15. For the differences between De Gasperi and Gronchi, see Luigi Somma's *De Gasperi o Gronchi* (Rome: Corso, 1953). For the *Sinistra Sindacale*, see Giorgio Galli and Paolo Facchi, *La Sinistra democristiana* (Milan: Feltrinelli, 1962), Part II, Chap. 4.

16. Galli and Facchi, *op. cit.*, Part II, Chap. 7.

17. Dr. Ugo Sciascia, in an interview with this writer on July 24, 1967.

18. Amintore Fanfani, *Centro-Sinistra '62* (Milan: Garzanti, 1963); Norman Kogan, *A Political History of Postwar Italy* (New York: Praeger, 1966), Chap. 12.

CHAPTER 5

SOCIALISM AND COMMUNISM IN ITALIAN POLITICAL LIFE

NORMAN KOGAN

The revolutionary movement emerged in Italy as an elitist movement of intellectuals, middle- and upper-class professionals, and the liberal aristocracy. The twin goals of national unification and social justice, best expressed in the fervent language of Giuseppe Mazzini, would be defined differently by moderates and radicals, by constitutional monarchists and republicans, by centralizers and federalists, or by free enterprisers and later socialists. The heroes of the Risorgimento achieved legal but not psychological and cultural unification. Italy was created, but not Italians. Social justice, an even more elusive concept to measure, was disputed as to its content, but generally recognized as absent in Italian society. Neither in its psychological sense of fraternity nor in its economic sense of well-being was it even approached. Italians remained, and still remain, fragmented and alienated, suspicious and skeptical of their fellow men, lacking (in comparison with the peoples of western and northern Europe) the quantity and variety of economic goods potentially available to them.

It has been argued that unification might have been accompanied by some degree of social justice if the revolutionary movement had not been so predominantly elitist, if the "popular masses" had played a more prominent role in the revolutionary process. This argument remains speculative; nor can we firmly decide the debated question of whether the masses were capable of being mobilized for revolutionary goals in nineteenth-century Italy. We do know that the elitist imprint on Italian politics and on Italian revolutionary movements, both Marxist and non-Marxist, has continued up to the present. This phenomenon has not been unique to Italy, but it has been especially marked there.

Although Mazzini and his followers dominated the left wing of the revolutionary movement during the Risorgimento, their republican bourgeois liberalism was challenged slightly by the early stirrings of socialist thought in the works of Giuseppe Ferrari and Carlo Pisacane. These were minor figures with little or no following whose utopian socialist ideas derived from Proudhon and Babeuf. Pisacane's concept of economic determinism is analogous to that of Marx, although there is no evidence that he knew of Marx or his writings. His anarchist principles were inspired by Proudhon, however, and his emphasis on the spontaneous and voluntaristic uprising of the masses became a recurring theme in Italian revolutionary debates,[1] carried on usually by intellectuals far removed from the real masses.

The unification of Italy under the House of Savoy, achieved through the skillful diplomacy of Cavour, undercut the influence of Mazzini on the Italian left. Mazzini's long years in exile further weakened the power of his ideas. In the decade after unification socialist ideas coming from outside the country gradually captured the younger generation of his followers. Mazzini's attacks on the Paris Commune in 1871 dealt the final blow to his influence. During the 1860s Bakunin was active in Italy, and Italian socialism in the early years of its formation reflected the anarchist and libertarian motives of this great Russian. Socialism in Italy, in other words, was dominated by libertarian rather than Marxist or authoritarian conceptions. Throughout the 1870s and early 1880s when Marx's Internationals were becoming the leading force among the socialists of northwestern Europe, anarcho-socialism held its preeminence in Italy. In the middle 1880s Marxism began to supplant it and by the 1890s had replaced it as predominant in Italian socialist thought. The organization of socialism on a mass and class basis, a developing labor movement and a political party to speak for it would now emerge, although anarchist groups would continue to exist and their influence revive in different forms in the early twentieth century.

Mutual aid organizations for workers had existed since early in the nineteenth century. Their transformation into trade unions generally took place in the 1880s, although the printers and typographers had organized earlier. The growth of local trade unions in the cities of the north led to the establishment of coordinating bodies, the Italian Chambers of Labor. Modeled after the French Bourses du Travail, the chambers have played an important role in Italian labor history. By the middle 1890s they were dominated by Socialists, as was most of the leadership of the local trade unions.

Foreign influences have always played an important role in modern Italian life, particularly so in the development of Italian socialism and the Italian labor movement. French and Russian influences have already been mentioned, and German influence was growing through the spread of Marxism and through the increasing prestige of the German Social Democratic party on the continent. The formation of the Italian Socialist party (PSI) in 1892 reflected not only the late beginnings of industrialism in Italy and the radicalization of the countryside, but also the impact of the German example.[2] The PSI was originally structured on the basis of an affiliation of workers' organizations, reflecting imported models. Government repression of workers' organizations in 1894 and 1895 following the uprising of the Sicilian *Fasci* led the Socialists to decide in 1895 to establish party sections and to provide for personal affiliation through individual membership in the local sections. This restructuring did not mean detaching the party from the trade unions and Chambers of Labor, however; on the contrary, the link between the party and the labor organizations became stronger, for the party was fighting the battles for both. The major struggle of the PSI in the 1890s, a decade of reaction and suppression, was to achieve the goals of democracy and liberty, neither specifically socialistic, in order to achieve the right for the party to organize politically and the right for the unions to organize economically. Linked to the organizational struggle was the drive to obtain the expansion of the suffrage through the elimination of property and income qualifications, as well as the adoption of an electoral system based on proportional representation rather than single-member constituencies. It took until 1913 to achieve almost universal male adult suffrage and until 1919 to achieve proportional representation.

While a small number of young intellectuals were being converted to socialism through the missionary work of foreign Marxists and through the reading of foreign socialist literature, a larger number became acquainted with Marxist ideas through the writing of Antonio Labriola, the first Italian Marxist philosopher. Labriola was not an original thinker. His presentation of socialist thought came straight from Marx and Engels. He was the disseminator of Marxist doctrines in Italy in the small academic and intellectual community.

The principal disseminator of socialism among the workers and peasants, primarily in the north, was Filippo Turati, one of the key founders of the party. Through Turati and his disciples socialism spread swiftly among the factory workers, in the textile industry and later in the mechanical industries. The first industrial revolution in Italy really got under way in 1900, and in the subsequent decade and a half the basis was laid for the conversion of northwestern Italy into an industrial triangle. The penetration of Marxist ideas from the intelligentsia was not confined to the workers of burgeoning industry. A rural base of considerable strength was established among the peasants of the Po Valley and later among the *mezzadri* of Tuscany, Umbria, and the Marches. Italy was exceptional among continental countries in the support given to a socialist party by the countryside. A key explanation is found in the Ghibelline inheritance, the anticlericalism and republicanism of these regions—itself a product of earlier papal misrule—and Garibaldian traditions of the Risorgimento.

Antonio Labriola's transmittal of Marxist doctrines to the Italian intelligentsia had to contend with the influence of pre-Marxist currents of thought, currents that very early led to the emergence of reformist or revisionist influences in Italian Marxism. Among these currents can be identified the positivism found in the work of Achille Loria, a continuing trace of Bakunin's anarchist or libertarian socialism, the sociologism of Italian evolutionists and social Darwinists, and, most important, the bourgeois liberalism of Benedetto Croce. Reinforcing Croce's criticisms of Marx's theory of surplus value and his argument on the declining rate of profit were the analyses of the liberal economists Maffeo Pantaleoni and Vilfredo Pareto.[3] This intellectual input quickly challenged the "crude determinism" of vulgar Marxism as well as the dialectical process. The end result was that even before Eduard Bernstein's major work of socialist revisionism appeared in Germany, the intellectual socialist climate in Italy was prepared for its reception. In fact some Italian scholars claim that Bernstein borrowed directly from the Italian revisionists or at least was aware of and influenced by their work. Bernstein's writings immediately stirred a major debate which went far beyond intellectual circles and undermined the unity and political effectiveness of the Italian Socialist party.

In the first decade of the twentieth century Italian Socialists were split by the rivalry and competition between the reformist, or revisionist, and the orthodox, or maximalist, currents in the party. The factors encouraging reformism were not only German and French developments and ideas like the revisionism of Jean Jaurès but were also domestic in origin and inspiration. Inside Italy the economy was growing. The domination of Giovanni Giolitti over Italian government and politics meant increasing democracy in the political realm and more progressive and advanced programs in the economic and social realm. An optimistic and pragmatic idealism pervaded the environment. Giolitti's efforts to attract the Socialists into the political system stirred a positive response among the reformists and a bitter rejection among the maximalists, who opposed collaboration with non-Socialist groups to achieve non-Socialist goals. Although it is outside the scope of this discussion to enter into the vicissitudes of the reformist-maximalist struggle, with the alternating victories and defeats of one wing over the other,[4] it should be emphasized that the long-range consequences were to leave Italian Marxists permanently divided. By the time of the First World War both reformists and maximalists were further subdivided.

In the 1900s revolutionary syndicalism emerged in Italy, nourished by the frustrations of unsatisfied rising expectations and by the impregnation in a new generation of young intellectuals of doctrines of nationalism and irrationalism. From France came the influence of Georges Sorel to reinforce an earlier Italian anarchistic tradition. The revolutionary syndicalists, identified by Robert Michels as neo-Marxists rather than anti-Marxists, found even the maximalist socialists inadequate as revolutionaries. They left the PSI in 1906, led by Arturo Labriola (not to be confused with Antonio Labriola), an advocate of "direct action." Later, with some of the maximalist Socialists, they became susceptible to the development of a nationalist socialism, and the majority of them ended up in Fascism. Gaetano Salvemini's judgment of them at the time is revealing: "Most were *spiriti arruffatti* [disturbed, demagogic], late romantics, apologists of violence for the sake of violence, prophets of revolt or *coup de main* for the thrill of the dangerous gesture." [5]

Between the years 1909 and 1912 the reformists became willing to collaborate in Giolitti's cabinets. They controlled the leadership of the General Confederation of Labor as well as the leadership of the vast majority of the Socialist unions. The rank and file of the unions remained maximalist, in all likelihood, but a minority of the unions went over to revolutionary syndicalism. The reformists found it hard to swallow Giolitti's imperialism in Libya in 1911 and 1912, but some of them, like Leonida Bissolati, finally endorsed it on the grounds of its presumed benefits to all the Italian people. The maximalists violently opposed the Libyan war. Their newly emerging leader Benito Mussolini tried to block troop trains headed for the ports to deliver soldiers destined for the North African front. In 1912 the maximalists under Mussolini's leadership forced part of the reformists out of the PSI and the future Duce took over the editorship of the official party newspaper *Avanti!*

The outbreak of the First World War found the PSI adhering to the classic dogma of socialist internationalism and opting for neutralism. This position distinguished it from the other socialist parties of Western Europe, which endorsed their respective countries' war efforts. Not all Italian socialist neutralists were neutral for the same reason, and not all of the socialists were neutralists. The reformists Bissolati and Ivanoe Bonomi joined the ranks of the democratic interventionists. Mussolini also abandoned the PSI; followed by other maximalists and revolutionary syndicalists, he created his first *Fascio di azione rivoluzionaria* (Bloc of Revolutionary Action), adopting a position of national intervention. The bulk of the Marxists held firm, however, and as long as Italy stayed out of the war, their position was more than tenable, shared as it was by the Vatican and by large numbers of bourgeois neutralists led by Giolitti in parliament. But the Italian commitment to the Treaty of London in April 1915 and the decision by the Italian government of Antonio Salandra to enter the war on the side of the Triple Entente was the watershed. All the other neutralists crumbled, leaving the Socialist deputies in parliament to alone oppose Italian ratification of the Treaty of London. Socialist isolation once the country was in war was difficult. The PSI adopted a policy of neither supporting nor sabotaging the war effort, a policy almost impossible to implement as national and patriotic sentiments developed throughout the country. The party ignored these sentiments and suffered thereby in the postwar period. After the Second World War both the Socialist and Communist parties avoided this error.

The strains and burdens of war left the Italians an exhausted and irritable people. Italian socialists were stimulated by the two Russian revolutions and strongly attracted to the optimistic vision of swift Marxist victories everywhere. The 1919 parliamentary elections, the first under the system of proportional representation, saw the emergence of the PSI as the largest single party, with approximately 35 percent of the vote. The new Popular party, founded by Don Luigi Sturzo, was second. The old liberal parliamentary cliques and factions appeared to be on the way to oblivion. The Socialists could not agree, however, on how to use their increased parliamentary power. Though temporarily reunited for electoral purposes the maximalists and reformists disagreed as to strategy. The maximalists refused to participate in any "bourgeois" government, while the reformists were more flexible. The maximalists won out, fortified by the optimistic belief of the period that the socialist revolution was near, and deterministically convinced of the inevitability of its triumph. In the words of the maximalist leader Giacinto Serrati, "Socialists interpret history, we don't make it."

Although they initially responded positively to the Russian invitation to join the Third International, the Italian Socialists finally rejected membership when it became clear to them that subordination to Soviet control was the price to be paid. At home postwar tensions reached a peak in 1920 and 1921 with the workers' occupation of the factories and the bitter aftermath of the failure of the occupation. The Socialists were splitting again, divided by conflicting factions, none of which could force a policy. The PSI executive bureau (*direzione*) was dominated by maximalists who were intransigent without being revolutionary. At the same time other movements, also revolutionary in their goals and rhetoric, had emerged to challenge Italian Socialists.

Early in 1919 Mussolini had converted his earlier *Fascio di azione rivoluzionaria* into the *Fasci di combattimento*. Fascist programs enunciated at this time still reveal the socialist heritage. They were antibourgeois, anticapitalist, antimonarchical, and anticlerical. Syndicalist and nationalist themes, outgrowths of intellectual and political currents of the prewar period, were added embellishments. The appeal these programs made to many disparate and divergent forces brought together persons who nevertheless shared a mutual hostility to a society and political system which they judged incapable of governing Italy.[6] This judgment coincided with the judgment of Italian Marxists of many varieties.

In January 1921, a small group of Socialists on the extreme left wing of the party broke off to found the Communist party of Italy. The leaders of this schismatic group were the Neapolitan intellectual Amadeo Bordiga and two university graduates in Turin, Antonio Gramsci and Palmiro Togliatti, who were ready to accept the discipline of the Third International. Bordiga was the party's first secretary-general and dominated it in the early years. He was a purist revolutionary with little sense of practical politics and an independence which within a few years got him into trouble with the Soviet leaders. During the years when parliamentary liberalism was dying in Italy and all Marxist movements were in danger of suffocation by an emerging Fascism, Bordiga constantly emphasized that bourgeois democracy was the enemy. This myopia concerning the Fascist threat can better be understood if it is appreciated that at first both Italian and international communism saw Fascism as a progressive revolutionary movement, not yet as a reactionary instrument of finance and industrial capitalism.

In 1924, with Fascism strangling all rival political movements, Gramsci, who had obtained Russian backing, replaced Bordiga in the Communist party hierarchy. Mussolini outlawed competing parties in 1925. Gramsci was jailed, and Togliatti, who escaped into exile, took over the leadership of the party. Both men opposed a "mechanistic determinism" in interpreting Marxism. Both were concerned with the role of the individual—especially the man of ideas and the man of action—in making history, not merely accommodating to it. They were not complete voluntarists, for they recognized that real conditions do limit what men can accomplish in a given era. Gramsci is not the great original thinker that the Italian Communist party after the Second World War has tried to make him. But he certainly is one of the most intriguing of the twentieth-century Marxist ideologists.[7]

The Fascist victory marked the temporary defeat of Italian Marxism (as well as Italian liberalism and Italian political Catholicism). The Marxist elements in Fascist thought were pushed aside, to reappear in a perverted form in the 1930s when the state took control of private industries in order to bail them out during the Great Depression. This partial nationalization of some heavy industry and the major banks would never be recognized by Marxists as genuine socialism, yet it would become the basis of economic policy in which Marxist parties would participate after the Second World War.

During the era of Fascist domination the Marxist parties were reduced to almost nothing inside Italy and led a fitful existence in exile. Only the

Communists were able to maintain a tiny underground organization inside the country. Their leadership in exile was able to survive because of Soviet help. Togliatti and most of his fellow exiles accepted, however reluctantly, the growing Stalinization of Soviet and international communism. A few Italian Communists such as Angelo Tasca and Ignazio Silone refused to take it and left the movement.

The Socialist leaders who fled into exile, mainly in France, suffered there the strains and disputes which other socialist parties were experiencing during the interwar years. Attempts to unite in defeat, among themselves and with other anti-Fascist exile groups, had occasional successes and discouraging failures. Long-held divergencies of outlook and differences of opinion over strategy made agreement difficult. Paris was the center of exile activity. In 1930 Pietro Nenni and Giuseppe Saragat, with some old-time socialist exiles, brought about a fusion of the maximalist and reformist wings under the label of the historic PSI. They also took the Socialists into coalition with another exile group, the Justice and Liberty movement.

The Justice and Liberty group was composed of intellectuals who were attempting to forge an ideological program synthesizing the liberal and Marxist traditions. The young Turinese thinker Piero Gobetti and the historian Gaetano Salvemini at Florence had been working in this direction. A group of their disciples carried on their ideas after Gobetti's early death and Salvemini's flight into exile in 1925. Inside Italy such men as Ferruccio Parri and Ernesto Rossi organized clandestine groups which suffered arrest, persecution, and attrition, but which would continue to survive throughout the interwar period. In the mid-thirties the philosopher Guido Calogero added his stimulating contribution to the heady mixture of ideas and personalities. In exile the movement was led by the dynamic Carlo Rosselli and his brother Nello. The efforts of the Justice and Liberty group to reconcile intellectually their two spiritual heritages were unsatisfactory. Most of the members remained basically either liberals or socialists. In 1931, when the group signed a working agreement with Nenni's reconstituted PSI, Rosselli and his friends decided that they should emphasize the socialistic aspects of their program.

By 1931 the various exile movements, except for the Communists, had joined together, albeit with reservations and internecine rivalry. The Communists were following the Soviet line of the period, which classified Socialists of the Second International as social fascists. After the Nazi victory in Germany, however, a gradual rethinking of strategy led to new attempts at rapprochement. In August 1934 the Socialists and Communists in Paris signed a unity of action pact, one year before the Communist International fully launched its strategy of popular front and united front. We can assume that the earlier agreement between the two Italian Marxist parties had clearance from Moscow—at least as a trial balloon. During this same period, however, the Justice and Liberty group had withdrawn from collaboration within the anti-Fascist concentration, with the standard recriminations and haggling over doctrinal differences which are typical of exile groups. The concentration formally expired in May 1934, three months before the creation of the unity of action pact.

The realignment of the Soviet position in international politics, the Fascist invasion of Ethiopia in October 1935, and Mussolini's intervention in the Spanish Civil War after July 1936 produced the stimulus to unity among anti-Fascist forces which enabled them to collaborate until August 1939. Only the Justice and Liberty group still went its independent way, although it, too, participated in the International Brigades during the Spanish Civil War. The Rosselli brothers were assassinated in 1937 by French fascist thugs in the hire of the Italian secret police. The movement had been dealt a serious blow.

The collaboration of Italian Marxists was destroyed by the bombshell of the Nazi-Soviet Nonaggression Pact of August 1939. Almost all the Italian Communists accepted it obediently, but the Socialists were outraged and broke the unity of action agreement immediately. Although Nenni was reluctant to break completely, his indignant comrades, especially in the reformist wing, forced him to resign as secretary of the party. The Italian Communists then embarked on the defeatist tactics required by Soviet policy during the years of war between September 1939 and June 1941. Non-Communist exiles in France made minor attempts to help the French war effort, but after the German defeat of France in June 1940, most anti-Fascists were captured and shipped back to Mussolini's Italy for imprisonment; some escaped to Britain, the United States, and other countries. Then the Nazi attack on Soviet Russia in June 1941 restored the premises for a popular front. In Toulouse during October 1941 a few Italian Communists and Socialists, this time joined by representatives of the Justice and Liberty group, created a Committee of Action for the Union of the Italian People.

Inside Italy, the Spanish Civil War and Mussolini's complicity and intervention in it turned some members of the new generation of young Italian university students into anti-Fascists, and there was a spurt of recruits into both Marxist and non-Marxist parties between 1936 and 1940. Mainly, these young men joined the Communist underground or the liberal socialist groups stimulated by the thinking and writing of Professor Calogero. Later the liberal socialists merged with the exiles of the Justice and Liberty movement to form the Action party.[8]

Italy's entry into the Second World War on June 10, 1940, and the succession of military reverses which followed in the next two years laid the groundwork for the renewal of agitation among the Italian people in

1942. As the collapse of Axis forces in North Africa became apparent, Communist infiltrators began the covert organization of the workers in the large cities of the north. In March 1943 the first major strike against the Axis erupted in Turin and Milan. During the same spring, efforts were made to form a broad coalition that would include Catholics and monarchists as well as Marxists and liberals. The dissolution of the Communist International by Stalin in April 1943 helped. That same month an Anti-Fascist United Freedom Front was created in Rome under the leadership of Ivanoe Bonomi, the ex-reformist Socialist. After the surrender of Italy to the Allies on September 8, 1943, the United Freedom Front became the Central Committee of National Liberation.

The liquidation of the Fascist regime and the overthrow of Mussolini on July 25, 1943, was carried out by the king and the generals of the armed forces, not by Marxist revolutionaries or ideological anti-Fascists. The Allied invasion of Sicily in July 1943 and the collapse of Italian military resistance had been responsible for the monarch's decision to terminate the Duce's government. Beginning in September the Italian peninsula from Salerno northward was occupied by German troops, and Anglo-American forces very slowly pushed their way forward. The country was cut in two, occupied by warring foreign armies; its own armed forces disintegrated, and a nascent civil war emerged behind the German lines.

On the day after the surrender the king and his generals fled from Rome to the southeastern city of Brindisi. Victor Emmanuel's contemptible flight, on top of all his other mistakes of the past two decades, deterred the Committees of National Liberation behind the Allied lines in the south from collaborating with the rump ministry in Brindisi. The king was supported by Winston Churchill, however, and the impasse between the rivals lasted until April 1944, when Palmiro Togliatti returned from Moscow to announce that Communists had no objection to collaboration in a royal government. A new cabinet was then formed by the southern Committees of National Liberation to carry forward the Italian contribution to the United Nations war effort under the king. In June 1944 after the Allies entered Rome, King Victor Emmanuel III turned over his authority to his son Umberto, giving him the title Lieutenant General of the Realm. The Communist shift of position, crucial to unblocking the situation, indicated the new basic strategy of Togliatti: to seek power from inside the system rather than to attack it from a position of revolutionary opposition.[9]

During the period of the war in Italy a vigorous partisan movement developed behind the Nazi lines, sparked by disbanded soldiers, anti-Fascist intellectuals, workers, and peasants. On September 12, 1943, Mussolini was rescued from prison by the Germans to create a Fascist Social Republic in the area occupied by Hitler's troops. The principles enunciated by his government were a return to the socialist and syndicalist doctrines of Fascism's early years. But the underground Resistance in the north was not taken in by his propaganda and organized to fight his Blackshirt troops and to sabotage the German armed forces. The Communist and Action parties were the most successful in organizing partisan brigades, although smaller Christian Democratic, Socialist, Liberal, and independent Resistance units were also created. A unified political command for the Resistance was established in Milan in the Committee of National Liberation of Northern Italy. This committee set up a coordinated military network, the Volunteers of Liberty Corps, under the leadership of the Communist Luigi Longo and the Actionist Ferruccio Parri. By 1945 a major Resistance army was created in the north, one of the most effective partisan armies in all of Europe. At the time of the final German collapse in northern Italy, the partisans were able to capture and liberate the key cities.[10]

The disappearance of the unifying stimulus provided by a common enemy, as well as differing positions on political and economic structures, led to intraparty and interparty disintegration. Within a year after the end of the war the Committees of National Liberation had fallen apart. The Action party disappeared by late 1946 and early 1947. Its *équipe* of intellectuals had not been able to reconcile the liberal and socialist components in their doctrines. The Marxists among them left to join the Socialist and Communist parties, while most of the liberals joined the Republican party.

The Socialists, under the name of the Italian Socialist Party of Proletarian Unity, continued their pact of unity with the Communists. It was Nenni's conviction that when Socialists fought Communists, reaction triumphed. He considered the Fascist victories in Italy and Germany the consequence of the disunity of the working class—hence the name of the party. The commitment to unity of action, however, subjected Socialist objectives to Communist strategy and tactics, and not because the Socialists were numerically inferior to the Communists. The first nationwide election in 1946, held to elect representatives to a constituent assembly, produced a Socialist vote of 20.7 percent. The Communists, in spite of their rapid growth in the last year of the war, received 19 percent of the total vote. It is interesting to compare this vote of 40 percent for the Marxist parties to the 1919 vote of 35 percent for the Socialists. A quarter of a century of Fascism culminating in a disastrous war had increased the Marxist vote only 5 percent.

The intensifying "cold war" put increasing strains upon Socialist unity. In January 1947 the reformist minority in the party, led by Giuseppe Saragat, split off to form a new political grouping. Subsequent schisms produced more Socialist splinter movements, which finally coalesced into the Italian Social Democratic party. The defectors included almost half (50 of 115) of the Socialist deputies in the Constituent Assembly and a smaller portion of the party apparatus and electoral support. The remaining Socialists under Nenni's leadership resumed the historic PSI name. They were ejected from the Italian cabinet in May 1947, along with the Communists, because of their opposition to the growing pro-Western orientation of Italian policy.

Togliatti's strategy of sharing power inside the government was being put to the test. Since 1944 he had followed the path of collaboration rather than the path of revolutionary opposition, always proclaiming, however, the revolutionary nature of Communist long-range goals. Within a few weeks after the end of the war, he had warned the Communist partisan leaders in northern Italy that the party had no choice but to follow the legal path to power. There was no Red Army available to provide cover for a revolt, and the Anglo-American forces were present to suppress one. Nenni agreed with this analysis. Togliatti directed his party's efforts to gain the goodwill and collaboration of other major forces in Italian society. Over Stalin's objections he opened the Italian Communist party to anyone willing to join, choosing a mass party over an elite or cadre party composed only of believing and knowledgeable Marxists. He promoted the unity of the labor movement by encouraging the formation of one Italian General Confederation of Labor (CGIL) led by three secretaries general: a Communist, a Socialist, and a Christian Democrat. He helped the Christian Democratic leader Alcide De Gasperi become prime minister in December 1945. He delivered the Communist vote in the Constitutional Assembly in favor of incorporating the Lateran Accords of 1929 into the new constitution of the republic. He muted traditional Marxist anticlericalism and tried to come to terms with the Catholic church by playing down such issues as birth control and divorce. He envisioned his party sharing power jointly with Catholics and Socialists, in a three-party government endorsed by the Vatican and by the Soviet Union. But the church rejected his advances, and the new Communist Information Bureau, created by Stalin to replace the old Comintern, attacked his strategy for being nonrevolutionary.

After the Communists and Socialists were ejected from the cabinet in 1947, they presented a joint slate in the general election of April 1948. The election campaign of that spring turned into a Catholic crusade against Marxism. The sweeping victory of the Christian Democrats in the election led to the creation of a new four-party "center" cabinet which included the Social Democrats but in which the Catholics had a majority all by themselves.

The Communist-Socialist isolation was further aggravated by a split in the trade-union movement. By 1950 the CGIL was faced with two competing federations, the Italian Confederation of Free Syndicates (CISL), and the Italian Union of Labor (UIL), the first dominated by Christian Democrats, the second by Social Democrats and Republicans (see Chapter 9, pages 216–217). The tripartite split was a repetition of a process well known in the history of Italian labor as well as in the history of labor movements in other European countries. Italy's decision to join the newly formed North Atlantic Treaty Organization over the opposition of the Communist and Socialist parties nailed down their political isolation in the country.

The 1948 election marked the definitive emergence of the Communists' dominance in the Italian left. Their discipline in the use of the preference vote for the selection of deputies from the joint slate gave the Communists almost twice as many deputies as the Socialists received. Although the Socialists renewed their unity of action pact with the Communists, they determined that in following elections they would run their own ticket.

Socialists formed coalition cabinets with Communists in numerous local and provincial governments, especially in central Italy, where the two parties could produce a winning majority. And while they were rarely able to win victories in the south, they continued to expand in that part of the country where they had been traditionally weak. By 1953, however, the Socialists began to speak of the possibility of their availability for an "opening to the left," for an alliance ranging from the Christian Democrats to the Socialists, if a suitable program could be elaborated. It would take ten more years before the opening was realized, but the potentiality for another split in Marxist ranks was present from 1953 on.

The isolation of the Marxist parties was primarily political. In the everyday life of the country the Marxists were always present; they were not on the margins of society. The CGIL collaborated with the other labor confederations to organize joint strikes. They negotiated joint contracts with businessmen. Marxists were active in professional, scholarly, and academic organizations, and they dominated in the fields of publishing and the fine arts. Even at the parliamentary level they played the role of a constitutional rather than a disloyal opposition. Their leaders were in daily contact with other leaders in the management of the regular business of parliament. Over the years they contributed, as the official opposition, to the shaping and modification of policies. By the late 1950s and the 1960s they were intimately involved in the committee work of parliament. Communists might denounce the government on the floor of the Chamber of Deputies, but at the same time they were bargaining and negotiating agreements on legislation, jobs, and appropriations in the privacy of committee rooms.

The united action of the Communist and Socialist parties was strained significantly in 1956. The first blow was the publication of Khrushchev's secret speech denouncing the crimes of the Stalin era. Nenni attacked the Stalinist record and declared that democracy was equally important to all good Socialists. His criticism of the Soviet model went beyond rejection of the cult of personality to an attack on the kind of regime that could permit the Stalinist terror to last for so many years. The Hungarian uprising in the fall of 1956, the Soviet invasion of that country, and the Italian Communists' embarrassed defense of Soviet behavior further exacerbated relations between the two Marxist parties. It also stimulated the defection of a number of key intellectuals from the PCI (Italian Communist Party), although the rank and file remained loyal.

Togliatti responded to these strains by publicly enunciating an "Italian way to Socialism" which would be a "democratic way to Socialism." The Italian Communists openly asserted that the days when the Soviet Union and its Communist party were the "guiding state" and "guiding party" were over. Togliatti elaborated the doctrine of "polycentrism." [11] If the Communist assertions were accepted at face value, the links with the Socialists might still be maintained and good relations with the Catholics could be reforged.

The opposite trend prevailed, however. By 1959 the Socialists formally severed the unity of action pact and embarked on the process which led to the opening to the left by 1963 and the participation of the PSI in the governing coalition. Only a small minority of Socialists considered this policy a betrayal of Marxist principles; they seceded from the party in January 1964 to form the Italian Socialist Party of Proletarian Unity (PSIUP). During these years the Communists alternated between denouncing the opening to the left and hoping that it could be extended to include them. The changing atmosphere in the Catholic world during the pontificate of Pope John XXIII encouraged Communist hopes of engaging in a dialogue with socially conscious and politically leftist Catholics (see Chapter 4). Pope Paul VI, however, quickly halted this dialogue in 1965.

The reality of center-left governments in Italy from the early 1960s on forced Togliatti to lead his party toward accepting political reformism. In 1962 he proclaimed that Italian Communists accepted the method of gradual reforms on a democratic basis, but with the goal of achieving a truly socialist society. His differences with the Social Democratic parties of Western Europe, he asserted, were not over the method of reform, but over their abandonment of socialism as the final goal. This put the Communists in line with the Socialists, who as late as 1965 were insisting they differed from the Social Democrats precisely because they were still committed to an ultimate radical transformation of society, while the Social Democrats were willing to settle for a society of well-being.

A year later the Socialists and Social Democrats had reunited, apparently ready to agree on the utility of working for a society of well-being. The reunification was managed at the leadership level of the two parties. It had not been sought by the rank and file, nor did it result in a true merger. All that was accomplished was to enlarge the number of factions within the reunified party. By 1969 the experiment had failed, and that July the Socialists split once more, with the old Social Democrats adopting the name of the Unified Socialist Party (PSU), which they later abandoned to return to their previous name.

Although the split was mainly the result of personality clashes and factional rivalries, it also revealed two substantive differences. The Socialists considered that the center-left experiment had failed, substantively because of the few and limited reforms actually achieved during the 1960s and politically in the realization that they had lost votes to the Communists rather than gaining votes for themselves. For the most part they were ready to accept the Communists as democratic allies once more; the radicalization of the political atmosphere from 1968 on encouraged this acceptance. On the other hand, the Social Democrats had a more favorable judgment of the results of the center-left experiment and were not ready to accept as bona fide the Communist commitment to democracy and reform.

Small but voluble groups of Communists both inside and outside the party, urged on by Chinese support, were challenging the PCI's reformist line. Particularly active among the university youth, they embarked on the tactics of sporadic violence, threats, and denunciations of the PCI as betrayers of the principles of the revolution and of the working class. While the PCI leaders tried to accommodate themselves to the radicalization of the political atmosphere, they held resolutely to their reformist line. In 1970 five members of the party's central committee were expelled for publishing a schismatic, pro-Maoist journal, *Il Manifesto*. In 1972 the *Manifesto* group organized a new Communist party under its own name to compete in the parliamentary election of May 1972. The PCI found itself contesting on two fronts, against the PSIUP and *Manifesto* parties on its left and the Socialists to its right. In this competition the PCI leadership, under Enrico Berlinguer, the new secretary-general, decisively opted for the conservative commitment. At the party congress of March 1972 Berlinguer emphasized the maturity and responsibility of the PCI, its readiness to participate in a grand coalition with Christian Democrats and Socialists, its preference for law and order, and its dislike for adventurism, violence, and inconclusive agitation. In the June 1972 election the *Manifesto* and the PSIUP failed to elect a single deputy. Shortly thereafter the PSIUP dissolved. This cycle of Italian Marxism appears to have closed.

The transformation of the Italian Communist party appears genuine, at least as far as the party elites are concerned. While factional differences exist inside the central committee, it is doubtful if any of the Communist leaders today believe in the feasibility of a revolution either in Italy or elsewhere in Western Europe. This same conclusion appears valid for the Socialists. Only marginal groups from the former PSIUP and *Manifesto*,[12] or scattered Trotskyites, anarchists, syndicalists, and some young leftwing Catholics still seem to believe in the revolution. Yet the transformation has not produced any deep-seated reevaluations of Marxist ideology, except from a few intellectuals who are not authoritative spokesmen for the principal Marxist parties.

From early socialist days until the present, Italian Marxist theorists have primarily concentrated on the political and philosophical aspects of Marxism rather than its economic aspects. Italy has yet to produce Marxist economists of a stature comparable to Rudolf Hilferding or Oskar Lange. Thus Italian Marxists cannot handle the necessary analysis of, nor provide adequate explanations for, the economic processes of the modern Western world. They have fallen back on a slogan word "neocapitalism," which hides more than it explains. Since 1961 Giorgio Amendola, a leading member of the *direzione* of the PCI, has been calling for a better analysis of contemporary economic phenomena, but the response by Marxist economists has been clearly inadequate. It is equally true that non-Marxist economists find similar difficulties in interpreting contemporary economic patterns in advanced societies, but they are not burdened with a tradition that claims to have a scientific answer to social phenomena and the capacity to forecast the direction of history.

The failure of Marx's major predictions has led some contemporary Marxist intellectuals to reject the claims of Marxism as a science and insist instead on Marxism as an ideology. Roberto Guiducci, an engineer, planner, and sociologist, finds that Marxist ideology can provide an understanding of countries at an early stage of industrial development. The judgments Marx made were valid only for the Europe of his day, although Marx stated them in universal terms. Guiducci recognizes that contemporary Italy is far beyond that stage of development. He also believes that the dialectic method is inappropriate to our time, especially if applied to the relations of nuclear superpowers, where the conflict of thesis and antithesis will more probably produce extermination than synthesis. Guiducci still calls himself a Marxist because of his commitment to democratic planning in a mixed economy.[13]

The philosopher Michele Salerno speculates on the role of automation in contemporary industry. He concludes that modern automation certainly does not confirm Marx's conclusions, which, Salerno (like Guiducci) asserts, were always concretely related to a given historical period and specific circumstances, although Marx presented them as abstractions or general laws. Salerno believes in Marxist methodology, but he finds that the Marxist approach to the study of new phenomena such as automation can at best demonstrate tendencies, not rules.[14]

These two thinkers are neither leading party activists nor spokesmen for the Marxist establishment. Closer to the centers of power, although not among key leaders, are Communist professors such as Ambrogio Donini and Lucio Lombardo Radice, who have stressed Marxist humanism, going back to the Philosophical Manuscripts of 1844, the "pre-Marxist Marx." Lombardo Radice, for example, lauds the "creative Marxism" of the Czech and Slovak "liberal" Communists who were suppressed by the Soviet invasion of Czechoslovakia in August 1968. He admires the aborted Czech model of a socialist system. It would have developed a pattern of economic "regulators." It would have stimulated "the spirit of socialist entrepreneurism" and liberated and developed the individual personality and creative initiative. The Czech model would have replaced orders from above and arbitrary rule with democratic self-administration, removed the restricted party mentality, and developed Communism as a humanistic movement.

Another Communist intellectual, Vincenzo Galetti, rejects various existing Eastern European models and substitutes his own conception of the Italian model of a socialist society, in both political and economic terms.

> In fact, we are already constructing our own "model." When we think about a lay state, neither atheistic nor confessional; when we refuse to give privileges to one ideology as against another; when we fight for social, political and state pluralism; when we speak of a democratically programmed mixed economy; when we struggle to establish an open relationship between representative democracy and "direct" democracy at the base—in all this we are already prefiguring our own conception of socialism. . . . It may seem superfluous to set all this down; but it is not, if one thinks of the many times when, in discussing with leading comrades of the Communist parties of socialist states the Italian situation, the tactics and strategy of the workers' and democratic movement in our country, we have often been told that all this is very well at present, in the struggle to win power, but that afterwards . . . afterwards nothing. We reject all forms of opportunism, because we know that tomorrow we shall have only what we have been able to gain today, through our struggle.[15]

Galetti's model describes, although in ideal terms, most of the characteristics of current Italian life; a pluralistic social and political order in a mixed economy that has produced, in the recent past, one of the highest rates of growth in the postwar world. Democratic programming became the law in 1964, and the first Italian five-year program went into effect in 1966. The government-controlled proportion of the economic mix has steadily expanded from the 1930s, when Mussolini bailed out many large industrial and financial institutions by placing them under government ownership. In 1962 the electric utility industry was nationalized. In subsequent years several of the largest private conglomerates have been taken over by government holding corporations. In 1971 the huge Montecatini-Edison chemical combine came under the influence of Ente Nazionale Idrocarburi (ENI), and in 1972 the Snia Viscosa artificial fiber monopoly was brought under the Istituto per la Ricostruzione Industriale (IRI). Now the Fiat-Pirelli combine remains the only large private monopolistic group which might be a target for Communist propaganda, the Communists having promised to leave small and medium-sized business alone. And in 1973 Giovanni Agnelli of Fiat and Giorgio Amendola of the PCI publicly agreed more than they disagreed on the requirements of the Italian economy.

Given this picture, a Communist or a joint Communist-Socialist takeover of the Italian political system would mean only a transfer of management. The new management might be more efficient and less corrupt than the present one, but it certainly would not produce a transformation of society, a new system of values, or a psychological "new man" no longer alienated from society or from himself. Those local and provincial governments now controlled by Communist-Socialist coalitions, mainly located in central Italy, have the reputation for good, sound government, sometimes conservative in the services provided and fiscally parsimonious. In fact some Christian Democratic cities have had more socially progressive municipal policies than have the Marxist-controlled cities.[16] This record hardly indicates any major social transformations.

Of course it can be argued that neither recent experience nor the model of the Italian way to socialism elaborated by some party leaders and academic intellectuals represents the real political and social system that would result from a Marxist takeover at the national level. Perhaps Galetti's Eastern European comrades are correct in claiming that the "Italian way to socialism" is only an opportunistic strategy in the struggle to win power. I believe that the history of Marxist thought in Italy supports the genuineness of the commitment to the "Italian way." From the beginning, reformism has been a major theme in Italian socialist thought. The need of the Italian intellectuals for independence of culture is found in the work of Gramsci and Togliatti as well as that of the re-

visionist socialists. The problem of freedom of thought, so pronounced
in the Italian Marxist intellectual heritage, reflects perhaps the centrality
of the presence of the Catholic church and the Holy See in Italian life.
The personalism and individualism in Italian social and political behavior,
the tradition of humanism and skepticism—all suggest rejection of a forecast of monolithic uniformity and submissive conformity. The voluntaristic tradition in the country's intellectual heritage dating back at least
to Machiavelli, the concern with the role of elites demonstrated in the
works of Gaetano Mosca and Vilfredo Pareto reinforce my belief. It is
true that Fascism also emphasized voluntarism and elitism in a totalitarian
framework, but Fascist efforts toward uniformity and conformity were
successfully undercut, in large part by this voluntarism and elitism. I feel
that these traditions would also defeat Marxists in any similar efforts.

Perhaps it is only the leaders at the national and local levels who have
rejected revolutionary dogmatism. In a recent study of a sample of
Italian Communist deputies, using an elaborate interview schedule, only
one out of twenty deputies exhibited attitudes characterized by the in-
vestigators as "genuinely revolutionary." [17] But studies of municipal performance and electoral behavior provide a variety of evidence that the
mass base of the Marxist parties and the voters from whom they obtain
their electoral support are not calling for either a genuine revolution or
a total transformation of society. In fact, contrary to classic Marxist doctrine, cultural factors such as attitudes towards the church have been
more influential in voting behavior for Italy as a whole than have been
class (socioeconomic status) factors. In Italy, as elsewhere in Europe, the
parties are becoming more heterogeneous in their class backing, and the
impact of socioeconomic characteristics as the primary influence on party
preference is declining.

Nor is there much evidence that the mass electorate of the Marxist
parties has significant influence on the leadership. They look upon their
leaders as different and separate from themselves. They have little sense
of subjective political competence, the feeling that they could influence
the political process if they tried.[18] A sense of political competence is
felt mainly by the minority of highly educated university graduates. In
central Italy, where the Marxist parties are strongest, the feeling of political competence among the masses is even lower than in northern or southern Italy.[19]

Prior to the First World War the Catholic and Marxist movements
denounced the "liberal oligarchy" ruling Italy as merely the legal rulers,
and both claimed to speak for the real masses. Since the Second World
War the Catholic and Marxist parties have ruled Italy, in the government
or in the loyal opposition. The Italian masses appear to be no more identified with the state and the current political system than they were under

its predecessors. The age-old problem of the commitment of the people to the political order has yet to be solved, and Italian Marxism has not produced a solution.

NOTES

1. Richard Hostetter, *The Italian Socialist Movement I: Origins (1860–1882)* (Princeton: Van Nostrand, 1958), pp. 17–26. There are numerous partisan histories of Italian socialism and communism. A reasonably good survey of Italian socialism is Aldo Romano, *Storia del movimento socialista in Italia*, 3 vols. (Milan: Fratelli Bocca, 1954–1956). The official party history of Italian communism is Paolo Spriano, *Storia del partito comunista italiano* (Turin: Einaudi, 1967–1970), of which the first three volumes have appeared, taking the story to 1945.

2. Ernesto Ragionieri, *Socialdemocrazia tedesca e socialisti italiani, 1875–1895: L'influenza della socialdemocrazia tedesca sulla formazione del Partito socialista italiano* (Milan: Feltrinelli, 1961).

3. Enzo Santarelli, *La revisione del marxismo in Italia* (Milan: Feltrinelli, 1964), pp. 40–41.

4. For a recent study of this period see Giuseppe Mammarella, *Riformisti e rivoluzionari nel Partito socialista italiano 1900–1912* (Padova: Marsilio, 1968).

5. Quoted in Santarelli, *op. cit.*, p. 124.

6. See Emiliana P. Noether, "Italian Intellectuals Under Fascism," *Journal of Modern History*, 43, No. 4 (December 1971), 636.

7. The literature on Gramsci in English is not extensive. The most thorough and scholarly examination of his ideas is contained in the book by John M. Cammet, *Antonio Gramsci and the Origins of Italian Communism* (Stanford: Stanford University Press, 1967). For a more popular biography see Giuseppe Fiori, *Antonio Gramsci: Life of a Revolutionary*, trans. Tom Nairn (New York: Dutton, 1971).

8. On the Italian Resistance movement see Charles F. Delzell, *Mussolini's Enemies: The Italian Anti-Fascist Resistance* (Princeton: Princeton University Press, 1961); see also Paolo Spriano, *op. cit.*

9. Norman Kogan, *Italy and the Allies* (Cambridge: Harvard University Press, 1956).

10. Delzell, *op. cit.*, pp. 261–576; see also Giorgio Bocca, *Storia dell'Italia partigiana* (Bari: Laterza, 1966).

11. Norman Kogan, "National Communism versus the National Way to Communism—An Italian Interpretation," *The Western Political Quarterly*, II, No. 3 (September 1958), 660–672; see also the chapter by Giorgio Galli in Walter Laqueur and Leopold Labedz, eds., *Polycentrism* (New York: Praeger, 1962).

12. For English translations of some of the major documents of the *Manifesto* groups, see *Politics and Society*, 1, No. 4 (Summer 1971), 409–477.

13. Roberto Guiducci, *Marx dopo Marx: dalla rivoluzione industriale alla rivoluzione del terziario* (Milan: Mondadori, 1970). The American economist Kenneth E. Boulding argues that the dialectical process, involving conflict and victory, is not the major process of history but provides only waves and turbulences on the great tides of evolution and development which are fundamentally nondialectical; see Kenneth E. Boulding, *A Primer on Social Dynamics: History as Dialectics and Development* (New York: The Free Press, 1970).

14. Michele Salerno, *Automazione e teoria marxista* (Cosenza: Pellegrini, 1971).

15. Vincenzo Galetti, "Il punto cruciale: la democrazia socialista," *Rinascita*, March 12, 1971, as translated and quoted by Kevin Devlin, "Radio Free Europe Research," mimeographed March 19, 1971, p. 7.

16. Robert C. Fried, "Communism, Urban Budgets, and the Two Italies: A Case Study in Comparative Urban Government," *The Journal of Politics*, 33, No. 4 (December 1971), 1036–1051; Robert H. Evans, *Coexistence: Communism and its Practice in Bologna, 1945–1965* (Notre Dame: University of Notre Dame Press, 1967).

17. Robert D. Putnam, "Studying Elite Political Culture: The Case of Ideology," *The American Political Science Review*, 65, No. 3 (September 1971), 667.

18. Gabriel Almond and Sidney Verba, *The Civic Culture* (Boston: Little, Brown, 1963), pp. 315–324.

19. Ann Serow, "Political Competence in Italy," unpublished manuscript, The University of Connecticut, pp. 26–31. See also Giorgio Galli and Alfonso Prandi, *Patterns of Political Participation in Italy* (New Haven: Yale University Press, 1970).

PART II

ECONOMIC AND
SOCIAL DEVELOPMENT

From the time of unification Italy's ruling elites tried to cope with the persistent forces of disunity with a combination of suppression and tokenism. This was particularly true of regionalism, which, except under Fascism, gained a certain revenge for its suppression by forcing each cabinet to include a minister from each region, whether he was suitable for the job or not. And local power and patronage remained largely in the hands of that very lower middle class that many reformers saw as the great enemy of progress and good government. The integration of Italy's vast peasant population, particularly in the south, was delayed by the reluctance of the dominant groups to relinquish their quasi-seignorial hold on agriculture. In 1939 the national secretary of the Fascist party—himself a southerner—simply announced that there was no more southern problem. Like the mafia, crimes of passion, and beggars in the streets, the Fascist regime had rendered it "invisible." In recent years, however, all of Italy's formerly "invisible" problems have reasserted themselves with a vengeance, and suppression and tokenism can no longer contain the rising level of expectations of all classes and regions. As economic growth changes the level of expectation, organized labor is playing an increasingly important role in Italy's social strife. No longer content to be a pawn in the hands of the political and economic elites, labor is becoming active in its own behalf.

The four chapters in this section deal with these problems as they have evolved since the 1860s. Denis Mack Smith shows how a belief in federalism or regional decentralization was held by major political groups—the liberals of the Risorgimento, the Fascists, the Christian Democrats—while they were the underdogs and still struggling to gain power. Once they achieved power, however, they became great centralizers and even authoritarian. Mack Smith also emphasizes the conspiracy of silence concerning the south until recent years. His theme is that regional differences remained such a dominant problem because (like so many others) they were regarded from two ideologically encumbered points of view, either as a healthy diversity that enriched the life of the country, or as pulling the nation apart. Leonard W. Moss views the south as the repository of both traditional values and the inherited social ills of a brutalized past. Only in the last two decades has the outflow of peasants to the expanding urban-industrial marketplace begun to change the social structure of the villages significantly. Moss dramatizes his analysis with an in-depth anthropological study of a typical village in southeast Italy. Jon Cohen deals mainly with the modern side of Italy's economy and its problems. In explaining the country's economic expansion he concentrates on three major factors: foreign trade, the economic activity of the government, and the organization and policies of the financial system. Nunzio Pernicone analyzes what is currently the most disruptive force in Italian life: organized labor. He traces the history of the labor movement, the hostility of Italy's ruling elites toward it, and its exploitation and fractionalization by competing ideological movements. Pernicone points out that Italy's recent waves of strikes were concerned not only with material gains but also with an intensified quest for power, participation, equality, and dignity in a society that had traditionally treated the working masses as "invisible."

CHAPTER 6

REGIONALISM

DENIS MACK SMITH

In any nation, however solidly constructed, there are bound to exist regional differences and traditions, and occasionally this constitutes a major political problem. Superficial distinctions of dress and dialect are relatively unimportant, but some divisions created by geography and history are such that Wales, or Sicily, or French Canada may be called nations or subnations of their own, and border regions such as Istria, Val d'Aosta, and Alto Adige present difficulties which are not easily solved. In Italy it is fairly obvious that substantially different cultures and degrees of economic development coexist simultaneously in neighbouring areas. These differences can be regarded from two points of view, either as a healthy diversity which enriches the life of the country, or as pulling the nation apart. This double aspect of the problem of regionalism in modern Italy, which dominates the whole of modern Italian history, is the theme of this chapter.

The leaders of the Risorgimento, in their struggle to fuse the various regions into a single whole, were acutely aware of the problem. Some of them saw regionalism as a demon that had to be crushed. Others, on the other hand, welcomed it as one of the great glories of Italy. In between these two attitudes, some people looked on it as something unavoidable which had to be accepted and if possible used to enhance the life of the community. Carlo Cattaneo wished to create a "united states of Italy"; for he thought that only some kind of federal organization would prove sufficiently resilient to contain the existing diversity of his fellow countrymen. But his view did not prevail, and in 1861 Italy became a unitary state, possessed of a strongly centralized legislation which was intended to iron out regional differences. Cattaneo was a great Italian patriot, who had the advantage or disadvantage of a detached point of view as he watched

125

events from his home in federal Switzerland. He observed, accurately enough, that the spirit of patriotism among Italians was frail, and he drew the conclusion that a unitary state would be unrealistic. He also feared that a unitary state would become authoritarian in the process of forcing the regions into a common mould.

At the other extreme, Giuseppe La Farina argued that a strongly centralized government was natural and desirable, for he started from the supposition that Italy should rightly and in every way become a great power. He ridiculed the Americans for believing (as Cattaneo believed) in the out-of-date doctrine of federalism: any European army would easily beat a federal America, he said, just as the Roman legions had beaten the undisciplined hordes of Mithridates. La Farina wanted a strong Italy with a strong government, and he managed to convince himself that no country in the world had so little regional sentiment as his own.[1]

La Farina's general views emerged victorious from the Risorgimento, whereas those of Cattaneo accordingly disappeared; and yet what La Farina said about the lack of regionalism in Italy was nonsense. Nineteenth-century Italian history is difficult to explain unless it is accepted, perhaps paradoxically, that patriotism was more a result than a cause of the Risorgimento. Despite what La Farina said, regionalism was much the stronger force of the two. Why else was there no great popular involvement at the time of the annexation of Venice by Italy in 1866 or that of Rome in 1870? Or how else, behind the inflated rhetoric of official pronouncements, can one explain Garibaldi's and Louis Napoleon's outraged protests in private at the lack of support they met in Lombardy during 1859? In contrast, the existence of tremendously powerful local loyalties is undeniable, for instance, in the five days of Milan in April 1848, or the ten days of Brescia in March 1849, or during the siege of Venice in the summer of 1849. Nor will this seem very surprising to anyone who can ignore the rhetoric and look at the kind of society that Italy was. The bitter quarrels between regions had an important, even decisive, part to play in the Risorgimento. It is hard, for instance, to conceive of how Italy could have been unified without the strongly regionalist and anti-Neapolitan loyalties of Sicily which touched off revolution during the decisive years 1848 and 1860.

The Risorgimento was not just as a series of national wars against Austria: it cannot be understood unless it is also seen as a continuous succession of "civil wars" in which there were Italians on both sides. In the famous battle of Magenta, no Italians were killed except those who were fighting on the Austrian side. To say that many Italians fought (and fought well) in the Austrian army is sometimes taken as being offensive, but it is no more offensive than the fact itself should be thought surprising. Italians possibly made up the bulk of the crews in the Austrian navy at the battle of Lissa against Italy in 1866; and when in the Nationalist congress at Florence in 1910 someone claimed that for this reason the Italians could be said to have won this battle, he was applauded for saying so. This may have been a rhetorical flourish, and the Italian historians of the campaign prefer not to so much as hint at such an unwelcome truth. Another almost unmentionable fact is that only 2 to 3 percent of the population of the peninsula had Italian as their first language at the time of national unification: [2] to most Italians, the "national language" would have been unintelligible, and the word *Italy* was unknown. No wonder that Cattaneo assumed that the creation of a united Italy ought to be balanced at the very least by recognition of individual regional administrations with wide delegated powers. Vincenzo Gioberti and even Giuseppe Mazzini himself were in this sense regionalists as well as nationalists. They saw that the nature of the country could not be denied without danger; nor could the hard facts of geography and economics.

Another obvious, but important and sometimes neglected, fact about the Risorgimento is that it happened according to no preconsidered plan, and its last stages caught everyone, including Camillo Benso di Cavour, so by surprise that not until the last moment did anyone think out any detailed constitutional procedure through which a united Italy could be organized. The officials of the Turin administration had absolutely no idea of what to do, and they certainly had no blueprint ready which took into account the possible alternatives of centralization or decentralization. When the Piedmontese annexed Lombardy in 1859, they desperately decided to impose the centralized Piedmontese system of administration, with just minor changes. Moreover, this fundamental and ultimately permanent decision was taken not by parliament, for parliament did not meet in the twelve decisive months between April 1859 and April 1860: it was imposed by royal decree. Of course strong opposition was encountered in Lombardy to such an arbitrary decision, for it was certainly not what the Milanese were expecting; but they were put off by statements from Turin that this was merely an emergency solution until Lombard representatives were elected to parliament and could discuss the matter there. When parliament finally met, Cavour did say he intended to change the law; yet substantially the same legislation was extended to Emilia, again by royal decree, and subsequently to Umbria and the Marches, then to Naples and Sicily, and finally to Tuscany, Venice, and Rome itself. This represents half a dozen quite separate decisions taken by successive governments; so we are not talking of a mistake, or of mere chance. Protests were made in one province after another, and again the reply came each time that centralization was just a temporary measure until Piedmont

had won the south, or Venice, or Rome. But the truth was that this centralized kind of administration, based on the French system of prefects,
had come to stay.

How Cavour let it happen is still not entirely clear, but his somewhat
muddled views on the question are important to know because centralization turned out to be a fundamental law of the Italian state, and it was he
who more than anyone else laid down the basic principles of constitutional
development. The question arises whether his decision was by intention
or by default. Cavour, during his early years in politics, had been no great
lover of centralization on the French pattern; indeed in 1850, before
entering the government, he claimed that it was the basic defect in modern society. He also made the challenging statement that Italy would
never be truly liberal until ordinary citizens had learned at the local level
the practice of self-government. Yet once in office he seemed to change. As
prime minister he found it increasingly hard to delegate responsibility: he
liked taking many ministries into his own hand, and at one time he was
running more than half of the government departments himself as well as
helping to administer some of the others.
    Cavour was never doctrinaire about practical politics and did not let
his theoretical approval of decentralization obtrude itself. He knew by
experience that the Piedmontese system worked, and that was enough.
Nor did he make any adequate study of other regions and their methods
of administration. He himself confessed to a friend privately that he
knew more about the laws of England than those of Tuscany or Naples,
and hence he had to act on very little evidence. He was not a man who
took kindly to other people's independent initiatives, and when he saw
decentralization at work in Ricasoli's Tuscany, he strongly resented this
apparent defiance of his own direction. Bettino Ricasoli, it will be recalled,
was for a time unwilling to surrender the last shreds of Tuscan autonomy
because he feared a duplication of what had happened in Lombardy. But
this reluctance was not at all well received in Turin, especially since
Cavour thought that what he called the feeble "Etruscan race" deserved
and needed forceful government from outside. He had an even greater
contempt for Sicilians, and hence Francesco Crispi encouraged a group of
prominent Sicilians in trying to preserve some of their old ways and laws.
So even though Cavour went on talking in public of the need to give the
regions a real element of local autonomy, in practice he worked in the
other direction and imposed the prefectoral system. He also got his cabinet
to agree that Piedmontese laws should be imposed quickly before local
conditions could be studied or local opinion consulted, and he explicitly
demanded that this should be done before parliament could meet and
create trouble. When Luigi Carlo Farini told Cavour that centralization

would arouse the same ill-feeling in Naples as it had previously in Milan and Florence, the answer came that local feeling must be sent to the devil, and armed force should be employed if necessary. When Michele Amari made a practical point that the jury system would mean a major perversion of justice if introduced into Sicily, he was given the irrelevant and entirely inaccurate answer that juries worked perfectly well on the island of Sardinia.[3]

We must remember that Cavour was under tremendous pressure at the time, and also, of course, that his disparaging remarks about the south were all made privately and to friends. In public he spoke differently, declaring his intention of setting up a liberal system of regional government as soon as north and south Italy were united. This regionalist scheme was, we know, never in fact placed by him or his successors before parliament, and some people have suggested that it was never meant seriously except as propaganda. Possibly, however, Cavour's highly pragmatic mind had at one point been feeling its way to a completely different and more regionalist solution of this problem from that which ultimately triumphed. It seems very likely that early in 1860 he was quite keen on the idea of regional devolution: first, because he needed an alternative policy to that of Urbano Rattazzi as a means of winning votes in Lombardy and replacing Rattazzi in power; second, because he desperately needed French backing, and Louis Napoleon preferred a regional Italy which was not too powerful or too strongly centralized; and third, too, because it was necessary not to antagonize the autonomist factions in the various regions—including, be it noted, the autonomists in Piedmont itself, who were by no means unimportant. There was a considerable propaganda value in advocating regionalism at a time when Piedmont was playing for local support in its policy of annexing one state after another, and we can prove that Cavour's assurances about introducing local self-government helped to win him powerful support in Tuscany, Naples, and Sicily. Thus, even if he seemed to favor a regional solution, it is possible that this was still largely a stratagem; and if so, it would have been a perfectly fair political stratagem, which in any case was, in retrospect, justified by success.

This appraisal may seem farfetched and oversubtle, but there are undeniably some ambiguities in Cavour's policy which need explaining. We know, for instance, that he encouraged Marco Minghetti to go ahead with a law to set up the regions; but we also know that he refused to regard this law as a question involving the government's survival, and such an attitude shows some lack of enthusiasm. With his left hand he also let others of his closest collaborators work in a quite different direction, and I am thinking here of La Farina, and of Giovanni Battista Cassinis, who was also in the cabinet. Cavour may well himself have been of two minds and wanting to see how public opinion would react to Minghetti's regions. Nor, if so, would this have been the only occasion when he employed different agents to pursue different and even contradictory policies, as he waited to see which alternative would come out on top.

But, having said this, there also seems little doubt that by early 1861 Cavour had changed, and that he was beginning to realize that regional differences would have to be overridden in the interests of national unification. At all events, it is hard to believe that members of the National Society would have been allowed to oppose Minghetti's scheme in the spring of 1861 if such opposition had been against Cavour's wishes. As for Cavour's motives, I have already mentioned his annoyance when Baron Ricasoli called into question the hegemony of Turin, and this, without any doubt, made him strongly suspicious of local autonomy. Even worse than the provincial feelings at Florence, he was horrified to discover that in Naples regionalism was likely to lead to the triumph of Garibaldinism and the left—or, equally bad, to the triumph of anarchy. The Neapolitan exiles seem to have been deliberately deceiving Cavour about the degree of enthusiasm he would find at Naples, but he soon learned the true situation. So I suggest that Cavour, as he received more information, may have changed his mind: at an earlier stage he seems to have favored regionalism as an inducement to make southerners accept annexation by Piedmont, but at a second stage he suddenly realized that regionalism threatened to give power to his political enemies and the enemies of Piedmont. In this second moment, possibly with reluctance, he was driven to burying the local autonomy of which he had lately claimed to be the champion. He now saw the need to create a strong state, so as to defeat the democrats and to foist the anticlerical legislation of Piedmont on a Catholic society in the south. He now told his agents in Naples to "impose unity on what is the most corrupt region of Italy"—if need be, using armed force to do so, and paying no mind to any local opposition.

When trying to analyze why regionalism failed in 1861, one other fact must be remembered, namely that it was Cavour's preferred technique of government to work with a coalition that contained many various views on most subjects, and not least on the subject of regional devolution. As well as Farini and Minghetti, who leaned in one direction, his coalition included Cassinis and La Farina, who leaned very strongly in the other; and, naturally, Cavour would hardly go out of his way to contemplate dividing this broad majority at such a critical moment. This, no doubt, was why he did not make Minghetti's proposed law a matter involving the government's survival. We have the evidence of such diverse friends of Cavour as Ruggero Bonghi and Francesco De Sanctis that the prime minister deliberately confused the issue of regionalism for this very reason

—to avoid having to make a clear-cut decision which might divide his coalition. With supreme irony, Agostino Depretis, the notorious confuser of parties, was another who blamed Cavour for letting decentralization be defeated by the requirements of transformism. Even Minghetti, when asked why he did not resign after the government dropped his scheme, replied cryptically: "the majority is a majority"—in other words the boat must not be rocked.

There is another aspect of Cavour's technique of government which is relevant to this point and which was adopted by his successors. After mis-judging badly about the elections of 1857, he had decided to take over the ministry of the interior himself so that the same mistakes should not be repeated in future. He subsequently learned in the elections of 1860 and 1861 the importance of using the prefects in each province and the mayors in each town as a means of influencing the voters. It was vital to have these officials dependent on the minister of the interior, and to that extent it would have been unwise to allow any real devolution or any increase in local self-government. That would have been another reason why Minghetti's scheme, which allowed for the election of mayors, could not be accepted without reserve.

I would hazard the guess that later governments, all of which, inciden-tally, went on speaking of the urgent need for administrative devolution, failed to take action precisely for these same reasons. Elections had to be won, and therefore governments needed a prefect who was strongly in control of the provincial deputation, as well as mayors of cities and villages who should preferably be appointed and not elected. Future premiers, too, saw that coalitions cohered far too flimsily to risk any fundamental debate on such a contentious topic as local self-government. Ricasoli remained in theory an advocate of decentralization, but after Cavour's death he was also eager to create a strong nation. His colleague General Luigi Federico Menabrea insisted on at once claiming great-power status for Italy, and Giovanni Lanza, true liberal though he was, said that all Italian youth should be organized militarily for this purpose. Nationalism was thus prov-ing a potential enemy of liberalism, just as Cattaneo had always said it would; and when Giuseppe Ferrari, a leading federalist, tried to speak in parliament about the different requirements of the different regions, he was ruled out of order by Rattazzi, the president of the chamber, who said: "The integrity of the Kingdom of Italy cannot be a matter for dis-cussion." [4] Vito D'Ondes Reggio complained in parliament that all the main laws on local government had been imposed by royal decree and without parliamentary approval, but he too was told by the president (Cassinis) that regional autonomy was now *ultra vires* and could not legally be raised even in parliament. D'Ondes Reggio had been speaking in particular about the law of 1865, the most important of all in determining that the provinces would come directly under government appointees. Yet this law of 1865 was not brought before parliament for approval, even though parliament was in session at the time.

One explanation for this attitude is that the dramatic events of Naples in 1860 and 1861 had taught many Italians to fear the results of too great a degree of democracy and self-government; the ugly possibility was raised that the victories of the Risorgimento might perhaps have been only paper-thin. There was a strong feeling that the country could possibly, even easily, fall apart again; and hence to create the regions might prove to be a gratuitous endangering of national unity.[5] The real problem for Italians, according to Azeglio, was to find how they could hate each other less, and he irreverently referred to the union with Naples as like going to bed with someone suffering from smallpox. Ricasoli, of course, had always been cynical about the capacity of Italians to govern themselves. "Nothing good can be hoped for from the Italian people," he once said. And during the Tuscan plebiscite he had insisted on marching his own peasants with strict discipline and under close supervision to register their votes in the public polling booths. Cavour too, though he had a more generous belief in his fellow countrymen, was determined to avoid giving any real powers of decision to the local elites and the *dottoruzzi di villaggio*. Then there was the argument used by Sebastiano Tecchio, who was speaking as the parliamentary committee chairman for Minghetti's project of decentralization. Could we possibly, asked Tecchio, think that the Italian people had genuinely wanted national unity? And he replied, no: unity had been a miracle, and must not be thrown away by allowing too much self-determination to people who might not want it.[6]

To sum up the argument so far, the history of regionalism during the Risorgimento can be viewed as a double paradox. The first paradox is that regional feelings were a powerful reason for the success of the Risorgimento; and I am not thinking here just of Sicily's fierce battle against Naples; I also think of Leghorn struggling against Florence, of Liguria against the domination of Piedmont, Treviso against Venice, and of the Neapolitan provinces against that of Naples. Secondly, the fear of regionalism, and of its possible effects in undermining national strength, was a powerful reason why northerners sought refuge after 1860 in a much more centralized and more authoritarian pattern of government than many Italian patriots (both conservative and radical) would ideally have liked.

Although the establishment of a centralized administrative system may at the time have seemed temporary, we now know that it lasted for nearly a century, and the reasons for its survival are therefore important to keep in mind. Chief among them was the fear that decentralization might imperil the fragile unity of the nation. Then there was the fear that it would destroy the far more fragile existence of each coalition cabinet. In the ten years between 1860 and 1870, there were seventeen changes of minister of the interior. This gave a very substantial power to the permanent bureaucracy, which was dominated by Piedmontese elements and which was reluctant to lose any authority to the regions. The bureaucrats understandably felt that the traditions and personnel of the old Piedmontese departments had to be preserved as indispensable to the healthy growth of the nation.

Any sweeping generalizations on this subject are likely to be wrong, which is a pity, but a lot can be learned from examining the many, sometimes contradictory, motives involved in what was a continuing debate over regionalism and decentralization. The champions of regionalism included the ideologues of the left, among them Cattaneo and Ferrari; but there were also some high-principled conservatives, Jacini and Amari, for example; and there were also some very strange characters indeed, for instance, Liborio Romano, who saw in regionalism a possible way of winning power locally, of organizing local jobbery and the proliferation of minor offices under their direct patronage and control.

On the other side, opposing regionalism, was another mixed bunch. There was Depretis of the left, but also Giovanni Lanza of the right. There were Piedmontese of right and left, but also exiles from other regions who found themselves strongly opposed by the entrenched local *notabili* when they returned home in 1860 and encountered jealous hostility. These men recognized from this experience that their own personal future depended on the total victory of Piedmont. I would guess that the Sicilians Filippo Cordova and La Farina helped as much as anyone to turn Cavour against regionalism after they had been chased out of Sicily. It was the Lombard exiles in the Commissione Giulini who did most to assist the absorption of Lombardy into Piedmont; and it was Sebastiano Tecchio, that Venetian of the left, who wrote the decisive report that condemned Minghetti's scheme to oblivion.

Another interesting fact is that La Farina and Cordova both came from eastern Sicily, which had a traditional war against Palermo, and such eastern Sicilians were inclined to regard Turin as their ally in this war against their western neighbours; just as Francesco Ferrara, who came from Palermo, opposed centralization for the very opposite reason. Similarly, Giuseppe Toscanelli voiced the opinion of provincial Tuscany, which feared the dominance of Florence over a regional administration; Giuseppe Massari, from Puglia, greatly preferred Turin to uncivilized Naples; Giuseppe Pica, the author of the hated law imposing martial law on the south, was himself a southerner, but he came from the provinces, not from Naples. Silvio Spaventa is another interesting case. He was an Abruzzese who returned to the south in 1860, only to be disgusted by what he roundly called "the filth and corruption," and he soon returned to seek more congenial company in the north. This not untypical attitude explains why Antonio Salandra in later years was able to reproach southerners for not staying to help solve the problems of the area. In these attitudes can be found a fundamental fact in the development of modern Italy.

To understand the effects of centralization on Italian society after 1861, one must be aware of later criticism—not because that criticism is necessarily right, but because it is at least informative. One objection, for instance, is that the lack of local self-government resulted, as Cavour foretold it would, in a lack of training in responsibility and political education; and this criticism is probably justified. Another is that centralization helped to jam public business in the national parliament, since already in 1862 it was being said that major issues were being swamped by *affari di campanile*. Minghetti had wished to transfer to the regions such matters as agriculture, irrigation, and higher education, but the failure of his project made these the responsibility of parliament; and as parliament had neither time nor knowledge to deal with them adequately, important decisions often went by default. One argument against the regions had been that only a strong central government could control local corruption and the tyranny of the local *notabili;* but, in practice, Turin (and later Rome) was so remote that centralization increased the growth of local clienteles dedicated to immobilism. In other ways, too, centralization led to the very condition that its champions had been aiming to prevent; thus, instead of minimizing regional sentiment, centralization helped to perpetuate it and by its very suppression render it a morbid fact in society.

Even though the battle for regionalism was lost in 1861, everyone or almost everyone continued to repeat that some degree of decentralization was absolutely essential. Ricasoli himself recognized that greater authority would have to be given one day to local institutions if the Italian system of government was to succeed. From the very beginning, Francesco De Blasiis was claiming that decentralization, far from imperiling unification, would assist it; and this view gradually took a secure hold. Depretis sympathized with it. Somewhat surprisingly even Crispi as prime minister acknowledged the absolute necessity of "administrative and governmental decentralization," and hoped to create a new kind of "interprovincial government." Crispi's opponent Marquis Antonio Di Rudinì spoke in the same sense: in particular he wanted government brought closer to ordinary citizens, and spoke of the unhealthy distortion of national politics when the government at Rome had to depend on local vested interests prepared to sell their support. Di Rudinì thought the answer was in grouping provinces into larger regions, and in 1896 he tried to create one such large administrative region in Sicily. Again and again in parliament, deputies of all parties seemed to agree on at least the principle and on the fact that the centralized system of 1861 was somehow unsuitable. Giuseppe Saredo worked out in detail that Italy ought probably to have thirteen regions,[7] roughly the figure that Mazzini had wanted. Similarly, Giovanni Giolitti and Baron Sidney Sonnino called decentralization about the most urgent need of all: as Giolitti said, decentralization of power was the one logical way to organize a country such as Italy, which had so many economic and social differences inside it.[8]

But these were words and not deeds. In practice the forces behind centralization remained strong, and coalition governments were understandably reluctant to commit suicide by going much further than talk on such a fundamental issue. Nor by any means was it just northerners who were unwilling to sacrifice the administrative unity of 1861. For, as Francesco Saverio Nitti admitted, it was his own fellow-southerners who were to a large extent responsible for what they subsequently turned against and blamed, using the pejorative term "Piedmontisation." [9] Most of the former exiles from the south, once they had transferred their residence to Turin, had had strong reasons for opposing the grant of regional autonomy; so at a later date did Giustino Fortunato, another southerner, who approved of decentralization up to a point but who saw clearly that regional autonomy would increase the power of the local oligarchies and clienteles, which were largely responsible for keeping the south backward and poor. Gaetano Salvemini came to share this same opinion, and he, like Fortunato, had seen the problem very much at first hand.[10]

But what was the alternative? I believe that even Salvemini came to recognize that the alternative was hardly more promising. Perhaps he had been right in suggesting that regional administrations would have been dominated by corrupt elements; and yet one must also admit that centralization in practice was equally corrupting, for it allowed the *notabili* an important role in both national and local politics. Their "clients" were largely made up of the very *piccola borghesia* which Salvemini and Napoleone Colajanni saw as the great enemy of progress and good government; and this *piccola borghesia* in general dominated the elections and voted for the candidates put up by the *latifondisti*. Thereby the government got the vote of the *ascari parlamentari*, as Giolitti's disciplined parliamentary followers were called; the *latifondisti* got as their share protective duties for grain, thus upsetting the social and economic life of the whole peninsula; and the *piccola borghesia* was allowed in return to keep its desiccating hold on local power and patronage. This was the unholy alliance that created, or to be more correct, perpetuated, the Southern Question.

The Southern Question has been the greatest manifestation of regionalism in modern Italian history, for it has perpetuated the division of Italians up into *nordici* and *sudici*—as the bitter saying went. Many northerners knew little of the people whom they spoke of contemptuously as *terroni* and *cafoni,* not at least until southerners started to pour north in search of jobs. What, after all, had Dante known of the south? Or Petrarch, or Machiavelli? Or, come to that, Mazzini, who did at least briefly visit Naples? Alessandro Manzoni never saw Rome, let alone any place further south. Nor did Cavour. Cavour once penetrated as far south as Florence for several days, but was too unhappy there to see much more than the four walls of his room. Yet Cavour was the man who annexed central and southern Italy; and it is important to realize that he did so under the impetus of some totally mistaken expectations. For instance, he apparently thought that in twenty years the south could be made into the richest part of Italy. Some northerners certainly came south; Massimo d'Azeglio made at least three journeys there, and he not only knew much more about the rest of Italy than did Cavour, but was aware that there was a serious southern problem. Yet Azeglio's views were not listened to very readily in government circles.

One basic fact about this southern problem was that over a hundred thousand Italian troops had to be sent to the southern third of the peninsula in the 1860s to control what could be described as a counter-revolution against the Risorgimento; and this "occupation" began a few months after Cavour's death. I am referring to a large army, twice as large a force as Cavour had ever fielded against the Austrians. Comparisons, as we know, are odious, and many other factors were present in this civil war after 1861, but the very size of the force employed is one index of the strength of regionalism.

Sicily, of course, is a special case, and here one may mention that Palermo was taken over for a week by rebels in 1866 with what was evidently a fair degree of popular backing. Cavour's viceroy in Naples had had to confess that Sicily's help to Garibaldi was due not to love of Italy but hatred of the mainland.[11] Regional autonomy seems to have been the wish of almost all Sicilian patriots in 1861; they wanted and expected to be given exclusive powers over education, public works, and the like; and it was on the strength of this expectation that they voted yes in the plebiscite on unification.[12] They proudly called themselves Italians, but they also belonged to what they called "the Sicilian nation." The mass of the people in Sicily went much further, for they knew nothing of Italy.

Even in 1901, according to Salandra, the fatal and irresponsible illusions about the fabled riches of the south were still alive, simply because northerners did not go anywhere off the beaten track. But 1901 was the year of Giuseppe Saredo's drastic report on Naples after revelations by a Socialist newspaper had broken the silence and exposed a sad tale of corruption among the dominant southern elites. It was the debate on Saredo's report which propelled Giuseppe Zanardelli to visit the Basilicata, and this must have been the first fact-finding visit made by a northern prime minister to the south. A good number of hard and not altogether welcome facts came to the surface in this debate. Colajanni made the point that a prosperous south, and hence a complete change of direction in official policy, was an indispensable condition for a healthy and prosperous nation. Pietro Lacava made another interesting point when he argued from his own experience as a minister that the early legislation of 1865, imposed on Italy by royal decree, could not possibly have worked or have been expected to work in the south, where conditions were so completely different. The conspiracy of silence had in the meantime played havoc with the life of society. It was in this debate that the Socialist Enrico Ferri made his famous—or infamous—statement that northern Italy had small enclaves of crime, while the south had just small oases of honesty. This brought the house down, and parliament had to be hurriedly closed.

But Ferri was voicing an attitude that was becoming fashionable as scholars and politicians groped for an explanation of what was amiss. Scipio Sighele had already argued as an anthropologist that there were two Italys, the north and the south, and he explained this difference in terms of race. Giuseppe Sergi was hard at work measuring skulls and had recently discovered that northern Italy was of Aryan blood—a fact, incidentally, which the noted agricultural economist Friedrich Vöchting still believes. Alfredo Niceforo had already coined the phrase "L'Italia barbara contemporanea" about southern Italy. Neapolitans, he said, "have always fled before their enemies"; and the result had been that the Italian army never won a battle.[13] Niceforo's book on *La delinquenza in Sardegna* argued that Sardinians were physically degenerate and driven inevitably to violence by some unknown chemical in their nervous cells. This anthropological interpretation of the Southern Question was of course not universally accepted, and it provoked southerners, Colajanni, for instance, to develop in rejoinder a sociological explanation that seems now to make far more sense.

Sardinia was another special case, as it still is today, for this was a region where local problems were very slow to meet serious study. This was the proud province from which the kings of the House of Savoy took their regal title, yet it had been left behind by history at a quite different level of civilization from Liguria and Piedmont. Feudal rights of justice continued here for longer than perhaps anywhere else in Europe, right up to the time of Charles Albert (1831 to 1849); and the feudatories then simply changed into absentee landowners who knew little about local conditions and still kept a quasi-feudal supremacy. Alberto Lamarmora's study of Sardinia was once borrowed by Depretis from the library of the Chamber of Deputies in order to prepare a report on the island, but the report was never written; the book was still marked out in Depretis's name ten years later, and perhaps no deputy had needed it in the interval. Cattaneo, who really did know something about Sardinia, described it as far more neglected by the Piedmontese than Sicily by the Bourbons, yet this was a conclusion which few other outsiders were sufficiently courageous or perceptive to accept. Even Cavour was quite as offhand as other prime ministers about this unfortunate island. He told parliament that talk about Sardinian poverty was greatly exaggerated: if people were unemployed there, he said, it must be because they refused to work; and he promised that what he called gigantic improvements were only a few years away. Yet when Sardinian deputies begged him to come and see things for himself, he had to decline, and his gigantic improvements took another century to appear. After Cavour's death a fair amount of money was spent on public works, but without a proper study of local conditions this was in many respects money thrown away. The Pais report to parliament in 1896 specially singled out the absurdity of undertaking public works without seeing first what purpose they would serve, whether anyone would find them truly useful, for instance, or whether there was enough money to maintain them once they had been constructed. Pais also stressed once again the damage done by trying to impose the same legislation simultaneously in both Lombardy and Sardinia at once. It was not only juries that did not work in this forgotten island. Northern property laws did not make the same sense in a countryside of wandering shepherds; the application of such laws to Sardinia, he explained, was one reason why so much money had been wasted and why so many of the fine old oak forests had now been unprofitably destroyed.

The report by Pais on Sardinia inaugurated a new period when special acts of parliament were introduced to mitigate conditions in the more backward areas of Italy. Individual regions could now be seen to have special problems and to need special treatment. But these laws were of very limited effectiveness, and one reason was that the money allocated had a political purpose. Every successive government, of whatever color, depended on the bloc southern vote which was organized by the prefects; for instance, promising the Apulian aqueduct could be a useful means of buying votes. Nor was there any great hurry. The Apulian aqueduct was first proposed in the 1880s; it was not complete forty years later. There was no new move, needless to say, toward granting regional autonomy because that would have upset the whole political system and many vested interests. Giolitti did not want regional autonomy because it might upset his transformist majority in parliament; nor did the new Socialist party or the new Nationalist association wish to reduce the central authority of the state.

Of the other new political currents in the country, it was notably the Sardinian Party of Action which, in 1919, finally made regionalism a political issue once again. The Partito Sardo d'Azione used to be called the Italian Sinn-Fein movement. Some of its members carried local autonomy to the point where it could be called Sardinian separatism. Such views were a not surprising product of the First World War, for wartime experience had intensified the bureaucratic stranglehold of Rome, thus convincing some people for the first time of the sheer waste and inefficiency of the 1861 solution. At the same time in 1919, the annexation of Venezia Giulia and of the Alto Adige forced the government to think anew, for these new provinces contained strong linguistic minorities that would need special treatment; they also had enjoyed a certain autonomous status under the Austrians and would hardly take kindly to a sudden transition to the rigors of the Italian system. The Italian government in fact gave assurances to these newly annexed provinces that their language, culture, and special economic interests would be preserved, but a year later Mussolini's thugs began a forcible "Italianization" more thorough and much more brutal than Piedmontization in the 1860s.

As late as 1919, even Mussolini had been proclaiming the virtues of decentralization—because he thought there were votes in it—and this fact, too, is an indication that public opinion must have been changed by the war. Strongest of all for regionalism were Don Luigi Sturzo and the new Catholic party, the Partito Popolare. The Catholics had been solidly in opposition after 1860, since it had been almost automatic for them to side against the anticlerical centralizers who had won in the Risorgimento. Hence the only way Catholics could affect public life had been through local government. Giuseppe Micheli, from the Popularists, who was a minister in 1921 and 1922, called for more than just administrative decentralization; he wanted recognition that the various regions of Italy were "profoundly different" from each other and needed a new constitutional status. He also emphasized that overcentralization was speedily killing • parliament as an institution, for parliamentary business was so choked with petty local matters that the big issues—for instance, postwar economic and social difficulties and, above all, the rise of Fascism—could not be discussed adequately.[14]

If this is true, even the victory of Fascism can in part be ascribed to the denial of that local self-government which Cavour had once said was so essential in Italy. Fascism in its turn, by the very opposition it eventually aroused, ultimately gave a great boost to the desire for self-government. As Salvemini said, before the time of Mussolini it was the south that had had firsthand experience of the bad side of a prefectoral regime; now the north also learned that centralization might be harmful and inefficient.[15] Especially harsh treatment was given by the Fascists to areas with linguistic minorities, and a tremendous regional opposition built up in the Val d'Aosta, in Alto Adige, and Venezia Giulia, where people were prevented from using local dialects and were even forced to change their family names if these sounded un-Italian. So hostile was Mussolini to any manifestations of regionalism, that in 1941 he decided on the ridiculous step of removing all Sicilian-born officials from Sicily, and one can just imagine how such a ridiculous decree was received. The sheer triviality of Fascism in its attitude to the south can be seen in a remark by Party-Secretary Achille Starace in 1939: "How absurd it is that there still exists an association for the interests of the south! Fascism has by now completely solved the so-called southern problem." [16]

The fact that the Fascists entirely and repeatedly deceived themselves and, in particular, the fact that they had *not* solved the Southern Question, was going to be a principal ingredient in the collapse of the Great Dictator. It was military defeat and the successes of the Resistance which then brought to the forefront another version of the regional solution which had been repudiated in 1861. This arose naturally from the experiences of 1943 to 1945, when Italy was divided virtually into four parts—one governed by Mussolini and the Germans, one directly by the Allies, one by Marshal Pietro Badoglio and the king, and one by the Committees of National Liberation—for this division broke the unity of the country. The partisans had perforce to work on their own and develop a new type of popular government. A correspondent of the London *Times* at Florence in October 1944 noted "a spontaneous experiment in self-government which may have considerable influence in determining what political system is ultimately to take the place of Fascism." [17] The so-called partisan republics, notably in Ossola in the northwest and Carnia in the extreme northeast, developed an individuality and even a legal individuality of their own; Carnia, for instance, abolished the death penalty; and Ossola had its own court, prison, and even its own *Carta bollata* (the stamped paper forms on which official business was transacted).[18] At one point this seemed to presage a truly autonomist reconstruction of society, especially when Sardinia and Sicily were being governed by high commissioners as semiindependent states of their own.

At the end of the Second World War, the various political parties reappeared and reconstituted themselves. Regionalism was thus an inescapable issue. The liberals were divided on it. The monarchists and the Uomo Qualunque party were some of the few who took a firm stand against regionalism because they still clung to the old nationalist myth of the strong state. Other individuals, for example Nitti and Orlando, opposed the regions because as southerners they doubted (as Massari, Spaventa, and La Farina had doubted in 1861) if the south was truly ready for self-government. Salvemini, too, saw the *piccoli borghesi intellettuali* of the south as still rotten to the core; hence regionalism would mean handing over power to the "agrarian bloc," and it was noticeable that Sicilian separatism found one of its main supports in the *latifondisti* and the mafia.

Salvemini was perhaps overpessimistic, and most of the Resistance Party of Action (mainly leftwing liberals and socialists) was true to the tradition of Cattaneo and strongly championed the regions. The Communists were lukewarm, and seem to have adapted their views to whatever they thought provided the most likely chances of winning power in a general election. The extreme left therefore gave merely qualified support to regionalism in the constitutional debates of 1946 and only became enthusiastic supporters when turned out of the government coalition a year later. Once in opposition, they were to realize that regional governments would at least give them power in Emilia, Umbria, and Tuscany.

For this same reason in reverse, the Christian Democrats changed their policy. They had begun life in 1919 and earlier as a party of opposition, and as such had been strongly regionalist; but after their overwhelming victory in the 1948 elections, they were notably less enthusiastic about sharing the spoils and patronage of office. In this respect they were not unlike those liberals of the Risorgimento who believed in federalism or regional decentralization while they were the underdogs and still on the make, but who became great centralizers and even authoritarian once they had achieved power.

The debate over regionalism in 1947 raised many fundamental issues. At long last there met a constituent assembly of the kind Cattaneo and Mazzini had wanted, and in which the representatives of the nation could discuss fundamentals. Cavour had set his face against allowing such a constituent assembly: with a finer political sense than his opponents, he had wanted not an entirely new nation with a new constitution but an extension of Piedmont with an administrative system that already had been tried at Turin and found to work. It is no discredit to Cavour that the centralized state he created did not seem so effective when extended to other regions which possessed traditions and problems outside his experience.

Only in 1947 was the Statuto of Charles Albert finally and formally abolished, and Italy then became something which Cavour had fought against strenuously: it became a republic—moreover a strongly Catholic republic—and one based on regional self-government. A century of centralization had not killed regionalism, but rather had almost exacerbated it. The different regions of Italy still often knew little about each other. In the early 1950s there were still 13 percent of Italians who did not speak Italian at all, and for four-fifths of the population the use of dialect was still habitual.[19] This of course helps to explain why it has been hard to develop a genuinely popular Italian literature.

As an admission of the facts about regional diversity, the new Constitution of 1947 wrote local autonomy into the fundamental statute of the republic. It provided for five regions with special powers: Sardinia, Sicily, Val d'Aosta, Trentino-Alto Adige, and Venezia-Giulia. The rest of Italy was to be split into fourteen ordinary regions, each of which would have lesser powers. These nineteen regional governments ought, by the terms of the constitution, to have come into existence within a year, that is to say, in 1949. But, as we know, a long succession of transformist coalitions were unwilling to enforce this law until 1970 because they feared it might upset the political balance of the country.

The five special regions all had compelling reasons for existence which were impossible to resist. Indeed the constituent assembly found that some of the main decisions had been taken already by force of circumstance and were in practice unalterable. In Sicily, for instance, a strong Sicilian separatist movement had come into existence to exploit the fact of occupation by the Allies, and an "army of independence" had been organized. Thus an urgent decision had to be taken by the Italian government to offer a wide measure of local autonomy. Many Sicilians had wanted and expected to be given regional autonomy in 1861; in 1944 it was better late than never, and a prudent acceptance of this fact was calculated to avoid the still more drastic step of separatism.

In the Val d'Aosta, too, the government's hand had already been forced by 1945. Some of the partisans had assumed that the only way to get autonomy would be to break from Italy and annex themselves to France. This threat of secession may not have been very great, but De Gaulle's troops at one point invaded the valley to support it, thus compelling the Committee of National Liberation to promise a wide degree of self-government.

Trentino-Alto Adige also had a formidable linguistic problem, which was much more complicated than in Aosta just because the area was less homogeneous. Here the De Gasperi-Grüber agreement of September 1946 agreed to allow some legislative powers to a locally elected regional government. De Gasperi himself came from this region. He accepted that Bolzano had a German-speaking majority, but he also ensured that the unit of government would be not the province of Bolzano but the whole region—in other words, an area with a convincing Italian majority. This still remains an enormously complex problem, and one to which an entirely fair solution is hardly conceivable. But successive Italian governments have tried hard to accept many demands made by the Südtiroler Volkspartei on behalf of the German-speaking inhabitants, though of course they have always stopped short of giving away the substance of power. Terrorist activity by partisans, especially after 1961, and protests by the Austrian foreign minister to the United Nations kept the issue alive; and it is easy now to recognize that the grant of regional autonomy was the very least that could have been conceded in 1947.

Until 1970 we had only the experience of the five special regions on which to form a judgment about regionalism under the new constitution. Nor in these five regions is it easy to discover the facts on which judgment can be based, for the story is hidden under mountains of paper with which a multiplicity of departments and committees have hoped to justify their own activities and use up public funds. Probably we must be content with calling them just a qualified success. Regional governments have at least ensured that money is no longer such an obstacle to development. Another gain is that the burden of work in the Rome parliament has been lightened by the decline in local business. Another positive point is that it is no longer possible to argue that regional governments are inimical to national unity; if anything, the reverse has now been proved to be true. Another advantage is that government has been brought nearer the citizen, and many more people than before are acquiring experience of administration and politics. Some people would say that this by itself would make the regions worthwhile.

On the other hand, one must recognize that these new units of government have incidentally led to a vast waste of money; a great deal has been spent on only partially effective agrarian reforms; there has been a good deal of duplication of effort between different official bodies; enormous bureaucracies have been set up, which in turn have become as centralized and unyielding as those of the central government. It is quite clear, too, that the central bureaucracies have not been reduced correspondingly in the way that the proponents of regionalism once imagined. State funds seem to have been often funneled through the regions into the patronage networks of the local bosses and into pork-barrel legislation of one kind or another.

Another difficulty is that while the regions have had considerable success in drawing attention at a national level to local problems, they have sometimes acted in an opposite sense in order to ward off state interference and conceal local scandals. I am thinking, for instance, of the repeated decision by the Sicilian Regional Assembly that the mafia was not a problem that required serious investigation by outsiders. In Sardinia, too, the president of the regional *giunta* once allowed himself to say that Sardinian banditism was something in books, not in real life. One can understand these attempts to keep dirty linen away from public scrutiny, but one also can learn from them why Salvemini and Fortunato were so anxious not to give the local bosses an absolute say in the management of public affairs.

This is why it is important to note that the pendulum has swung a good way back from the enthusiasm for regional autonomy which was so common twenty years ago. The powers enjoyed by at least some of the special regions have been considerably curbed since then. There has never

been much trouble in Sardinia, where the Christian Democrats have had
an easier run than elsewhere and where few conflicts of jurisdiction with
Rome have arisen; but even there, out of 287 local laws passed in ten
years, the central government used its powers to suspend 80 and entirely
block 10; nor could they stop the Consiglio Regionale at Cagliari from
having a debate on the Vietnam war. In three years after 1964, about a
third of the regional laws of the new Venezia Giulia region were challenged by Rome. In the Val d'Aosta there was not much difficulty so
long as the Union Valdôtaine party supported the Christian Democrats;
but there was big trouble when the Communists won power, and in the
end the Communist president of the region had to be escorted from his
office by the police.

Sicily, too, had its difficulties, especially when the Communists, with
neofascist support, joined some disobedient Christian Democrats under
Silvio Milazzo in forming a highly unorthodox government in defiance
of all the rules. This brought the word *Milazzismo* into the language to
describe a refinement of transformism that is hard for a foreigner to comprehend. Even though Sicily, under the constitution, had some exclusive
rights of legislation, especially in the field of economic life and education,
the constitutional court lately has adopted an increasingly centralist
standpoint. Apart from challenging laws which seem to conflict with national legislation, the government has the right to dissolve the regional
government in certain circumstances. They also have the supreme
weapon: the regions still rely on the central government for most of their
income, and this lack of financial autonomy is fundamental.

Despite all this, a modus vivendi is being established. The governments
of Aldo Moro and Mariano Rumor eventually decided to purge their
contempt of the constitution and establish the fourteen other regions
which should have been created in 1949. Strong vested interests have still
to be overcome, and on a recent occasion when the issue of regionalism
came seriously before parliament there were a thousand different amend-
ments proposed by Liberals and neofascists in an attempt to wreck what
they called the breaking up of the nation. But despite long years of opposition, Italy is now, strictly speaking, a regionalist state. Cavour and Mazzini, who were kept apart by almost everything else, might have come
fairly close to each other in accepting the fact.

NOTES

1. There are no specific studies on the problem of regionalism in modern Italian history. The following, however, are helpful for an understanding of the issues involved: Luigi Carbonicri, *Della Regione in Italia*
(Modena: Cappelli, 1861); Denis Mack Smith, *Victor Emanuel, Cavour,*

and the Risorgimento (London: Oxford University Press, 1971); Francesco De Sanctis, *Il mezzogiorno e lo stato unitario*, ed. F. Ferri (Bari: Laterza, 1960); Manlio Rossi-Doria, ed., *Giustino Fortunato, antologia dei suoi scritti* (Bari: Laterza, 1948); Adriana Petracchi, *Le origini dell'ordinamento comunale e provinciale italiano* (Venice: Pozza, 1962); Gaetano Salvemini, *Scritti sulla questione meridionale (1896–1955)* (Turin: Einaudi, 1958); Rosario Villari, ed., *Il sud nella storia d'Italia* (Bari: Laterza, 1961); Friedrich Vöchting, *Die italienische Südfrage* (Berlin: Duncker, 1951); Michele Viterbo, *Il mezzogiorno e l'accentramento statale* (Bologna: Cappelli, 1923); Umberto Zanotti-Bianco, *Meridione e meridionalisti* (Rome: Collezione Meridionale, 1964); Ettore Rotelli, *L'avvento della regione in Italia (1943–1947)* (Milan: Giuffré, 1964).

2. Tullio De Mauro, *Storia linguistica dell'Italia unita* (Bari: Laterza, 1963), p. 41.

3. Virgilio Rossi, "Sul regionalismo in Italia," *Appunti al nuovo codice penale* (Turin: Unione Tipografico-Editrice, 1889), p. 92.

4. April 4, 1861, recorded in *Il parlamento dell'unità d'Italia (1859–1861), atti e documenti della Camera dei Deputati* (Rome, 1961), II, 352.

5. Carlo Tivaroni, *Storia critica del risorgimento italiano* (Turin: Roux, 1894), VI, 469; Rossi-Doria, *op. cit.*, pp. 25, 35, 42.

6. June 22, 1861, Tecchio's report printed in *Il parlamento dell'unità d'Italia*, III, 129–131.

7. *La legge sulla amministrazione comunale e provinciale, commentata da G. Saredo* (Turin: Unione Tipografico-Editrice, 1901), pp. 177–178, 197–204.

8. Giovanni Giolitti, *Discorsi extraparlamentari*, ed. Nino Valeri (Turin: Einaudi, 1952), speech of October 29, 1899 at Dronero, p. 223–224.

9. Francesco Saverio Nitti, *Napoli e la questione meridionale* (Naples: Pierro, 1903), p. 32; A. Petracchi, *op. cit.*, I, 213, 286–287, 366.

10. Gaetano Salvemini, *op. cit.*, pp. xxxvi–xxxvii.

11. December 18, 1860, Montezemolo to Cavour, in *La liberazione del mezzogiorno e la formazione del regno d'Italia* (Bologna: Zanichelli, 1954), IV, 104; see also the similar report dated January 9, 1861, *ibid.*, p. 195. Similarly, the Neapolitan provinces, according to the governor, L. C. Farini, believed in Italian unity partly from dislike of Naples, *ibid.*, III, 131.

12. August 30, 1860, Cordova to Cavour, *ibid.*, II, 189; October 19, 1860, Cavour to Carini, *ibid.*, III, 145; *Carteggio di Michele Amari*, ed. Alessandro d'Ancona (Turin: Roux, 1896), II, 130, 132, 141, 144; report of Sicilian Council of State (November 1860), quoted in Villari, *Il sud nella storia d'Italia*, pp. 72–73.

13. Alfredo Niceforo, *L'Italia barbara contemporanea* (Milan: Sandron, 1898), pp. 251, 260; also see essays by Sergi, Sighele, and Colajanni in Antonio Renda, ed., *La questione meridionale* (Milan: Sandron, 1900), pp. 53, 75–76, 141–142; Vöchting, *op. cit.*, pp. 36–38.

14. See speech of Luigi Sturzo on October 23, 1921, in L. Sturzo, *I discorsi politici* (Rome: Istituto Sturzo, 1951), pp. 148, 155, 165. Giuseppe Micheli, *Problemi nazionali* (Parma: Fresching, 1922), pp. 103–105.

15. *Il Ponte*, 5 (1949), 831–832.

16. Quoted by Zanotti-Bianco, *op. cit.*, p. xxii.

17. *Times*, October 25, 1944, p. 5.

18. Rotelli, *op. cit.*, p. 31.

19. Figures from Rüegg, quoted by De Mauro, *op. cit.*, p. 116.

CHAPTER 7

THE PASSING OF
TRADITIONAL PEASANT SOCIETY
IN THE SOUTH

Leonard W. Moss

Inescapably, the history of the peasantry in Italy is a history of crisis. The turmoil of a segment of society alternating between revolutionary movements and ultraconservatism stems directly from that nation's agrarian heritage.[1] The rapid social changes occurring today are, perhaps, unprecedented. Indeed, it is possible to foresee the end of traditional peasant society in the immediate future. Although the Italian peasantry has certainly not occupied an unchanging position to the present day, tradition has played an important role in the preservation of an earlier stable society. As one southern peasant so aptly worded it: "History is fastened to my shoulders. At times it is a burden greater than I can bear."

Italy's rural cultivators form a large folk culture, subordinate to the townfolk and gentry, who are the bearers of the "great traditions" of the dominant culture. Not all who work the land are peasants, and not all who own the land are farmers. The farmer is the capitalist of the soil. He has a regular and established relationship with the market; it is predicated and dependent upon a planned, predictable surplus productivity. The farmer is a producer of a marketable surplus, an investor in capital, and a consumer of economic goods obtained through either a cash or barter exchange. The peasant, or *contadino*, is more characteristically a self-sustaining, subsistence-level agriculturalist. His connection with the market is irregular and dependent upon a relatively unplanned and somewhat fortuitous surplus productivity. As Eric Wolf notes: "Peasants . . . are rural cultivators whose surpluses are transferred to a dominant group of rulers that uses the surpluses both to underwrite its own standard of living and to distribute the remainder to groups in society that do not farm but must be fed for their specific services in turn." [2]

The past one hundred years of Italian history have hastened the transformation of traditional peasant society throughout the nation. At the time of the Risorgimento, nearly 70 percent of the total labor force was employed in agriculture. Not until after the turn of the century did the figure go below 60 percent, and only after the Second World War was the agricultural labor force reduced to less than 50 percent of the working population. By 1961, exactly a century after unification, Italy joined the rest of Western Europe with fewer than 30 percent of its workers in agriculture (see Figure 1).

The Mezzogiorno—the old kingdom of Naples and Sicily—has lagged behind the rest of the nation increasingly since unification. Even today no region of the south has an agricultural labor force below 30 percent of its total working population. From a low of 35.9 percent (1961) in Campania to a high of 57.4 percent in Basilicata, southern agriculture gives evidence to the oft-repeated expression *Siamo ritardati* (we are retarded). To a great extent, therefore, this paper will be devoted to an analysis of the peasant in the south.

Though pockets of peasantry have existed and continue to exist in northern and central Italy, the exacerbation of the problem has reached its ultimate levels in the history of the Mezzogiorno. For the most part, northern agriculture has become economically rationalized and has taken on the characteristics of entrepreneurial farming, much like that of Western Europe, Canada, and the United States. In central Italy the system of *parziari* (partial sharecropping) or, more specifically, *mezzadri* (fifty-fifty sharecropping) agriculture had given the peasant a major stake in production. Only in the recent past have we witnessed the breakdown of this system, with the consequent creation of major problems in this once fertile region. The lure of urban industrialism has beckoned the central Italian peasant from the fields. Perhaps a more enlightened propertied class might have been able to instill initiative into the peasantry by greater investment in capital goods, but that is a moot question at this juncture.

The long history of the Mezzogiorno is not a happy one. Foreign domination has played a crucial role in determining the destiny of the southern peasantry. Since the days of Greek settlement, the south has endured the onslaughts of Romans, Arabs, Normans, Hohenstaufen Germans, Angevin French, Florentines, Genoese, Venetians, and Aragonese Spaniards. The onetime "bread basket" of ancient Rome had been reduced by the time of the Risorgimento to an impoverished land despised and disowned by the rest of Italy. The Southern Question continues to embroil every political party in debate. The southern peasant remains "an African" in the eye of the northern urbanite; even though much of the old social order is changing, many of the stereotypes remain.

There is much evidence to suggest that the lot of the southern peas-

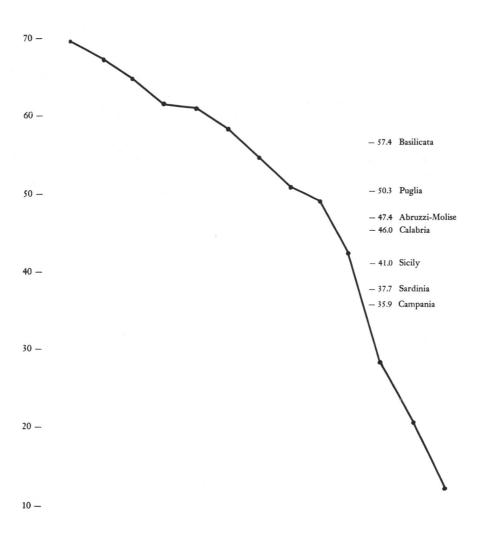

Figure 1

Agricultural Labor Force in Italy
Expressed As Percentage of Total
Labor Force, 1861–1981 *

* Statistics and projections adapted from *Annali di Statistica, Sviluppo della Popola-zione Italiana dal 1861 al 1961*, Anno 94, Serie VIII, Vol. 17.

antry worsened after the unification of Italy. It is doubtful that the peasant ever enjoyed real prosperity in the past, but there appear to have been happier times. The exhibits of peasant costumes and jewelry at the National Museum of Popular Arts and Traditions in Rome indicate a relative degree of affluence in the south in the early years of the nineteenth century. In addition, the archives of provincial and national museums contain notations of folk songs of a bygone age. But this observer has never heard a peasant singing in the fields, either at planting time or at harvest.

Gabriele Gaetani D'Aragona, the noted agricultural economist, suggests that the worsened condition of the southern peasant began in the sixteenth century. By then, Spanish imperialism had been imposed on the south by the Aragonese, and the exploitation of that area continued. During the seventeenth and eighteenth centuries tax upon tax was levied until productivity and peasant life sank into that morass which is so poignantly described as *miseria*. The ill-fated land redistribution instituted by Joseph Bonaparte in 1806 did little to breathe new life into the impoverished economy. Most of the peasants who gained small parcels of land could not make a living on them and soon had to sell them to the big landowners. Those few peasants who were able to retain their small landholdings soon wiped out the gains of the reform; through the chaotic inheritance pattern of the south, these small holdings became smaller as the father bequeathed bits and parcels to this child and that. Soon, the landowning peasantry were left with *fazzoletti* (handkerchief-sized plots). The period of the Risorgimento dawned with an impoverished south reeling from the ravages of exploitation. During the last days of the Bourbon kings, the bread of the poor remained untaxed, to be sure, but even this little protection was swept away after unification.

From the high middle ages to the early sixteenth century, a virtually static economic equilibrium had been achieved, with a population approximating 1,500,000 existing at slightly above the threshold of starvation. By 1530 the population reached 1,700,000 and continued to increase to 2,700,-000 in the early years of the seventeenth century. High mortality rates induced by epidemics (plague in 1656), malarial infections, and famines (at close intervals throughout the sixteenth and seventeenth centuries) served to reduce the southern population to approximately 1,973,000 in 1669.[3]

The inability to increase wheat production stemmed from a variety of socioeconomic causes. Ravages of war, feudal land tenure, demesnial rights, uncertainty of landownership, lack of lease rights, inadequate communications, and a host of other factors conspired against the extension of agriculture. There was actually a decline of cereal production, including the minor grains that formed the black breads of the poor: oats, buckwheat, and rye.

From the third decade of the eighteenth century, political and economic changes instituted under the Bourbon dynasty permitted stimulation of the agricultural organization. New lands were added through swamp drainage and terracing; olive and vine plantings increased. Agricultural expansion was able to keep pace, for a short time, with demographic increase. The population rose from 3,000,000 (1734) to 6,700,000 (1861).

During the early nineteenth century there was further expansion in the agricultural sector. The process of formation of free property continued in the Mezzogiorno from the Napoleonic era to the unification. This process, which affected nonpeasant landowners most, brought a decline in feudal entail. Ecclesiastical property had already been redistributed beginning in the late eighteenth century, and thereafter much land under private and public control had been given unencumbered titles of ownership. As a result, a new propertied bourgeoisie grew in numbers and wealth.

At precisely the time that the alteration of southern agriculture was taking place, other technological changes were occurring which soon proved to be mixed blessings to the peasantry. It is difficult to date the beginnings of modern sanitation practices in the south, but the introduction of simple techniques of medicine probably began in the early eighteenth century. Swamp drainage and controlled disposal of wastes significantly lowered the mortality rates among newborn babies, young children, and postpartum mothers, and the stable equilibrium between population and food supply began to disintegrate as population shot upward. Then population doubled from 1861 to 1901 (12 million) and increased to nearly 18 million by 1961. During the crucial years following unification, many of the gains were wiped out by an unchecked demographic increase.

The standard of living of the peasant entered a downward spiral as a result of population growth without a corresponding increase in agricultural productivity. One lesson could be learned from this latter period of history. The conditions of the Mezzogiorno were not irreversible. Neither geography nor climate were the determinants of southern agriculture. Rather, social, political, and economic factors were responsible for the plight of the south.

During the Risorgimento southern peasants showed considerable revolutionary potential in the Revolution of 1848 and again in 1860, when Garibaldi and his Thousand conquered the Kingdom of the Two Sicilies. But most of them were less interested in political independence than in acquiring land. Seizure of land in sporadic rebellions took place prior to the unification and continued in a number of places and at a number of times since 1861.

The monarchies, north and south, received the grudging support of the peasants. The unknown evil represented by Garibaldi and the forces for nationalism was to be feared. Local tyrants—landlord, usurer, police —were the targets of the peasant's ire. Even into the twentieth century the political loyalties of the peasants, such as they were, belonged to the monarchist parties. As a recent study has noted, "Partly through traditional loyalty to the *baroni*, partly through fear of reprisals, partly through religious fanaticism, and partly through self-interest in the case of the wealthier peasants who dream of becoming themselves small landowners, the peasantry . . . votes monarchist." [4]

Huddled in the misery of their hilltop villages, the *contadini* cared little for the promises of political independence or unity in 1860. These villages, built centuries ago at the crests of the least desirable and least workable land, epitomized the problems of Italy as a whole and the south in particular. Although other reasons may be advanced for hill villages —banditry, malaria, "Mediterranean gregariousness"—all arguments pale in comparison to the desperate need and hope for arable land. A plot of land represented the aspirations of the struggling peasant, even though it might be distant from the village and despoiled by centuries of wanton cutting of timber, continued planting of wheat on top of wheat, exhaustion of soil, torrents of winter rainfall, and erosion. Garibaldi promised land redistribution in the hope of winning the Sicilian peasants to his cause, but once on the mainland he used military force to oust peasants from lands they had occupied illegally.

Over the years the issue of agrarian reform has plagued the entire peninsula. Various measures were attempted, particularly in the south, but to little or no avail: shortly after unification in 1861 and again in 1884, 1893, 1902, 1904, 1924, and after the Second World War. But the slogan "Land Reform," so easily mouthed by peasant and politician, belies the enormity of the issue. Division of land into economically inefficient units worked by an impoverished and illiterate peasantry does not resolve the basic problems. Agricultural self-sufficiency in the modern world is rarely achieved. The thousands of abandoned farmsteads in Calabria, Sicily, and the Maremma give testimony to the bankruptcy of land reform. Here and there some reform schemes have met with success. On the larger scale, success has been achieved when the reform has gone beyond simple land division and has included regional planning, conservation, and the creation of the infrastructure to attract industry and/or tourism. On the smaller scale, a simple truism emerges regarding success or failure: where the peasant has received fertile land, there has been success; where the peasant has received poor land, there has been failure—all other factors being equal. We have seen that the Napoleonic reforms which broke up the *latifondi* in the south did little to resolve the problems of Italian agriculture. Even the *mezzadria* pattern of Tuscany, though it provided great social stability, was not the answer.

In the decades following unification, the southern peasant sank deeper into his *miseria*. Caring little for the distant government in Rome or its foreign representatives on the local scene, he erected psychological barriers of suspicion, diffidence, and political apathy. Parliamentary inquiries revealed the shocking conditions of the landed and landless poor, but to no avail. From 1861 to 1901, the number of landowners declined and the power of the landed estates increased. Only the safety valve of emigration prevented the complete collapse of the system. Disease and famine wreaked havoc among the impoverished population; malaria, cholera, pellagra, vitamin deficiencies, dysentery, and other health hazards served to reduce the will of the southerner to survive.

Governmental policies of the last part of the nineteenth century further served to cripple the south. The grist tax (see Chapter 2, page 31) and the salt tax hit hardest at the poor. Protectionist tariffs for northern industry and monetary policies lowering the value of agricultural products further discriminated against the south. Italian agriculture, lacking risk capital and transportation, was unable to compete in any sector of foreign trade against the inroads of France (wine), the United States (citrus fruits), and Greece and Spain (olive oil).

The alienation of the southern peasants from the unfeeling bureaucracy in distant Rome made them begin to establish a defensive network of social relations to protect themselves. The intricate interlocking web of mutual obligation is evident in a variety of social forms. The system of patronage and *raccomandazioni* (recommendations) worked to undermine an inefficient bureaucracy by making it more inefficient. The reliance on personal strength or the pooled strengths of a small circle of intimates gave rise to such organizations as the mafia in western Sicily and the *camorra* in Naples, as well as widespread banditry.[5] Lack of faith in a government the peasant viewed as corrupt and without justice undercut any belief in systems of legality. Although not of peasant origin, the mafia symbolized the power that was needed in a dog-eat-dog world. The protests went on, erupting here in the form of land seizure, there in the destruction of town-hall tax records, and in the next place as open insurrection.

Although in the late nineteenth century the state attempted to deal with the Southern Question, it usually settled for half measures. Mindful of the pressures, the national regime began to create the infrastructure of modernization: railroads, highways, water supply, and so on. Yet, nature seemed to conspire against the south. Natural disasters such as volcanic eruptions, earthquakes, landslides, and droughts wiped out many of the gains. Usurious rates of interest dried up sources of capital for the exten-

sion of agriculture and industry, leaving the south as impoverished as
before. Repressive taxation further destroyed the initiative of the Mezzogiorno. Perhaps unintentional, taxes on farm buildings favored the north,
where these were in the sparse countryside, and worked against the south
where the peasant dwelled in village clusters.

Meanwhile the gap between north and south began to grow ever wider.
For the southerner, totally disillusioned with what he perceived as a do-
nothing government, there was but one avenue of escape—emigration.
The floodgates opened wide—over six hundred thousand Italians a year
were leaving the country in the early 1900s—and the southerner sought
his fortune abroad. Yet despite the resultant mitigation of local population
pressure and despite remittances from Italian workers in France, the
United States, and Argentina, the economy of the south showed no improvement. By the First World War the gap between the two Italys
seemed unbridgeable, despite all well-meaning interventions on the part
of Rome.

The war and the immediate postwar period further dislocated the
Italian peasantry. Itinerant workers who had migrated to industrial centers
and peasants who had been called into military service had had their eyes
opened to a larger world. They returned to their *paese* with a growing
discontent. Land seizures and the mobilization of peasants by Socialist
and Catholic unions frightened the landlords into early support of the
Fascists. Although great strides had been made by the postwar government in altering the condition of the peasant, these gains were soon to be
wiped away. Various benefits were created to permit the peasant a larger
stake in the south: cooperative enterprises, rent controls, favorable interest rates, increased farm labor wages. These gains were all destroyed
with the advent of Fascism. Once again, the Italian peasants settled in for
a long hard night. In their own way, some of them tried to resist Fascist
control, but in a totalitarian system the unorganized are helpless.

"Life is hell and work is a beast." These words of one of my peasant
informants evoke more clearly than any statistics the brutal heritage of
the Italian peasantry by the end of the Second World War.[6] As Italy
began the slow painful process of picking up the pieces after the war, the
Southern Question emerged once again, and formulas doomed to failure
were once again applied. The poverty of the peasant had ground him
into the soil of the arid south. Reduced to a near animal existence he
viewed the loss of a mule as a greater personal tragedy than the loss of a
grandparent, for the mule represented an economically productive factor.
In 1947 the conscience of the north had been pricked by Carlo Levi's
book *Christ Stopped at Eboli*. Political pressure from many quarters compelled yet another land reform.

The Cassa per il Mezzogiorno was created in 1950, and the long, slow, tedious process of transforming the south began. Though it is clear that progress in altering the south has still fallen short of expectations, irreversible steps were taken to jog the status quo. Forces set in motion by planned socioeconomic change have begun to reshape the south. Industry is being attracted by governmental subsidies, low rates of taxation, and long-term low interest loans. The building of the infrastructure to support a variety of industries is well under way. Highways have opened parts of the Mezzogiorno to tourism, which has already brought the modern world to such regions as the Sila and the once sleepy villages of the Ionian coast. Yet, as one peasant noted: "Tourism! I will never be a servant to another man!"

The social costs of long years of neglect, repression, and exploitation have been high and are evident in statistics that indicate the causes of unrest and tension. Though the south may be looked upon as the repository of traditional values of the society, it also exhibits the inherited social ills of a brutalized past. For one thing, its labor force remains heavily agricultural and has the highest rates of unemployment and underemployment; when employed, the average *bracciante* (day laborer) can anticipate a daily wage of 2200 Lire (about three and a half dollars).[7] But this is only for a few months out of each year. The south also has the highest incidence of bedridden patients but the lowest incidence of hospital beds (fewer than 4 per 1000 population). Sixty-three percent of all cases of typhoid fever occur in the Mezzogiorno; and infant mortality rates in Campania (52.3 per 1000 live births), Puglia (46.5), and Basilicata (44.4) outstrip the national average (34.7).

Although great strides have been made in the battle against illiteracy, the problem remains uniquely a southern one. In 1871 in Calabria, a typical southern province, 79 percent of all males over six and 94 percent of all females over six were illiterate. By 1951, this figure had been reduced to 23 percent of the males and 39 percent of the females. (A factor analysis in which the children of school age would be dropped out would reveal much higher rates of illiteracy for the adult population. Indeed, one may seriously question that the ability to sign one's name to the census document is a test of literacy.) By 1951, 68 percent of all illiterates in Italy were to be found in the south.[8]

The seething discontent of the population is revealed in statistics on crime and delinquency. Although the south has 34 percent of the resident population of Italy, 70 percent of first-degree murders occur there. Killings of unwanted infants account for 37 percent of the national total. Forty-six percent of arsons take place in the south. Business fraud 49 percent, sale of nongenuine food 45 percent, and extortion 55 percent are obviously related to the social conditions in the Mezzogiorno. Delinquent acts by minors are higher in the south: against persons 61 percent, against property 52 percent, and against the state 52 percent.

Against this turbulent, volatile backdrop the drama of renewal is being played. Teams of agricultural agents, technicians, social workers, community organizers, and political parties are struggling to alter the conditions of the peasantry. The modernization of agriculture is an uphill battle. The peasant, with real effort, can be induced to change his traditional ways. By nature a pragmatist, the man of the soil can be brought to appreciate the results of hybrid seeds, modern fertilizers, agricultural diversification, and the use of mechanical equipment. With even greater effort he can be instructed in the establishment of production and marketing cooperatives that would give him a competitive edge in world markets. He can see the ready advantages of plastic greenhouses, which permit twelve months of cultivating tomatoes, squash, other truck crops, and flowers for the expanding urban market. Like the peasant, the fisherman can learn to appreciate modern technology. The fishing trades have quickly adopted sonar, radar, depth gauges, and other advances which promote the catch. Yet, all of this takes time and great capital investment. And time is short and the funds inadequate.

The self-reliance that has been the hallmark of the southern peasant now stands in the way of further change. Even where agricultural production has been increased, the new farmers lack the marketing facilities to compete. Israel has surpassed Italy as a marketer of citrus fruits to northern Europe; interviews with merchants in Britain and Scotland reveal a distrust of Italian products because there is little quality control. It is in the arena of social organization that changes must occur. The studied unwillingness to cooperate has been cracked in some cases, but, again, time is short.

Modern agriculture, like modern industry, creates few new jobs. Indeed, as industry becomes more automated, fewer hands are needed in the production process. The same can be seen in the coming mechanization of agriculture. Yet population growth continues unabated and threatens to destroy what gains might be made, while the old safety valve of emigration now functions imperfectly.

In summary, then, the traditional peasant society of southern Italy does not work well on any level. The peasants remain in a position of subordination to the townfolk and the gentry. Their death-oriented ethos includes a marked antipathy toward the predatory nature of all "superiors." Even where the nobility no longer exist or have moved away, the peasants' antipathy is focused on other authority figures. As in other backward areas of southern and eastern Europe, the local village or town intelligentsia are viewed by the peasants as representatives of powerful outside institutions.[9] They are seen as exploiters who bleed away whatever surplus might accrue to the peasants for the benefit of a distant government or to fill the coffers of the landlord. Much more than mere antipathy is involved here, for there is considerable evidence for such other attitudes as awe, fear, reverence, and jealousy in the characteristic outlook of the peasant. Perhaps to gird himself against the desire for the impossible, the peasant surrounds himself with suspicion toward all outsiders.

This suspicious nature of the peasant extends to his fellow villagers as well. But the *campanilismo,* or village centered outlook, of the Italian peasant does not create a sense of community for him. Rather, according to Edward C. Banfield, the "amoral familism" of the Italian peasant works against cooperation with his fellow villagers.[10] We might add that there is little that can be described as sustained, intimate interpersonal relations in the village setting. There are, of course, contacts beyond the confines of kin and fictive-kin groups; friendship groups, and patron-client relationships exist within the village setting, but we fail to find a *community*. Rather, the patterns of interaction outside the family might be better described as discontinuous circles of intimacy. For the distrust of the peasant is pervasive; he merely distrusts his fellow villagers a little less than outsiders.

We also fail to find among southern Italian peasants the love for the soil which has been said to characterize other peasant societies. Exploitation, both real and assumed, of the peasant by the elite, together with the niggardly return of the soil for a heavy investment of labor, evoke apathy and antipathy toward the land which he works but often does not own.

The peasant's reverential attitude toward the traditional ways of his local culture does not necessarily extend to Roman Catholicism. Although he has been told of the equality of all men in the sight of God, the peasant stands, cap in hand, at the rear of the village church, while the gentry sit in front.

In this relatively stable society, which seems to have resisted change for so long a time, many factors contribute to the maintenance of the status quo. The members of the elite are reluctant to release their monopoly of power and loose the peasant from their grasp. The craftsmen likewise have an interest in keeping the situation stable, even though the peasant consumes but little of their production. In his subsistence-level, self-sustaining role, the peasant does not place a positive value on the consumption of economic goods. Gideon Sjoberg identifies the craftsman as a check against the diffusion of the industrial-urban complex.[11] However, in southern Italy it has been seen that little or no diffusion of the new technology takes place even when the craftsman's ability to maintain his position has broken down. For when that occurs, the craftsman becomes mobile and leaves the village. The status quo is perpetuated, and the peasant remains.

Only in the last two decades has this picture begun to change. The outflow of peasants to seek their fortunes in the expanding urban-industrial marketplace has begun to have a profound effect on the social structure of the villages. The revolutionary potential of the peasant seems to have been channeled away from the desire for land. As he becomes an urban proletarian, the unskilled peasant finds himself at a distinct disadvantage in an industrial world that demands high skills. He finds himself pushed into marginal service trades that grant him as perilous a living in the crowded urban environment as he had once had in the rural scene.

Perhaps the following anthropological case study will illustrate at the level of the microcosm the forces and trends which are reshaping the macrocosm of Italy.

Land reform and the deliberate introduction of technological innovations in depressed agricultural areas constitute basic problems for anthropologists. There is a growing body of literature devoted to community-development schemes in zones that are undergoing prescribed social change. In Italy, particularly, many researchers have produced excellent studies of peasant society under the impact of planned change. Nevertheless, little attention has been paid to the communities in non-land-reform areas. Such villages provide a natural setting for the analysis of unplanned change and its consequences.

Cortina (a pseudonym for a village in southeast Italy) is a commune with a high incidence of individual landownership. Following the Napoleonic reforms of 1806 to 1808, the pattern of individual local landownership became established. Even now the vast majority of the agricultural labor force (86 percent) own their land. There has been no attempt on the part of land-reform agencies to alter the existing pattern. There has been no effort to introduce technological innovation. Hence, to a great extent, the events that have occurred in Cortina have been fortuitous and unplanned.

The mountain village was studied by Stephen C. Cappannari in 1954 to 1955 and Leonard W. Moss in 1955 to 1956 (see note 6). The original site exploration utilized standard ethnographic techniques: intensive interviewing as well as statistical analysis of census data and other techniques of data gathering. Although major emphasis was upon social organization, family structure, and social stratification, other aspects of community culture and folklore came under scrutiny. The study served as a baseline for continued investigation of the community and its émigrés in other Italian cities and in the United States and Canada. The village was restudied by Moss in 1962, revisited by Moss and Cappannari in 1963, and again by Moss in 1968 and 1969 in an attempt to evaluate the impact of out-migration and technological change upon the village.

At the time of the original study, the local economy was based to a great extent upon a self-sufficient peasantry engaged in a familial pattern of subsistence-level agriculture. Fragmented landholdings provided the local peasants with plots of land averaging less than five hectares in size (one hectare = 2.47 acres). Although each peasant could take pride in landownership, the size of his holdings limited his ability to produce for the market. For the most part, he raised crops and domestic animals for family use. Surplus production, dependent upon fortuitous conditions, might be used for cash or barter in the marketplace. Given the historical conditions of individual landownership, land remained a basic value, much as it had before the Napoleonic reform.

Cortina is also a center for truck transport serving the local region. This was an innovation introduced after the First World War by a returned American who brought a truck with him. Since the early 1920s, aside from some small-scale stone quarrying, the trucking industry has constituted the major economic activity outside of agriculture.

Given the basic orientation toward a landed, barter economy, the village retained a system of social stratification much more closely akin to the old regime, which also placed a premium upon one's relation to landownership.

Within the village we found long-standing interparish rivalries and feuds. The two parishes were so divided in loyalties, based primarily upon endogamous kin ties, that the local residents claimed separate ethnic origins for the two parishes. Indeed, the gulf between the factions was so great that villagers claimed that each parish group spoke mutually unintelligible dialects. There is little linguistic evidence to support the notion of separate ethnic origins, but some differences in the parish dialects do exist. The significant point here is that villagers exaggerated the differences between the two parish dialects. The older persons apparently refused to believe that they could understand a dialect speaker from the other parish, even though they often conversed easily with each other using dialect rather than standard Italian. Subsequent linguistic analysis indicates that a person in Parish A could, in fact, understand a person in Parish B, even though he might have difficulty with a few expressions. What is important, however, is the social definition that the dialects are different in origin, for people seemed to act as if this definition were true.

The concept of cooperation to solve mutual problems was, by and large, unknown in Cortina. The concept of community, aside from geographical identification, was nonexistent. Indeed, the term *comunità* (meaning community in the contemporary American usage) did not exist in the Italian vocabulary until the late 1950s. Banfield noted the "amoral" quality of working for the support of one's nuclear family with the tacit assumption that all others will also attempt to maximize the immediate advantages for their own families. Given these preconditions, it is obvious that community did not constitute an ultimate common value for the peasant. Of course, Banfield ignored the very important social network of patronage—mutual obligation—which forms the normative base of the village social system.[12]

If one can speak of a prevailing ethos in the 1950s, it was the longing of the younger members of the village to emigrate. The stable economy of the village worked against economic opportunity for those entering the labor market in this period. Sufficient contact had been maintained with relatives who had emigrated abroad and found the lands where streets are paved with gold. The dream of movement to America, Canada, and Australia dominated conversations with the adolescent males of the village.

There was another ethos evident in the village: the older residents longed for death. For them there was no future. Their life, spent in toil, offered little hope, and they had entered the downward spiral of despair which is so adequately described by the Italian term *miseria*. Death became a welcome relief, indeed an aspiration.

Fairly continuous contact with Italian sources and residents of the village since 1956 had forewarned us of a diminishing population. Upon our return in 1962 and 1963 we learned that the village had indeed shrunk in size from 3200 to 2500. By 1969 the population had dropped below 2000. Neither increasing death rates nor declining birth rates could account for the population change that had occurred. After many years of relative demographic stability (births balancing deaths and emigration), new socioeconomic factors contributed to the population loss.

Most of these factors are related to the economic modernization of Italy as a whole, including a 6 to 8 percent annual increase in the gross national product and expanded agricultural productivity in several regions. Rapid industrialization in the north increased economic opportunities, not in automated factories, which require highly skilled workers, but in the adjunct service occupations. These opportunities became especially important to southern peasants after 1957, when all restrictions on internal migration were removed. In that same year, the Treaty of Rome also opened the prospect of unrestricted migration across international frontiers within the newly created European Common Market. With the introduction of television, these and other prospects became immediately communicated and accessible to the inhabitants of Cortina and every remote mountain village. Also, a new provincial highway within three miles of the village made daily bus service possible and eased the problems of truck transport.

All these outside developments have brought visible changes in the social organization of our village. Most important, it is unusual to see males in the age range of nineteen to forty. When young men leave for their military service, they often do not return to resume permanent residency. They tend to marry girls from the village who emigrate as soon as possible after their husbands have established economic stability elsewhere.

As Joseph Lopreato has noted in his study of Stefanaconi, the contributions of relatives abroad or in industrial centers of Italy have also served as stimuli to changes in the residents' socioeconomic position.[13] While we found no great shift in social position, there is considerable evidence to support the argument that these funds from external sources have alleviated many family economic problems and, in some instances, have brought about increased agricultural productivity. Seemingly, possession of desired consumer goods has begun to confer prestige upon the consumers.

During the summer months, a number of Cortinese return from Rome and elsewhere to spend their vacations in the village. Often, their children spend the entire summer with grandparents who remain permanently resident in the *paese*. By August, the period of the two local festivals, the population of the village has doubled. This influx brings a good deal of money into the local economy.

Social change has been affected by the changing economic base of the village itself. The system of barter-exchange has given way to a money economy. Abandonment of small but prospectively productive tracts of land has occurred as members of the agricultural labor force have left the village to seek their fortunes elsewhere. The increased economic activity in the nation as a whole has stimulated (or forced) some peasants to abandon their family-subsistence orientation and has caused them to enter into the role of the market-oriented farmer.

Furthermore, increasing agricultural productivity throughout the province has stimulated the growth of truck transport activity. Through historical accident Cortina remains the trucking center for the immediate region. This phenomenon has brought about increased communication between Cortina and its provincial capital as well as other centers, such as Rome and Naples.

Although television has been used primarily as an entertainment medium, its educative functions cannot be dismissed. Specific programs have been aimed at the illiterate adult population. We are not prepared, however, to evaluate their success in Cortina. The most visible effect has occurred among the younger inhabitants; school children are immediately aware of events which occur in Rome, Paris, London, New York, and, indeed, everywhere in the world. This new awareness has brought about a dramatic shift in orientation on the part of the children. The church bell no longer defines the limits of their universe.

Finally, the local intelligentsia have brought pressure on the ministry of public instruction to provide more than the traditional classical education for the children of the village. Heretofore, Cortina has had only an elementary school providing education to the fifth grade. These pressures have been rewarded by the creation of a vocational-technical middle school.

One aspect of Cortina's social life which has not changed is the rivalry between the endogamous parishes. This rivalry had led to violence in the past, and in our early impression of the village, we thought the manifest hostility completely a disruptive force. As our familiarity with the village increased, we began to speculate that this division did serve to unify persons within a parish. In a sense, it could be called functional conflict. A person could derive some satisfaction in the identification with his parish because at least he *was* superior to those wretched souls in the other parish. Since this village was completely lacking in voluntary organizations on the community level, any device that promoted unity was especially important.

The position of those older persons who have remained in the village is illustrated by the following example. One of our good friends, Zio (Uncle) Vittorio, became a widower in 1959. Shortly after his wife died, her sister, who had been a widow for some twenty-five years, moved into his home. They had jointly worked in the same fields for many years, and they continue to do so in the same manner and with the same tools. He is in his eighties, she is over seventy, but they continue to work long hours on the land. They do not read a newspaper and do not own a radio or television set. They seem to view the latter as a curiosity that apparently has meaning for their children and grandchildren, who seem to be entering a different world.

Zio Vittorio and Maria Bosco maintain a strong, effective bond with the younger members of their family who come from Rome to spend some of the summer in the village. Their own meals are frugal and largely vegetarian, as they prefer to save the *prosciutto* (ham) and *salciccia* (sausage) for the youngsters. They do not seem to disapprove of change for the younger generation. On the contrary, they often express pleasure and pride with the apparent progress being made by their attractive grandson. They themselves remain peasants in activity and orientation, and their world is peopled with those imaginary witches and werewolves and possessors of the evil eye who have always lived in Cortina.

During our last visit, a minor but touching incident occurred which serves to illustrate how one elderly man views change going on within the village. The steep old rounded-cobblestone street leading from the upper to the lower village had been torn up and replaced with flat paving stone, and this in turn was being covered with a wash of cement. Zi' Angelo, in whose home we were guests, watched the men working on the street. "It won't be so slippery in winter," he commented, and then added sadly, "but our shoes will wear out much faster."

Although many visible changes have occurred, further alterations of the social structure are yet to come (see Figure 2 and Table 7-1). The basic structure of the village has been maintained since at least 1806, and most of the essential problems remain intact. There were no voluntary associations within the village aside from the limited circle of the local

Figure 2

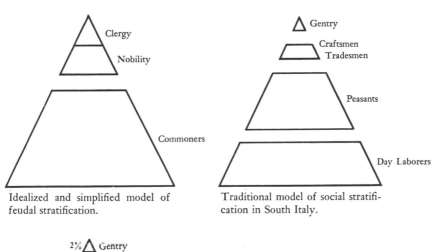

Idealized and simplified model of feudal stratification.

Traditional model of social stratification in South Italy.

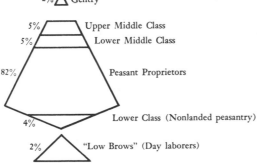

Model of social stratification in Cortina, circa 1954 to 1961.

intelligentsia. Little value is attached to intravillage cooperation, and mutual problems still remain without much hope of mutual solution. Interparish rivalries continue to erupt from time to time. The new vocational-technical school remained unbuilt for several years since the town council could not provide the ministry of public instruction with a specific site. Each parish contended that it was the one which was entitled to the new edifice, and there was no indication that either side would concede simply because it would benefit the village as a whole. After five years of conflict, a compromise was reached. The old school, which nearly straddles the parish boundary lines, was remodeled to include the vocational-technical school. The social-stratification system (Figure 2) still retains vestiges of the old regime but is beginning to reflect the repercussions of a money economy, with the shift from possession of land to the possession of consumer goods as a major value change. A death orientation continues to dominate the thoughts and life-styles of the older residents.

The abandonment of land—if one may speak of the tiny fragments of soil as land—makes possible the reconsolidation of holdings on an economically rational basis. Adventurous, risk-taking members of the village have been able to purchase some landholdings of the émigrés and are attempting to bring about modernization of agricultural techniques. The transmittal of funds from émigrés makes possible the purchase of land, tractors, combines, trucks, and other means of increasing agricultural yields. There is even some evidence for arguing that a changing orientation is coming about among older peasants whose yields have increased. In 1955 a peasant was asked what the future held for him. He responded, "For me there is only death." In 1962 the same old man remarked, "There is for me no hope, but for my son, there is!" This same peasant, in 1968, was asked the same question: "Uncle Giovanni, what is the future?" He replied: "On television I heard that the weather was going to be nice. This will give us a chance to harvest the hazelnuts while they are dry.

Table 7-1
Demographic Change in Cortina

Year	Total Population	Percentage of Labor Force Employed in Agriculture
1936	4,094	90.1
1951	3,532	86
1956	3,500 (est.)	82 (est.)
1961	2,727	60
1962	2,500 (est.)	59 (est.)
1969	1,800 (est.)	43 (est.)

The *nocciolini* (hazelnuts) are bringing 300 lire a kilo in the market." From a distinctly death-oriented ethos, a new attitude toward life has emerged.

In 1969 we witnessed some striking changes in the community. An agricultural technical assistant had helped the local *contadini* to form a cooperative, and indeed a second cooperative association was in the talking stage. This external intervention stimulated the local peasants to think in terms of larger social units than their own families. There was also increased participation in other voluntary associations related to agriculture.

In other attitudes, however, the peasant is slow to change. He still tends to view the government in Rome with fear and suspicion. He thinks of it as distant, and uninterested in the problems of the *contadini*. This belief—right or wrong—is expressed in the old statement: *E piove, governo ladro* (It is raining, thief of a government). Although there are many governmental schemes and programs to aid the peasants, many peasants perceive these attempts to be tied to bureaucracy. They feel that without the aid of politically influential friends, they themselves cannot participate in the programs and derive the just benefits which are due them. Their fear, suspicion, and distrust work against their own best interests.

The Italian anthropologist Tullio Tentori suggests that the peasant is ill-equipped to enter the modern role demanded of him because his heritage from manorial society has stifled his initiative.[14] The peasant in his role as the exploited has been cast as illiterate, genetically inferior, and uneducable. However, technological change has dealt an irreversible blow to traditional peasant society. The isolated peasant village, for better or worse, is dead; localism in the contemporary world is rapidly disappearing. Although there has always been a relation between peasant and town, it is in a stage of redefinition.

In a sense, the peasant-farmer will probably emerge from his position of semiisolation. The values of the urban-industrial market center will impose themselves upon the farmer and dominate his life-style. The prototype that has emerged in American culture may well appear in other cultures undergoing this pattern of change. The farmers will deal directly with the values of the city even though they continue to make their chief residence in the village.

In many ways Cortina is typical of southern Italy as a whole; indeed, the impact of out-migration and social, economic, and technological change can be generalized to other villages throughout Italy.

The entire land surface of Italy is slightly smaller than the state of California. The total arable land approximates 26 million hectares (67.6 million acres); however, only 8 million hectares (20.8 million acres) are plains. Mountainous terrain is not suited for mechanized farming. Although Italy is generally considered a Mediterranean country, its climatology varies from Alpine to Continental to Mediterranean Littoral. Hence, the amount of land adaptable to modern agriculture is severely limited. Where the right combination of land and climate are to be found, Italy has the potential of being the garden of Europe.

In recent years Italian agriculture has become less self-sufficient than ever. Although great strides have been made in the reduction of the agricultural labor force, the percentage of the population employed in all phases of farming (21.4) is the highest within the Common Market. The movement of people from the farms to the towns and cities continues at an unslackened pace. In 1969, 5.3 percent of the rural population moved to urban areas. In the long run, perhaps, there may be salutary effects as some 250 thousand persons leave the rural areas each year. The picture, however, is far from clear. On the one hand, consolidation of abandoned tracts of land could aid in the economic rationalization of agriculture. On the other hand, many former members of the farm-labor force leave their families on the land or refuse to sell the land, using it as an economic cushion or a vacation site.

The typical Italian farm is too small for efficient management. In 1967, there were 2.3 million farms of three hectares (7.8 acres) or less. Despite a decline in small farms since 1961, the growth of larger farms has not occurred. Although it is true that those who leave refuse to sell their land, other factors seem to account for the current inability of agriculture to keep pace with Italy's growing needs.

In foreign trade, agriculture contributes to an overall imbalance of payments (see Table 7-2). The only exceptions are leather, hides, and wine. Italy is the largest producer of wine in the world, and the provision of the Common Market permitting free trade in wine will benefit Italy's economic position. By and large, however, Italian agriculture has failed to generate sufficient capital to bolster this segment of the economy. Indeed, the gross product of agriculture (4,591,000 million lire at current prices) is lower by 4.2 percent in real terms and by 5.8 percent in monetary terms than in 1967.[15] Inflationary tendencies, coupled with loss of reserves, have produced an adverse effect on the cost of financing. The higher interest rates, which continued through 1970, made it difficult to undertake long-term expansion in the private sector of agriculture. There has also been a considerable drain on the internal economy through illegal exportation of banknotes. Yet, ironically, although Italian agriculture has not attained a competitive position in the world market, the nation's exports of tractors and farm machinery yielded a surplus over imports equal to 33 million lire in 1969.

Meanwhile rural depopulation continues in both the northern and central regions of Italy. In the Mezzogiorno the outflow of population has

Table 7-2

Italian Foreign Trade in Agriculture
and Related Sectors, 1969 *

	Imports (Million Lire)	Export (Million Lire)	Difference (Million Lire)
Livestock	371,973	4,495	−367,478
Agricultural products	723,854	378,285	−345,569
Foodstuffs	536,167	204,106	−332,151
Animal feed	194,975	16,959	−178,016
Forestry	132,805	7,698	−125,107
Paper and paperboard	178,729	74,406	−104,323
Timber and cork	157,862	118,049	−39,183
Tobacco	19,028	362	−18,666
Leather and hides	48,448	70,374	+21,926
Beverages	24,397	68,144	+43,747

* Figures adapted from *Italian Business*, No. 4, 1970, p. 14. Statistics relating to the textile industry have been excluded since such figures include man-made fibers, reprocessing, importation for processing, etc.

been called a "hemorrhage." It is highly unlikely that any measures within the sphere of agriculture will halt this population movement. More likely, any modernization of farming will contribute to further reductions in the agricultural labor force. The process of rural out-migration is not immune to general economic pressures. In 1971 hundreds of thousands of workers returned to the southern villages as a result of the economic recession in Europe. This countermovement, barring an economic cataclysm, must be viewed as a temporary phenomenon in the overall picture of agricultural modernization. By 1980 it is entirely possible that fewer than 12 percent of the total labor force will be in the agricultural sector. As agriculture becomes economically more rationalized and begins to approach on a technological basis industrialized farming, there will be simply no room for the relatively uneducated and unskilled farmer.

The peasant needs help as he confronts a future of increasingly rapid changes. His individualism stands in marked contrast to the need for mutually derived solutions to community problems. He has, thus far, been unable to overcome his fear, distrust, and diffidence regarding a distant government and an overwhelming bureaucracy. Technical assistants and social workers, hand in hand with the peasant, can help him to form voluntary associations with others who share similar problems. The essential pressure groups, so necessary for sociopolitical activity in the complex modern world, can do much to ameliorate the conditions of the peasant. They can make his small voice heard. Though there will be a loss of individualism, there may be a gain in individual human dignity. There is also some evidence that the peasant is beginning to lose his political apathy in that he is taking some interest in the substantive matters of the elections. However, until he rids himself of his fear of participation, the peasant will remain outside of the democratic process.

Two conversations with informants in the village of Cortina during the summer of 1969 are revealing of the changes as perceived by the local inhabitants. A stonemason, in discussing the future, suggested that the best that can be done is to educate the youth, teach them a skill, and give them a bus ticket to Rome. A government functionary speaking to this anthropologist observed, "You have been privileged to witness the passage of traditional society—for better or for worse."

NOTES

1. In preparing this chapter I found the following works particularly useful: Franco Alberoni and G. Baglioni, *L'integrazione del immigrato nella società industriale* (Bologna: Il Mulino, 1965); Anna Anfossi, Magda Talamo, and Francesco Indovina, *Ragusa, comunità in transizione* (Turin: Taylor Torino Editore, 1959); Margaret Carlyle, *The Awakening of Southern Italy* (New York: Oxford University Press, 1962); Franco Ferrarotti, et al., *La piccola città* (Milan: Edizione di Communità, 1959); Frederick G. Friedman, *The Hoe and the Book* (Ithaca: Cornell University Press, 1960); Gabriele Gaetani D'Aragona, "Evoluzione agricola e incremento demografico nel mezzogiorno all'unità (1500–1860); una ipotesi e la sua possibile conferma," *Rivista di economia agraria*, 13 (September 1958); D'Aragona, "L'economia agricola della Basilicata nel cinquantennio 1860–1914 e le inchieste Iacini e Faina," *Annali del Mezzogiorno* (December 1964); D'Aragona, *Politica dello sviluppo agrario* (Milan: Giuffrè, 1964); Gustavo Iacono, "An Affiliative Society Facing Innovations," *Journal of Social Issues*, 24 (1968); Carlo Levi, *Christ Stopped at Eboli* (New York: Farrar, Straus, 1947); Gavino Musio, *La cultura solitaria* (Bologna: Il Mulino, 1968); Donald Pitkin, *Land Tenure and Family Organization in an Italian Village*, unpublished Ph.D. dissertation, Harvard University, 1954; Donald Pitkin, "A Consideration of Asymmetry in the Peasant-City Relationship," *Anthropological Quarterly*, 33 (January 1959); Robert Redfield, *The Little Community and Peasant Society and Culture* (Chicago: University of Chicago Press, Phoenix Books, 1960); Allan Rodgers, "Migration and Industrial Development: The South Italian Experience," *Economic Geography*, 46 (April 1970); Manlio Rossi Doria, "Cos'è il Mezzogiorno agrario," in Bruno Caizzi, ed.,

Antologia della questione meridionale (Milan: Edizioni di Comunità, 1955); Manlio Rossi Doria, *Dieci anni di politica agraria nel Mezzogiorno* (Bari: Laterza, 1958); Gustav Schachter, *The Italian South: Economic Development in Mediterranean Europe* (New York: Random House, 1965); Gideon Sjoberg, "Folk and 'Feudal' Societies," *American Journal of Sociology*, 58 (1952); Sidney G. Tarrow, *Peasant Communism in South Italy* (New Haven: Yale University Press, 1967).

2. Eric R. Wolf, *Peasants* (Englewood Cliffs, N.J.: Prentice-Hall, 1966), pp. 3–4.

3. Statistics adapted from *Annali di Statistica: Sviluppo della popolazione italiana dal 1861 al 1961* (Rome: Istituto Centrale di Statistica, 1965) and D'Aragona, 1958.

4. A. L. Maraspini, *The Study of an Italian Village* (Paris: Mouton, 1968), pp. 106–107.

5. Friedrich Vöchting, *La questione meridionale* (Naples: Istituto Editoriale del Mezzogiorno, 1955), p. 52.

6. A number of peasant informants were interviewed during the author's residence in Cortina (pseudonym), a hill village in southeast Italy. For other details of this research: Leonard W. Moss, "Interazione tra mutamento tecnologico e sviluppo socio-culturale nell'Italia meridionale," *Sociologia*, 3 (May 1969), 67–78; Leonard W. Moss and Walter H. Thomson, "The South Italian Family: Literature and Observation," *Human Organization*, 18 (1959), 35–41; Leonard W. Moss and S. C. Cappannari, "Patterns of Kinship, Comparaggio, and Community in a South Italian Village," *Anthropological Quarterly*, 33 (January 1960), 24–32; Leonard W. Moss and S. C. Cappannari, "Folklore and Medicine in an Italian Village," *Journal of American Folklore*, 73 (April-June 1960), 95–102; Leonard W. Moss and S. C. Cappannari, "Estate and Class in a South Italian Hill Village," *American Anthropologist*, 64 (April 1962), 287–300.

7. This figure represents an average of daily wages paid in the south in 1967, although there is variation in wages in different southern regions. These and other statistics used here have been adopted from the *Annuario statistico italiano* (Rome: Istituto Centrale di Statistica, 1968).

8. These figures are from the *Annali di statistica: Sviluppo della popolazione italiana dal 1861 al 1961* (Rome: Istituto Centrale di Statistica, 1965).

9. Irwin T. Sanders, *Balkan Village* (Lexington: University of Kentucky Press, 1949), pp. 7–13 and 273.

10. Edward C. Banfield, *The Moral Basis of a Backward Society* (Glencoe, Ill.: The Free Press, 1958), pp. 115–116.

11. Gideon Sjoberg, "The Preindustrial City," *American Journal of Sociology*, 60 (1955), 444.

12. Banfield, *op. cit.*, pp. 115–116.

13. Joseph Lopreato, *Peasants No More: Social Class and Social Change in an Underdeveloped Society* (San Francisco: Chandler, 1967), pp. 246–257.

14. Tullio Tentori, "Evolving Forms of Italian Peasantry," unpublished paper presented to the Central States Anthropological Society in 1959.

15. "Economic Facts and Figures," *Italian Business* (Rome: Confindustria), No. 5 (October 1969), p. 1.

CHAPTER 8

ECONOMIC GROWTH

JON S. COHEN

At the time of Italy's unification in 1861, the country was poor by the standards of northwestern Europe.[1] The national product was composed mainly of agricultural goods, and the majority of the labor force was employed in agriculture. The industry that existed was, for the most part, small and backward in comparison with that of Italy's northern neighbors. By 1900, while trade and industrial activity had expanded noticeably in the north, most of the south remained rural, isolated, and backward. Indeed, much of Sicily had yet to escape from semimedieval relations in both agriculture and industry.[2] In 1961, a century after unification, the gross product of industry was almost double that of agriculture, while employment in industry and services was almost three times that in agriculture.[3] Poverty and backwardness continued to exist, especially in the south, but the extent and degree of these conditions had changed drastically since 1900. This chapter will sketch the main features of Italy's economic growth from the time of unification to the present to provide a picture of the changes that have made Italy a modern industrial nation.

Such a vast subject requires some focus. Economic growth is measured by changes over time in the real value of national income and product per capita. Most economic growth models contain some type of functional relationship between income expansion and growth of the capital stock, that is, of plant and equipment. By and large, the rate of capital formation in Italy was strongly influenced by fluctuations in the pattern and composition of foreign trade, the economic activities of the government, and by developments within the financial sector. This discussion will therefore focus on these factors and their role in Italy's long-term growth.

A word of caution to dispel any misconceptions: economic growth as described above is not necessarily a good or a bad thing; a higher or lower rate of growth is simply that. Until economists perfect standards for measuring social welfare and techniques for estimating the distribution of costs and benefits of economic change, growth rates will remain indications of changes in the size and number of economic activities which are recorded by national income accountants. They will be unable to measure, except in a gross manner, improvements in the economic well-being of individuals.

Particular aspects of Italy's economy throughout most of the period since unification have caused trade, the government, and the financial system to assume important roles in economic expansion. Italy was and remains an open economy. Its lack of industrial raw materials has caused a rise in the quantity of imports to accompany most of its spurts in industrial production. Although improvements in transportation and the exploitation of new energy sources have reduced the burden of a poor resource base, they have not eliminated Italy's dependence on foreign trade. In addition to a dependence on foreign sources for industrial raw materials, Italy has been a net importer of agricultural products since the 1870s. Whereas foreign lending to industry and the government has tended to reduce Italy's balance-of-payments deficits, short-term capital flows into and out of the country have occasionally subjected the economy to severe financial strains. In the light of these considerations, it is understandable that Italy's ability to export goods and services has played a major role in its economic growth and stability.

Agriculture was the largest sector in Italy from 1861 until the years just prior to the Second World War. In most industrially advanced countries, sizeable gains in agricultural productivity appear to have preceded or accompanied rapid industrial expansion, and most economists agree that these advances in the agrarian sector were essential for continued industrial growth. They permitted agriculture to release capital and labor without a reduction in output or a rise in prices. Higher output per unit of input in agriculture meant larger per capita incomes and an expanding domestic market for manufactured goods. In many cases, agricultural commodities served as a source of foreign exchange that was needed to finance inputs of capital equipment from more advanced countries. In Italy, however, agricultural productivity rose very slowly. Domestic markets were restricted, saving out of income was limited, capital transfers out of agriculture were hampered, and because Italian farm products for the most part were not competitive on world markets, a potentially large source of foreign-exchange earnings was not fully exploited.

This situation was in part a consequence of the backwardness of the south, but it would be a mistake to regard it solely as a regional problem. At the turn of the century we have ample evidence of serious poverty and primitive farming practices in such supposedly advanced regions as the Po Valley. Since the Second World War the situation is much improved; but productivity levels in agriculture are still low relative to those in most northern European countries, and productivity increases have been noticeably smaller in Italy than in many countries in southern Europe.

Italian industry has faced two major problems for most of the years since unification. It has lacked a domestic market for its products and an adequate supply of funds to finance its capital formation. To foster industrialization, the government became a major customer of heavy industry, while the government together with the financial system provided both the incentives to invest in industry and the funds necessary to finance these investments.

To facilitate our analysis, we will divide the period 1861 to 1969 into growth phases. A growth phase is a purely descriptive device that groups together a series of years during which the growth rate of national income and its components was constant and in which existing trends in structural change (or lack of change) were maintained. Italy's long-term growth can be separated into five phases: 1861 to 1886, 1896 to 1913, 1920 to 1926, 1929 to 1938, and 1950 to 1969.[4]

Between unification and 1886, Italy's rate of expansion in terms of total and per capita income was low, not only compared to the national average over time, but also in terms of the performance of other countries during these years. According to most calculations, Italy ranked lower in terms of growth per capita product than any other industrial country during the nineteenth century.[5] Trends in saving and investment were equally low in relative terms. Saving exceeded 8 percent of national income in only two years between 1861 and 1886; the annual average rate was less than 4 percent. It is not surprising that only a small fraction of any increase in income was saved. Although the growth in gross fixed investment was more impressive, it barely exceeded levels achieved in many less-developed countries today.[6]

By and large, government expenditure and revenue policies during this period constrained rather than encouraged industrial expansion. Defense spending, railroad building, and public works were the main expenditure items in the government's budgets, and on paper these would seem to form an ideal pattern of demand for domestic industrial goods. But, for the most part, the rails, rolling stock, arms, and ammunition were all purchased abroad. Jobs were provided, and a stock of socially useful capital goods was built up, but the direct impact on industry was minimal.

Furthermore, the imports had to be paid for, and the outflow of funds contributed to the country's balance-of-payments problems.

The government's budgets were constantly in the red during this period in spite of tax rates that exceeded those of other European nations. The high tax rates kept disposable incomes per capita low, and potential savings were siphoned off from the public to the government. Had the government conceived and pursued a rational development strategy, it could be argued that economic growth demanded this type of income transfer. But all our evidence suggests that no such strategy existed. At the same time, the persistent deficits forced the government to borrow heavily on domestic and international capital markets, thus raising the overall cost of funds. This does not mean that deficits are necessarily detrimental to economic growth, but in the context of the Italian government's expenditure policies, they probably were.

In the 1880s, the situation began to alter. Under pressure from the military and certain financial and industrial groups, a modern steel works was established with governmental assistance at Terni, a town north of Rome.[7] In 1887 a tariff was introduced which gave substantial protection to iron and steel producers. These actions represented a decisive break with the past. Although their positive effects on industrial activity were initially dampened by the combined impact of a downturn in the business cycle and a serious financial crisis, it would be a mistake to underemphasize these changes in the government's commitment to industrial growth.

Although the financial system was virtually destroyed by the crisis of 1893 to 1894, the long-range results of the debacle were probably salutary. The system was totally inadequate to meet the credit needs of a rapidly expanding economy. Only two banks, the Credito Mobiliare Italiano and the Banca Generale, provided funds for industry, and their resources were limited. Loans for small-scale investments in agriculture or industry could be had through the cooperative banks (*banche popolari*), but as they depended in large part on the resources of their members, only the more prosperous areas could support such institutions.[8] Agricultural credit facilities were in general poorly developed, an unfortunate situation for a country so dependent on this sector.

No consensus exists among economists about the connection between the money supply and the level of economic activity in a modern economy, but most would agree that a mismanaged money supply can create serious economic problems. Italy's financial history before 1893 is a perfect case in point.

The main component of the money supply was currency, and this was controlled primarily by the National Bank of the Kingdom of Italy until 1871, and by five additional banks from then until 1893. The government, in extreme need of financial assistance, granted extraordinary privileges to these banks and, in effect, sanctioned excessive note issues. By the late 1880s, these note-issuing banks, along with the industrial credit banks, had portfolios filled with high-risk paper and large outstanding liabilities. In 1892, the details of these excesses were exposed to public scrutiny, and the financial system collapsed. Although the industrial credit banks were not directly involved in the affairs of these banks, a loss of confidence by the public in the financial system in general led to withdrawals by depositors and demand for payment by other creditors. The industrial credit banks were unable to withstand this pressure and were forced to declare bankruptcy.

A better organized and more closely regulated system of money and credit might have allowed a more rapid expansion of industry and improvements in agriculture before the 1890s. As it was, industrial growth was slow (except for the years 1880 to 1885), while total agricultural production remained almost unchanged. In terms of value added to total product, the proportional contributions of agriculture, industry, and commerce were unchanged; agriculture was the largest sector, and it also employed over 50 percent of the working male population. Although agriculture did make slight gains in value added during the first decade after unification, a depression began in 1875 from which the sector only fully recovered twenty years later.[9]

With one major exception, economic growth was so handicapped by the factors mentioned that it is not surprising to find that rates of expansion were generally moderate. The exception was foreign trade, which rose almost three times and increased from 12 percent to 25 percent of national income. The rise in inputs of industrial raw materials and capital goods was partly balanced by the sharp expansion in foreign sales of wine and other traditionally exported commodities. Heavy borrowing on international markets by the government and, to a lesser extent, by industry provided a welcome source of foreign exchange to finance imports. But in spite of this impressive trade expansion, it was only after 1896, with a reorganized financial system and a government sympathetic to the needs of industry, that substantial economic expansion occurred.

As the data in Table 1 show, the growth rate of national income accelerated in Phase II (see statistical appendix to this chapter). The rate of increase compares favorably with those achieved by other industrial countries in the nineteenth and early twentieth centuries. The performance of the economy in the first part of this period was particularly striking when contrasted with the social and political unrest which prevailed at the time. Saving rose to over 10 percent of national income and remained relatively constant until 1926. Gross fixed investment jumped ten times and equaled 15.4 percent of national income by 1913. Investment in industry rose sharply, and with it, the net capital stock. Although agricultural production was up, investment in that sector was constant.

In 1894 the government constructed the Bank of Italy out of the rubble of the old note-issuing banks, and almost simultaneously a group of new industrial credit banks were started: the Banca Commerciale Italiana, the Credito Italiano, the Banco di Roma, and later the Società Bancaria Italiana. The Bank of Italy assumed the role of a central bank, although it continued to share the right of note issue with the Bank of Naples and the Bank of Sicily. It regulated the money supply, was a source of financial assistance for other banks, and on one occasion directed a salvage operation that saved the Società Bancaria Italiana from bankruptcy. Since the Bank of Italy demonstrated its willingness to assist commercial banks in temporary difficulties, the industrial credit banks were able to hold a large percentage of their assets in the form of industrial paper. This arrangement increased the flow of capital to industry. At the same time, the public's confidence in the banking system rose, thus increasing demand savings deposits with commercial and investment banks. The financial system's role as an intermediary, particularly as a source of industrial capital, thus expanded swiftly during these years.

The government's expenditure policies were now directly beneficial to industry. The state no longer sought foreign suppliers for military equipment and railroads but instead bought from Italian manufacturers. It was often the case that prices were higher and quality lower, but this now appeared to be a cost worth bearing. Investment in industry grew, plant size with it, and in some cases unit production costs fell as scale increased.

While government purchases of the products of domestic industry rose, government spending as a whole declined as a percentage of net national product. Thus a substantial change occurred in the pattern of expenditures. Aside from the exceptional outlays for the Libyan campaign, defense spending fell as a proportion of the total, while subsidies to industry, shipping rebates, public works and the like all rose as a percentage of the total.[10] In particular, larger subsidies to the merchant marine indirectly provided greater assistance to domestic shipbuilding and iron and steel firms.[11] Between 1905 and 1908 the government undertook an extensive program of railroad rebuilding which led to a sharp rise in this category of spending. Spending for education, social services, and welfare showed little tendency to rise. The government did assume responsibility (on a voluntary basis) for old age and sickness insurance for workers, but it was merely replacing the mutual aid societies that had provided this insurance in the past.[12] The government was active in building up the physical capital of industry, but was little concerned with raising the economic quality of human capital—the people.

The tax structure remained virtually unchanged, in spite of the removal of the bread tax in 1902. But during much of the period the government managed to balance its administrative budget, and in 1905 it successfully reduced the cost of its outstanding debt by refunding it at a lower rate of interest. Since it now borrowed less both domestically and internationally, competition with private industry on capital markets was reduced. Effective rates of interest declined through 1908, and the cost of capital for industry was lower than it had been since unification.[13]

Along with these factors, external conditions contributed greatly to Italy's growth. A half-century decline in world prices was reversed, and world trade in both primary and manufactured goods rose dramatically in a period of relative peace and prosperity. Under these circumstances, it is not surprising that Italy's foreign trade flourished. As we would expect, imports tended to run ahead of exports, but with capital markets wide open and emigrant remittances flowing in, a balance-of-payments deficit was no constraint on behavior.

Even more important than overall trends was the commodity composition of trade, especially of exports. Manufactured cotton textiles and to some extent heavy machinery for the first time began to bulk large in the value of total exports. This development suggests that Italian industry was advanced enough in some sectors to compete with other industrial nations for markets in places such as Argentina, Brazil, Turkey, and Egypt. Trade with Italy's traditional partners expanded, but trade in these new markets grew even more.

In some respects Italy's commercial policy did not allow industry to exploit fully its potential or to benefit completely from these favorable trends in world trade. The tariff of 1887 raised the price of iron and steel products above world market prices and consequently placed Italy's machine industry at a competitive disadvantage both at home and in export markets. A major unresolved controversy in Italian economic historiography is the exact benefits and costs of this tariff in terms of overall growth. Although we cannot settle the question here, it is quite certain that the tariff did limit the extent to which ouput growth of textiles, chemicals, and other products stimulated the domestic machine industry, thereby holding down the impact that this sector could have had elsewhere in the economy.[14]

The tariff is more clear-cut in agriculture since it fostered misallocation of resources in this sector. Protection for wheat production promoted increases in the amount of land under wheat cultivation at a time when Italy's competitive edge lay in the cultivation of fruits and vegetables. Giolitti attempted to win foreign markets for Italian citrus fruits, wine, olive oil, and other specialty crops through a series of commercial treaties, but the tariff of 1887 gave wheat growers an indirect subsidy. The consequences of this subsidy were manifold, especially in the south. It gave support to extensive, low-productivity farming, a special feature of the *latifondi* in the south. It prevented the creation of new land-tenure arrangements and farming practices that were essential for a more productive agriculture and higher incomes. Agriculture was thus unable to break completely free of its past and become more economically efficient.

In spite of the drawbacks of the tariff, industrial production grew more swiftly than it had ever done. The importance of agriculture in the economy fell relative to that of industry and services. This can be seen in all the aggregate figures: in the relative sizes of the capital stock, labor force, and real output. It should be noted that the decline in the working population in agriculture was caused not only by the lure of higher wages in domestic industry but also by the chance to emigrate. It was during these years that over eight million Italians left for the United States and South America as well as for France, Germany, and Switzerland for shorter stays. This loss of labor in agriculture had only a minor influence on production and labor costs, thus suggesting that some underemployment may have existed among the peasantry.

Certain features of the economic growth during this phase were to persist and sharply influence the nature of subsequent economic and political developments. Industrialists expected the government to support their interests by protecting property, insuring an acceptable return on capital, and maintaining a market for their products. Financiers had similar expectations, in part at least because they were the same people. The banks wanted governmental assistance in their banking business and in their entrepreneurial functions. By and large, these groups got what they wanted. It can be argued that this paradigm holds for other countries of Western Europe as well, and to some extent it does. What makes Italy unique is the extent to which these groups relied on governmental favors, their economic and political power, and their unwillingness to compromise.

The First World War increased industry's dependence on government demand and led to the creation of huge industrial complexes and the concentration of industrial production. To insure an adequate supply of war materiel, the government provided credit to industry either directly or through permission to write off new investments quickly. Wartime contracts, because of their terms, yielded enormous profits and were eagerly sought by industry. The larger firms were better able to meet the initial wartime demand and were better placed to secure new contracts. Indeed, those individuals charged with the responsibility of distributing government orders were frequently heads of large industrial firms or close banking associates. Furthermore, the war interrupted foreign trade and placed Italian industry in a precarious position because of the shortage of raw materials. Licenses were issued for the right to import coal and similar natural resources, and the government strictly regulated the distribution of these imports. Once again, the large firms benefited since they could control the distribution of imports. By the war's end, a number of new industrial giants were largely dependent on the government for their sales and profits.

The metallurgical and machinery sectors, chemicals, textiles, rubber, and cement were major beneficiaries of wartime demand. In many firms technology improved and productivity rose. But the urge toward bigness often overshadowed strict cost calculations so that expansion sometimes occurred without proper planning and with little knowledge of the full array of new machinery available. Technological obsolescence was common, and organizational inefficiencies were widespread. The rush to profit from governmental demand encouraged excessive investment even among the giants; easy credit terms and rapid depreciation allowances facilitated these excesses. As a result, two of Italy's largest industrial complexes, Ansaldo and Ilva, were left with enormous excess capacity in 1918 and eventually declared bankruptcy.

At the end of the war the government was under pressure to maintain the support it had provided industry—or at least to bear part of the costs of conversion—and at the same time to meet new demands from the masses. The complexion of the electorate changed in the 1919 elections. Over 50 percent of the male population voted, and two mass parties, the Socialists and the Populists, gained a majority of the votes. These two parties voiced the demands of agricultural and industrial workers for drastic changes in the tax structure, in landholdings, and in welfare policies. Inflation compounded the problems of the government. It had financed the war through direct borrowing from the Bank of Italy and the sale of securities to the public. In particular, the value of short-term treasury bills had risen sharply during the war, and these, combined with the increase in the money supply, vastly expanded liquidity and purchasing power in relation to the supply of goods. The government's inability to solve the nation's postwar economic problems and satisfy new popular demands helped to discredit the liberal regime, thus paving the way for Fascism.

Actually, recovery from the postwar slump began before Mussolini's assumption of power (statistics indicate a rise in industrial and agricultural production in 1921) and continued until 1926. During Phase III the annual rate of increase of income per capita (in real terms) was the highest recorded by the economy since unification. Gross fixed investment almost doubled in value and continued to be directed increasingly to industry.

The policies of Alberto De Stefani, Mussolini's minister of finance from 1922 to 1925, provided both psychological and tangible encouragements to business. De Stefani was a true nineteenth-century liberal in his economic policy; he reduced government participation in the private sector directly and through legislation. Government expenditures fell by 50 percent between 1922 and 1925 and declined sharply as a percentage of national income. De Stefani reduced or removed duties on a large number of products that had received generous protection from the tariff of 1921. Taxes fell both absolutely and as a percentage of national income. Interference in business activities was curtailed over a wide range: stock certificates were no longer required to bear the owner's name and thus became difficult to tax; private Italian and foreign life insurance companies were permitted to operate freely alongside the nationalized insurance system; rent control laws were removed.[15] Although reduction in government spending caused some decline in government demand for industrial goods, the government's destruction of labor unions (see Chapter 9) and its control over wage increases allowed industry to keep costs down and obtain large gains from the moderate inflation during this period.

Chemicals, electric power, and machinery experienced the highest rates of increase in production during this phase, whereas the performance of textiles was mixed. Textiles was one of the largest industries in terms of value added and employment throughout the years 1861 to 1938, and its growth was relatively moderate in all phases. These results, however, are deceiving. Between 1880 and 1914, cotton textile production had risen swiftly; indirect but adequate evidence of this was the rapid growth of imports of raw cotton during those years. In the aggregate data, this expansion was offset by the unimpressive performance of the silk industry, the largest and least dynamic branch of the textile industry. Between 1920 and 1938, Italy began to produce synthetic fabrics and was second in the world to the United States in the production of these goods in the 1920s. While output of traditional textiles (which included cotton goods by this time) lagged, that of synthetic fabrics soared. Again the aggregate data hide this remarkable growth.

The most dynamic sectors during this phase were those in which capital formation was most pronounced. War demand, as noted, had led to heavy investment in chemicals, rubber, cement, machinery, and iron and steel. The potential of this wartime capital formation was realized in the postwar period. The greatest increases in productivity between 1911 and 1927 were in chemicals, processed food products, and construction. The sectors that grew most rapidly between 1920 and 1926 in terms of value added were consequently those in which investment and productivity gains were highest. In this context, note that the sectors that were to suffer *least* during the depression of the early 1930s were those that had maintained the highest rates of output per man-hour.

Agricultural production rose rapidly between 1920 and 1926; it surpassed rates of expansion achieved in the past, even though Mussolini's major expenditures for land reclamation and improvement began only in 1928. In most years weather was favorable, credit was more available, and farmers—generally a debtor class—gained from inflation. Equally important, the fact that the tariff on wheat was removed in 1915 and reintroduced only in 1926 gave a greater incentive to cultivate crops for which international markets existed. In this respect, agriculture shared with industry the growth of demand for Italian exports prompted by the depreciation of the lira. De Stefani's successful attempts to reduce trade barriers led to concessions on the part of foreign countries for the crops of southern Italy. Hence even southern agriculture prospered.

It can be argued that between 1920 and 1926 Italy's domestic expansion was led by exports. Up to 1925 exports expanded even more rapidly than imports, although the nation continued to run a trade deficit. The most dynamic sectors domestically were precisely those for which foreign demand grew most rapidly. This holds true for the products of industry such as artificial silks, industrial chemicals, and automobiles as well as for olive oil, citrus fruits, wine, and other agricultural commodities.

Italian exports expanded in spite of unfavorable trends in world trade. Textile exports expanded at a time when international demand for these goods declined, and chemical exports grew in the face of a stable world demand.[16] World demand for machinery and transport equipment expanded most during the 1920s and 1930s. Thus, of Italy's export industries, only automobiles were favored by the shift in the commodity composition of world trade.[17] Italy had become an able competitor indeed in world markets.

By this period Italy possessed a well-trained core of industrial workers and still had a large reserve of underemployed labor in agriculture. Financial capital, controlled by the large industrial credit banks, was quick to move into new investment opportunities. The linkages between the major export sectors and the rest of the economy promoted expansion elsewhere. The demand for power stimulated further growth in electric power production, while heavy investment in plant and equipment raised the demand for building materials and for construction. Furthermore, industrial growth brought more workers to the city and triggered a demand for new housing.

By 1926 most industrial sections were dominated by a few large firms: Fiat in automobile production, Montecatini in chemicals, Snia Viscosa in artificial textiles, and the Edison group in electric power production. Such concentration, along with the tariff of 1921, removed the threat of competition at home and gave export industries the possibility of charging higher prices on the domestic market than on the foreign one. By and large, this type of price discrimination was tremendously lucrative for industry; for the average Italian it meant higher prices.

By 1925, as the international value of the lira began to decline rapidly, inflationary pressure mounted at home. Mussolini had, in fact, done nothing to control inflation; the rapid expansion in economic activity had at least temporarily eased demand-induced inflationary pressures. The Fascist government now had to deal with this problem. Between May 1925 and December 1927 it took decisive steps to reduce domestic liquidity. It lengthened the maturity of government bonds and reduced the money supply. This mopping-up operation was combined with, and facilitated by, institutional changes. In particular, bank notes of the Bank of Italy became the official currency of the country, and this bank became the official banker for the treasury. This move gave the government greater control over the money supply and more flexibility in its management of the national debt. Government expenditures were kept low, and for a few years the budget was in the black. The regime was aware of the need to follow a deflationary domestic policy in order to revalue the lira.

Between May 1925 and June 1926 the government began its efforts to stabilize the lira; at first it pegged it at 120 to the pound, but in July 1926 the lira's value began to fall again. In December of that year Mussolini decided to stabilize the lira at 90 to the pound sterling. This rate, the *Quota novanta*, became official a year later. The rate was higher than any since 1921, far higher than that anticipated or desired by industry. But Mussolini pushed through his decision for reasons of international prestige and domestic control.

While industrial production recovered from the deflationary pressure in 1928 and the first half of 1929, the rate of expansion slowed. Exports still provided some stimulus, but their force was weakened. The value of exports did not grow at all between 1927 and 1937. During the period when exports had been the main factor in economic growth, Italy's terms of trade had not improved relative to its European competitors; its gains from trade had come through an expansion in the total volume of foreign commerce. Whereas the revaluation of the lira did improve Italy's terms of trade, it seems that the high price elasticity of its export products led to a decline in total volume. This decline more than offset the savings in raw-material costs.

Between 1925 and 1927 a marked change occurred in Fascist economic policies. Giovanni Volpi di Misurata, an old associate of the Banca Commerciale Italiana and a substantial man of affairs (industrialist, speculator, and so on), replaced De Stefani as minister of finance and very quickly made it clear that even more than his predecessor he had the best interests of industry at heart. A duty was reintroduced on wheat, commercial treaties were permitted to lapse, and heavy protection was once more accorded to industry. A phase of direct and active intervention by the government had begun.[18] After 1927 government expenditures expanded as a percentage of national income and an increasingly large share of spending went to maintain a growing bureaucracy. Industry was favored by stiff tariff protection and a package of subsidies, rebates, tax breaks, and purchases of finished products. Labor costs were kept down through a squeeze on wages made possible by the Labor Charter of 1927 (see Chapter 3, page 69). The Fascist regime increased the number of social services it provided labor, although the data suggests that initially at least expenditures on social services fell relative to those on defense and public works.

The performance of the economy during the depression was poor, even by international standards. From 1929 to 1938 national income expanded at an annual average rate of 1 percent, while gross private product rose at less than 1 percent per year; real per capita income exhibited a similarly unimpressive rise. A modest upswing in economic activity began after 1935 in response to a rise in demand for arms and war materiel to support Mussolini's aggressive international policy, but by 1939 per capita income barely exceeded its 1929 level.

The reduced rate of growth in real per capita product was reflected in savings rates, which declined to an average of less than 8 percent a year between 1928 and 1939, the lowest since the turn of the century. Gross fixed investment rose as a percentage of national product throughout the depression, largely because of heavy government investment in agriculture and public works. Private investment in industry declined continuously after 1929. Total agricultural investment actually expanded because of the government's decision to finance land reclamation.

It is important that the government's role in the private sector be interpreted correctly. Government intervention during the 1930s represented an attempt to save the existing economic system (as it did in most industrial countries). It did not represent, as Fascist propaganda suggested, the introduction of a new economic system, the corporative state. The Istituto Mobiliare Italiano (IMI), the Industrial Reconstruction Institute (IRI), and other state-owned holding companies used government funds to salvage industry and the banks. The reorganization of the financial structure in 1936 was motivated by a similar desire to save what remained of the old system. In fact, the state assumed the role that the industrial credit banks had played in the previous periods of Italy's economic growth and thus was able to coordinate government policy and industrial expansion more effectively. No attempt was made to redistribute wealth, nor did government participation in the private sector alter the distribution of profits.

An increase in international trade restrictions in connection with the autarchic policies of the government reinforced the regressive nature of the tax system. During this phase taxes on consumption accounted for half of total tax receipts. The relative weight of indirect taxes declined after 1935, not because of legislation, but simply because of reduced consumption expenditures.

The autarchic policies of the government did not differ greatly from the protectionist policies and competitive devaluations pursued by other industrial nations. The Battle of Wheat (an effort to increase production and reduce imports) and the Bonifica Integrale (Integrated Land Reclamation), main components of the push toward self-sufficiency, had both positive and negative results. The Bonifica Integrale in particular raised productivity in those areas in which funds for land reclamation and improvement projects were concentrated. Some people felt that a major objective of land reclamation was to force landowners to improve farming practices and modernize tenure arrangements on land which was reclaimed, especially on large estates. But Mussolini had other ideas. Although the law permitted the government to expropriate unimproved land after reclamation, no expropriation took place; consequently only insignificant changes in land use and tenure systems occurred. Because of this, improvements in agriculture through the Bonifica Integrale were hardly equal to the value of funds invested by the government, which frequently supported the least productive aspects of Italian agriculture.

The investment banks in Italy, as elsewhere, were hit hard by the depression. Decline in the value of industrial securities led to a sharp reduction in the value of the portfolios held by these banks. Various attempts were made to salvage the banks and industrial firms. Finally in 1933, IRI was created and took over management of the securities' portfolios of the major investment banks. In March 1936 the entire financial system underwent another reorganization. The Bank of Italy became a publicly owned and controlled central bank, the three major industrial credit banks—the Banca Commerciale Italiana, the Credito Italiano, and the Banco di Roma—became pure commercial banks, whereas the Banca Nazionale del Lavoro, the Bank of Sicily, and the Bank of Naples became government-controlled and publicly owned credit institutions. The latter were allowed to provide some medium- and long-term credit, but the old industrial credit banks were permitted to engage only in short-term credit operations. Most industrial financing was left to the state-run holding companies, IRI and IMI, and the government began to supervise the activities of the banks more closely. The reorganization was done out of extreme necessity but proved both durable and efficient in the period after the Second World War.[19]

Foreign trade virtually ceased during the depression. Imports fell more than exports, but the improved trade balance was accompanied by a greatly reduced overall volume of total trade and a reduction in income earned from exports. The decline in exports was felt most among those industries that had experienced rapid increases in the preceding phase, especially machinery production. Just as the economy had prospered with the export expansion before 1927, so it suffered from a reduction between 1929 and 1935.

Italy's foreign trade collapsed along with the worldwide shrinkage in trade brought on by the depression, the restrictive policies of other industrial nations, and the growth of import substitution among both the industrial and the less developed countries. The government made efforts to promote Italian exports: special clearing arrangements were established with certain countries, and export industries were given subsidies on the basis of imports required for finished products.[20] Mussolini's reluctance to abandon the *Quota novanta*, however, severely handicapped export industries by keeping the prices of Italian goods and services artificially high in the world market.

When, in 1936, Mussolini was persuaded to devalue the lira, exports rose almost at once. At the same time, Italy's trade pattern altered as commerce with its colonies in Africa rose sharply. Between 1934 and 1938, exports to Africa increased from 10 percent to 28 percent of Italy's total exports, while its trade with Europe declined from 68 percent of the total to 51 percent. This expansion of trade, a result in part of Italy's colonial policy, permitted Italian exports, especially machinery, textiles, and chemicals, to grow once again. But the upswing in both exports and economic activity was moderate since the capacity of these colonial markets to absorb Italian manufactures was limited.

By 1938 real per capita income exceeded slightly the value reached in 1925, and total value added was equal to that in 1925. Real value added by manufacturing in 1938 exceeded that of 1913, while value added by agriculture was unchanged. Industrial recovery began after 1935, partly in response to increased foreign demand, but largely as a result of military expenditures by the government. Thus, machinery, iron and steel, chemicals, and electric power production all rose after 1936. In an attempt to prop up the economy, Mussolini encouraged cartelization and similar arrangements that increased concentration and reduced competition at home. These restrictive agreements maintained domestic prices but, combined with the restrictive international trade policy, led to inefficiency in production techniques and obsolescence in equipment.

Value added in agriculture declined between 1926 and 1938 as a result of the worldwide crisis in agriculture, the depression, the closing of export markets, and the poorly conceived agricultural policies of the government. Not only were wheat and industrial crops such as sugar beets encouraged at the expense of vegetables, citrus fruits, and animal husbandry, but labor mobility in agriculture was also restricted. Many technical-assistance agencies and corporations which had grown up during the early postwar years became bureaucratic strongholds and lost much of their flexibility. As already noted, the Bonifica Integrale was unable to realize its potential because the government was unwilling to force the changes in land tenure and production methods which were necessary to raise productivity in agriculture. The south, of course, lost most from these events; it suffered most from the decline in agricultural exports and benefited least from the land reclamation expenditures.

The Second World War had far more disastrous effects on Italian production and income than the First. Equipment in industry was run down, and inventories were depleted. Agricultural production in 1945 was 65 percent of its 1939 value, industrial production 50 percent, and national income less than half its prewar value. Port facilities were almost totally destroyed, railway lines and rolling stock sharply reduced; the merchant marine lost almost 90 percent of its gross tonnage; roads and bridges were severely damaged. The housing shortage in 1945 was acute, especially in the major northern cities, where bombing had been particularly heavy. It is useless to try to estimate the cost of the war; it is easy, however, to imagine the suffering it caused.

Italy financed its war effort through loans from the central bank and through heavy borrowing from the public. Inflation had begun during the war, and by 1945 with extreme shortages of goods and materials and a swollen money supply the economy was threatened with hyperinflation. Prices remained stable through the first half of 1946 and then began to climb at an alarming rate. The immediate and crucial task of the government was to reduce the liquidity of the banks and the public.

Between 1947 and 1950 monetary policy operations by the government did manage to reduce liquidity and curb the inflation. New reserve deposits on commercial bank deposits were imposed in September 1947, and the Bank of Italy was given powers to enforce them. Access by the treasury to financing by the central bank was restricted. These and other measures had immediate effects on the money supply and total liquidity. The new reserve requirements in particular cut free reserves held by commercial banks from 110 billion lire to 3.2 billion. The rate of expansion in bank loans and deposits slowed, interest rates rose, and prices were stabilized. Inventory speculation was halted, and the public began to build up its cash balances. The money supply was allowed to increase at a moderate rate, but the impact was no longer inflationary. A brief decline did occur in industrial production at the end of 1947, but by February 1948 output began to rise again. The mopping-up operation was successful, and the costs in unemployment and idle resources were relatively minor.[21]

Italy's postwar boom dates from 1948. The performance of the economy during this period far outstripped that of any past period. Total real product grew at an annual average rate of 5.8 percent and per capita product at 5.2 percent between 1948 and 1960. It has been calculated that total fixed investment rose from 17.2 percent to 24.5 percent of GNP between 1950 and 1963, while saving rose from 18.1 percent to 22.3 percent.[22] Between 1950 and 1964, the total net capital stock almost doubled; its rate of growth was actually higher in agriculture than in industry, although housing grew most as a percentage of total net capital.

One of the most remarkable features of Italian economic growth after 1948 was its smoothness. Up through 1968, the swift expansion of the economy slowed in 1952, 1958, and 1963 to 1964; in each instance the slowdown was brief and relatively mild. Italy's steady growth was a result of stability in the level of domestic investment. While private investment in plant, equipment, and inventories fluctuated, public investment rose steadily and compensated for changes in the private sector. Thus, total fixed investment rose continuously between 1950 and 1963, declined slightly between 1963 and 1965, and resumed its rise again in 1966.

The governments in the postwar period were better equipped to deal with problems of growth and stability than they had been in the past. Changes in the structure of the financial system gave the government powerful monetary policy instruments. In addition, state-owned holding companies such as IRI, IMI, ENI (Ente Nazionale Idrocaburi—mineral fuels) and development organizations such as the Cassa per il Mezzogiorno (a government-run and funded institute established to finance and generally encourage economic activities in the south) gave the government useful tools with which to manipulate the allocation of resources and the level and composition of the GNP. These new instruments were used to achieve a variety of ends, in particular to preserve both rapid growth and reasonably stable prices.

Two long-term problems faced the postwar governments in Italy: the existence of high rates of unemployment and underemployment and, closely related, the economic backwardness of the south. The latter was still viewed as a regional problem, although it was finally understood that such regional imbalance had national consequences. Both problems manifested themselves in low levels of real income per capita among workers and peasants. Most government economic policies between 1950 and the present have been concerned directly or indirectly with the resolution of these two problems.

The government approached the development of the south directly: first through the creation of the Cassa in 1951, then through special loans and funds earmarked for particularly backward regions (Calabria and Basilicata) and finally through informal directions to the state holding companies to promote investment by their firms in the south. Although governmental attempts to reduce the disparity between real income per capita in the north and in the south were unsuccessful, heavy investments in the south at least kept the gap from growing as it had been since unification.[23]

The policies designed to combat unemployment and underemployment, especially in agriculture, were made part of the government's decision to promote rapid long-term economic growth. Throughout the 1950s and early 1960s, as a result of government policies, the money supply grew at a rapid average annual rate, while the treasury ran a deficit in every year between 1950 and 1961. The desire, unstated but clear, was to promote a high rate of investment to modernize plants and equipment especially in industry, thereby providing a growing number of jobs in high productivity occupations. It was estimated that in 1962 the capacity of the economy to create new jobs was approximately 500,000 to 600,000 per year, whereas in 1950 the capacity had been 200,000 per year. In 1962 the growth rate of new jobs exceeded by a ratio of 2:1 the natural growth in the labor force, whereas in 1950 the labor force had been growing at a more rapid pace than new job openings.[24]

Italy's monetary and fiscal policies were combined with direct expenditures to promote growth. The government gave funds to the state-owned holding companies but withdrew no dividends or profits. This policy served as a mechanism to redistribute income to promote industrial growth. In addition, the government encouraged the rapid depreciation of new investments in order to maintain a high rate of reinvested profits. The government's total expenditures rose swiftly between 1949 and 1966, both absolutely and as a percentage of national income.[25] A dramatic shift occurred in these expenditures: the most rapid growth occurred in expenditures for health, education, and welfare; the largest single item came to be public-works expenditures. Although the government still has not undertaken a major tax reform, various piecemeal changes in the tax structure have reduced the regressive nature of Italian taxation. But indirect taxes in 1964 still exceeded all other categories of taxes and accounted for over one-third of government tax revenue.

Government health and welfare policies were not designed to redistribute income among classes. The solution to the unemployment-underemployment-low-income problem was new, higher paying jobs. Old age, sickness, and disability insurance was designed to distribute risks among workers and income over time. For certain social insurance or welfare arrangements employers were expected to pay the premiums. These payment arrangements generally acted as substitutes for higher pay or reduced the total wage bill. Lump sum payments especially encouraged more intensive use of existing employees and discouraged increasing their number.

Postwar government economic policy was designed to facilitate economic growth; rapid expansion in exports and a widening of the domestic market for manufactured goods were the main elements in this growth. Exports took a leading role in promoting industrial expansion. World trade in manufactured goods almost doubled in the first decade or so after the war, and Italian exports of these goods increased at a much more rapid pace than total world exports.[26] Increased exports were particularly noticeable in the newer lines—metallurgy, machinery, and metal products; motor vehicles; and chemicals and synthetic fibers—in which technological change was most rapid. The newer industries' share of total exports rose from less than 50 percent to almost 60 percent between 1950 and 1963, and their share has continued to rise since then.[27] These branches of manufacturing accounted for an increasing portion of domestic value added during these years, and the growth of total production in these areas outstripped that in the more traditional branches. Not only did these industries' share of total exports rise, but a growing percentage of their total output was exported as well. It should be noted, however, that export sales of certain traditional goods also increased, particularly textiles and clothing.

Export expansion was a strong stimulus to investment in manufacturing and, indirectly, in the rest of the economy. While economists have been unable to establish a strong relationship between investment and productivity in companies with large export sales, they have shown that reductions in unit labor costs and export prices due to productivity increases were important factors in Italy's ability to increase exports.[28] Trends in world demand, domestic productivity, and prices all favored Italy's export sectors, while the economic policies of the government abetted industry in taking full advantage of these new opportunities.

Although it is impossible to evaluate here the significance of the European Economic Community, or Common Market, on Italy's economic growth, the pattern of Italy's trade does demonstrate the impact of the customs union on the country's imports and exports. Imports from EEC members rose from about 23 percent of total imports in 1957 to almost 35 percent in 1968, while exports to those countries almost doubled during the same period. The other countries of Western Europe and North and South America suffered most in terms of sales to Italy, and Italian exports to those countries declined proportionately. It seems likely that general reductions in world trade barriers had a positive influence on Italy's postwar growth. The common tariffs of the EEC on goods from other countries were lower than the ones Italy had prior to the creation of the customs union; Italian industry was thus faced with a kind of carrot-and-stick situation. A much larger market for Italian goods was freed from trade barriers, and at the same time Italian manufacturers received less protection from foreign competitors than they had previously. The results noted above speak for themselves. Finally, the Common Market reduced restrictions on labor mobility, enabling large numbers of Italian workers to migrate north to Belgium, Germany, and France. Their remittances helped Italy maintain a favorable balance of payments, and in cases of repatriation, their newly acquired skills represented a costless rise in the value of human capital.

Industrial growth in general far outstripped the expansion in agriculture. The annual average rate of increase in agricultural production between 1949 and 1964 was 2.4 percent; this rate, though the highest Italy had achieved so far, was below that of most countries in Western Europe. The growth rate peaked in 1953 and again in 1959. Both peaks were due to structural changes in production; the first was a result of reorganization and investment after the war, the second was due to a sharp rise in emigration and a reduction in subsidies given to soft wheat production.[29] Nevertheless, major structural changes must still occur in agriculture, accompanied by large investment, if this sector is to undergo an expansion similar to that experienced by industry. As in the past, the main restraint to growth in Italian agriculture is low productivity, particularly in comparison with other industrial nations.

In the immediate postwar period it was hoped that land reform and public investment in land reclamation and improvement would provide the push needed to begin a major spurt in agricultural production. By 1960 the government redistributed 673,000 hectares (about 1.7 million acres) of land and directly invested 43 billion lira in reclamation projects connected with the land reform.[30] Although improvements in productivity did occur on the redistributed land, the reform was too restricted in scope to promote a structural transformation throughout the agricultural sector. In addition, the actual policy of the government was to encourage people to leave agriculture and move into higher productivity jobs in industry. It was estimated that between 1950 and 1973 the labor force in agriculture would decline from 40 percent of the total to 18 percent—an annual average rate of decline of 2.6 percent.[31] With the removal of trade restrictions on agricultural products within the Common Market, Italian agriculture will have to specialize even more in the production of high-quality fruits, vegetables, and wine.

Although some economists feared that the recession of 1963 to 1964 was the prelude to a period of slower economic expansion, growth rates regained their earlier levels in 1965 and remained high through 1968. The slowdown was partly created by a restrictive monetary policy pursued by the Bank of Italy in an attempt to moderate price increases and to combat a worsening in Italy's balance-of-payments position. But the recession was short lived, and restrictive policies of the Bank of Italy were successful. In 1969 prices began to rise once again, investment in industry declined, money flowed out of Italy, and the balance-of-payments position was once again in jeopardy. That crisis resembled the earlier one, although the resolution of such problems seem more difficult than in the past. The rate of expansion in international demand has slowed, and the labor market in Italy has tightened considerably. Labor, in particular, has begun to force the government to face problems of distribution which it has previously avoided.

By 1970 it looked as if the south would play a strategic role in the nation's economic recovery and expansion. If the southern market continues to grow and if investment and income in the south continue to rise, it is conceivable that the region will take a leading part in the further economic expansion of the country.

In the 1950s and 1960s the south provided cheap labor, thus giving Italian goods an advantage on world markets. In the 1970s the economy may benefit from the expansion of aggregate demand in the south.

Italy must now confront some of the problems created by its own prosperity. Venice is becoming a casualty of industrial growth in the surrounding area. Rome, Florence, and other major cities have been seriously damaged by automobiles. Much of Italy's coast line is polluted to some extent by the wastes of industry and agriculture and the untreated refuse of municipalities. But pollution is only one of the country's problems. Economic growth has served as a panacea for a variety of economic ills including a highly unequal distribution of income, a regressive tax system, and an extremely low level of publicly provided social services. It appears that labor is increasingly impatient with a pie-in-the-sky rhetoric, and serious confrontations between labor and management (and the government) show no sign of abating. We are unable to predict how these problems will be resolved, but the present government, like most of its recent predecessors, is doing nothing. It is difficult to avoid comparing this sort of colossal inaction to the failure of liberal politicians to deal with the social and economic problems that confronted Italy just prior to the rise of Fascism.

STATISTICAL APPENDIX

The tables in this appendix provide some aggregate data on Italy's economic growth between 1861 and 1969. Strict space limitations forced us to keep the number of tables to a minimum. Data on the pattern and composition of Italy's foreign trade, on value added per man hour in industry for the years 1911, 1927, and 1938 to 1940, and value added by sectors are available upon request from the author at Scarborough College, University of Toronto, West Hill, Ontario.

Table 1

Average Annual Percentage Changes in National Income, Per
Capita Income, and Gross Private Product, 1861–1938, by Phases
(1938 values)

	National Income	Per Capita Income	Gross Private Product
Phase I (1861–63– 1885–87)	.7	.2	3.5
Phase II (1895–97– 1911–13)	2.2	1.5	2.0
Phase III (1920–22– 1925–27)	2.4	1.9	4.7
Phase IV (1926–28– 1936–38)	1.2	.6	1.1
Overall	1.2	.7	1.5

Sources: Percentage changes in national income and per capita income based on data
in Istituto Centrale di Statistica (Istat), *Annali di Statistica*, Serie VIII, Vol. 9, 251
(1938 values). Gross private product estimates were taken from *Annali*, 243–244.

Table 2

Gross National Product, Consumption, Investment,
Exports and Imports, 1949–1968
(1968 values, billions of lire)

	1949–51	Percentage of GNP	1966–68	Percentage of GNP	Average Annual Percentage Change
Gross national product	10611	100.0	42442	100.0	GNP 6
Consumption	8049	75.8	32839	77.3	
Investment	1970	18.6	8476	20.0	GNP per capita
Exports	1237	11.6	8174	19.3	5.7
Imports	1380	13.0	7048	16.6	

Sources: Istituto Centrale di Statistica, *Annuario Statistico Italiano*, 1951, 1952, 1968,
1969.

Table 3

Annual Average Rate of Increase of Gross Capital
Stock, 1881–1938, by Phases

	Total Reproducible Capital in Industry (percentage)	Total Reproducible Capital (percentage)
Phase I[a] (1881–1886)	3.2	1.8
Phase II (1895–97– 1911–13)	2.9	1.8
Phase III (1920–22– 1925–27)	2.4	1.7
Phase IV (1926–28– 1936–38)	2.4	3.1
Phase V[b] (1950–52– 1962–64)	3.5	3.9

[a] The data begin with 1881 so that it is impossible to calculate the rate of increase during the entire first phase. The annual average rate of growth is higher between 1881–1886 than it is for the first phase as a whole because of the moderate rise in economic activity during these years.

[b] 1950–1964 in 1964 values.

Sources: Ornello Vitali, "Nuova Stima Disaggregata dello Stock di Capitale in Italia," *Rassegna di Lavori dell'Istituto Nazionale per lo Studio della Congiuntura* (January 1968), Table 16.

NOTES

1. See, for example, Gino Luzzatto, *L'economia italiana dal 1861 al 1914*, Vol. I (Milano: Banca Commerciale Italiana, 1963), Chapter 1.

2. See Denis Mack Smith, *Modern Sicily* (London: Chatto & Windus, 1968), Chapter 51.

3. P. Ercolani, "Documentazione statistica di base," in Giorgio Fuà, ed., *Lo sviluppo economico in Italia* (Milan: Franco Angeli, 1969), Vol. III, Table XII.1.3.A. and XII.2.4. Unless otherwise noted, all statistical data and estimates in this chapter come from articles in Volumes II and III of Fuà's work.

4. The war years are excluded from this breakdown because of the special nature of wartime economic activity. The impact that Italy's two major wars had on postwar economic activity is included in the analysis. We must consider such figures as crude approximations. The choice of a base year to deflate prices incorrectly weights the product mix, the more

so the more distant the year in question from the base year. In addition, exclusion of price change may remove an element of quality change. We have excluded the years after the Second World War from the overall average since such a long-term average lacks any meaning.

5. Simon Kuznets, *Modern Economic Growth* (New Haven: Yale University Press, 1966), pp. 64–65. Unless otherwise noted, comparisons with other countries are from this book.

6. Based on data in Ercolani, *op. cit.*, Table XII.4.14.A.

7. On the creation of Terni and the government's role, see E. Guaita, "Alle origini del capitalismo industriale italiano: la nascita della *Terni*," in *Studi storici* (April–June 1970).

8. See Jon S. Cohen, "Italy: 1861–1914," in Rondo Cameron, *Banking and Economic Development* (New York: Oxford University Press, 1972).

9. The decline in the price of agricultural products and in production was not limited to Italy. It was a Europe-wide phenomenon caused, it seems, by the introduction of cheap American grains in European markets. In Italy, the crisis was prolonged and made more severe by the tariff war with France after 1887 since this closed the French market to Italian wines and other agricultural products.

10. Francesco Repaci, *La finanza pubblica italiana nel secolo, 1861–1960* (Bologna: Zanichelli, 1962). Most of my statements about government expenditures come from this book.

11. Rosario Romeo, *Breve storia della grande industria in Italia* (Bari: Laterza, 1963), p. 84.

12. Arnaldo Cherubini, "Profilo del mutuo soccorso in Italia dal origine al 1924," in Istituto Nazionale per la Previdenza Sociale, *Per una storia della previdenza sociale in Italia* (Rome: INPS, 1962).

13. In many cases capital for industry was available where it had been lacking in the past. In a sense, this brought the cost down from infinity to something more manageable.

It is necessary to comment briefly on fiscal policy in Italy during these years. As such, there was no fiscal policy, although government policies did influence economic activities in the private sector. That the government managed to run a surplus during many of the years between 1896 and 1914 does not mean that fiscal policy was deflationary. The budget which the government balanced was the one which included ordinary expenditures and receipts—it did not include many of the autonomous and semiautonomous institutions connected to the state, nor did it include movements on capital account or patrimony. Thus, while this budget was indeed balanced and gave policy makers more flexibility in debt refunding, the budget which represented total government activities was in deficit, as usual.

14. Gerschenkron's criticism of the tariff is based on this type of argument. See Alexander Gerschenkron, *Economic Backwardness in Historical Perspective* (Cambridge: Belknap, 1962), Chapter 4.

15. Felice Guarnieri, *Battaglie economiche* (Milan: Garzanti, 1953), I, 89–91.

16. Ingvar Svennilson, *Growth and Stagnation in the European Economy* (Geneva: U. N. Publications, 1954), p. 175.

17. See Robert E. Baldwin, "The Commodity Composition of Trade: Selected Industrial Countries, 1900–1954," *Review of Economics and Statistics* (February 1958), p. 54. It is worth noting that if international trade data were more detailed, they would probably reveal a sharp rise in the demand for synthetic textile fibers and for certain industrial chemicals.

18. Guarnieri, *op. cit.*, p. 114.

19. For a complete description of these changes see R. S. Sayers, ed., *Banking in Western Europe* (Oxford: Clarendon Press, 1962), Chapter 3.

20. On these policies, see Guarnieri, *op. cit.*, II, 86–92.

21. George Hildebrand, *Growth and Structure in the Economy of Modern Italy* (Cambridge: Harvard University Press, 1965), pp. 14–43, provides a lucid discussion of monetary policy during this period, as does P. Baffi, *Studi sulla moneta* (Milan: Giuffrè, 1965), pp. 133–317.

22. Robert M. Stern, *Foreign Trade and Economic Growth in Italy* (New York: Praeger, 1967), p. 7.

23. Public spending of this sort also contributed to the stability of aggregate demand. While total public investment varied inversely with private investment, public spending in the south, through the Cassa and other agencies, increased at a constant rate; see Hildebrand, *op. cit.*, p. 68.

24. Pasquale Saraceno, *Lo Stato e l'economia* (Rome: Cinque Lune, 1965), p. 22.

25. For data on government expenditure and revenue in recent years, see Istituto Centrale di Statistica (ISTAT), *Annuario Statistico Italiano*.

26. See Alfred Maizels, *Industrial Growth and World Trade* (Cambridge, Eng.: Cambridge University Press, 1965), p. 58; and Stern, *op. cit.*, p. 23.

27. For documentation of this trend, see Stern, *op. cit.*, pp. 85–90 and Luigi Bruni, "Analisi disaggregata dello sviluppo manifatturiero dopo la seconda guerra mondiale," in Fuà, *op. cit.*, III, 294.

28. See Stern, *op. cit.*, pp. 107–109 and A. Graziani, *Sviluppo del Mezzogiorno e produttività delle risorse* (Napoli: Edizioni Scientifiche Italiane, 1964).

29. The migration out of agriculture, especially in the south has not ended. In 1967 an average of over 12 percent of the total population of the regions of Calabria, the Abruzzi and Molise, and Basilicata emigrated

to northern Italian cities, to northwestern Europe, or overseas, particularly to Australia. The majority of these emigrants were agricultural workers. See Comitato dei ministri per il Mezzogiorno, *Studi monografici sul Mezzogiorno* (Rome: Istituto Poligrafico dello Stato, 1968).

30. Giovanni Marciani, *L'esperienze di riforma agraria in Italia* (Milan: Giuffrè, 1966).

31. P. Saraceno, *L'Italia verso la piena occupazione* (Milan: Feltrinelli, 1963), p. 174.

CHAPTER 9

THE ITALIAN LABOR MOVEMENT

Nunzio Pernicone

Italy experienced more labor agitation between 1968 and 1973 than in the preceding twenty years. Strikes and demonstrations followed each other in seemingly endless waves. Although terribly disruptive of normal routine, they became almost an integral feature of life in Italy. In Rome, for example, there was a certain telephone number that one could dial to find out who would be on strike that day. Virtually every category of worker struck at one time or another. In fact, journalists took crude pleasure in commenting that only the priests and prostitutes had not yet declared a strike.

This tendency to reduce labor trouble in Italy to the level of *opera buffa* is as misleading as it is cynical. For all the panegyrics written about the Italian "economic miracle," Italy has remained a poor country beset by an incredibly vast range of problems. When workers by the tens of thousands struck for higher wages, pensions, housing, schools, tax reforms, and so on, they were of course protesting the imbalances and failings that weigh most heavily upon the laboring classes of every industrial society. Yet there was more to the ferment stirring within the labor movement than the Italian workers' perennial struggle for material security. At the height of the turmoil in the "hot autumn" of 1969, Minister of Labor Carlo Donat-Cattin observed: "Today the workers are not asking for bread, but rather for more power, a greater participation, more equality and more dignity." [1] Donat-Cattin, a former union leader, was correct in differentiating between the mass movement of 1969 and the days "when the starving masses descended on the cities to ask for bread." Though no longer starving, the workers of Italy are continuing a quest for power, participation, equality, and dignity which has been at the heart of the Italian labor movement for more than a century. The brief

197

survey that follows will attempt to illustrate the course of this century-old struggle.²

No single year can be designated as having marked the birth of the Italian labor movement. Indeed, in the period before unification, there was no movement to speak of—only mutual aid societies. These were self-help organizations that provided workers with financial assistance for sickness, old age, burial, and so on. They did not concern themselves with wages, hours, and working conditions, and they abstained from any form of illegal action such as strikes. Although most of their members were craftsmen, the mutual aid societies were not restricted to any particular trade. They even included honorary members from the upper classes who provided leadership and financial assistance. By the end of the 1850s, there were over one hundred and fifty mutual aid societies in all Italy, ninety-eight of which were located in Piedmont.

The astute Piedmontese moderates understood that organizations preoccupied with self-help rather than social and economic reform were invaluable instruments of conservatism. Consequently, they also encouraged the first cooperatives, workers' congresses, and workers' newspapers—lest the initiative otherwise be seized by the radicals. It is surely true that Piedmont was the cradle of the labor movement. But, had it remained forever dominated by paternalistic representatives of the very classes most interested in maintaining the status quo, the labor movement would never have shed its swaddling clothes.

In the 1860s, inspired by the radicalism of Giuseppe Mazzini, a gradual metamorphosis began which ultimately gave birth to new forms of workers' societies whose interests and methods presaged those of modern trade unions. Mazzini's political and social doctrines constituted the first program of action offered to the working class. Whether accepted or rejected, his ideas provoked passionate debate. The result was a gradual awakening of the political and social consciousness of great numbers of the working class. This was Mazzini's greatest legacy to the Italian labor movement. Once aware of their own rights, needs, and potential strength, workers came to reject Mazzini's essentially political program, for it was unrealizable and had little to offer them. Furthermore, Mazzini's insistence upon class collaboration was recognized as a serious obstacle to working-class interests. Higher pay would never be forthcoming unless workers availed themselves of the means to force these concessions from their employers. Workers therefore resorted to strikes and demonstrations with increasing frequency during the 1860s, and many mutual aid societies began to transform themselves into Leagues of Resistance—the proto-unions of the 1870s and 1880s.

Once class conflict supplanted class collaboration as the guiding principle of the working class, the Mazzinian dream was doomed. In fact, by the early 1870s the rising militancy and class consciousness which the old conspirator had done so much to generate among the workers virtually assured the triumph of a new and formidable rival to the Mazzinian ethos. This rival was socialism.

Although socialism had taken root in Italy after the founding of the International Workingmen's Association (First International) in September 1864, the movement did not begin its ascendancy until Mazzini finally lost his hold over the young radicals. An Italian Federation of the IWA was founded in August 1872; and since the Italian Internationalists, with few exceptions, were aligned with Mikhail Bakunin against Karl Marx, they espoused the anarcho-socialism of the great Russian revolutionary. Marx, the sting of defeat having sharpened his normal propensity for vilification, described the Italian Internationalists in the following manner:

> The Alliance in Italy is not a "Workers League" (*Fascio operaio*), but a gang of *déclassés*, the refuse of the bourgeoisie. All the so-called sections of the Italian International are led by lawyers without clients, by doctors without patients or knowledge, by billiard-playing students, by commercial travelers and other salesmen, and especially by journalists of the minor press, of more or less dubious reputation.[3]

This description, repeated ad nauseum by Marxists and other detractors of anarchism, had little basis in fact.

The Italian Federation of the International was never intended to be an exclusively working-class organization because the anarchists' transcendent objective was the emancipation of all mankind, not merely the liberation of labor from capital. Membership was therefore open to anyone, regardless of class, but inevitably its leaders tended to be drawn from the bourgeoisie, given the backward state of the working class as a whole. Far from being misfits, Carlo Cafiero, Andrea Costa, and Errico Malatesta were men of great intelligence and ability. They were "declassed" in the sense that they had voluntarily severed all ties with the social class into which they had been born. But the rank and file of the International in Italy was unquestionably composed of genuine laborers and artisans, usually affiliated with the organization through mutual aid societies, *Fasci operai* (Workers' Leagues), Leagues of Resistance, and cooperatives. Concentrated mainly in Tuscany, Romagna, Naples, and Sicily, the organization had more than thirty thousand members in 1874.

Committed to the destruction of the state, capitalism, and religion, the Italian Internationalists thought in terms of immediate revolution, not gradual reform. They ascribed only minor significance to piecemeal gains, which are the primary focus of most labor movements. In their view, the working class would remain oppressed until the wage system itself was abolished and the means of production owned by the workers. Thus, while the Internationalists went to great pains to organize the workers into Leagues of Resistance, they believed that the main function of these leagues was to provide soldiers for the revolution. For these reasons the International's contribution to the growth of institutions and methods characteristic of modern trade unionism was limited in Italy. The International might possibly have done more in the labor sphere if the syndicalist tendencies present in embryo had had time to develop, an alternative precluded by the internal dissension and government persecution which combined to destroy the organization by 1880. But for all its limitations, the International, like Mazzini, did much to awaken the class consciousness of the workers, particularly in central Italy. Moreover, through its propaganda, its organizing, and even its insurrectionary attempts, the International succeeded in disseminating the ideas of socialism among a sizable segment of the Italian masses, thereby establishing a link between labor and the socialist movement which was never to be broken.

After the demise of the International in Italy, the axis of the labor movement shifted from the central regions back to the north, where industrialization was now accelerating and a modern proletariat beginning to emerge. Thereafter, the industrial triangle formed by Genoa, Turin, and Milan constituted the heartland of the labor movement.

It was among this young proletariat of the north that Italian labor's sole experiment in political exclusivism was undertaken. In 1882 the Partito Operaio Italiano (POI: Italian Workers' Party) was founded in Milan by Costantino Lazzari and Giuseppe Croce. The POI's starting premise was that the Italian working class had to emancipate itself by its own efforts, that is, without "bourgeois tutelage." Membership in the POI was therefore restricted to men with "calloused hands." The party's program called for action on two fronts: against the state and against capital. However, the actual demands of the POI were rather moderate: universal suffrage, the right to strike, legal recognition of labor organizations, profit sharing, public works projects for worker cooperatives, and so on.

Although sporadically active for nearly a decade, the POI never attained prominence as a political party. Far more successful were its efforts in the sphere of trade unionism. Through the League of the Sons of Labor, the economic arm of the POI founded in 1883, workers in Milan and other Lombard districts were organized along horizontal and vertical lines, that is, they formed nuclei of mixed occupations on a territorial basis which tended to section themselves into groups according to trade and industry. In this manner, the Sons of Labor established the foundation for the Chambers of Labor and the national unions that were to arise in Lombardy within the next two decades.

Intermittently persecuted by the government after 1885, the POI gradually overcame its resentment of "bourgeois tutelage" and drew ever closer to the socialists. Ultimately, in the oft-quoted words of Roberto Michels, "The Workers Party died neither a violent nor a natural death. With a slow organic process, protracted for an entire decade, it passed almost inadvertently into the Socialist party." [4]

The advances made by the labor movement in the 1880s were by no means limited to the industrial sector, for that decade also saw the rise of agricultural unionism. With leadership provided by middle-class professionals of radical and socialist conviction, the *braccianti* (day laborers) of the Po Valley organized themselves into Leagues of Resistance. These highly militant leagues launched innumerable strikes in the mid-1880s, but the landowners rejected every demand for higher wages, while the government tried to destroy the peasant organizations by persecuting their leaders and using soldiers to harvest the crops. Nevertheless, repression failed to achieve its purpose; by the 1890s agricultural unionism had become an integral feature of the labor movement. Moreover, the *braccianti* of the Po Valley—especially in Emilia—soon became the most impassioned disciples of socialism to be found anywhere in Italy.

Indeed, on August 14 to 15, 1892, representatives of the peasant leagues of the Po Valley, the Partito Operaio, and the middle-class intellectuals of the Milan Socialist League met in Genoa to found the Partito dei Lavoratori Italiani (Italian Laborers' Party). The symbiotic relationship developing between the socialist and labor movements thus achieved formal coherence in Italy's first socialist party.

Meanwhile, the creation of Chambers of Labor in 1891 had marked another great milestone in the history of the labor movement. The Chambers of Labor were central coordinating bodies for all the local unions and other working-class organizations of a given commune or province. The scope of their activities was extremely wide: strike control, conciliation of strike disputes, arbitration of disputes between workers and unions, organization and propaganda, education, medical and legal aid, research and statistics. Originating in Milan, Turin, and Piacenza, they quickly spread to many provincial capitals of northern and central Italy. By 1894 there were sixteen Chambers, claiming more than two hundred sections and forty thousand members. Thus the Chambers of Labor within only a few years became the nerve centers of the labor movement.

This precipitous expansion of the labor movement was abruptly halted when Prime Minister Francesco Crispi declared war on the Socialists and their allies (see Chapter 2, page 40). On October 22, 1894, he ordered the dissolution of the Partito Socialista dei Lavoratori Italiani—the name the party adopted from 1893 to 1895—and the more than three hundred workers' organizations affiliated with it. Party leaders, trade-union officials, and even ordinary workingmen were condemned to *domicilio coatto* (confinement) by the hundreds. However, after the reactionary tide receded with Crispi's fall in March 1896, the labor movement began to rebuild almost as if nothing had happened. This new round of activity and growth was abruptly terminated when the upheaval in Milan of May 7 to 10, 1898, known commonly as the *Fatti di maggio* (May Events), triggered another wave of repression even more extensive than that of 1894. But the labor movement once again demonstrated amazing powers of resiliency, and within two years, nineteen Chambers of Labor were back in operation. More important, Italy's experiment in political reaction was over with the fall of the Pelloux government (see Chapter 2, page 42).

When Giovanni Giolitti became minister of the interior in 1901 and then prime minister in 1903, a new era began in the history of Italian labor. Giolitti viewed the emancipation of the lower classes as an invincible movement, one common to all civilized nations. Past governments, he observed, had attempted to forcibly prevent the masses from acquiring their share of political and economic influence, but repression had only served to alienate the workers from existing institutions and to drive them into the waiting arms of the Socialists. Giolitti believed, therefore, that the state should remain neutral in conflicts between labor and capital. So long as their aims were economic and not revolutionary, Giolitti would permit the workers and peasants to organize trade unions and to engage in strikes without fear of repression. He told parliament on June 21, 1901, that "socialism can be fought against only on the field of liberty."

With the onset of Giolittian rule the Italian labor movement truly came alive. The whirlwind of strikes which swept the industrial and agricultural sectors in 1901 (1042 and 629 strikes, respectively) was completely without precedent; so was the increase in the number of new union organizations. Scores of local unions arose, many of them recruiting workers never before organized. Even more important, the need for stronger and unified organization was met by federating local unions of the same industry into national unions or federations. By mid-1902, there were twenty-seven national federations representing approximately 480,-000 workers. Half of this total was claimed by the National Federation of Land Workers. In the industrial and transportation sectors the most important federations were those of the metal-mechanical workers (50,000 members), the railroad workers (41,000), the construction workers (29,-000), the textile workers (18,000), the merchant seamen (12,000), and the chemical workers (6000).

The rise of national federations did not interfere with the expansion of the Chambers of Labor, whose number increased to fifty-five by late 1901, but jurisdictional and other disputes created a strong rivalry between the partisans of the two organizations. In the long run, although the national federations steadily increased their strength and jurisdiction at the expense of the Chambers, the latter always remained powerful centers of trade-union activity and the primary institution to which most workers paid allegiance. Not surprisingly, the deeper roots of this conflict within the labor movement were ideological, a reflection of the parallel struggle being waged within the socialist movement between reformists and revolutionaries, the syndicalists in particular.

According to revolutionary syndicalist doctrine, trade unions were both instruments of class warfare and the nuclei around which a stateless society would be constructed. Strikes were to be conducted incessantly, less for the conquest of economic gains than for the intensification of the class consciousness of the masses and the mobilization of their revolutionary drive. Ultimately, a chain reaction of strikes would culminate in one great "general strike," thereby accomplishing the destruction of the state and the expropriation of the means of production.

The syndicalists usually sought to control the Chambers of Labor. The Chambers were a logical target for infiltration because they held sway over a heterogeneous labor force, including many elements so poor and oppressed that they eagerly embraced a violent creed promising immediate redemption. Furthermore, since the Chambers could influence an entire local labor movement, they were in a perfect position to order the sympathy strikes that were the stock-in-trade of the syndicalists. The reformists, in contrast, usually controlled the national federations. Concerned with the day-to-day interests of particular categories of workers —groups which often tended to comprise the "aristocracy" of skilled workers—the federationists reckoned in terms of moderate and realizable economic conquests. Accordingly, they advocated temperate behavior, collective bargaining, and strikes only as a last resort.

In the end, the reformist current within the labor movement was to triumph over the revolutionary, but first the movement had to survive the syndicalist-inspired storms of 1904 to 1906. The most furious one was the general strike that brought Italy to a virtual standstill between September 16 and 20, 1904. Yet it achieved little, and the negative repercussions were enormous. The attempt to foment another general strike during the railwaymen's walkout in April 1905 had similar results. Far from energizing the workers, as the syndicalists maintained, these cyclone tactics merely constituted what Rinaldo Rigola called a "psychological depressant" that left many workers skeptical of both revolutionary syndicalism and reformism. This skepticism, combined with mounting employer resistance and the disillusioning spectacle of labor leaders at war with each other, plunged great numbers of workers into a state of utter demoralization. The net result was that by 1906 the labor movement had suffered a severe contraction. Tens of thousands of workers and peasants had abandoned their unions, federations, and Chambers.

In this time of crisis the federationists seized the initiative by convening a congress for the avowed purpose of establishing a national confederation of labor. In this manner, the Confederazione Generale del Lavoro (CGL) was founded in Milan between September 29 and October 1, 1906. The syndicalists quit the congress in the face of a reformist majority, which soon shaped the structure and policy of the CGL to fit its own outlook. Although the national federations, not the Chambers of Labor, played the dominant role within it, the CGL never became highly centralized, and the degree of control it exercised over its affiliates was always slight. On political issues, the CGL's attitudes essentially paralleled those of the reformist current within the Socialist party. However, the CGL zealously resisted political interference in labor matters, a task that became increasingly difficult after the maximalists (see Chapter 5, page 106) gained control of the party in 1912. The fact that the political and economic policies of the confederation remained permanently reformist in orientation was an achievement attributable in no small measure to the efforts of Rinaldo Rigola, the CGL's secretary-general from 1906 to 1918. Membership in the CGL rose steadily from the 190,422 registered in 1907 to 383,700 in 1911, but declined to 320,858 by 1914.

Though they were never able to displace the reformists as the dominant force in the Italian labor movement, the revolutionary syndicalists remained their strongest rivals in the prewar years. Among the urban blue-collar workers the syndicalists drew support from seamen and dockworkers, from certain sections of the engineering industry in Lombardy, and from railroad workers, although the important Federation of Italian Railroad Workers remained independent despite its ideological sympathy for revolutionary syndicalism. Also, there were periods (1904 to 1906) when they controlled the Milan Chamber of Labor, the most important labor organization in Italy. But they drew the bulk of their following from the agricultural day laborers of Emilia and the Romagna; the nerve center of their movement was the Chamber of Labor of Parma. There the activities of the revolutionary syndicalists were highlighted during the summer of 1908 by one of the most desperate strikes ever waged in Italy. This strike by the *braccianti* of Parma province collapsed only in the face of the employers' often violent resistance and the armed intervention of the police. Four years later, undaunted, the syndicalists formed the Unione Sindacale Italiana (USI) with the support of anarchists and revolutionary republicans. Imbued with an anarchistic hostility toward bureaucracy and hierarchical regimentation, they attacked the national federations, preferring to operate through the Chambers of Labor. In several northern cities the USI organized its own Chambers in order to compete with those dominated by the CGL. Claiming around one hundred thousand members at the time of its founding in 1912, the USI perhaps doubled its following by the outbreak of the First World War.

On the eve of war the revolutionary syndicalists were no longer the CGL's sole competitors; a Catholic trade-union movement, though a late arrival, had also established roots. Fear of socialism was the principal motive behind the Catholics' entry onto the labor scene, yet the Catholics found it enormously difficult to compete with the Socialists. In this regard they were their own worst enemies. Since 1874 the Catholic social movement had been dominated by the ultraconservative Opera dei Congressi (see Chapter 11, pages 258–261), whose old-guard leaders considered organizations composed exclusively of workers dangerous because they might foster class hatred. Instead, taking the medieval guilds as their ideal model, they stressed the collaboration of upper and lower classes in "mixed" corporations. Meanwhile, the Catholics had concentrated their efforts on creating mutual aid societies, of which 274 were under their sponsorship by 1891. In that year Pope Leo XIII's famous encyclical *Rerum novarum* condemning socialism and laissez faire capitalism gave moral support to the Christian Democratic minority's view that the only way Catholics could compete with the Socialists was to organize genuine labor unions. But the pope's highly equivocal pronouncement also urged the formation of "mixed" corporations of workers and employers. Thus Catholics made almost no attempt to organize trade unions during the 1890s, concentrating their efforts instead upon creating conservative labor institutions such as cooperatives, rural banks, and credit unions.

During the first three years of this century, 229 local unions were organized by Catholics. The Christian Democrats received a setback in 1904 when Pius X, the new pope, dissolved the Opera as part of the campaign to check the progressive elements within the church. Nevertheless, by 1907 the recently formed Economic-Social Union for Catholics of Italy injected new life into the movement, and within the next three years Catholic labor made its most significant gains. The overwhelming majority of Catholic unions were concentrated in northern Italy, 73.5 percent in Lombardy and Venetia in 1910. By 1914, two-thirds of their members were in agriculture. In the industrial sector Catholics had their largest following (41.5 percent) among the textile workers, two-thirds of whom were women. In agriculture, reflecting Catholic emphasis on the acquisition of property, the movement was supported mainly by small landowners, tenant farmers, and sharecroppers, rather than *braccianti*. Strikes were employed only as a last resort. Catholic unions remained under ecclesiastical control until 1919.

A numerically small labor movement divided into conservative, moderate, and revolutionary currents inevitably lacked the strength it might have possessed if united. Moreover, the negative effects of disunity were compounded by the antagonistic aims of the three major competitors: Socialists, revolutionary syndicalists, and Catholics often expended more energy combating each other than fighting for the interests of labor. Total trade-union membership in 1914 stood at 662,000 out of a labor force of more than 7 million; more than 90 percent of the potentially organizable workers and peasants remained outside the labor movement. Many problems inherent to the Italian masses were responsible for this situation—poverty (many workers could not afford union dues), ignorance, fear—but it can also be attributed in part to trade-union neglect. The CGL bears the principal blame in this regard for concentrating its attention almost exclusively (save the peasants of Emilia-Romagna) upon the labor aristocracy, the skilled workers of the industrial north. Working-class solidarity was therefore a fiction, and the labor movement suffered accordingly.

The structure of Italian trade unionism also left much to be desired. Despite their expansion after 1901, the national federations were still weak by 1914, and, worse, union locals did not exist. Nor was there adequate union representation within the factory itself; the employers fiercely resisted the creation even of grievance committees in their plants. Furthermore, the national federations had limited success in organizing those industries (textiles, clothing) which employed great numbers of workers. Small membership meant empty coffers, another crippling weakness. Without financial resources the unions were severely handicapped in their ability to bargain collectively because if recourse to strikes were necessary, the work stoppages could only be of short duration. Italian employers, whose standard arsenal included the blacklist, the lockout, and the scab, often deliberately provoked the workers into striking, knowing that after a prolonged struggle they would literally be starved into submission and the unions destroyed through bankruptcy. Finally, the weakness of the national federations perpetuated the horizontal organization of labor through the Chambers of Labor, the institutions most susceptible to infiltration and domination by revolutionary elements whose aims were political rather than trade-unionist.

Yet the Italian labor movement, for all its weaknesses, had made tremendous progress by the eve of the First World War: like Italian democracy, it was in the making. To have overcome the problems plaguing the movement at that time, many decades of peaceful development would have been required. Unfortunately, free trade unionism in Italy had only eight years of life remaining. In fact, once Italy declared war in May 1915, trade-union activities were extremely restricted for the duration.

And, like the rest of the country, the issue of entering and supporting the war divided and weakened the labor movement further.

The CGL willingly cooperated with the Industrial Mobilization Committees established by the government to minimize labor conflict in factories producing war materiel, thus counterbalancing socialist opposition to the war.[5] All labor disputes had to go before these committees for conciliation or arbitration. What made their decisions so binding, however, was the fact that all factories and personnel declared essential to the war effort came under military jurisdiction. Military codes do not recognize the right to strike; hence violators could be convicted of a variety of crimes ranging from abandonment of one's post to desertion. Particularly troublesome workers (usually revolutionary syndicalists, socialists, and anarchists), if not brought before a military tribunal, were often stripped of their draft exemptions and sent to the front. A more effective method for insuring industrial peace could not have been found.[6]

Bristling under the surveillance and harsh discipline of the military, workers in Italy's industrial centers found themselves toiling as many as sixteen hours a day by 1917. The scant consumer goods that were available could scarcely be bought, as inflation reduced the workers' real wages to 27 percent of their 1913 level. As these hardships multiplied, news of the March Revolution in Russia was received. Knowledge that revolution at last had triumphed somewhere in Europe stiffened the workers' will to resist and imbued the extremists with new hope. By the summer of 1917 unrest was spreading throughout central and northern Italy as protests against the cost of living escalated spontaneously into antiwar demonstrations and riots. The major eruption occurred in Turin, where the workers mounted a full-scale rebellion on August 23. Their pleas for support in the form of a general strike having been ignored by the CGL and the Socialist party, the Turin workers were crushed by the military and the police after a three-day struggle. The death toll has been estimated at anywhere between fifty and five hundred.

This bloodiest of episodes in the history of Italian labor was soon overshadowed by the two colossal events of late 1917: Caporetto and the Bolshevik Revolution. The military debacle at Caporetto, like the question of intervention, precipitated a crisis of conscience for many reformist Socialists within the party and the CGL. Ultimately, the stand taken by the CGL savored not merely of patriotism but of outright collaborationism; its official organ declared: "We may philosophize as much as we like . . . [but] when the enemy treads upon our soil we have only one duty: to resist." At the very moment the confederationists were rallying to the fatherland, however, the leftwing Socialists were hoping that the survivors of Caporetto would emulate their Russian brothers by deserting the trenches and turning their guns against the capitalist order. This aspiration had no basis in reality. The Italian soldier did not want to wage a revolution; he wanted to go home. Nevertheless, this vision of revolution was soon fortified by news of the Bolshevik triumph. Hereafter, the formula of the leftwing Socialists was *fare come in Russia*.

This obsession to "do as in Russia" did not infect the leaders of the CGL, whose outlook and program remained thoroughly reformist. A clash with the intransigents now directing the Socialist party was therefore inevitable. It came in July 1918, when the party directorate forbade the participation of the CGL and the Socialist deputies in a government commission for the study of postwar problems. Unfortunately, the CGL bowed before the command of the party's leaders. In protest against this encroachment upon the autonomy of the labor confederation, Rigola resigned as head of the CGL. Although his successor Ludovico D'Aragona was a competent man of reformist views, Rigola's departure constituted a serious loss for Italian labor.

Rigola's dramatic gesture clearly underlined the need for clarifying the relationship between the CGL and the Socialist party. This was presumably accomplished with the Pact of Alliance signed by the CGL and the party on September 29, 1918. But, far from a reaffirmation of the CGL's autonomy and independence as claimed, the pact merely revealed the degree to which the fate of the confederation was now inextricably linked with that of the Socialist party; the next four years would demonstrate at what great cost to Italian labor.

Revolution became the idée fixe of 1919, but the revolutionary expectations of the Italian working class were not necessarily synonymous with barricades and the millennium. To be sure, thousands of militant workers, stirred by the rhetoric of the revolutionaries, were eagerly awaiting the order to "do as in Russia." For others, the victories promised by the future were an eight-hour day, higher wages, grievance committees in the factories, or even workers' control. To an agricultural laborer the "revolution" was that piece of land promised by the government during the war. To a demobilized soldier the dream evoked by peace was perhaps a good job awaiting him at home. More often than not, the expectations of the working class in 1919 were not even articulated. The atmosphere they breathed was electrified, and the senses were alerted for a great change fated to come.

Whatever their expectations, many workers and peasants looked to the trade unions as the instruments to fulfill them. The result was an avalanche of new recruits. Within a single year, membership in the CGL soared from 249,039 to 1,150,062. By 1920 it reached the astonishing figure of 2,200,100. The Socialist labor confederation was not the only beneficiary of a burgeoning labor movement. The USI claimed eight hundred thousand members in 1920 and was deprived of even greater strength by the presence of the Unione Italiana del Lavoro (UIL), founded in May 1918 by the National Syndicalists (former USI leaders who had supported intervention in 1914). The UIL acquired a following of approximately two hundred thousand by the end of 1920. The independent railwaymen's union accounted for another two hundred thousand. The most impressive gains, however, were reaped by the Catholics.

In March 1918 Catholic laymen had created the Confederazione Italiana dei Lavoratori (CIL). The movement's primary objective was to challenge the Socialists for the allegiance of the working class with a progressive program. Within a year of its founding, the CIL had half a million members. By 1920 and 1921 its membership rose to 1.25 million, 80 percent of which was in agriculture. By securing the support of more members in the countryside than the CGL, the "white leagues" of the CIL effectively hampered any revolutionary alliance between the rural and urban proletariats.

Inevitably, the mushrooming of trade-union membership was accompanied by mounting aggressiveness on the part of the working class, spurred on by the material hardships and rising expectations of the postwar period. The problem of controlling this army of raw recruits, untutored in the disciplined tactics of trade unionism, was naturally enormous. Thus, in the highly volatile atmosphere of 1919 and 1920, when even veteran labor leaders cherished visions of a utopia about to be born, trade unions often found themselves enmeshed in titanic struggles that under normal circumstances they would never have dreamed of waging.

In 1919 disciplined trade-union activity ultimately gave way to violence. At first, fearing that resistance might provoke revolution, employers accepted the eight-hour day, which industrial workers had sought for thirty years. Another long-standing demand granted early in 1919 was the establishment of *commissioni interne* (grievance committees) in the factories. Then Italy was swept by a wave of demonstrations protesting food shortages and rising prices. Warehouses, shops, even cooperatives were sacked, government buildings occupied, and "soviets" set up. The Socialist party poured forth the rhetoric of revolution but made no attempt to channel these spontaneous outbursts in that direction. Usually the Chambers of Labor, which had done nothing to provoke these disorders, found themselves the only authority the masses would heed. They invariably urged calm. After the food riots finally subsided, the nation's attention was riveted on the general strike of July 20 and 21, 1919, called in protest against Allied intervention in the Russian Civil War. Again the revolutionaries preferred talk to action, but the fears of the bourgeoisie mounted steadily. The general strike was followed by land seizures in the Roman countryside in August 1919 and in Sicily during the spring of 1920. Led by Catholics rather than Socialists, the peasants involved were mainly returning soldiers who believed it was time that the government fulfill its promise of land.

The agrarian agitation in the south was mild compared with its counterpart in Emilia, Romagna, Tuscany, and lower Lombardy. The northern peasants were more militant and better organized. The CGL and CIL were in fierce competition and spared no efforts to retain the allegiance of their followers and to win new ones. Class conflict was most intense in Emilia, where the Socialist leagues and the Chambers of Labor had become so powerful after the war that they could sometimes dictate terms to the landlords. But they wielded their power so despotically that they fed the hatred of the entire propertied class, from the big landowner down to the small proprietor, tenant farmer, and shopkeeper. The Socialists of "Red Emilia" were not the only ones to earn the lasting enmity of the rural bourgeoisie. In the Soresina province of Cremona the Catholic peasant leagues led by Guido Miglioli fought so tenaciously to win laborers a share in the management of the large dairy farms that landowners came to speak of "white Bolshevism." The end result of this rural agitation was predictable: the landowners, as Gaetano Salvemini observed, wanted revenge against "serfs who had dreamed of becoming masters."

Postwar unrest reached a climax with the workers' occupation of many northern factories in September 1920.[7] The concatenation of events resulting in these occupations went back to the establishment of grievance committees in February 1919. Shortly thereafter, the communist *Ordine Nuovo* (New Order) group, led by Antonio Gramsci in Turin, initiated a campaign to transform these committees into factory councils (*consigli di fabbrica*). "The factory council," in Gramsci's words, "is the model of the proletarian state." [8] Thus they were not trade-union bodies, but revolutionary organs to train the workers in the communist management of the individual factory and ultimately of all society. By the fall of 1919, factory councils began to emerge in the metalworking plants of Turin. Union leaders of the Italian Federation of Metal-Mechanical Workers (FIOM) were wary of this new threat to their authority but could not openly oppose worker control of the factories. The FIOM eventually accepted the council movement, hoping nevertheless to moderate its radical tendencies.

In the spring of 1920, the FIOM, the Turin Chamber of Labor, and the *Ordine Nuovo* sought to win recognition of the councils from the industrialists. Determined to crush the council movement at all cost, the powerful General Confederation of Italian Industry (Confindustria) remained obdurate. The result was a general strike in Turin. After eleven days the strike collapsed in the face of employer resistance and the refusal of the CGL and the Socialist party to extend the strike to the rest of Italy. This was labor's worst defeat in the postwar period, setting the stage for the final disaster.

Encouraged by their victory in Turin, the industrialists were eager for any opportunity to further weaken the labor movement. It came the following summer when the FIOM presented new wage demands. In the face of refusal, the FIOM resorted to slowdown tactics rather than risk a new round of strikes which its empty coffers could not sustain. Hoping to force the union into striking under these difficult circumstances, the management of Alfa Romeo in Milan ordered a lockout on August 28, 1920. The FIOM, correctly anticipating that the lockout would be extended throughout the metalworking industry, ordered its members to occupy the factories on August 30. The occupations spread rapidly from Milan to Turin, Genoa, and other parts of Italy, ultimately involving hundreds of factories and a half-million workers.

Was the occupation of the factories the signal for the revolution so feared by the bourgeoisie? Gramsci's *Ordine Nuovo* group believed that in the absence of a general rising the Turin workers, if they left the factories and attempted to seize the city, would be isolated and crushed. Only the Socialist party and the CGL could carry out the revolution. The burden of decision, however, was placed on the leadership of the CGL. On September 10 and 11, 1920, the CGL National Council, declining the party's invitation to push the proletariat to suicide, voted against transforming the factory occupation into full-scale revolution. The workers, meanwhile, led by the factory councils, attempted with minimal success to run the factories themselves. The government, with Giolitti back at the helm, merely waited for the inevitable to happen. On September 25, 1920, the workers went home.

The occupation of the factories marked the beginning of the end for the Italian labor movement. Only one revolutionary in Italy had correctly assessed the situation, the old anarchist Errico Malatesta: "If we do not carry on to the end, we will pay with tears of blood for the fear we now instill in the bourgeoisie." Indeed, the Fascist squads were already exacting the price in full.

A counterrevolution against a revolution that never took place, Fascism set out to undo the gains so arduously won by the working class during the preceding forty years; the Fascists accomplished their mission by use of the bludgeon, the torch, and castor oil. Workers and peasants, fearful for their lives, abandoned their traditional labor organizations en masse. The losses sustained by the CGL testified to the efficiency of the Fascist onslaught: from a membership of 2,200,000 in 1920 to 201,049 in 1924. The other confederations suffered a comparable decline. Outright resistance having become impossible after 1922, the confederations attempted to continue functioning as best they could. But this proved increasingly difficult, not only in the face of Blackshirt violence but also because employer associations in 1923 and 1924 tended to exclude the free trade unions from negotiation and to sign agreements only with Fascist unions. In an understandable quest for self-preservation, workers began to drift into the Fascist unions in increasing numbers. In 1923, the National Confederation of Fascist Syndical Unions, headed by the ex-syndicalist Edmondo Rossoni, claimed a membership of 850,000. By 1924 and 1925, all attempts made by free labor unions to establish some sort of modus vivendi with the regime had failed. Free trade unionism was given the last rites by the Palazzo Vidoni Pact of October 2, 1925, and was buried by the Rocco Law of April 3, 1926.

Ultimately, far greater percentages of workers were organized in labor associations under Fascism than in the days of free trade unionism: 87 percent in industry, 70 percent in agriculture, 62 percent in commerce, and 77 percent in banking, according to official statistics for 1933. Total membership in Fascist unions reached 8,507,300 by the end of 1938. As early as 1926, the regime made it perfectly clear to employers that only workers belonging to Fascist unions were to be hired. Moreover, when the depression struck and employment of almost any kind was considered a blessing, membership in a Fascist union often meant the difference between subsistence and destitution. Thus the high levels of membership, far from indicating widespread support for Fascist labor associations, were another index of the Italian worker's ceaseless struggle to survive.

Since the primary function of the local unions under Fascism was to control the workers, important labor matters such as collective bargaining over wages, hours, benefits, and so on were handled by the national federations and confederations. Collective labor agreements negotiated between corresponding employer and labor associations at the national or provincial level were legally binding on *all* employers and workers of the given category. Certain minimums were thereby guaranteed (although circumvention was not uncommon) to the workers. For this reason national collective labor agreements are usually ranked among the regime's positive achievements. Yet the Fascists did not originate this system. The CGL had negotiated collective agreements in the agricultural sector before 1914 (especially for the *braccianti* of the Po Valley) and introduced their use into the industrial sector (especially the metalworking industry) in 1920. Had free trade unionism survived, the minimums guaranteed to the workers would certainly have been greater than those obtained under Fascism. In any case, the system of national collective agreements—inherited with few changes by the Republic—constituted one of Fascism's most important legacies.

Some might argue that labor's complete loss of freedom under Fascism would have been a tolerable price to pay if the regime had provided adequately for the well-being of the working class. But throughout the Fascist era labor endured one economic travail after another: the inflation of 1922 to 1926, the "stabilization crisis" of the late 1920s, the Great Depression, and the Second World War. Obviously, Mussolini was not responsible for worldwide disasters like the depression, but this fact brought little consolation to the 1,129,000 officially listed as unemployed in 1932, a figure that did not include agricultural laborers or self-employed craftsmen. Apart from emergency relief measures, Fascist economic policies were intentionally geared to insure that the major burden of hardship was borne by the working class. Until 1936 the government's answer to every new economic problem was invariably the same: wage cuts. But even thereafter, despite efforts in 1938 to raise real wages, these sank to their 1913 level and after a slight rise in 1939 plummeted during the war years.

The Fascist regime did introduce paid vacations, family allowances, and other fringe benefits for the urban workers, but charges for these benefits were withheld from the workers' weekly paychecks, and the benefits were distributed unevenly. Agricultural day laborers, whom the Fascists had hoped to convert into independent farmers, were worse off by the end of the 1930s than they had been before 1922. Not only were they ineligible for most fringe benefits, but also, because few of them could now emigrate, they glutted the limited labor market in the countryside, particularly in the south. In the final analysis, then, the regime's policies generally failed to improve the conditions of the working class and in many instances actually caused them to deteriorate.

The rebirth of the Italian labor movement in 1943 and 1944 coincided with the efforts of the Armed Resistance to bring about a national regeneration, sometimes called the "Second Risorgimento." The traditionally leftist workers of the industrial north made the greatest contribution to the Resistance. Their activities extended from the factories, where they subverted the Nazi-Fascists by means of strikes and sabotage, to the battlefield itself, where they fought in partisan units.

While factory agitation and partisan warfare flared in the north, labor leaders in the south returned to the task of rebuilding the free trade unions. In the spring of 1944, with the Germans still in control of Rome, the Socialist Bruno Buozzi, the Communist Giuseppe Di Vittorio, and the Christian Democrat Achille Grandi entered into negotiations that effectively committed their respective parties to a unified labor movement. On June 3, 1944, a Pact of Rome was signed providing for the same horizontal and vertical labor units that had existed in pre-Fascist days: a single national confederation, the Confederazione Generale Italiana del Lavoro

(CGIL), national federations, Chambers of Labor, and local and provincial unions. The pact also specified that the workings of the CGIL were to be based on the "fullest internal democracy," with proportional representation of the political minorities and free elections from below of all officials. The CGIL was declared independent of all political parties, but, good intentions notwithstanding, the professed principles of the Pact of Rome were violated at the very outset.

The circumstances of 1944 forced the relationship of the new-born CGIL to be one of dependency vis-à-vis the major anti-Fascist parties. A strong, democratic, and independent labor movement could not be created *ex novo*. The great tragedy that lay in store for the Italian working class was that the dependency and subordination of the labor movement to the political parties, unavoidable within the context of the anti-Fascist struggle, was to become a permanent state of affairs.

The reconstruction of the trade-union movement was accomplished within an amazingly brief period of time. By the summer of 1945 the number of workers enrolled in the CGIL exceeded three million. This massive influx of workers into the CGIL, occurring in an atmosphere bursting with revolutionary expectations, was reminiscent of what had taken place in 1919. This time, however, the factory workers and partisans (who still had guns) would undoubtedly have attempted a violent seizure of power. But such a course of action was vetoed by Communist leaders, who knew full well that any attempt at revolution would be crushed by the Allied armies. Nevertheless, while their official party line stressed cooperation with all parties in the reconstruction of a democratic and capitalist Italy, the Communists were not adverse to the idea of a gradual "backdoor revolution." [9]

The instruments through which this objective might ostensibly have been attained were the *consigli di gestione* (councils of administration), a latter-day version of the factory councils of 1919 and 1920. Ironically, it was Mussolini who had introduced these councils of administration into the northern factories as a last-ditch effort to rally the workers to his puppet regime at Salò. Although Mussolini's program for the "socialization" of industry was regarded as a hoax, the idea of worker control of the factories was tenaciously embraced. After the war, despite Catholic reluctance, the CGIL and the parties of the far left attempted to pressure the government into passing measures that would make the creation of the councils compulsory. These efforts proved futile. Perhaps five hundred councils came into existence, though they never functioned as originally intended. Gradually, as the Communists and Socialists were thrown on the defensive by 1947 and 1948, they abandoned the idea of using the councils as a means to control industry and manipulated them instead as political instruments. Once the political hegemony of the

Christian Democrats was assured by April 1948, the CGIL and the Communist and Socialist parties gave up on the councils altogether, and they rapidly disappeared from the factories. The "backdoor" to the revolution remained closed.

Meanwhile, the tripartite division of power laid down by the Pact of Rome no longer had any real basis in the CGIL; by 1947 Communist domination was already an accomplished fact. Nor could it have been otherwise. As even their enemies admitted, the Communists' talent for leadership and organization was unrivaled; Di Vittorio, for example, had transformed the general secretariat into a one-man operation. Moreover, their brilliant war record and their militant stand on labor issues assured the Communists the continuing support of the CGIL's rank and file. In the face of soaring inflation, the CGIL negotiated a number of interconfederal accords with Confindustria between 1945 and 1947 which brought the workers many crucial benefits (family and cost-of-living allowances, bread bonuses, and so on) in addition to wage increases. Thus at the Florence congress of June 1 to 7, 1947, where the CGIL claimed a membership of 5,735,000, the delegation strength was divided as follows: the Communists commanded 57.8 percent of the votes; their junior partners the Socialists won 22.6 percent; the Christian Democrats 14.4 percent; the short-lived Italian Workers' Socialist Party 2.2 percent; and the Republicans 2.0 percent. The Communists also controlled 80 percent of the Chambers of Labor.

The marriage of convenience contracted and consummated during the period of the Resistance had lost its raison d'être. By all logic the time had come for a split. But the same reasons that had held the CGIL intact since 1945 still restrained a secessionist movement: since the workers unquestionably desired labor unity, whoever instigated a split might lose their support at the polls. Political necessity required that the fiction of labor unity be perpetuated. At the same time, however, the Italian labor movement was transformed into a major battleground of an even greater conflict: the "cold war."

The CGIL, having become a *longa manus* of Soviet foreign policy, organized a seemingly endless wave of demonstrations, work stoppages, slowdowns, and general strikes throughout late 1947 and early 1948 for the purpose of compelling Prime Minister De Gasperi to reject the American aid forthcoming through the Marshall Plan. This campaign failed. Then, on April 18, 1948, the Christian Democrats won a landslide victory in the general elections. Once their political hegemony was assured, the Catholic faction within the CGIL had no further reason to fear the wrath of the workers should it secede. All that was needed was a pretext.

It came on July 14, 1948, when a young rightist student shot and wounded Palmiro Togliatti, the head of the Communist party. At six o'clock that evening the CGIL proclaimed a general strike, but this gesture merely recognized an accomplished fact. Workers by the tens of thousands had already massed in the piazzas, erecting barricades and occupying government buildings. In Genoa the demonstrations had assumed the proportions of a spontaneous insurrection, as ex-partisans patrolled the streets with weapons in hand. Whereas Communist leaders, hoped, at most, that the general strike might topple De Gasperi, the workers seemed anxious for a revolution. Now the Communists' principal objective was to regain control of their followers, since De Gasperi had warned Di Vittorio that unless the strike was called off, measures would be taken against the CGIL. On July 16, 1948, the CGIL executive committee issued orders to halt the strike.

For De Gasperi and Christian Democracy another decisive victory had been won. Ironically, the Communists, too, salvaged a victory from this near debacle. They emerged with their position at the head of a mass party intact and assured the perpetuation of their role as the major opposition party within the parliamentary system. Those for whom the general strike had constituted an unmitigated disaster were the workers. From this moment on, the Italian labor movement began a decline that would last for nearly twenty years.[10]

Between the late summer of 1948 and the end of 1950 the Italian labor movement split into three main confederations. On October 16 through 18, 1948, the Christian Democrats who seceded from the CGIL joined a section of Catholic Action devoted to worker education and assistance to found the Libera Confederazione Generale Italiana del Lavoro (LCGIL). Supported by the Christian Democratic party and plied with financial assistance from the United States government and American labor unions, it had an initial strength of perhaps six hundred thousand. A second secession involved Social Democrats and Republicans who, on June 4, 1949, founded the Federazione Italiana del Lavoro (FIL). No sooner was the FIL born than American and Catholic pressures were brought to bear urging it to fuse with the LCGIL. In February of the following year the leaders of the FIL, in flagrant disregard for the wishes of their own rank and file, decided upon unification with the LCGIL, which was achieved on April 30, 1950. The "new" organization, which also included a few autonomous unions, was called the Confederazione Italiana Sindacati Lavoratori (CISL); its main executive positions remained in the hands of Christian Democrats. By the end of 1950, the CISL claimed an official membership of 1,489,682. The third major confederation, the Unione Italiana del Lavoro (UIL), was founded on March 5, 1950, by the anti-fusionists of the FIL, who retained the allegiance of the overwhelming majority of its anticlerical followers. In addition, the UIL attracted a number of dissident Socialist leaders of such important national federations as the textile workers, chemical workers, and metalworkers. By the end of 1950 the UIL claimed a membership of 401,527.

Although certainly weakened as a result of the secessionist movement, the CGIL still towered over its young rivals in numerical strength, claiming a membership of 4,782,090 at the end of 1950. The losses sustained by the CGIL might have been far more severe—or, conversely, the gains of the CISL and UIL far more significant—had the new labor confederations impressed the CGIL rank and file as worthy alternatives. But the CISL, identified with the government and the church, was simply unable at this early stage to lure an appreciable number of workers away from the CGIL, apart from those who put their Catholicism before their class interests. A real threat to the CGIL might have come from the FIL, which initially promised to be a militant trade union rather than a tool of the Communist party or a lackey of the government. But thousands of potential recruits were lost the moment the FIL announced its imminent unification with the LCGIL. The petty wranglings between fusionists and antifusionists which followed succeeded in alienating many others. When the UIL finally emerged, its appeal as an alternative to the CGIL had already diminished considerably. As a result, many workers bore their dissatisfaction and remained in the CGIL. Others, angered at having been manipulated for political ends not related to their interests, disgusted by the opportunism of the secessionists, or disillusioned because "the Revolution" had failed to materialize, dropped out of trade unions entirely. Between 1947 and 1950 hundreds of thousands of workers may have taken this drastic step, thereby reducing the proportion of workers who belonged to unions to about 30 percent. Indeed, the worker apathy that dates from this period was to become as significant a cause of labor's weakness as trade-union disunity.

The factors causing the prolonged weakness of labor were numerous and omnipresent. The 1950s were the heyday of Christian Democratic hegemony, and the interests of labor were invariably among the government's lowest priorities. Worse than official neglect, labor suffered terrible consequences because trade unionism remained trapped in the vortex of the continuing struggles of the "cold war." For years the CISL was obliged to expend an inordinate amount of energy competing with the CGIL for membership in order to score political points for the Christian Democrats. The Communists, in turn, were preoccupied above all with maintaining and expanding their strength as a political party. The main function of the CGIL, therefore, was to serve as an instrument—a "transmission belt," in Communist terminology—for the party in its struggle for political ascendancy. The industrialists, too, found it expedient to politicize their relations with labor. In 1955, Ambassador Clare Booth Luce devised a policy whereby the "offshore" contracts awarded by the United States

Defense Department for the production of military equipment would be withheld from those Italian companies whose internal commission elections resulted in a vote of more than 50 percent for the CGIL. Although they hardly needed prodding to break the strength of the militant CGIL, companies like Fiat went to great pains to insure the decline of Communist representation on the internal commissions. In the end, Fiat and others exploited the situation to weaken labor generally, as the CISL discovered to its dismay.

Actually, by voting in accordance with the wishes of their employers, workers at Fiat and other companies were really voting for their jobs. Job security was the Italian workers' primary concern in the 1950s, and with good reason. Despite economic recovery and expansion, unemployment was chronic throughout the decade, with an average of at least 1.5 to 2 million workers out of work, a figure representing close to 10 percent of the labor force. Levels of underemployment were equally high. Thus, millions of workers enjoyed none of the fruits of Italy's "economic miracle." Others, those fortunate enough to have a job, enjoyed less than their fair share because real wages did not rise as much as productivity and profits. The result was that the Italians remained the lowest paid workers of any major Western European country. Under these circumstances, there was no way workers could engage in protracted economic strikes to improve their lot. The funds for such action were simply lacking, and the possibility of being replaced by someone eager for any job was great. Mutually reinforcing, low wages and unemployment made for a very docile labor movement.

Besides political rivalry, employer resistance, financial penury, and unemployment, another important factor that contributed to the weakness of labor in the 1950s was "the proclivity . . . to organize itself from the top downward under predominantly horizontal rather than vertical leadership," a tendency which Maurice Neufeld considers "the central defect of unionism in Italy." [11] The organizational units described in connection with the founding of the CGIL still existed in the 1950s, except that now the entire system had been reproduced in triplicate. Given the political orientation of postwar trade unionism, the confederations insured the continuance of a centralized organization with power concentrated at the top. This power was administered through those traditional centers of political influence, the provincial Chambers of Labor. The national federations and their subdivisions, save for rare exceptions like the metalworking industry, remained weak and dependent upon the parent confederation. But the real Achilles heel of trade-union organization was at the local and plant level, where no effective organs existed at all. The councils of administration had disappeared by 1950. The internal commissions, originally endowed with important functions, were viewed by the confederations as potential rivals for the allegiance of the workers; hence, they were often stripped of any real power. The employers, too, were intransigently hostile to the commissions. They either refused to allow them in the factories or, like Fiat, they attempted to manipulate them as foils against the unions. All the fanfare devoted to the elections of the internal commissions was much ado about nothing. A campaign initiated by CISL in 1953 and supported by CGIL after 1956 to establish factory unions unfortunately bore negligible results.

What made the whole question of local units so vital was the unique system of collective bargaining employed in Italy during the 1950s. Labor confederations and employer associations, such as Confindustria, would negotiate what are termed "interconfederal accords." Until 1954, the interconfederal accords applied to virtually everything: dismissals, the sliding-scale mechanism for cost of living adjustments, internal commissions, and even wages. Between 1954 and 1962 collective bargaining between the confederations and Confindustria focused more on national agreements for every occupational category, establishing minimum wage rates and working conditions for entire branches of industry (metalworking, chemicals, textiles, and so on). Agreements of this type, binding only on employers who signed them, reflected the cost conditions of the least efficient and marginal producers, thereby assuring great profits for the large and powerful firms. Worse, the unions had no means—in the absence of effective local units—either of improving upon these national agreements or even of insuring their enforcement. Employer violation of agreements was usually widespread. In sum, the system of interconfederal accords and industry-wide agreements did not secure adequate wages and conditions for the Italian workers.

Although in the 1950s the CISL and the UIL wanted to supplement industry-wide agreements with plant-level bargaining, not until 1962 and 1963 did trade unions and employers shift from the system of exclusively national bargaining to a new system known as "articulated" bargaining. As first employed in the metalworking industry, articulated bargaining involved three separate levels: (1) the national level, which provided for agreements applicable to the whole industry, usually covering issues not determined at other levels; (2) the sectorial level (iron and steel, automobiles, electrical engineering, and so on), each with different regulations concerning minimum wages, hours, and classification of worker categories; and (3) the plant level, which allowed bargaining for piecework rates, job evaluation, and productivity bonuses. Within two years of the metalworkers' victory, the system of articulated bargaining spread to other industries and has since become an accepted pattern of negotiation. Although interconfederal accords have become a thing of the past, industry-wide agreements have remained a typical feature of Italian collective bargaining. Plant-level negotiations, although increasing in number and scope, are still a bone of contention between employers and unions.[12]

The introduction of new methods of collective bargaining was only one manifestation of the resurgence experienced by the labor movement in the early 1960s. This resurgence was a direct outcome of the economic boom of 1959 to 1963 and the favorable political climate that came with the "opening to the left" and the formation of a center-left government.

As industrial expansion in the early 1960s reached unprecedented heights, unemployment shrank to around 3.6 percent of the labor force in 1963, as opposed to 10 percent during much of the 1950s. A shrinking labor supply actually forced wages up by 80 percent between 1958 and 1964. Job security and decent wages brought about a profound change in the psychology of the workers. No longer demoralized by fear of unemployment, workers grew increasingly militant and willing to strike. Moreover, higher pay and employment for perhaps several members of a family meant that strike funds could be accumulated, thereby enabling the workers to engage in protracted strikes that put effective pressure on their employers. This new-found zeal was not diminished by the recession of 1963 and 1964. On the contrary, having at last tasted the fruits of Italy's "economic miracle," workers were more determined than ever to fight for still greater gains.

In this atmosphere of rising expectations and working-class militancy, Italian trade unionism at last emerged from the doldrums of the 1950s. But to become truly effective in the changing world of the 1960s, the trade unions had to undergo a thorough transformation in ideas and policies. Above all, the unions now had to contend with a new generation of workers. Expanding industry had absorbed great numbers of peasants, southern immigrants, and women. These new elements, together with young northern workers, were less ideologically oriented than the older generation of trade-union and party militants who had formerly comprised the vanguard of the labor movement. The political trade unionism of the past had little appeal to a young generation of workers who were primarily concerned with their own economic and social improvement. Consequently, only those unions that could produce positive results on this level would enjoy the support of the "new workers."

The CISL and the UIL had a head start on the CGIL in this regard. Since the mid-1950s, they had concentrated mainly on bread-and-butter issues, usually by attempting to supplement industry-wide contracts with plant-level agreements on such essential items as productivity bonuses, incentive payments, and job evaluation. For this reason, among others, the CISL increased its membership by approximately eight hundred thousand between 1950 and 1958. In contrast, the CGIL in the early 1950s had neglected many important economic issues, such as the *conglobamento* of 1954 (a nationwide salary agreement), and had strenuously opposed plant-level agreements as a capitulation to capitalist ideology which undermined working-class solidarity. Neglect of worker interests at the plant level, plus the repercussions of the Soviet Twentieth Party Congress and the crushing of the Polish and Hungarian revolutions, resulted in a loss of nearly a million members between 1956 and 1958. But the CGIL was able to recoup these losses within a few years by adapting itself to the trends already established by its rivals and by devoting considerable attention to plant-level problems. Once the three confederations began striving for similar objectives, they found it possible to collaborate for the first time in a decade. Their parallel efforts now gravitated in two directions: toward the employers, from whom they sought to win even greater gains for their members, and toward the government, which they sought to pressure into granting labor a bigger voice in long-range economic planning. This concern with long-range planning was one important manifestation of labor's mounting insistence upon playing a greater role in the economic, social, and political life of Italian society.

But a greater role in Italian society continued to elude the trade unions as long as they remained subordinate to political parties. Over the years both the CGIL and the CISL had become increasingly self-conscious about their reputation for political subservience. As early as 1956, Di Vittorio called for the "definitive liquidation of the theory of the 'transmission belt' " which had governed relations between the CGIL and the Communist party. Nevertheless, while many Communist trade unionists chafed under the yoke of the party, trade-union autonomy did not become a real issue until the leftwing Socialists joined the center-left government in 1963. Now the possibility of these Socialists' abandoning the CGIL was a threat that had to be taken seriously. Therefore, by 1965 the principle that leadership in the CGIL should be incompatible with party office was accepted, though not yet put into practice. With the CGIL progressing along these lines, the CISL—no less open to the charge of being a "transmission belt"—was also compelled to change its image. However, in contrast to the CGIL, ever since the early 1950s the CISL had had within its ranks a group (centered around the young leaders from the confederation's training school in Florence) that strenuously supported the position that political office was incompatible with trade unionism. Eventually, the principle of incompatibility also gained ascendancy within the Catholic confederation.

Actually, the developments of the early and mid-1960s had provided only a surface glimpse of the profound metamorphosis the labor movement was experiencing. Thus, few observers—among the employers, the government, or even the trade unions—anticipated the veritable cyclone of strikes and demonstrations which swept Italy in 1968 and 1969. Once the fury subsided enough to permit a backward glance, a stunning discovery was made: labor had emerged as a major power in Italian society.

The driving force behind the labor movement's great march forward was the "new workers." Determined to win a strong position in the Italian power structure, the workers threw down the gauntlet to both employers and labor leaders when in early January 1968 they rejected a union-negotiated contract with the Pirelli rubber company. The campaign was led by new groups, known as the Comitati Unitari di Base (Unitary Base Committees), which had sprung up at the Pirelli plant outside of, and in opposition to, the trade-union organizations. Many of the activists in the base committees were young southerners employed at the most arduous jobs. Frustrated, angry, and tough, they exuded a kind of populist radicalism that labor had not seen for decades. Neither employers nor union leaders could control the base committees as they spread from factory to factory, stimulating the workers to action. Experts believe, however, that radical students sparked the full-scale agitation of that fall by contacting the workers through the base committees.[13] The ensuing dialogue unquestionably increased the workers' awareness of the larger context of their problems. But, perhaps most important, the student movement, by desecrating the sanctity of authority, had shown the workers that there were alternative methods, outside the institutionalized channels, for challenging the power relations in Italian society. In the end, the workers followed their unions rather than the students, but this brief exposure to novel ideas and methods resulted in mounting support for the base committees. Thus, by the end of 1968, the committees at Pirelli won a new contract that was considerably better than the earlier one negotiated by the unions. Elsewhere, the base committees continued to bypass the unions and to engage in innumerable wildcat strikes during the spring of 1969, often so vehemently that employers were forced to negotiate with the radicals and give in to their workers' demands.

The labor confederations quickly closed ranks in the face of this threat to their authority and succeeded in circumscribing the influence of the base committees. Nevertheless, in order to maintain their hold over the workers, the unions had to outperform these committees. The year 1969 gave them ample opportunity to do so because dozens of national contracts were due for renegotiation in the metalworking, chemical, and construction industries. Once united in action, the unions discovered themselves to be stronger than they had ever imagined. Indeed, the ensuing wave of strikes and demonstrations under union leadership was so overwhelming during the "hot autumn" of 1969 that by the end of the year labor emerged victorious on every front. Among others, its gains included large pay increases, reduction of working hours, the abolition of the discriminatory wage-zone (regional) system, and the right to call factory meetings. According to one employer, the right to hold meetings in the factory—which would strengthen labor organizations at the local level—meant "a new era in labor relations."

The years 1968 and 1969 unquestionably did mark the beginning of a new era for the labor movement in Italy. Tremendous pressures accumulated at the base of the labor movement during those tumultuous years, pressures that accelerated the process of internal transformation already evident in the early 1960s. Thus far, the most significant results of this continuing transformation have been preliminary steps in the direction of trade-union autonomy and unification.

Central to the whole question of autonomy was the principle of incompatibility. According to this principle, no trade-union official can hold political office or a directive post in a political party. This does not mean that Italian trade unionism must cease to be political; even without external political ties of an official nature, unions may continue to pursue an active political role because so many of labor's demands (pensions, public housing, tax reforms, and so on) involve changes only the national government can make.

By 1968 the confederations could no longer pay mere lip service to the principle of incompatibility as they had done in the 1950s lest they risk compromising their integrity in the eyes of the workers. At their respective national congresses in 1969, each confederation officially approved the principle of incompatibility, and most trade-union officials subsequently resigned from parliament. Another step toward political autonomy was the mutual decision not to participate in the electoral campaign preceding Italy's first regional elections in June 1970. Of the three confederations, the UIL was the most reluctant to sever its political ties. The CGIL, though willing to deem elected office incompatible, hedged on applying the principle to directive office in political parties. In contrast, the CISL appears to have made the greatest strides toward autonomy, some authorities claiming that it is now independent of the Christian Democratic party. But it is exceedingly difficult to determine the genuine realities behind the facade of official pronouncements; this holds true for all three confederations.

For most Italian workers, labor unity is probably a more important issue than autonomy. Because the victories of the "hot autumn" of 1969 were so clearly the result of the unity-of-action policy pursued for the first time at the national level by the CGIL, CISL, and UIL, workers and trade unionists alike became inspired with hope for the eventual reunification of the three confederations. This desire for unity is especially intense among the younger generation of workers and labor leaders, who view the divisions as a political anachronism serving only to diminish the potential strength of organized labor. The metallurgical industry is the best case in point. Reflecting a growing tendency for militant national federations to bypass the more cautious confederations, the metal-mechanical unions (FIOM, FIM, and UILM) were unwilling to relinquish the influence and strength derived from the common front forged in 1969, and they continued thereafter to make remarkable headway toward achieving autonomy, democratization, and unity. Many experts in 1972 regarded the unification of the metal-mechanical unions as an accomplished fact.

That progress toward unification at the confederal level should have proceeded slowly is hardly surprising in light of the bureaucratic inertia and irrepressible politicism of the three major confederations.[14] The leadership of the CISL, in opposition to a majority within its own ranks, opted to move cautiously. Thus, at the beginning of 1970, Bruno Storti, the CISL secretary general, advocated "experimentation" with the effective possibilities of labor unity by intensifying the existing trend toward unity of action. Even more resistant to the prospect of unification was the UIL. The Social Democrats within the UIL, determined to fight the Communists on every conceivable issue, threatened to break away and form their own organization if unity was effected. Only the CGIL, which obviously stood to gain the most, had been outspoken in its support for unification. Finally, on October 26, 1970, the general committees of the three confederations met in Florence to discuss the issue, and the conference ended with a joint declaration (opposed by the Social Democrats) advocating future unification.

Despite official pronouncements, at the beginning of 1971 the likelihood of unification at the confederal level seemed still very remote. Nevertheless, within the next year and a half, a host of factors—fiscal instability, spiraling inflation, rising unemployment, the fall of the center-left government, and the advance of neo-Fascism—combined to rouse top labor leaders from their complacency and intransigence. Threatened by a deteriorating economic and political situation, they realized that labor would again face hard times unless the movement succeeded in consolidating its new-found strength. Thus on July 24, 1972, the three confederations signed a pact creating the Federazione CGIL-CISL-UIL. Structured vertically and horizontally at the national, regional, and provincial levels, the Federazione has two governing bodies: a directorate and secretariat composed of 90 and 15 members respectively, the three confederations being equally represented. Included as members of the secretariat were the secretary generals Luciano Lama of the CGIL, Bruno Storti of the CISL, and Raffaele Vanni of the UIL. Although the Federazione was entrusted with not inconsiderable responsibilities on paper, real power remained in the hands of the confederations. At best, therefore, the formation of the Federazione CGIL-CISL-UIL represented only an intermediary step toward genuine unification, a step hardly commensurate with the pressing needs of the workers.

Thus the Italian labor movement stood at the crossroads in the early 1970s. A new era in which labor could realize its full potential seemed possible only if autonomy, democratization, and unity were achieved. Short of attaining these objectives, experts feared that the labor movement would be thrown into retreat. Given the disasters that have befallen the movement in the past and the myriad problems that will confront it in the future, one can understand why the Italians were not optimistic. Meanwhile, at the time of this writing, the strikes and demonstrations continued unabated. The Italian workers were still fighting for a position of real power, equality, and dignity in modern technological society.

NOTES

1. Quoted in an interview between Carlo Donat-Cattin and Gianni Baldi; cf. "Beyond the Labor Conflict, What's Next," *Successo*, Yr. 11, No. 10 (October 1969), 56.

2. Limitations of space require that the documentation for this essay be kept to a minimum. Those books which have been relied upon most heavily for basic information are the following: Rinaldo Rigola, *Storia del movimento operaio italiano* (Milan: Editoriale Domus, 1947); Roberto Michels, *Storia critica del movimento socialista italiano dagli inizi fino al 1911* (Florence: Società An. Editrice "La Voce," 1926); Maurice F. Neufeld, *Italy: School for Awakening Countries* (Ithaca: New York State School of Industrial and Labor Relations, Cornell University, 1961); Daniel L. Horowitz, *The Italian Labor Movement* (Cambridge: Harvard University Press, 1963); Humbert L. Gualtieri, *The Labor Movement in Italy* (New York: Vanni, 1946); Joseph La Palombara, *The Italian Labor Movement: Problems and Prospects* (Ithaca: Cornell University Press, 1957); Alfredo Gradilone, *Storia del sindacalismo* (Milan: Giuffrè, 1959), Vol. III, Parts 1 and 2; Christopher Seton-Watson, *Italy from Liberalism to Fascism, 1870–1925* (London: Methuen, 1967). Unfortunately, none of the major accounts listed above traces the history of Italian labor beyond 1962. For the early and mid-1960s, see Norman Kogan, *A Political History of Postwar Italy* (New York: Praeger, 1966); H. Stuart Hughes, *The United States and Italy*, rev. ed. (New York: Norton, 1965); Donald L. M. Blackmer, *Unity in Diversity: Italian Communism and the Communist World* (Cambridge: The M.I.T. Press, 1968); F. Roy Willis, *Italy Chooses Europe* (New York: Oxford University Press, 1971). For information concerning Italian labor in the late 1960s and early 1970s, the reader must consult the periodical literature. See, for

example, the following articles: Giorgio Lauzi, "Tre nodi per il movimento sindacale," *Il Ponte*, Yr. 25, No. 4 (April 1969), 515–520; Giorgio Lauzi, " 'Stagione dei contratti' e unità sindacale," *Il Ponte*, Yr. 25, No. 11 (November 1969), 1382–1384; Fabrizio Cicchitto, "Classe operaia, sindacati e partiti all'inizio degli anni settanta," *Il Ponte*, Yr. 26, No. 1 (January 1970), 25–50; Giorgio Lauzi, "Sindacati e unità: Non è più tempo di sperimentare," *Il Ponte*, Yr. 26, No. 2 (February 1970), 188–190; Giorgio Lauzi, "La 'punta' dei metalmeccanici," *Il Ponte*, Yr. 26, No. 3 (March 1970), 333–335; Alberto Asor Rosa, "Tesi sul dopo-autunno," *Il Ponte*, Yr. 26, No. 3 (March 1970), 350–362; Bruno Di Pol, "Problems of the Italian Labor Movement," *New Politics*, 2, No. 2 (Winter 1963), 132–139; Gino Giugni, "Recent Developments in Collective Bargaining in Italy," *International Labour Review*, 91, No. 4 (April 1965), 273–291; Wilton Wynn, "Behind the Current Labor Troubles in Italy Is a Drive for Radical Social Change," *Fortune*, 81 (January 1970), 51, 54; Donato Speroni, "Will Discount Rates Cause a Strike, Too?" *Successo*, Yr. 11, No. 10 (October, 1969), 62–64, 158; Ettore Massacesi, "Unionism's Deceptive Triumph," *Successo*, Yr. 11, No. 11 (November 1969), 75–76, 78; Donato Speroni, "The New Workers," *Successo*, Yr. 12, No. 3 (March 1970), 76–78, 80; Giorgio Galli, "Extreme Trade Unionism: An Infantile Disorder," *Successo*, Yr. 12, No. 6 (June 1970), 71–72, 74; Donato Speroni, "Are the Unions Running Wild?" *Successo*, Yr. 12, No. 8 (August 1970), 42–45; Donato Speroni, "Liberty, Equality, Comfort," *Successo*, Yr. 13, No. 1 (January 1971), 54–57.

3. *Ein Complot gegen die Internationale Arbeiter-Association. Im Auftrage des Haager Congresses verfasster Bericht über das Treiben Bakunin's und der Allianz der socialistischen Demokratie* (Braunschweiger, 1874), in Karl Marx and Friedrich Engels, *Werke* (Berlin: Dietz Verlag Berlin, 1962), XVIII, 382–383.

4. Michels, *op. cit.*, pp. 95–96.

5. Alfonso Leonetti, *Mouvements ouvriers et socialistes (chronologie et bibliographie): L'Italie (des origines à 1922)* (Paris: Les Editions Ouvrières, 1952), p. 126.

6. Guido Neppi Modona, *Sciopero, potere politico e magistratura 1870/1922* (Bari: Laterza, 1969), pp. 197–201.

7. The standard account of the occupations is Paolo Spriano, *L'occupazione delle fabbriche, settembre, 1920* (Turin: Einaudi, 1964); see also the special issue of *Il Ponte*, Yr. 26, No. 10 (October 1970), entitled *1920. La grande speranza: L'occupazione delle fabbriche in Italia.*

8. *Opere di Antonio Gramsci* (Turin: Einaudi, 1954), IX, 37, as quoted in John M. Cammett, *Antonio Gramsci and the Origins of Italian Communism* (Stanford: Stanford University Press, 1967), p. 82.

9. The expression is Neufeld's, *op. cit.*, p. 463.

10. On this very controversial issue, I have relied upon the interpretation of Giorgio Galli; see his *La sinistra italiana nel dopoguerra* (Bologna: Il Mulino, 1958), pp. 196–238 *passim*.

11. Neufeld, *op. cit.*, p. 502.

12. Information on collective bargaining in Italy is extremely scarce. My account is based entirely upon the article by Gino Giugni, "Recent Developments in Collective Bargaining in Italy," *International Labour Review*, 91, No. 4 (April 1965), 273–291.

13. See Fabrizio Cicchitto, "Classe operaia, sindacati e partiti all'inizio degli anni settanta," *Il Ponte*, Yr. 26, No. 1 (January 1970), 30–31.

14. It should be remembered that the three confederations do not include the independent unions of teachers and civil servants. Also, by the spring of 1972, the neo-Fascist Confederation of National Workers' Syndicates claimed a membership of half a million.

PART III

INTELLECTUAL, RELIGIOUS, AND CULTURAL DEVELOPMENTS

More than any other nation the Italians considered themselves the direct heirs of the ancient Greeks and Romans. This heritage was most obvious in the Roman Catholic church, in the arts, and in formal education. Italians gave the church its lasting form during the Middle Ages. With their Renaissance they were also the first to initiate a classical revival as the basis for the intellectual and cultural modernization of the Western world. Unfortunately the heritage of their illustrious past became a burden after the nation was finally unified politically. In education it continued to foster an outlook ill-suited to the needs of a modern industrial society. In the church it hindered the loosening of traditional shackles on individual and social development. And in Fascist party rhetoric it led to the disastrous delusion that the Roman Empire could be recreated with the inadequate means available to Mussolini. Although most of Italy's intellectuals beginning with the Risorgimento believed that their country had to seek a new basis for its "primacy," they have never been able to agree on what this should be. Also, as in other modernizing countries, they have remained divided between mandarins and activists, leftists and rightists, thus dissipating what moral authority they might have had as an elite.

The following four chapters deal with various intellectual, religious, and cultural efforts to cope with a changing world. Edward R. Tannenbaum describes the ways in which traditional bourgeois values have dominated all levels of Italy's educational system from the mid-nineteenth century to the 1960s. As elsewhere, Italy's elementary schools tried to integrate the masses into the national society by fostering literacy and good citizenship, but with less success in the countryside than in urban areas. According to Tannenbaum, the recent crisis in Italian higher and secondary education has been caused by the difficulty in adapting to the needs of the vast influx

229

of new lower middle- and lower-class students who care nothing for Virgil or Dante and who balk at qualifying examinations that discriminate against them. Raymond Grew argues that the Catholic church has been more intrinsic to the dynamic forces that shaped Italian development than any other element in the nation's history. But its influence on the process of modernization has been problematic at best. Its institutional voice has stressed old benefits undermined by economic and social change, while its spiritual voice has denied that anything is altered and has continued to uphold visions of how much better life might be. Emiliana P. Noether analyzes the important role of Italy's intellectuals in the Risorgimento and their disillusionment during the liberal era, when almost all of them criticized the parliamentary system from some ideological point of view. She emphasizes the roles of Croce, who educated the pre-1914 intellectuals, and of D'Annunzio, who dominated them. Although the majority of intellectuals conformed outwardly to the Fascist regime, Noether describes how two generations of anti-Fascists found their vindication in the Armed Resistance. Rosario Romeo concentrates on the influence of Germany on Italian intellectuals and on Italian affairs generally during the period up to the Second World War. He points out that after unification pro-German sympathies involved a cultural and political judgment about the future of European civilization and that they accompanied a growing disenchantment with France. Italy thus followed the path of many modernizing countries in seeking some more "advanced" nation as a model. Since the Second World War, Italy's intellectuals have tended to look either to the United States or to the Soviet Union.

CHAPTER 10

EDUCATION

Edward R. Tannenbaum

In modern times schools have been a bourgeois preserve. One of their basic purposes has been to help young people maintain or improve their status within the existing order. The traditional nobility and peasantry had little interest in formal education, and until the late nineteenth century neither did the common people in the cities. Of course schools have served other purposes than helping bourgeois youngsters "make it" socially and professionally; at the lower levels they have taught children to read and write and have instilled religious and civic values; at the higher levels they have met society's need for army and navy officers, priests, doctors, and other trained specialists. Nevertheless, with the possible exceptions of theology and the military, almost all schools in all modern societies have been operated by and for the middle classes. Even the Communists have tried to open bourgeois forms of education to the masses, rather than create new kinds of schools with new purposes.[1]

The basically bourgeois character of modern education must be kept in mind in discussing Italy's educational system from the time of its foundation over a century ago to the most recent efforts to reform it.[2] Bourgeois does not necessarily mean capitalist; Giovanni Gentile was just as bourgeois as Giovanni Agnelli and had a good deal more influence on public education. Indeed, until very recent years, Italy's schools served the country's capitalist economy so badly that the Agnellis at Fiat instituted their own training programs. It is not surprising that the homeland of the Renaissance should have clung to the classical curriculum in its secondary schools more doggedly than any other modern country; throughout the Western world this curriculum made it possible for a bourgeois to become a gentleman, thus setting up cultural as well as economic barriers between his class and the lower orders. In status-ridden Italy such barriers have

231

been particularly important. Aside from the curriculum, the leading educational philosophies of the liberal era and beyond also represented nineteenth-century bourgeois notions: laicism, positivism, idealism, pragmatism. Finally, when the leaders of united Italy decided to use the elementary schools to integrate the masses into the nation, they did so by means of the values, images, and even the language of the middle classes.

Language as taught in the schools has had a special role in the cultural and social life of Italy. Well into the twentieth century most Italians habitually spoke their local dialect outside the elementary school or the army; standard Italian was a second language for them. Among the masses only those people who worked in places where it was spoken constantly—shops, offices, schools—began to use Italian in preference to dialect when away from work. Another linguistic division between the middle and lower classes resulted from the fact that in the secondary schools the former had been required to study Latin. (The snob appeal of being acquainted with a "dead" language presumably compensated for the mechanical way in which it was usually taught.) A major argument for retaining Latin in the secondary schools was that it prepared students for the study of letters and law at the university level. Needless to say, many graduates in these fields gave themselves special airs as a cultured elite within the bourgeoisie. People like this have controlled educational policy in Italy and have tried to maintain the same standards that put them where they were.

Part of the crisis in Italian higher and secondary education today is that having been created to serve a relatively small bourgeois elite, its institutions could not adapt themselves to the needs of—or even find room for—the masses of young people who have swamped them during the past two decades of economic boom. Many of these new students are the sons and daughters of white-collar employees, workers, and even peasants. They care nothing for Virgil or Dante, resent the aloofness of many of their professors, and balk at qualifying examinations and proficiency tests whose "bourgeois" language and symbols discriminate against them.

Before unification the governments of most Italian states had done little to promote public education. During the Napoleonic period *licei*, secondary schools modeled on the French *lycée*, had been established in many parts of the peninsula, but these came under clerical control after 1815. Religious orders, local authorities, and private groups still ran most elementary schools where these existed, mainly in the north. The very idea that the state should provide elementary education to people of all classes seemed subversive to Italy's reactionary rulers, particularly since its most zealous advocates were nationalists and liberals. Only in Piedmont, beginning in 1848, were there any significant advances in the field of public education. Based on Cavour's doctrine of "a free church in a free state," these advances had a marked anticlerical character; the privileges of the religious orders in education were abolished, and the influence of the ecclesiastical authorities in the state schools was ended. This change, plus the reorganization and expansion of the state schools, paved the way for the Casati Law in 1859.

This law, named after Count Gabrio Casati (1789–1873), provided the basis for liberal Italy's educational system. Promulgated shortly after the annexation of Lombardy to the Kingdom of Piedmont-Sardinia, it incorporated the most modern ideas of the first half of the nineteenth century concerning pedagogical principles, church-state relations, and the role of education in a developing society. Casati himself had been a reforming political leader in his native Milan until the failure of the Revolution of 1848 forced him to flee to Piedmont, along with many other liberals from the rest of Italy. During the 1850s he supported Cavour's ideas in the Senate and as minister for public instruction in the second half of 1859. Indeed, the Casati Law may be considered Cavour's most enduring legacy aside from political unification itself. Until the Fascists came to power, the educational system set up by this law and extended to all the annexed territories in 1877 underwent fewer changes than any other aspect of the liberal regime. Even the Fascists did not destroy it completely, and parts of it have survived down to the present.

The Casati Law established a system of state-sponsored elementary, secondary, and higher education. Most of its 374 articles dealt with administrative matters, spelling out the functions and powers of the Ministry of Public Instruction and its local representatives. The ministry exerted its greatest control over the universities, which the state alone financed and whose professors were appointed by the king. These professors had a good deal of autonomy in academic affairs, but the highest university administrators were responsible to the central government. The main secondary schools were the classical *ginnasio* (first five years) and *liceo* (last three years). Although the state financed the *licei* and some of the *ginnasî*, a number of communal and private secondary schools were allowed to conduct their own affairs as long as they met national standards. Technical and normal schools were also provided at the secondary level, but these did not teach Latin and hence did not give access to the universities. In fact, for inspection purposes, they were lumped together with the elementary schools, which were financed and run by the communes.

The organizational structure of the Casati Law reflected the priorities of its rightwing liberal founders. Although they paid lip service to the idea of rudimentary education and vocational instruction for the masses, their main concern was the education of the nation's elites and the preservation of preindustrial bourgeois cultural values. (In this respect they differed little from their British and French counterparts.) Elementary education might be extended and improved, but it was to remain completely separate from secondary education. The secondary schools, particularly the classical *licei*, were the ones that really educated, the universities being considered primarily professional schools.

Until the end of the nineteenth century very little was done for elementary education, especially in the south. There were several reasons for this: inadequate finances, resistance in rural areas, and relative indifference among the nation's liberal leaders. The problem of inadequate finances was aggravated by the determination of Italy's political leaders, whether of the right or the left, to make their nation a great power. Given Italy's relatively backward economy, they had to spend a much larger proportion of the national revenue than the more advanced nations on the army, navy, and merchant marine. In the late 1880s the Italian government spent over 25 percent of its income on these three services and 2.4 percent on education. This would have been a paltry amount in an advanced society; it was woefully inadequate for a country that had to cope with widespread illiteracy and enforce compulsory education at the most elementary level. Of course the communes were supposed to provide the bulk of the financial support for their local schools, so the low national figure is somewhat misleading. But it was difficult for the national government to force the communes to fulfill their obligations, particularly in the south, where poverty and peasant hostility to any kind of forced instruction kept progress slower than in the rest of the country.

The dreary statistics of high illiteracy rates and erratic school attendance in liberal Italy are well known. In 1861, 78 percent of the total population was illiterate; ten years later the figures were 72 percent for the kingdom as a whole and 90 percent for the south.[3] By 1881 the national figure had declined to 62 percent; by 1901 to 48.5 percent. But in 1901 the regional figures varied considerably: 17.7 percent illiterate in Piedmont, 78.7 percent in Calabria. Thus, in education, as in almost everything else, north and south were two different worlds. The differences were increasing as the north moved forward while the south virtually stood still, despite all the reports and lamentations of liberal leaders about the Southern Question.

Figures for school attendance during the liberal period are also misleading for the poorer parts of the kingdom. In 1871, 51.3 percent of all children between six and ten were supposedly in school, but those who completed the first two grades satisfactorily were usually not required to continue any further. (With only two grades of schooling behind them the majority of these children soon relapsed into illiteracy.) By 1879 the national figure rose to 59.5 percent and reached 75 percent in the mid-

1890s. Few percentages are available thereafter until the mid-1920s (81 percent in 1926), but we may presume that the average was under 80 percent. Again, however, school attendance varied and had different meanings in different parts of the country. Of the three million children enrolled in elementary school in 1910, two and three-quarters million were in the first three grades alone. In many parts of the south not more than half the enrolled children were still in school by the end of the school year. As late as 1920 an informal local survey of the commune of Reggio Calabria showed that of the 3875 children of school age supposedly attending regular schools, 664 in the city's poor rural hinterland were getting only occasional instruction from unlicensed part-time teachers; hence the official figure of 49.54 percent in school should have been reduced to 32.41 percent.

The reforms of the early 1900s were designed to combat illiteracy and give more people a better elementary education. The Orlando reform of 1904, which tried by means of a kind of popular junior high school (*corso popolare*) to raise the compulsory-schooling age to twelve, was preceded by much debate on the needs of the masses for more general culture and more vocational training. Many lower middle- and working-class parents, eager to push their children up a rung in the social ladder, were sending them to the technical high schools. But in trying to become substitutes for the classical *ginnasî-licei*, these technical schools lost much of their technical character without really giving a humanistic education either. The reformers therefore decided to save the technical schools by providing more instruction at the elementary level. They proposed a novel type of "people's school," with a three-year course (fifth, sixth, and seventh grades) in which time schedules and courses would meet the needs of different localities, in which pupils would be prepared for life by developing the natural inclinations of their souls and the better qualities of their hearts and characters, while at the same time giving them enough basic skills so that they could find jobs in any branch of the economy. The actual reform of 1904 was much more modest. It merely added a sixth grade which, together with the fifth, formed the new "postgraduate" elementary school. The new "people's school" was a failure in two ways: the existing elementary school in effect lost its fifth grade, and in 1905 and 1906 four times as many new pupils entered the technical schools as the average for the preceding two years.

The Orlando reform provided other measures for combating illiteracy and strengthening elementary education, measures that were consolidated in the Daneo-Credaro reform of 1911. This law relieved the majority of the communes of much of the burden of running the local elementary schools by transferring it to the Ministry of Public Instruction. Centralization encouraged minimum standards of instruction for all regions and improved the salaries and working conditions of rural teachers. Finally, the law fostered local service organizations (*Patronati scolastici*) that provided food and clothing to needy children, as well as kindergartens, libraries, and other forms of assistance. Another aid in combating illiteracy was the provision of regular courses of elementary education for young men during their period of military service.

It is difficult to generalize about the quality of elementary education and the attitudes of pupils and teachers at the turn of the century. Surely the pupils in Collodi's *Pinocchio* were more typical than those in Edmondo De Amicis's *Cuore*, for whom school seems all-important and who are portrayed as models of good-heartedness. De Amicis has been called a sentimental socialist, but he was more of a bourgeois populist. He attributed virtuous qualities and humanitarian feelings to humble people and contrasted these with the corruption of society, the injustices of destiny and of men, and the brutal violence resulting from the inequality of classes. Although hardly a good source for the quality of elementary education, De Amicis's *Il romanzo d'un maestro* did awaken the public conscience of his day to the plight of poorly paid, overworked elementary school teachers. More important in ameliorating this plight was the teachers' union (Unione Magistrale Nazionale), founded in 1900 by Luigi Credaro and indirectly supported by the socialist movement. Yet until 1911, when "community control" was reduced in most places, even this union could do little more than give the teachers a sense of social responsibility.

Before the First World War Italy's inadequate effort to raise the level of literacy and elementary education had political as well as cultural and social consequences. First, it limited the number of voters, since literacy (until 1912) was a requirement for the franchise; many illiterate Italian workers supported the Socialists mainly because they championed their right to vote. Second, self-distrust, inexperience, and a sense of inferiority among such workers forced them to turn to middle-class ideologues to help them organize a labor movement (in contrast to Great Britain, France, the United States, and even Germany, where educated workers provided such leadership). On the other hand, like many developing countries, Italy produced an intellectual proletariat. "Unreconciled to human suffering, deprived by conviction as well as by the lack of opportunity from seeking normal channels for the exercise of their talents, these restive individuals turned against the kind of society which seemed to have betrayed them and most other Italians." [4]

By 1913 Italy had reached the degree of economic development attained by Germany fifty years earlier—roughly the same total income and the same income per capita. But whereas in Germany in the 1860s the proportion of children of school age attending school was already close to 100 percent, in Italy in 1913 the proportion of children between six and ten registered at the beginning of the school year was barely 80 percent, and the proportion of those between eleven and fourteen was less than 10 percent.[5] By the standards of the 1860s Prussia was a greater power than Italy was by the standards of 1913; in other words, with a similar economic base, Prussia far outstripped Italy in both military strength and educational achievement.

Greater efficiency in the utilization of resources and manpower would seem to be the obvious explanation for this difference, but there were also differences in the character and content of elementary education in the two countries. Most important was Italy's lack of the German tradition that it was to the state's advantage to have a moral and strong citizenry by educating it—that schooling was the cornerstone of the social edifice, which, in turn, existed for the needs of the state. Second, the very antiquity of the German system reduced the amount of time and effort required to instill basic neatness and decorum and allowed more concentration on actual instruction. (At the turn of the century in most countries the main task of compulsory elementary schools was to "debarbarize" the first generation of schoolchildren from culturally deprived backgrounds.) Third, the German system, by permitting access from the middle to the secondary grades, allowed some selection of talent, at least in urban areas; in Italy, as in much of Western Europe, very few poor children with talent had any opportunity to gain a secondary education and hence add to the nation's pool of trained manpower. The fact that Italy's educational philosophy was more liberal than Germany's was morally edifying for those who propounded it, but it did little to alleviate the poverty and segregation of the masses. Democracy was for the middle classes, and even they, despite their humanistic education, were soon to show few compunctions about abandoning it for Fascism.

Whereas elementary education was deficient in quality, secondary and higher education were deficient in quantity. In 1910, out of almost 6.4 million children between eleven and nineteen, 63,304 were enrolled in classical preparatory schools; 45,262 of these were in *ginnasi-licei* run by the state, and 18,042 in private or semiprivate schools. Thus, barely 1 percent of Italy's adolescents were in these preparatory schools (as compared with almost 2 percent in technical high schools). All of these students planned to go to a university for at least three years in order to become *laureati*[6] or to obtain some professional degree. Since 31,693 students were enrolled in all Italian institutions of higher learning in 1910, we may presume that only those *liceo* graduates who failed the entrance examinations (roughly one third) were not enrolled. Unlike France, Italy gave no baccalaureate degree; a student who did not complete his studies in the university had no academic credentials and hence no prospect of a good professional career.

Modern aspirations toward democracy, called the "revolt of the masses," have often been misunderstood. Rather than leveling (You're no better than I), the emphasis is usually on upward mobility (I'm as good as you). The demand for equality alternates with a demand for marks of distinction and even privilege. In Italy at the turn of the century these alternating demands from the ranks of the lower middle class posed a threat—or so it seemed—to the classical preparatory schools and even to the universities.

The "revolt of the masses" in education and culture at the turn of the century was noted by the philosopher Benedetto Croce, the publicist Giuseppe Prezzolini, and a number of professional educators. Aristide Gabelli, the country's outstanding pedagogical theorist at the time, attributed it to a vulgar rush for academic diplomas that "open the door to the professions and bring home the bread." Augusto Monti, a young high school teacher of Latin, blamed the "crisis" on the poor quality of students and teachers from the lower middle classes, whom he treated as a different race from the "intellectual bourgeoisie" that had traditionally dominated the classical high schools. But the higher standards and the more genuine devotion to classical culture of the good old days were largely mythical, as Monti's own description of the old-style teacher indicates. What the "intellectual bourgeoisie" was really objecting to was a growing professionalism in the schools and universities, a development caused as much by industrialization as by the utilitarian aspirations of uncultured *piccoli borghesi*. Furthermore, the aspirations of these people were snobbish as well as utilitarian; they wanted culture (including Latin) because the better people had it—a perfect example of the dual desire for equality and distinction.

The snobbery of the lower middle classes did far less harm to the nation as a whole than did that of their bourgeois betters. In no other modern European country did a class of would-be mandarins cling so blindly to a fixed classical tradition as did the Italian "intellectual bourgeoisie" during the liberal period. It is a Marxist oversimplification to identify these would-be mandarins exclusively with the conservative ruling classes, although it is true that the political conservatives were the main defenders of the classics, whereas the proponents of the sciences often tended to be politically radical. This mixing of political and social concerns with educational matters not only slowed the pace of Italy's modernization, but it also made reforms in secondary and higher education almost impossible before the Fascists came to power. As in so many other matters, liberal coalition governments made concessions under pressure—particularly in the creation of the scientific *liceo*—without going so far as to antagonize possible future allies, be they Socialists or Catholics. The would-be educational reformers were often more concerned with ideological issues—laicism versus clericalism, positivism versus neoidealism—or with teachers' rights than with adapting the nation's schools to the needs of a modern democratic society.

During the Fascist period a number of changes were made in the Italian education system: the chief ones were initiated by the Gentile reform of 1923 and the Bottai reform of 1939 (*Carta della Scuola*). Aside from Balilla activities (see page 243) and loaded textbooks, which disappeared with the regime itself, many of these changes might have occurred without the Fascists. Probably the rates of school attendance and literacy would have risen just as fast.[7] Changes in secondary education were long overdue and were carried out under Fascism by liberals who had been proposing them for two decades; but these changes did little to improve social mobility and select talent. Fascist efforts to promote technical and scientific training met with much resistance. The one area in which the Fascists did something different and more successfully than the liberal regime was in partially integrating the masses into the national society.

From the moment he sent the *squadristi* home after the March on Rome, Mussolini sought help from other quarters in his effort to build a viable personal dictatorship. Big business, the army, the monarchy, the state administration, and the church furnished his most important supporters, but he also wanted to gain some respectability in the intellectual community. Hence, until the late 1920s, Mussolini created the impression that Giovanni Gentile was the regime's philosopher in residence.[8] As one of Italy's leading interventionist intellectuals Gentile had obvious appeal in nationalist circles; as a long-time advocate of raising educational standards he had a considerable following in the liberal educational establishment. Indeed, his goal of "poche scuole, ma buone [few schools, but good ones]" was shared by his archrival Croce as well as by Giuseppe Lombardo-Radice, the archevangelist of education as the key to the creation of a truly national society.

After the end of the First World War several movements were trying to remake Italian society, and it would be a mistake to question the good faith of those intellectuals and educators who, by the end of 1922, threw in their lot with Fascism as the movement most likely to succeed in such an effort. Three years earlier these men, led by Lombardo-Radice and Ernesto Codignola, a follower of Gentile and a leader of the Federation of Secondary School Teachers, had founded the *Fascio di educazione nazionale* after Codignola had publicly accused the majority of the secondary school teachers of responsibility for Italian failures in the war.[9] This *Fascio* had no connection with the *Fasci di combattimento*, and a

number of its members (Piero Gobetti, for example) never supported the
Fascist regime. What brought the two groups together was their nationalist orientation. The nature of this orientation was best expressed by
Lombardo-Radice in his appeal to the teachers to join the new *Fascio* in
the January 15, 1920 issue of the review *Educazione Nazionale:*

> We must renovate the conscience of the new generations, if we
> want to reap suitable benefits. . . . The bitter ordeal of the war—
> notwithstanding the marvelous, spontaneous gifts of our people,
> second to none—has laid bare serious gaps in the spiritual framework
> of the nation, particularly in those classes whose studies should have
> given them a devout feeling for the law and for the subordination of
> the individual to the supreme collective interests, an active faith,
> moral training, a realistic view of things, and a sense of the concrete.

In late 1922 Gentile became Mussolini's first minister of education, with
Lombardo-Radice in the post of director general of elementary instruction: their reforms were set forth in a series of decrees during the following year.

The spirit of the Gentile reform involved two principles: the identification of philosophy and pedagogy and the unification of teacher and
pupil in the learning process. According to Gentile, the teacher is not
somebody who "instructs" his pupils by giving them information, formulas, laws, or arguments. The truth of all such things resides in the conscious act of the one who utters, hears, or thinks them. Hence, the teacher
"educates" his pupils by bringing them into his sphere of thought and
making them share in his enlightened life. Since the nature of "spirit" is
movement and perpetual creation, every teacher and every pupil are
something new in comparison with all others. Hence, pedagogic rules can
only hamper the progress of truth and should be abolished. (In fact,
Gentile abolished the teaching of pedagogics in his new teacher-training
colleges, including even practice teaching.) Pedagogy can only acquire
meaning by becoming subsumed to philosophy; there is no distinction
between "spirit" becoming conscious of truth and "spirit" extending its
truth through education. Thus, the "spirit of the reform" resided more
in the authoritarian way teachers taught than in any changes in curriculum, examinations, or administration.

Gentile made sure that the "spirit of the reform" would be carried out
by strengthening the authority of school administrators at all levels: the
authority of principals and headmasters over teachers, of superintendents
over them, and of the minister of education over all. Although the universities were officially recognized as autonomous bodies with regard to
educational policy and their own administrative affairs, the professors

lost the right to elect their rectors and deans. Thus, one major aspect of the Gentile reform was its authoritarianism and its extension of the power of the state at all educational levels. This move was justified by Gentile's conception of the state as partaking of the nature of "spirit" itself: the state embodies all the experiences and happenings that take place in it; it represents the combined expression of the minds and wills of its citizens and rules over them for their, and its, own good.

Gentile's philosophy of the state and its responsibilities also gave theoretical justification to another major reform, the introduction of a state examination at the end of each three- or four-year cycle of study. Not only did the certificates, diplomas, and degrees gained by passing these examinations guarantee the same standards in all public schools, but they also gave equality of opportunity to pupils from private schools. Educators have argued the pros and cons of state examinations for generations—how, on the one hand, they do the good things just mentioned as well as creating better relations between teachers and pupils (before the teacher was feared as the examiner; now the pupils viewed him as an ally in helping them pass the state examinations); how, on the other hand, they place culturally deprived sections of society at a disadvantage, how they thwart an interest in learning anything not in the syllabus for the examinations, and so on. In the 1920s, however, state examinations were a definite improvement over existing conditions in Italy.

The Gentile reform reinforced the humanistic character of the Italian schools at all levels. The elementary schools gained from the fact that their new teachers no longer came from the catchall normal schools but from new teacher-training colleges in whose lower grades philosophy and Latin were compulsory courses. The old normal schools and the lower technical schools were abolished, as were substandard secondary schools of all kinds. The *ginnasio-liceo* remained *the* institution for educating the nation's bourgeois elite in a humanistic way, with the introduction of philosophy for the first time and with more emphasis in Latin classes on the reading of classics and the study of the life they revealed.

It was extremely ironical, not to say hypocritical, for Mussolini to call the Gentile reform "the most Fascist of reforms." The conservatives welcomed it because it required no financial sacrifices or organizational efforts and because putting the formula "poche scuole ma buone" into practice restricted the number of lower-middle- and lower-class children who could aspire to a humanistic education. The Catholics welcomed the state examination because it put their schools on the same level as the state schools. But what true Fascist could like a reform that was designed to revive and reinforce the nineteenth-century bourgeois elitist conception of culture and education? The Gentile reform and the ideas that inspired it were the antithesis of what the "Fascist Revolution" stood for, namely the overthrow of the liberal establishment and the exaltation of more plebeian leadership and values. (Ortega y Gasset was right; Fascism was a form of the "revolt of the masses.") Mussolini wanted to placate the conservatives and gain respectability, but in so far as he did so he was not a typical Fascist. The typical Fascists were Roberto Farinacci, Augusto Turati, Giuseppe Bottai, Cesare Maria De Vecchi—the very types whom the "intellectual bourgeoisie" despised (and who reciprocated the feeling). The obvious proof of this was the way the Fascist leaders "retouched" the Gentile reform and the way Gentile reacted.

The retouching of the Gentile reform began as soon as he left office; so did his objections. In early March 1925 Gentile wrote a letter to Roberto Forges-Davanzati, editor of *L'Idea Nazionale*, violently criticizing the new minister of public instruction, Pietro Fedele, for modifying his rule that high school students who failed one or two out of ten comprehensive examinations in June had to repeat the whole year's work. Fedele decreed that for a transitional period of four years the old system would prevail, whereby such students could retake these examinations in September. (In fact, Fedele's "transitional" decree remained in effect throughout the Fascist period.) This contretemps was the first in a series of examples of the contrast between Gentile's bourgeois elitist outlook and the plebeian, "democratic" outlook of most Fascists.

There were many other examples, but one more will have to do here. On January 9, 1929, another minister of public instruction, Giuseppe Belluzzo, wrote a letter to Mussolini explaining Gentile's rejection of the post of president of the council for a separate section of the lower grades of the *ginnasio-liceo*. Gentile argued that the new detached section would not have prestige and that the classical secondary school should remain intact. Belluzzo argued that each section served a useful purpose, implying that some students could benefit from two more years of schooling in specialized subjects, even though they could not cope adequately with general classical subjects, especially Latin. (A comparable dispute arose in this country when the first junior colleges were set up.)

Despite Gentile's complaints that the Ministry of Public Instruction was giving unqualified party members important positions, the "Fascistization" of the schools did not really begin until February 1929. In that same month elementary and secondary school teachers had to take a loyalty oath to the regime, and the Concordat with the Vatican, by introducing religious instruction into the secondary schools, dealt a blow to Gentile and his neo-idealist followers, who opposed the teaching of any dogma and who wanted secondary school students to read the great philosophers instead.[10] Later in 1929 the Ministry of Public Instruction was renamed the Ministry of National Education; since the word *educazione* means the total upbringing of the child, the name change was meant to be more than symbolic. Also in 1929, the Opera Nazionale Balilla, created in 1926 specifically to give moral guidance and physical education to the young, was transferred from the jurisdiction of the party to that of the renamed ministry.

The process of Fascistization accelerated during the 1930s. In 1931 the turn of the universities came when the professors had to swear loyalty to the regime in order to keep their chairs. In early 1935 premilitary training was introduced into all secondary schools. Fascistization went into full swing when Cesare Maria De Vecchi (one of the four triumvirs of the March on Rome) was minister of education (January 1935 to November 1936). His main target was the universities, whose autonomy he destroyed and whose professors he harassed in many ways. Under De Vecchi tighter controls were also instituted over the curriculum and textbooks of the elementary schools: courses in "Fascist culture" were added; about half of all the material in the first- through fifth-grade readers was Fascist propaganda.[11] During the mid-1930s propaganda radio broadcasts beamed to the classroom were particularly effective because of their novelty. As everywhere, such broadcasts had the greatest impact among smaller children in smaller communities; sophisticated students in the urban *licei* were less impressed.

As in popular culture and the youth organizations, the Fascists wanted to alter the bourgeois character of Italian education. In typical "totalitarian" fashion they decreed that the purpose of the schools was to train young people to serve the state: hence the infiltration of Balilla activities and the introduction of premilitary training into the curriculum. They also wanted to make the secondary schools more democratic than under the liberal regime. Here is how one high school principal put it: "Just as in Napoleon's army every soldier could aspire to a marshal's baton, so in the corporative order every worker can become a senator. The classical high school is no longer the only road to power, as it seems to have been in the days of parliamentarianism." In practice, however, most students went on seeking the kinds of bourgeois professional careers they wanted, rather than those the state might have needed. By 1940, in almost all Italian universities the schools of education had the largest number of students (five thousand new ones each year), and almost all of these wanted to teach in the classical preparatory schools. Since there were more than enough teachers of this kind already, most of these graduates would have to find less rewarding jobs and join the ranks of dissatisfied intellectuals. How different from Nazi Germany, where the total number of university students was markedly curtailed in the late 1930s, particularly outside strictly technical fields!

The Fascist regime tried to foster scientific and technical education in order to bolster its modernizing image, to increase the number of technically trained people, and to allow more mobility and selection of talent. In 1930 it created a new category of vocational junior high schools to replace the moribund "postgraduate" elementary training schools. The new schools, called *scuole di avviamento professionale*, were the most effective and popular educational institutions created by the regime. However, at the university level the old bourgeois desire to be *laureati* caused resistance to all pressures toward scientific and technical training. This resistance was due partly to snobbery, partly to skepticism concerning the availability of jobs in engineering and other technical fields in a period of economic depression, and partly to the belief (in some measure justified) that the examinations were easier in law and letters.

Many educators who were active during the Fascist period now argue that "Fascistization" was least effective in the secondary schools; what they really mean is in the state-run classical preparatory schools, as if the kinds of people who went to them are the only ones who mattered. In the first place, there is no justification for the argument that the humanistic spirit—which supposedly immunized young people against Fascism—was necessarily liberal; the Jesuits and even Gentile were authoritarian humanists. In the second place, the majority of Italian students in secondary schools did not attend the state-run *ginnasî-licei*. In the academic year 1939 to 1940 there were 162,797 students in these schools and 50,242—or almost a third—in private (mostly Catholic) and semiprivate preparatory schools of the same type; private and semiprivate teacher-training schools enrolled just over half the number of students as those run by the state (56,757 as opposed to 108,343). The priests and nuns in these private schools were far more likely to instill conformity to the regime than their colleagues in the state-run preparatory schools. There were also over 375,000 students in state-run secondary technical and vocational schools, which had no strong humanistic tradition. The most that can be said is that most teachers over thirty-five did not propagate Fascist ideals with much real conviction and that this was perhaps especially true in the state-run classical preparatory schools. Still, teen-age students in the late 1930s were more likely to be Fascist-oriented than not, having already been indoctrinated in the elementary schools and the Balilla.

Under Fascism the schools were more successful in integrating the masses into the nation than in breaking down bourgeois prejudices. For one thing, the education ministry banished translations from dialect in the elementary schools in 1934. The fact that Catholicism now had a significant place in the Fascists' ideal national society also helped to break down traditional barriers. But the most important integrating theme was patriotism. Members of the "intellectual bourgeoisie" look back with utter contempt at the propagandistic glorifications of the regime in the schools. But for most pupils at the time the regime *was* the nation, just as today unsophisticated Cuban and Chinese school children equate their regimes with the nation. (Like Mussolini, Mao is "always right.")

The most concerted effort to put Fascist educational principles into practice was the *Carta della Scuola* (1939), whose author, Giuseppe Bottai, was minister of education from November 1936 until February 1943. Here is its credo:

> To all the effective possibility of enrolling in school and following a course of study, but to each one the duty of fulfilling his scholastic obligation in the interest of the State, that is, according to his truest aptitudes, committing all his faculties and his entire responsibility in such a way that the schools may be the reserve from which the State continually draws all the fresh energy it needs and not simply the agency in which thoughtless bourgeois vanity looks for seals and diplomas for its sterile ambitions.

Another goal of the new charter was to unite the activities of the schools with those of the Fascist youth organization GIL (Gioventù Italiana del Littorio—formerly Balilla). Bottai believed that this union would greatly aid the cultural, political, and militaristic development of the new generation. He also believed that manual training should be introduced into the schools so that all children could learn that even the humblest forms of labor have their dignity and humanity. Finally, the *Carta della Scuola* instituted a so-called unified junior high school (*scuola media unica*).

The Second World War prevented most of the goals of the charter from being realized, but the unified junior high school was a misnomer to start with since it served only those pupils who intended to go on to the higher secondary schools. Latin remained the requirement that kept out pupils from the vocational junior high schools who might have wanted to change their course of study; it was also the one that tested aptitude for the classical *liceo*. Bottai's *scuola unica* was a step away from Gentile's elitism, but not until 1963 were all Italian school children to go to the same kind of school up to age fourteen. As for the universities, according to a survey in Bottai's own literary review *Primato* (issues of April through November 1941), they remained the bastion of the "intellectual bourgeoisie."

In 1944 and 1945 Allied military operations and the civil war between Resistance fighters and the Nazis and their Fascist puppets disrupted Italian education both physically and morally. Yet during those two years the "de-Fascistization" of the schools was virtually completed by the Allied Commission for Education under the direction of a renowned American educator, Carleton Washburne. In cooperation with the Italian authorities Washburne's staff saw to it that all Fascist propaganda was eliminated from textbooks and course plans. There was also a purge of the more notorious Fascist teachers and administrators, though this effort, as elsewhere, was inconclusive. At the same time two eminent liberal scholars tried to prepare the way for permanent reforms in their brief tenures as minister of education: Adolfo Omodeo (April to June 1944) and Guido De Ruggiero (June 1944 to January 1945). The universities regained their autonomy and academic freedom. Omodeo also tried to make the curricula of the secondary schools more dynamic and open-ended, but more conservative views soon prevailed.

After the end of the war the work of physical reconstruction of the schools went on despite the country's poor economic condition, but little change was made in their scholastic and administrative structures. The famous compromise between the Christian Democrats and the Communists on keeping the Concordat of 1929 in the Constitution of 1947 meant that religious instruction was retained in both elementary and secondary schools for all pupils except those excused at the request of their parents. Otherwise, the basic structure of Italian public education remained that of the Casati Law of 1859. Reforms in the elementary schools did not begin until the mid-1950s, and in the secondary schools not until a decade later.

In sheer numbers of students at all levels Italy has made great strides since the Second World War. By 1961 over 90 percent of all children from age six through ten were already in elementary school. At that time only 54.4 percent of all children between ages eleven and fourteen attended junior high school; today over 75 percent attend. In 1961 only 18.7 percent of Italy's adolescents attended an advanced high school; today the figure is over 35 percent. One of the most encouraging changes has been the growth of school attendance in the south, which has almost caught up with the north in this respect (though it must still "export" many of its junior high and high school graduates to the north or abroad because of lack of economic opportunities at home).

This rise in school attendance is a function of rapid modernization. Increased per capita income has allowed more and more parents to keep their children in school longer before sending them out to work. Urban people tend to value education more than rural people, and Italy is becoming urbanized at an unprecedented rate (the percentage of rural inhabitants declined from 50 percent in the late 1940s to less than 20 percent by the early 1970s). The more complex the economy, the more skilled personnel are needed to operate it; this is another obvious reason for children to stay in school longer for more training. Finally, society, through the state, has spent more money than ever before on education. The proportion of state revenue devoted to education grew from 9.5 percent in

1950 to 14 percent in 1961 to 22 percent in 1968, as compared with 6 percent during the Fascist period and 3 percent at the turn of the century.

Italy's elementary schools have fared somewhat better than its high schools and universities, although they are still inadequate for the new needs ascribed to them. The nation's cumbersome bureaucracy has proved unable to spend the huge funds for school construction which parliament appropriated in the 1950s and 1960s. Consequently, by the fall of 1972, there was a desperate lack of classrooms and equipment. In 1955 the curriculum was reformed according to the "activist" educational philosophy —combining ideas from Maria Montessori and John Dewey—which makes the child the center of the educational process and stresses the interaction of the individual and society. Beginning in 1964 textbooks were distributed free to all elementary school pupils. Unfortunately, an increasing number of elementary school teachers are now poorly trained, inexperienced, and insensitive to the problems of underprivileged children. As long as most parents, teachers, and pupils continue to view the elementary school primarily as a glorified nursery, the quality of the present teaching staff is probably adequate. If, however, the elementary school is supposed to act as a corrective to vast social and cultural differences and to give all pupils an equal educational basis for bettering themselves, then the teachers cannot be merely substitute parents. But this is precisely what they are in Italy, where the same teacher stays with his or her pupils through all five grades.

The elementary school teachers are criticized from all sides these days, and it is unfair to expect them to perform tasks for which they are not equipped. Nevertheless, as the main problem in Italian elementary education is the teachers, something must be said about them. Traditionally the poorer students who wanted some professional qualification went to a normal school and then began teaching in their late teens. Only since the Fascist period have most elementary school teachers themselves risen to the lower ranks of the *piccola borghesia* as a result of their new status and better salaries as civil servants and of the humanistic education they received in Gentile's *istituti magistrali*. Now Italy's educational reformers want to abolish these institutions, train teachers in college-level courses, and have them return later on for refresher courses—as in America. But we all know that college training and refresher courses do not give the typical teacher the ability, the time, or the incentive to understand why some children perform poorly—whether it is because they are abused or neglected at home or because they are unfamiliar with the language, symbols, and values of the school environment. It is simply easier to say that they have little intelligence or little will to learn.

These attitudes among Italy's elementary school teachers are part of a larger phenomenon that has already been mentioned: the middle-class character of the school environment at all levels. The middle- or lower middle-class child entering this environment finds the language and values familiar; the working-class or peasant child finds them strange and often distasteful. It is particularly difficult to bring poor children who speak dialect most of the time up to the level of middle-class children in Italian composition. The elimination of entrance examinations for junior high school and high school in 1968 has removed one handicap to further study without really tackling the problem of how to give all children equal facility in the national language. More basic is the problem of motivating poor children to conform to petty-bourgeois standards of worldly success, duty, and law and order, which are often viewed negatively in the environment to which these children return at the end of the school day. This is not a new problem, of course, but it is especially serious today, when a child who resists the school environment and drops out of it at fourteen has difficulty competing in the job market. A possible solution would be to find more sensitive teachers, give them smaller classes, and supplement them with dedicated social workers who could reach the disadvantaged children on their own terms. But neither the money nor the personnel is available for such a vast undertaking.

The principal reform in Italian education since the Second World War was the creation of the unified junior high school (*scuola media unica*) in 1963. Until then, children who had completed the fifth year of elementary school could choose either a regular junior high school (*scuola media*) or a vocational school (*scuola di avviamento*) for a three-year course. Even though there was an entrance examination for the regular junior high school, 57 percent of the students could not complete the three-year course in three years. Since the reform, all children must attend the unified junior high school, which instead of selecting students out of the educational mill is supposed to continue the work of the elementary school in giving them all a common orientation up to age fourteen or fifteen. In order to keep all options open for the higher secondary schools, especially the *ginnasio-liceo*, Latin is offered in the third year. Otherwise the program of instruction is uniform for everyone, with more science courses than before and with emphasis on learning in groups, as prescribed by the "activist" school of educational philosophy.

Lamberto Borghi, one of the early champions of the *scuola media unica*, believes that it is a great step toward the democratization of Italian society as well as of the educational process itself. As a Marxist this is important to him. On the other hand, as a follower of John Dewey, Borghi insists that the schools, especially the *scuola media unica*, "help their pupils to develop their own inventiveness and creativeness." [12] He acknowledges the fact that this task can be accomplished only by training new teachers and retraining old ones but says that this is a problem for schools of education in the universities.

As in the past, the largest number of students in higher secondary education are in the technical schools.[13] Most of these students are upwardly mobile youngsters who hope to get better-paying jobs as white-collar workers and technicians than they would as graduates of the vocational schools (the latter can only hope to become skilled blue-collar workers). In the technical schools (as opposed to the vocational schools) the perennial problem is that of teachers who are unqualified to teach technical subjects, especially those concerned with specialized industries. But, as everywhere, the students in these schools are relatively docile and politically indifferent.

The major thrust of student protest in the *licei* and the universities in recent years has been against outmoded and impersonal institutions and practices; but the problem is twofold, for it also involves increased numbers of students, whom these institutions are hard-pressed to accommodate.

One major target has been the examination system. Until the creation of the *scuola media unica*, examinations had been used to "select out" children from going on in secondary education at age eleven. Then the abolition of entrance examinations to both this new school and the higher secondary schools postponed the selecting-out process until the examinations at the end of the first year in the *ginnasio-liceo*. If a student failed one or two courses, he had to take the examinations over in September; if he failed them again, he had to repeat the whole year's work in all his courses. Finally, after having completed the five years of course work, the student had to pass a comprehensive examination—*maturità* in the *liceo, abilitazione* in the teacher-training school—in order to be eligible to go on to a university. In 1969 the September make-up examinations were abolished, and the *maturità* examination was made broader, with less emphasis on factual data and more on the cultural maturity of the candidate, as its name implies. In all these reforms the goal has been to cut down the number of students selected out before the university level.

As in many modern countries, antielitism seems to have become a favorite battle cry for many radical students in Italy. Ironically, in the name of antibourgeois slogans, they are expressing a typically bourgeois form of self-indulgence: guilt feelings about their privileged position in society. The following excerpt from an article in the December 18, 1968 issue of *La Stampa* concerning demonstrations at the Liceo D'Azeglio speaks for itself:

> Even in Turin unrest has cropped up in a liceo with glorious traditions, but the students have no pride in the past; they feel that it is

an unjust privilege to go to a school for "the elite." They back
courageous reforms set forth by some of their teachers but they also
demand active participation in the whole life of the school and a
social reform of the system. Above all they are opposed to the PTA
[*comitati scuola-famiglia*]: "Our parents are further to the right
than the teachers."

All the ingredients of recent student protest are mentioned here: the
revolt against the parents, who represent the past (the "right"); the
search for understanding leadership among the teachers, even though
most of them also represent the past; the youthful oversimplification of
blaming institutions for the ways in which people misuse them and for
the values that sustain them; the demand for power to change the world.
But the real motive of the antielitists is that they do not want to belong
to the *old* elite because they see that its cultural values neither justify its
privileges nor help a person find his sense of identity in today's world.

The main reason that the extremists have been able to gain such a wide
following in Italy and elsewhere (aside from demagogic acts like provoking police "brutality") is that masses of young people resent the schools
for not giving them new cultural values that tell them who they are and
what to do in a new kind of world. Since the schools do not do this, the
institutions are attacked for all the things that have always been wrong
with them—from their curriculum and teaching methods to their "elitism."
Alma mater becomes simply another disappointing parent at a time when
young people are desperate for guidance.

Predictably, the upshot of Italian student unrest in 1968 and 1969 has
been a reform plan for the universities. Several provisions of the plan have
to do with the professors—making them work full time, increasing their
number, and reducing the differences in status and power between the
full professors and the rest of the teaching staff. Students as well as the
lower ranks of teachers are to have a voice, particularly in the newly
created departments, each one of which is to coordinate and direct research and courses for at least four similar disciplines. But at the time of
this writing (March 1973) the proposed university reforms were only
partially implemented, and both students and teachers were confused and
demoralized. In the academic year 1972 to 1973 there were over seven
hundred thousand full-time students in Italy's institutions of higher learning; since 1968 their total number has grown at an annual rate of 12 percent. This swarm of new students has resulted partly from opening admission to all branches of the university for all high school graduates and
partly from increasing the number of scholarships. The University of
Rome has 90,000 registered students; Milan State University, 60,000.

Thus the "revolt of the masses" has assaulted the last bastion of the "intellectual bourgeoisie," but, aside from reducing the privileges of the full professors, this assault is not likely to change the character of the universities very much. Once some semblance of equality—or "participation"—is achieved, the emphasis will shift, as it usually does, to acquiring the distinctions of one's new status. Or, to put it another way, believing that they have "captured" the universities, most of the students and younger staff members will surely want to nurture their prize. The real revolutionaries—Maoists, anarchists, et al.—know this and have opposed the current university reform because they know that it is designed to win the majority of dissidents away from *them*. As elsewhere, the university will undoubtedly become the principal agency of *embourgeoisement* in Italy. And for every bourgeois youth who wants to opt out of his class there will be ten from the lower classes who will want to take his place.

NOTES

1. This has been so not only in countries like Italy, where the Communists have never controlled the national government, but also in countries where the Communists have been in power for many years. The "new class" in the Communist states of Eastern Europe is very bourgeois in its attitude toward education, especially at the higher level. By the 1960s even in Mao's China the universities seemed to be producing a dangerously career-oriented intelligentsia, as evidenced by the great pains the government has taken to counteract this trend—such as restricting the curriculum in the liberal arts and forcing students to spend time living with the peasants.

2. The following works on the history of Italian education since unification are useful: Dina Bertoni Jovine, *La scuola italiana dal 1870 ai giorni nostri*, 2nd ed. (Rome: Editori Riuniti, 1967); Lamberto Borghi, *Educazione e autorità nell'Italia moderna* (Florence: La Nuova Italia, 1951); Giacomo Cives, ed., *Cento anni di vita scolastica in Italia. Ispezioni e inchieste* (Rome: Armando, 1960); Lorenzo Minio-Paluello, *Education in Fascist Italy* (London: Oxford University Press, 1946); Angelo Broccoli, *Educazione e politica nel Mezzogiorno d'Italia* (Florence: La Nuova Italia, 1968). The most recent description of the Italian school system is Anna Laura Fadiga Zanatta, *Il sistema scolastico italiano* (Bologna: Il Mulino, 1971).

3. Istituto Centrale di Statistica, *Annuario statistico italiana, 1886*, p. 954. All statistics in this chapter come from this annual publication unless otherwise noted.

4. Maurice Neufeld, *Italy: School for Awakening Countries* (Ithaca,

N.Y.: New York School of Industrial and Labor Relations, 1960), p. 129.

5. Allied Commission, *La politica e la legislazione scolastica in Italia dal 1922 al 1943* (Milan: Garzanti, 1947), pp. 428–429.

6. The Italian *laurea* is somewhere between an American master's and doctor's degree; in any case it entitles its holder to be called "doctor." Actually, on the eve of the First World War, over one third of all Italian university students were studying law; the next largest group was in medicine. Then came pharmacy, mathematical, physical, and biological sciences, engineering, and philosophy and letters (see Allied Commission, *op. cit.*, pp. 454–455). A person with a law degree was (and is) called "lawyer," rather than "doctor"; an engineer, "engineer."

7. The national illiteracy rate was down from 48.5 percent in 1901 to 30 percent in 1921 (27 percent for those over six years old—a more realistic measure). The decline to 23 percent by 1931 could easily have been matched under the liberal regime. By 1939, 75 percent of all children between six and fourteen were in school; 93 percent began the first grade, but only one out of six was still attending in his fourteenth year (see Allied Commission, *op. cit.*, pp. 150–151).

8. The two men's loyalty to one another lasted beyond 1929, when the combined hostility of the Vatican and the more zealous Fascist bigwigs forced Mussolini to deprive Gentile of this role. During the 1930s Mussolini continued to flatter the philosopher and to shield him from attacks from the Fascist hierarchy. In 1944 Gentile, in turn, came out of retirement to support the fallen Duce's Italian Social Republic.

9. The naïveté of Codignola's accusation, "La Scuola Media ha preparato Caporetto," reminds one of Picasso's explanation of the Fall of France in 1940: "C'est la faute des Beaux Arts." Picasso was referring to the conservatism of the Ecole des Beaux Arts, whereas Codignola was referring to the pacifistic socialism of Italy's high school teachers.

10. It should be noted, however, that Gentile had instituted religious teaching in the elementary schools because, according to his philosophy of "spirit," religion anticipates some universal views that will be fully understood only through philosophy. But since the overwhelming majority of children never went on to secondary school to study philosophy, it also seems clear that Gentile was using religious teaching in a typically conservative way, namely to instill obedience and respect for authority. Gentile's ideas about education are discussed in H. S. Harris, *The Social Philosophy of Giovanni Gentile* (Urbana: University of Illinois Press, 1960).

11. The most famous and best written of these were the fifth-grade reader *Il balilla Vittorio* by Roberto Forges-Davanzati and the fourth-grade reader by Piero Bargellini. In the first-grade reader one little story says that when Mussolini was shown on horseback in a newsreel, everyone

applauded and cried in unison: "Duce, Duce!"; the children would thus know how to behave when *they* went to the movies.

12. Lamberto Borghi, "Pedagogia moderna e scuola media," *Scuola e Città*, Nos. 4–5 (April-May 1966), p. 143.

13. In 1970 and 1971 there were 676,601 students in the various technical institutes (*istituti tecnici*) for business subjects, industry, agriculture, nautical studies, and so on, as compared with 655,105 in liberal arts and teacher-training schools.

CATHOLICISM
IN A CHANGING ITALY

RAYMOND GREW

In every generation hundreds of Italians have dreamed rich visions of a better world, encouraged "because Italy is great in the eyes of the Lord." The certitude so simply expressed by Niccolò Tommaseo, a mid-nineteenth-century Venetian liberal, describes a sense of mission common to many Catholic patriots, a sense so vibrant in Vincenzo Gioberti that his influence and something of his vision survived the disastrous disproof of politics. In all nineteenth-century definitions of Italy's historic calling there was a Catholic component, resonant in Giuseppe Mazzini, palely echoed by the statesmen of the old right. It encouraged the use of moral criteria as the measure of political achievement, thereby assuring that disillusionment, first with the Risorgimento and then with Italy itself, would remain the stigmata of Italian politics.

This Catholic vision of a new Italy was most open and optimistic in the transient glory of neo-Guelfism, when Italy united under the pope appeared to be a real possibility and when patriotism could be presented as the application of Christian teaching to the affairs of this world. Although the events of 1848 and the teachings of the Jesuits suggested that no easy consonance was likely between the commandments of God and the demands of a modern state, the hope for such harmony has remained especially strong in Italy, even when it has contributed to discord. Neo-Guelfism suggested the possibility of a social transformation that would be extensive but painless. The church remained suspicious of such optimism, and the denunciations of modernism early in the twentieth century included warnings against facile programs for religious and social reform.[1] But Catholicism represented more than a part of Italy's national identity; it contributed what may be called a religious utopianism to Italian political life, a utopianism that spread far beyond Catholic circles.

254

In Italy, however, almost any campaign for social or political change led to talk about reform of the institutional church, an important theme in Italian thought, inspiring much of liberal Catholicism, weaving through literature from Alessandro Manzoni to Antonio Fogazzaro, moving so sober and secular a figure as Bettino Ricasoli, giving life to many an anticlerical attack, and finding perhaps its simplest expression in Giuseppe Garibaldi's complaint that the pope was not a Christian. The hint that political and religious reforms were related, explosive enough anywhere, was bound to raise special complications in the homeland of the Roman church. It was almost a tradition that the Catholic intellectuals who reached the widest public were tainted with heresy: Gioberti, of course, but Manzoni by Jansenism, Rosmini by ontologism, Gioacchino Ventura through Felicité de Lamennais, Romolo Murri and Fogazzaro by modernism. Liberal Catholicism, so vital in France, was associated with neo-Guelfism in Italy and was therefore far more liable to the penalties of failure. Ultramontanism elsewhere could support many different political programs, but in Italy it stood for the intransigent rejection of a liberal state.

By the 1890s, an organization of Catholic laymen, the Opera dei Congressi, was filled with enthusiasm for the Christian regeneration of Italy and had become one of the most active and extensive such movements in the world; but it was also more directly subordinate to the Vatican than other lay movements, until the political implications of its energy and the inevitable disagreements within it became such an embarrassment that Pius X ordered its dissolution. It is now commonplace to note that Italy did not contribute its proportionate share to the intellectual vitality of Catholicism in nineteenth-century Europe. One reason must surely be the special circumstances of Italy, where the *Syllabus of Errors,* many of whose propositions came from papal comments on Italian affairs, had such immediate and practical implications. Most Italian Catholics probably continued to feel in their hearts that their patriotism and their faith were reconcilable; but it was a difficult subject for public exploration.

Clearly the church has been important to the process of modernization in Italy, but its role is difficult to identify, not only because unambiguous evidence is scarce (one wishes anthropologists had been studying Italian villages a century ago) but because religion anywhere and especially Catholicism in Italy is too fundamental a part of life to be easily isolated for analysis. We know that the great moments of the Risorgimento were usually celebrated by a *Te Deum;* and however uncomfortable that made some bishops, the people undoubtedly felt it right. Not only lay Catholics but even priests often supported national union, just as priests played a part in the revolts of 1821, 1848, and 1860, and in the Sicilian *fasci* at the end of the century. The collection of funds for Garibaldi in 1860—which was perhaps the Risorgimento's moment of greatest popular participation —was begun in frank imitation of a Catholic device, the collections for a beleaguered pope called peter's pence.

But the church affected social change in more fundamental ways. Nineteenth-century believers in progress could not forgive the church for Italy's high rate of illiteracy; nevertheless, most Italians who could read had learned their letters from the clergy.[2] To this day the curriculum even in state schools bears the stamp of what Catholic tradition once considered the education appropriate to particular social stations. Despite their fear of Voltairean ideas, Catholics remained as confident that education brought social benefits as they were that they should provide it.

Charity, too, was a Catholic undertaking. Thirteen percent of the population, according to one informed estimate, received such aid at mid-century; and though by then most of the money came from taxes, it was still largely distributed by Catholic agencies (and Italy compared well with the rest of Europe in the number and size of such institutions). Most of these activities were certainly not intended to assist the process of social change, but they were important in making bearable its cost in human misery. Many charitable enterprises did reflect a changing society: mutual aid societies for typographers (as well as music professors and physicians) in Milan; burgeoning orphanages that attempted to teach a useful trade; a home for street sweepers in Venice, open to any who could present a certificate from his parish priest. Much admired was the school established by Anatole Demidoff in the suburbs of Florence. There, poor children were boarded, paid for simple manual labor, taught geometry, instructed in mechanical drawing as well as piety, and then apprenticed in "industrial professions." These professions were those of artisans, making straw hats or shoes or harness. Many feared the dangers of giving too much education to the lower orders, but they were assured that the school presented only that part of a subject important for the useful arts.

When the laborers and children in these hundreds of workhouses, asylums, and orphanages were lectured on the virtues of thrift and hard work, their tutors were, after all, serving the cause of economic growth. So, in a different way, was the clergy of Tuscany in October 1830, when they told their parishioners of winter and spring jobs in the Maremma. If some priests helped their parishioners find new jobs, others could praise the inventions of their age as confidently as any economist; and the businessmen of the Papal States believed in the 1850s that their applications for subvention would be strengthened by describing how they made use of steam within their enterprises. The church provided much of whatever comfort and guidance there was for men learning to sell their labor in a larger and more demanding market.

Although the church controlled education, charity, and communication during most of the century, its position was eroded with unification. An ambitious yet insecure state deliberately attempted to restrict the social influence of the church, and these attempts produced some of the loudest outcries in the running battle between church and state. But the church's losses in these spheres were more relative than absolute, the result in large part of competition from a more efficient bureaucracy, from tax-supported schools, from newspapers and public meetings. Catholics, of course, lamented this change; in doing so they exaggerated it. They represented the church as weaker and more on the defensive than it was or needed to be, and they created a romantic picture of a previous corporative world in which monasteries and priests had cooperated with statesmen, artisans, and peasants for the general welfare. Less elaborate but similar theories developed in France and Germany; these ideas of corporative cooperation helped Catholics to become outspoken critics of the social irresponsibility of liberal government. This in itself was as significant as the loss of old privileges.

Furthermore, a church with fewer formal connections to government was less implicated in official policies and potentially freer to act as a center of resistance, a possibility anticlericals never forgot. In practice, complex organization and multiple obligations guaranteed that the hierarchy would remain cautious from prudence as well as lack of imagination. The clergy's role in social change is, in any case, obscured for the historian by the enormous variation among local conditions and individuals. The renewed dedication to the cure of souls which marks the nineteenth-century clergy certainly includes considerable social awareness, and the less-inhibited laity with their militant organizations were a new social fact, a conscious response to the social environment with, more often than not, a social purpose.

These organizations, which had begun to grow in the Napoleonic period, blossomed in the restoration. Usually based on some small and private circle of friends, sometimes secret, they were closely tied to the aristocracy. The best known of them, the Amicizia cattolica in Turin, was as well-connected at court as the Congrégation in France, and, similarly, it died from the suspicions of intrigue which had made it famous. Such circles won broader and more lasting effect through a remarkable array of newspapers and reviews.[3] Dedicated to combating revolution, they understood it to result from original sin and bad books. While doing battle in the name of the Word, however, the Catholic press was establishing connections between religious concern and every aspect of social life. Such efforts helped to make sense of a changing world, and the Catholic press continued to prosper in the 1860s and after unification, often encouraged by Pius IX who insisted, for example, that the Jesuits publish *La Civiltà Cattolica* in Italian rather than the Latin with which they felt safer. In the government repression of 1898 there were twenty-five Catholic papers frightening enough to be shut down.

Other lay organizations, dedicated to accompanying the viaticum and to dozens of other pious observances, sprang up in circles of less social and intellectual distinction; but these unnumbered societies, active in towns across Italy, were more than personal expressions of renewed fervor. They were public and sometimes defiant efforts to establish (they would have said to reestablish) the place of religion in an alien world. And from these efforts grew the sense of the lay apostolate, the need to make one's Witness an act with some effect upon society. Less dynamic than in France—perhaps because such movements appear to have gained their strength primarily from the middle class—they tended like the Society of Saint Vincent de Paul to increase the awareness of social ills among the well-to-do and to sponsor projects of amelioration. In 1854 when there were more than eight hundred conferences of the society in France, there were only a tenth as many in Italy; but the society grew steadily, spreading from Genoa and Rome to Piedmont and then throughout the north. Its receipts from Italy suggest its relative strength. Even in 1860 it collected about as much as the Italian National Society was able to gather in individual gifts for Garibaldi, and the Society of Saint Vincent de Paul maintained an impressive level of contributions from 1855 to 1871. Local conferences visited the poor, established pawnshops, supported some schoolchildren and apprentices. By the 1870s, the conferences in the district of Genoa were supporting over four hundred apprentices, and those under the Bologna conference, with half as many more, even ventured upon a project of ocean bathing for the poor. The society itself began to meet in national assemblies.

More active still were the youth associations; Gioventù cattolica, founded in 1868 and the Opera dei Congressi, established in 1874. This latter, a sprawling organization, of which the Catholic youth and most other lay movements became a part, saw itself first of all in symbolic terms, its every act a gesture of defiance and a testimonial of loyalty to the pope. The rape of the temporal power was the issue that moved it most. Organized in parish and diocesan councils, it encouraged its members in special devotions to the Eucharist and to the Virgin, collected peter's pence, disseminated propaganda, and campaigned for Sunday observance. Led by intransigents quite willing to affront a secular society, its very militance drew it more and more into social action. The growth of the Opera was impressive; its nearly seven hundred parish committees in 1879 had become more than thirteen hundred by 1884 and reached nearly four thousand in 1897. By the 1890s it sponsored hundreds of mutual aid societies, associations of Catholic workers, and rural banks, as well as newspapers, periodicals, and youth groups. Catholics, ready to view liberal society with a jaundiced eye and organized in behalf of social cohesion, did much to make comfortable men aware of the misery of their brethren.

All such ventures into Catholic social action thrived primarily in the north. Giovanni Bosco founded his famed Society of Saint Francis de Sales in Turin during the fateful year of 1859; and though it spread beyond Italy, the most extensive application of his methods for teaching unruly city boys and for reaching workers was always in Piedmont. Leonardo Murialdo's Union of Catholic Workers was established in Turin in 1871, becoming the Subalpine Workers' Federation in 1887. The Society of Saint Vincent de Paul was strongest in Liguria and active throughout Piedmont, Tuscany, Lombardy, and Venetia, with only its Roman conference (strongly supported by the French colony there) a more southern exception. The first national organization of Italian laymen, the Italian Catholic Association for the Defense of the Freedom of the Church in Italy, founded in the 1860s, fared well in northern cities but not in the south, which, Cardinal Sforza explained, was less "up-to-date." The Opera dei Congressi was centered in Bologna and Venice; though its strength spread into central Italy, even at its height the Opera's councils in the south were fewer and less active, except for a significant flurry in Sicily.

The Bolognese leaders of the Opera tended to be the most vigorous advocates of social involvement, and the fact is suggestive. Bologna, like Lyons, another great center of Catholic action, was a thriving commercial city where manufacturing kept its artisan style. Like Lyons, it had a long tradition of radical agitation and resistance to policies determined in a distant capital. Catholics in both cities were quick to learn the importance of social issues and were imaginative in seeking a Christian response. Two other centers of the Opera's strength, Venetia and Sicily, shared a tradition of separation and of opposition to foreign rule which could make alienation fruitful. In Sicily, Don Luigi Sturzo sought to spur real economic change, and the Casse rurali spread in Venetia as nowhere else (nearly two-thirds of them were there), where the use of irrigation must have made small sums of capital especially important to the farmer seeking improvement. Catholic action was most vigorous, apparently, among societies modernized enough to feel the pressures of an international market and to adopt new technology but in which the scale of production remained small and the pain of slow transition real.[4]

Italian Catholics were discovering the social interstices in which they could win a special place with their sensitivity to immediate needs and their belief in the dignity of the struggle for economic well-being. These

Catholics who intruded with such vigor upon a society they disapproved felt a sympathy for those less fortunate that is remarkable among men well fed. Their varied programs and the tone of their expression often revealed the underlying coherence in their view of the world; yet that view remained vague and general. Combining social awareness with Christian concern for individual souls, these social activists could denounce (and even exaggerate) the radical wrongs about them with little temptation to radical solutions. Thus, though they sought to aid the poor of every degree, their programs meant most to a thin layer of society on the edge of economic and social respectability. Whenever possible, Catholic unions were called professional associations. The wish that employers would also join was only slowly abandoned, and so antagonistic a weapon as the strike still more slowly adopted. Mutual aid societies, savings banks, and even pawnshops were useful primarily to those who could hope for lasting gain through a little insurance or small amounts of capital. Like the paternalism so earnestly preached or the clublike atmosphere of weekly meetings, these were measures most appropriate to skilled workers, small shopkeepers, and artisans. Similarly, rural banks and cooperatives were important to those who owned their own equipment or livestock. The Opera dei Congressi had many of the marks of a mass movement in a society that had yet to experience one, but the strength of its social action rested more narrowly upon those groups acutely sensitive to the current of social change who had something to lose and much to hope for. By the turn of the century, the Opera had begun to organize among women and university students, two other groups belonging to middle-class society but not fully integrated into it.

In 1904, however, the Opera dei Congressi, was dissolved on papal instructions. The period marks a major turning point in the social role of Catholics. The new Unioni Cattoliche which replaced the Opera were far more firmly subordinate to the bishops, a change which reflects both the Vatican's determination to direct the church in its social action (as in its war on modernism) and some concern for the growing accommodation of Catholics to Italian society. The dissolution of the Opera had seemed at first a defeat for the growing numbers of Christian democrats within its ranks, a new generation determined to press on to mass organization and legislative programs. But even in politics the position of the intransigents, who had so disdainfully refused to take part in the elections of a liberal state, was being undermined. From the election of 1904 on, the public participation of Catholics steadily increased, making the first experience of universal suffrage in 1913 far less frightening to Giolitti and his supporters. Now there were bishops like Radini Tedeschi in Bergamo who supported labor unions and accepted strikes. The writings of Giuseppe Toniolo, leading Catholic economist and reformer, gave Italian social

Catholicism broader horizons and invited more sweeping programs, and its local leaders were developing more aggressive methods (see Chapter 4).

The Opera dei Congressi had in fact been weakened by the exhaustion of older forms of social action as well as by internal dissension. The intransigents had built on regional ties of declining relevance to a national economy. They had taught that society's privileged had a responsibility to lead by example, but young Christian democrats rejected that aristocratic precept and noted instead the influence of leaders working through organization. Intransigents had argued for the cooperation of classes, insisting that the peasant be given a just price and the worker a just wage, but workers and peasants were likely to learn from this that they were being cheated by those in power. Catholic propaganda—emphasizing the dignity of honest work, the virtues of thrift and sobriety, and the evils of avarice in landlord and employer—had contributed to the class antagonism it denied. It was no longer enough to appeal to those resentful of modernization whose voices were coming to count for less or to build upon subcultures of artisans and farmers, helping to inject them into society at large. Yet thousands of Italians had learned to cope more effectively with the modern world through cooperative action, savings banks, organized interest groups, and special training—thanks to the activities and concerns of Catholics, most of whom never employed the word modern as an adjective of praise.

The formal separation of Italian Catholics from liberal society was neither vague nor subtle. Their abstention from national elections gave silence the power of symbol; and the simple act of not voting, multiplied by thousands and recurring regularly, added an air of immeasurable threat to elections which were otherwise liberalism's most appealing and sacred rite. "Ne eletti, ne elettori [Neither elected officeholders nor voters]," Don Giacomo Margotti's ringing challenge in *Armonia*, took its place with "Italia farà da se" among the famous phrases of the national experience. Don Margotti had been looking back to the elections of 1857 when Cavourians unseated legitimately elected but conservative Catholics; distrust of liberalism was no reason not to pillory liberals for violating their own principles. By the 1870s the tactic of abstention, dignified with the sanction of the papal *Non expedit*, was a challenge to the legitimacy of the liberal state.

Always ready to assert that the church was in touch with the "real" Italy, the Catholic press regularly reminded its readers of how the Italian state had been the creation of sheer force. The more intransigent periodicals consistently confounded the Risorgimento with the French Revolution, thus denying even that bourgeois moderation which radicals denounced. Nonparticipation, begun as a tactic of outraged principle and continued as a challenge to the state's legitimacy, implied the disturbing prediction that this state, too, would pass away. Resting on force rather than the popular will, without deep roots in Italian history, it was inherently ephemeral, a historic stage to be survived. Most Catholics did not go so far and were never this explicit, but a fundamental challenge to the legitimacy of the state was kept alive as a significant part of Italian political life. Reactionaries were the most outspoken, just as they were the first to assail the Risorgimento as the work of narrow economic and class interests, but such judgments could also spur demands for reform and quite radical proposals. Whatever its political thrust, the Catholic challenge contributed to the "isolative character" of Italian politics.[5] A society not suffering from any excess of machinery became sensitive to the perils of industrialization even before they were widespread. By associating the mechanistic device of counting votes with a social system that treated man only as an economic animal, Catholics could present liberalism as a more selfish expression of class interest than most Marxists would allege. The confiscation of church property was not only an act of irreligion but one that benefited the rich at the expense of the poor.

These various strains of opposition to liberalism were brought together and given new sophistication by Luigi Sturzo, for whom the combination of traditional political theory, practical Catholic action, and modern social analysis was made easier by the fact that Italian Catholics had been even less tempted by nineteenth-century economic thought than Catholics in countries where industrialization had come earlier.[6] He felt no need to acknowledge any of its apparent benefits as he denounced "the canon of *lasciar fare* and *lasciar passare*—founded on the theory of the prevalence of stronger forces over the less strong as an absolute law of progress— an egoistic and pagan theory which had in liberalism its crude realization. . . ." He considered "profoundly real" the criticisms of "atomistic liberalism, powerful capitalism, state centralism, dishonest administration, oppressive pauperism . . . the abnormal and precarious conditions of the proletariat, the debasement of labor thanks to unchecked competition, to egoistical, militaristic, and wasteful policy, to monopolistic liberalism." [7] Through propaganda and organization, Italian Catholics sought to take advantage of all the liberties the law permitted; but for many of them even these opportunities represented not the virtues of liberalism but its weakness, one more contradiction in a feeble and fallacious system.

Because they tended to equate liberalism with simple egoism, many Catholic writers added an ethical judgment. Liberalism could be blamed not only for political corruption and social injustice but for a more fundamental emptiness. In Catholic eyes liberalism lacked any useful sense of the common good, any doctrine of corporate responsibility, and any theory of culture. Art and literature, they argued, were social expressions:

at their highest, achievements of Christian society. Out of their own sense of alienation, out of particular political wrongs and general social ills, Catholics made an important contribution to a ferment of discontent that viewed everything from rural poverty to bad art as one more symptom that contemporary civilization was sick. For some Catholics, at least, it was easy to add with complacent disdain that this was the necessary fate of a society based on error.

Understandably, the leaders of an insecure, liberal state reacted strongly. The Cavourians of the old right had hoped through separation and political freedom to resolve the legal issues between church and state. Sometimes they had even imagined that a thriving liberal culture might revitalize a modern church which would inspire the new Italy. As the conflict proved intractable, these visions faded, and questions of religion were discussed in more narrowly legal terms. The tactic was artificial, but it became almost a tradition among moderate men, accounting for the strange silence about the larger role of religion in Italian life which left uneasy gaps in political discourse then and in historiography later.[8] The left, less tempted by dreams of the church reformed, confronted the threat to liberalism more aggressively; and the descriptions by Catholic writers of Masonic conspiracies poisoning the schools, the press, and the theater were matched by a very similar picture of clerical armies subverting the new order. Indeed, widespread belief in conspiracies may itself be an important characteristic of Catholic culture in an apparently secularizing society. If the left often conceived of the church as some vast, wealthy, and disciplined political army, its fears of clerical propaganda and influence were reinforced by the Catholic tendency to attribute the changes of a century to the influence of a few Voltairean ideas. Sella in 1874 had labeled the "black international" more dangerous than the red, and Sonnino at the end of the century spoke of socialism and clerical organization as the two revolutionary forces to be feared.[9]

These comparisons are significant, for they indicate the isolation of Italian liberals. Anticlericalism was useful to Crispi, but it could not for long win reliable support from the groups on the left which were becoming increasingly important. No Dreyfus case arose in Italy to unite half the nation in support of a liberal government. At the theoretical level, anticlericalism was a part of the more far-reaching efforts to define the proper role of a laic state;[10] but it failed to mobilize the masses, while it offended the liberal gentry.

Thus the anticlerical forays of the 1880s and 1890s were a source of serious turmoil and division but not of political strength, and conflict easily degenerated into battles of symbols more than principles. The attacks on the casket of Pius IX in 1881, the statue of Giordano Bruno, speeches in Rome, and proposals for anticlerical legislation sustained a perilous atmosphere, and that is important; but they did not give focus to political life. Even the issue of public education proved less explosive in a poor society badly divided than it did in France. Legislation on divorce remained only a threat. The politics of anticlericalism was further inhibited by international complications; for the central issue between church and state remained the temporal power. Italy did not quite experience either a war between church and state in the style of Bismarck or the great battle of ideas that sundered France. When the state directly attacked the social role of the church, disbanding Catholic Action and suppressing Catholic papers in 1898, it was part of a general panic, the crisis of a narrow liberalism terrified by spectres on both the left and right. By associating Catholicism and socialism, the Marquis Antonio di Rudinì acknowledged that both were among the vital forces in a changing society. On the eve of the First World War Gaetano Salvemini could comfortably insist that Italy was an anticlerical country, but he scorned as delusive any efforts to attack the church through restrictive legislation. The real issues were education and social programs; in these spheres the state needed only to outperform the church, a challenge which, he added, required new parties, new policies, and full democracy.[11]

Fear of Catholic influence was a primary fact in Italian politics. It was less important, however, in electoral campaigns and official policies than as a limitless source of insecurity and as the most effective argument against enlarging the suffrage. Francesco De Sanctis's fear in 1864 that universal suffrage would give power to the priests and to the rich had not been forgotten fifty years later. In Italy even the most determined secularists could not claim that the church was a foreign influence; nor, after the 1880s, that it was strong only among the ignorant and backward. In a sense, both sides had found their conflict useful. Catholics, unimplicated in the disappointments of the new Italy, were freed for imaginative participation in social programs. The church of the committed proved in many ways more vital than the church of everyone. Liberals, on the other hand, anxious to recapture the enthusiasm of the Risorgimento, pointed to the perils Italy still faced, and the church was pictured as a domestic and international threat before which patriots must remain united despite high taxes or the postponement of democracy. Politicians, disheartened by their inability to reach the Italian masses, found solace in blaming the priests. Even as Catholics formally reentered the political arena, they sought to maintain their defensive posture: they would vote and be candidates only to defeat the greater evil of materialistic socialism. And the very government that encouraged their participation and benefited by their support made it a condition of joining the cause of the Entente in 1915 that the papacy would not be represented at the peace conference.

Toward the end of the nineteenth century, the disagreements among

Catholics were becoming a matter of public, and not always benevolent, comment. But conflict over participation in local elections, forms of social action, and the subordination of the laity to the hierarchy was in itself the result of their greater involvement in society and the awareness it brought of social complexity. Catholics had become public participants in a modern world, using all the available techniques of organization and propaganda. To Catholics, however, these open disagreements were a shock. For years, proud of a militant unanimity, they had fondly fostered the myth of their social isolation. There was a loss in having to admit that Catholics, too, were subject to society's confusions. When they seemed the victims of their era, Catholic leaders had responded by raising the spiritual and practical standards of what it meant to be a Catholic. The faithful were urged to take part in special worship and frequent communion and to demonstrate their loyalty to church and pope by the newspapers they read, the schools they supported, the clubs they joined, and the elections they boycotted. There was something heroic in demanding from outside the practical world that Italians be provided better working conditions and improved credit, but that quality was diminished as Catholic programs became more detailed and specific. Militant Catholic unity and self-discipline were more easily maintained in isolation.

The bitter conflict of the 1890s opened the way for a limited reconciliation between liberal government and Catholic church. Neither the church, concerned for its institutional security, nor the state, anxious for any supporters it could find, was quite so fervently opposed to the other as rhetorical custom made both sound. With no large Catholic bloc in politics, the army, or the bureaucracy, the government could abandon some traditional fears; so could a church more challenged in France where the *ralliement* had failed than in Italy where the Risorgimento had won.

In fact, Catholics and liberals were discovering some interests in common. Both made a distinction between state and society which left some room for accommodation. They shared a respect for order, and in the twentieth century each could see the utility of cooperating to maintain it. They shared, too, a detestation of political sects and were anxious to avoid becoming sects themselves. Beneath institutional conflict, strong ties remained. Many Catholics were patriots whose nationalism was irrepressible during the Libyan campaign or the First World War. The correspondence between Pius IX and Victor Emmanuel II or the friendly dealings of Mgr. Chavaz with Cavour represented a tradition of private relations which found some counterpart in the experience of nearly every prefect and bishop. The southern clergy, Italy's least educated and most conservative, had never really resisted cooperation with the state but rather had extended old patterns of clientelism and local influence to make that cooperation safe. In the north and in Sicily social activism led a new generation to seek further involvement. Gradually, public Catholic political participation was added to the traditional expressions of Catholic presence —militant opposition, social action, institutional negotiation, and private accommodation.

The founding of the Partito Popolare in 1919, the culmination of this change, had been facilitated by the test of war, for the Vatican's autonomy had been respected by the state, and Italian Catholics had proved loyal patriots. At the same time, Don Sturzo viewed the war itself as a product of bourgeois politics and unfettered capitalism, an interpretation that fit well with Italy's disillusionment and domestic strife. If the Popularists represented the massive reentry of Catholics into public life, they came on new terms. The party, antiliberal, was unwilling to assist the Giolittian moderates in their tangled compromises; instead it demanded democracy and substantial reform. More striking still, it claimed to be "aconfessional"; by proclaiming its independence of the hierarchy and the Vatican, it was abandoning the old insistence on Catholic unity. To Antonio Gramsci the new party was a sign of the "spiritual renewal of the Italian people."

Immediately successful, the party gained one-fifth of the total vote in both 1919 and 1921 to become second by only a little to the Socialists. In the new game of mass politics, the network of Catholic societies and newspapers had proved invaluable. Not only did the new party effectively pull together traditional Catholic groups, Catholic Action (Azione Cattolica), and Catholic unions (which now claimed millions of workers), but it also recruited into political life rural elements whose voice had rarely been heard before. From the first, the Popularists, despite their internal divisions, showed themselves remarkably tempted by a share of power. Beginning in late 1922 their presence in government seemed of itself a dramatic change, an end to old evils. Their own program was hardly monolithic, and the new opportunity to have even some of it effected—to have a Catholic voice heard, for example, on education—was irresistible. Men who considered themselves outside the traditional political system, whose principles were proclaimed to be above the petty interests of older parties, felt themselves untainted by the very politics they played. Sharing power, especially in a time of crisis, seemed so natural that it was easily extended, despite the doubts of Sturzo and others, to Mussolini's first government. Only later did the Partito Popolare establish itself as part of the fixed opposition to Fascism, most of its deputies joining with the socialists in the futile gestures of democracy's last years. A favorite target of Fascist violence, the party was steadily bludgeoned until its dissolution in 1926, unwept by hierarchy or pope. Indeed, the Vatican clearly considered the cooperation of Catholics and socialists an error far graver than leaving the political field to the Fascists.

The implications of Don Sturzo's brave claim to have mobilized the democratic majority of Italian Catholics were never fairly tested.

With some notable exceptions, Catholics were on the whole surprisingly slow to recognize the special threat Fascism presented them. Experienced in long conflict with the state, they had developed a keen sense of those symbolic acts that expressed a whole position (or foretold an impending crisis); and they were peculiarly vulnerable to the cynical use of gesture. Mussolini's display of respect for the papacy or the government's benevolence toward religious processions were welcomed like the abrupt cessation of a pain long endured. Fascism offered concrete benefits as well (and then cited them as evidence that a separate political party to defend Catholic interests was no longer needed). The proposal to restore religious education in the primary schools moved a Catholic congress meeting in 1923 to send a telegram to Mussolini, naïvely praising "the government's noble proposal to honor once more the precious moral and spiritual values and the centuries-old heritage of the nation." [12] Fascism benefited enormously from Catholic joy at seeing the church once more in the mainstream of Italian public life, and even in conflict Fascism recognized the church as a social and political force, a welcome change from secularist contempt.

Nor did Fascist theories provoke automatic distrust, for vigorous denunciation of liberal hypocrisy and bourgeois self-interest, along with vague visions of corporativist cooperation, had long been a part of Catholic culture. Indeed, Fascist behavior at its crudest was, after all, only worse by degree than the descriptions of secularist atrocities against religion that for years filled *La Civiltà Cattolica*. Two generations of hyperbole dimmed the senses and lessened the immediate shock that might have made pious men respond more effectively to brutal beatings and pagan praise of force. Believing themselves so long beleaguered, they were all the more tempted to welcome the enemy of their enemies, and fear of communism made such temptations seem pragmatic good sense. To many, an honored public place for the church as an institution seemed a gain well worth the loss of political freedom or an independent Catholic party insistent on divisive social reform.

The Lateran Accords of 1929 were instantly Fascism's most popular achievement, and they have proved perhaps its most enduring. The treaty and the Concordat that accompanied it not only ended the Roman Question by establishing Vatican City but also recognized Catholicism as the religion of state, provided for religious education in public elementary and secondary schools, and recognized canon law in matters of marriage and family rights. Patriots could cheer that Italy was united at last, her Catholics no longer either opposed to or separate from the Italian state. Catholics could hail the concessions won, especially in the Concordat, which gave official recognition and considerable autonomy to their church. To opponents of Fascism, the church seemed in the next decade to become inextricably implicated in Fascist policy, particularly during the Ethiopian War, for which bishops and clergy frequently expressed the most unrestrained support. Even the denunciations of particular Fascist policies were expressed in temperate tones that seemed a significant contrast with the fulminations against the liberal monarchy.

Yet the church, although more inhibited than at any time in modern Italian history, did resist the persistent attacks on the remaining forms of Catholic Action and did formally denounce Mussolini's racial policy in late 1938. No opposition to a complete totalitarianization of Italian life was more formidable.[13] A few years later, as Allied armies slowly moved up the peninsula, Catholic laymen and clergy were often active in the Resistance, rebuilding the base from which a Catholic party would come to dominate Italy's postwar political life. The Christian Democrats, however, were heir to more than the Popularist tradition, for they also replaced the secular parties as the major voice of the political center and absorbed most of the right as the leading opponent of communism in the bifurcated "cold war" world. The church and all the various shades of opinion and interest it encompassed was from the first an integral part of the republican fabric.

Even so brief a sketch suggests something of the ways in which Catholic belief and the Catholic church have helped to shape modern Italy. The most important point, perhaps, is the one historians most easily overlook: that influence has been far broader, deeper, and more varied than mere conflict between church and state, however central that may have been.

First, Italian views of marriage, the family, and social justice, Italian cultural values, and Italian education in form and content have remained very largely Catholic.

Second, the church was an important factor in the process of modernization, providing education and job training, networks of communication, and social relief which stimulated the process of change even when seeking to slow it. Catholic activity gave millions of Italians their first experience of how to combine and to act in their own interests, teaching the techniques of organization, propaganda, demonstration, and coercion necessary for influence in a complex, mass society. And participants in such activities came thereby to see themselves as part of national life.

Third, at the same time Catholic activities greatly complicated that modernization process. They did not permit the painful death of a pre-industrial society to go ignored but injected the anguish of the unheeded —artisans, peasants, aristocrats—into national life. Whether this was done with reactionary regret or radical indignation—and there were Catholics of both sorts—the effect was to strengthen resistance to the liberal bourgeoisie and to accelerate the political mobilization of backward areas. Catholic organizations and propaganda provided all those people who had reason to distrust a world of middle-class rationalism with arguments and tactics far more effective than they could have devised on their own. The weaknesses of modernization as an ideal and as experienced in Italy were precociously exposed, and the process itself was presented as an alien imposition, the result of foreign ideologies and special interests. Vast social changes may sometimes be easier to adjust to if perceived as separate, but Catholic critics argued even before taught by experience that a commercial economy, factory life, urbanization, social mobility, secularization, and a more intrusive government were all interconnected and in turn related to unemployment, class conflict, and high taxes. Their propaganda contributed to a pessimism that, even in times of prosperity, leaves Italians disposed to doubt that economic growth can be indigenous or lasting.

Catholic critics of industrialization were aided by an intellectual tradition rich in its perceptions of human nature and social needs while relatively unencumbered by commitment to specific solutions. They thus proved readier than most to adapt elements from the solutions of others, to try propaganda, cooperatives, land banks, paternalism, unions, and political action. Stimulated by their own sense of isolation and resentment as well as by their traditions of organization, they mobilized *padroni* and artisans, peasants and elites to more effective resistance.

The effects of this opposition often moved beyond the ideas on which it rested. Catholic writers discussed corporativism in terms that simultaneously encompassed simpleminded nostalgia and modern sophistication, terms that proved useful to tired aristocrats, socialists, and Fascists. In a society with one of Europe's oldest urban traditions, Catholics often spoke of rural life with the voice of the Vicomte De Bonald; but out of this affection for the countryside there grew a strong movement for social reform. The paternalism so prevalent in Catholic social theory, happily mocked by Marxists, was not irrelevant to a nation of tiny workshops and rented land; and if few employers behaved like Christian fathers, that justified organizing against them. As Toniolo put it, the church first gave the aristocracy its chance, then the bourgeoisie; now it was up to the people. Opposition to class conflict in principle could sometimes fan its flames in practice. After all, Sturzo argued, class conflict was merely the translation to groups of that individual warfare cherished by liberal economists. Similarly, the church was more willing than any other respectable institution to acknowledge the misery around it and readier to inform others about the realities of land contracts and urban housing.

Italians were allowed few of the nineteenth century's comforting illusions about the social cost of industrialization and rapid change.

Fourth, Catholics contributed significantly and in several ways to that negative view of government which many American social scientists have regretfully established as a characteristic of Italian civic life. Not only were Catholics for two generations the state's most consistent and effective critics, but the church frequently displayed an ability to penetrate deep into society which a liberal regime could not match. While advertising the dangers of statism, Catholics in their militant autonomy made the state seem weak. Anticlericals, believing that the church competed with the state, were thus further frustrated and tempted to substitute coercion for strength. The earnest leaders of united Italy wanted badly to believe in the will of the people; confronted with popular ignorance and social rigidity, they often escaped despair by blaming the priests. Inadvertently, then, the church helped sustain the unrealistic visions of the left which, while joining in contempt for the existing regime, anticipated religion's decay and imagined an intractable society become suddenly malleable. Yet accommodation was unavoidable, and so two opposed sets of institutions seemed constantly to be making arrangements that belied their public policies, providing fodder for increased rumor and suspicion and a model of how one dealt with the forces of government which has been much copied by political parties, industrialists, local patrons, and labor unions. While denied the ability to accomplish durable solutions, politics in Italy was credited with a capacity for infinite deals.

Fifth, Catholicism has obviously influenced the terms and tone of Italian political debate. While liberals lectured on the role of economic forces beyond political control, Catholics had insisted that politics and politicians bore responsibility for social conditions. That alone was enough to make Catholics seem the more modern, but their influence had no single political direction. The church could, of course, be a bulwark of social order; and Giolitti therefore encouraged a more direct Catholic participation in politics. But just as the denunciations by Catholic writers of middle-class avarice stimulated class resentment, so their critique of liberalism frequently coincided with socialist arguments. Vigorous opponents of socialism, Catholics helped to make the movement more familiar and less frightening by labeling it the natural extension of liberalism and by advertising a communist menace as early as 1847 (and frequently thereafter). Catholic sensitivity to the plight of the humble, Catholic visions of a socially active state and Catholic descriptions of the good society also affected the Italian left. So did the feeling that a comprehensive ideology and righteous indignation were more admirable than pragmatic compromise or the tradition of a rhetoric aflame with moral fervor and anathema. When Filippo Turati took the chair before the constitutional parties meeting to honor the death of Matteotti and mark the Aventine secession of anti-Fascists, he expressed their anguish in moving terms. "The miracle of Galilee," argued the leader of Italian socialism, "is renewed." [14]

Sixth, both the notable continuity and sense of high tension that have marked modern Italian history are related to the vital presence of the church. Through the French Revolution and Restoration, the Risorgimento, the liberal monarchy, Fascism, the Resistance, and the republic, Catholic institutions have provided important connecting links that restrained effort at radical change. The continuity that contributes to national identity is, however, also a source of frustration in an era of social transformation. Problems of industrial production, social interest, and national policy were in Italy still discussed in terms of family, corporate, and Christian responsibility—terms that bring to bear a rich philosophic heritage but risk burying specific issues and obscuring awareness of concrete change. The very ambiguity of social change is underscored by a church that tends with its institutional voice to stress old benefits undermined by modernization, while with its spiritual voice denying that anything is altered and upholding visions of how much better life might be. Similarly, in defending itself, the church has helped to make Italy a pluralistic society while deploring pluralism. As firmly as the propagandists of the Risorgimento, of Marxism, or of Fascism, Catholics have been inclined to consider unanimity on great issues the mark of a healthy civilization and to confuse its absence in Italy with decadence.

External critic, independent institution, and integral part of the social fabric, the Catholic church is ubiquitous in Italy; yet it has no fixed position on the mundane issues of politics and economics, a matter of grave frustration for politicians who have sought some durable basis of understanding. Such a force, always present but in secular matters neither predictable nor controllable, produces fears of conspiracy (on both sides), the temptation to seek relief in the extremes of clerical obscurantism or priest-baiting, and the uncomfortable feeling, strong even among moderates, that most of what matters in public life is hidden from public view. Secularists from Sella to Salvemini and Gramsci have tended to predict the church's decline, citing the inadequacies of its social programs; but those are expendable, merely a manifestation of its closeness to society. Catholic social influence has thus proved far more lasting than the particular issues and programs that seemed to be its source; yet who knows what issue will next evoke a "Catholic" response? Some Catholics saw the Libyan war as a crusade against the Turk and perceived the First World War as the battle of Catholic Austria against schismatic Russia. Leading social Catholics not only felt closely attached to kindred spirits in other countries but contributed to making social reform in Britain, France, and Germany a part of Italian discussion, thereby thrusting Italy still more into the European mainstream, just as admirers of De Maistre or Lamennais had done a half-century before. The church has been both closely tied to Italian national pride and a vehicle for foreign influence. Alcide De Gasperi's significantly titled *Renaissance of Christian Democracy* treated in detail the tribulations of Cardinal Manning, Vogelsang, and La Tour du Pin; and Italian Christian Democrats have been strong advocates of European cooperation.

These multiple connections and complications have been confounded by a parallel trend in politics (from Giolitti through Fascism and postwar Christian Democracy) and in the church (from Pius IX up to Pope John XXIII): the greater and greater injection of Catholics into Italian political life was accompanied by increased effort on the part of the Vatican to maintain central direction over Catholic social action. Thus, the conflicts, maneuvers, and disagreements within church life (at once theological, political, and personal) have been part of the interests, intrigues, and prejudices of Italian politics since the turn of the century—from the battle against modernism in 1909 through the reorganizations of Catholic Action in the early 1920s, the Concordat in 1929, and the triumph of the Christian Democratic party in the late 1940s.

A central point emerges clearly and challengingly for all students of Italian society: the Catholic church in Italy has been more than part of the Italian heritage, like ancient Rome or the Renaissance; more than a social complication like regionalism, more than the locus of powerful social and intellectual movements, more, above all, than the shrewd monolithic institution so often described; for Catholicism has both pushed and resisted, and therefore in part determined the effect of the dynamic forces that shaped Italian development.

NOTES

1. Works dealing with different aspects of Catholicism in Italian life are: Arturo Carlo Jemolo, *Chiesa e Stato in Italia negli ultimi cento anni* (Turin: Einaudi, 1952); Gabriele De Rosa, *Storia del movimento cattolico in Italia;* Vol. I, *Dalla restaurazione all'età giolittiana;* Vol. II, *Il Partito popolare* (Bari: Laterza, 1966); Dino Secco Suardo, *I cattolici intransigenti* (Brescia: Morcelliana, 1962); L. Riva Sanseverino, *Il movimento sindacale cristiano* (Rome: Zuffi, 1950); Giovanni Spadolini, *L'opposizione cattolica da Porta Pia al '98* (Florence: Vallecchi, 1955) and *Giolitti e i cattolici* (Florence: Le Monnier, 1959); S. William Halperin, *The Separation of Church and State in Italian Thought* (Chicago: University of Chicago Press, 1937) and *Italy and the Vatican at War*

(Chicago: University of Chicago Press, 1939); R. A. Webster, *The Cross and the Fasces* (Stanford: Stanford University Press, 1960); D. A. Binchy, *Church and State in Fascist Italy* (Oxford: Oxford University Press, 1941).

2. Suardo thinks literacy was higher in the "Catholic" areas of Lombardy-Venetia in 1900 as a result of Catholic schools (*op. cit.*, pp. 80–81), but comparative statistics are generally lacking.

3. An account of these efforts before unification can be found in De Rosa, *op. cit.*, I, 16–72.

4. De Rosa, *op. cit.*, I, 80–81, 154–155, 181–189, 208–209, 280, 368.

5. Joseph La Palombara, "Italy: Fragmentation, Isolation, Alienation," in Lucian Pye and Sidney Verba, eds., *Political Culture and Political Development* (Princeton: Princeton University Press, 1965), pp. 301–302.

6. G. De Rosa, *op. cit.*, I, 84–85, makes this point—though I think with some misunderstanding of the thought of French Catholic economists—in comparing the Society of St. Vincent de Paul in France and Italy.

7. From a speech of 1902 reprinted in *Opera omnia di Luigi Sturzo*, seconda serie, I, *Sintesi sociali* (Bologna: 1961), pp. 9, 13.

8. The point is nicely discussed in Suardo, *op. cit.*, pp. 7–16.

9. De Rosa, *op. cit.*, I, 309; Jemolo, *op. cit.*, pp. 319–320. The general question of anticlericalism in the 1870s is subtly analyzed in Federico Chabod, *Storia della politica estera italiana dal 1870 al 1890;* Vol. I, *Le premesse* (Bari: Laterza, 1951), 210–283.

10. Halperin, *op. cit.*, pp. 40–58.

11. G. Salvemini, *"Il ministro della mala vita,"* e altri scritti sull'Italia giolittiana (Milan: Feltrinelli, 1962), pp. 353, 365–369.

12. Cited in G. De Rosa, *op. cit.*, II, 383.

13. The relations of church and Fascism are among the few aspects of the church's role in modern Italian history which have been the subject of balanced studies in English; see Webster, *op. cit.*, and Binchy, *op. cit.*

14. Quoted in De Rosa, *op. cit.*, II, 482.

CHAPTER 12

ITALIAN INTELLECTUALS

EMILIANA P. NOETHER

For centuries, while Italy remained divided into states with different laws, economies, and often antagonistic governments, its intellectuals developed a common language and laid the bases for a national culture.[1] The poets Dante Alighieri and Francesco Petrarca, the philosophers Giordano Bruno and Tommaso Campanella, the historians Ludovico Muratori and Giambattista Vico—each contributed to the formation of an Italian cultural identity. By the eighteenth century this identity was strong enough to survive two decades of French hegemony.[2] While most Italian intellectuals accepted French revolutionary ideas and served Napoleon, men like the poet and soldier Ugo Foscolo and the publicist Vincenzo Cuoco ultimately reaffirmed their belief in a distinct Italian tradition.

After the Congress of Vienna those who wrote for the *Conciliatore* at Milan were asserting their right to think for themselves. They wanted economic and social reforms and preferred romanticism to the now arid classicism supported by Austria. Thus, intellectual rebellion against superseded ideas and concepts marked the beginning of the Risorgimento. Men of diverse interests and political outlook like the philosophers and theologians Antonio Romagnosi and Raffaele Lambruschini, the historian and reformer Gino Capponi, the writer Alessandro Manzoni, the economist Carlo Cattaneo, the critic Niccolò Tommaseo, and the editor Gian Pietro Vieusseux shared an awareness of the need for change and modernization in Italian life. Vitally concerned with the state of their society, they sought the causes of Italy's decline and suggested reforms. But only with Giuseppe Mazzini and Vincenzo Gioberti did a new commitment to the national cause emerge.

Going beyond the social, economic, and educational programs of the Capponis and Cattaneos, Mazzini and Gioberti called for a political organization of Italy in which Italians would rule themselves. Without unity, they asserted, reforms would be meaningless. For Gioberti this unity was to be achieved by a federation under papal leadership. Mazzini wanted a centralized people's republic. In both men intellectual speculation rested on well-defined political goals to be achieved through action. In their writings both considered the role of the intellectual in the national movement to be paramount. In the early 1840s Gioberti claimed that whoever wrote well would transform public opinion and would become the leader of free men because they would accept his ideas. After describing at some length the responsibilities of intellectuals, Gioberti concluded that there was only one "source of progress: the creative force of ideas." [3] Keeping his faith in the indissolubility of thought and action, Mazzini survived the vicissitudes of imprisonment, exile, conspiracy, and revolution to see the ultimate failure of his republican ideals.

Ideas, programs, goals were necessary, but Mazzini insisted that they would accomplish little by themselves. Action was needed to give substance to the world of ideas. Thus, thought and action, translated into a working relationship between intellectuals and the masses, dominated Mazzini's thinking and writing. More than any other thinker during the Risorgimento, Mazzini wanted to reach the Italian masses. He realized that if Italy were truly to *risorgere* it had to be through the involvement of all its people. "Revolution," he wrote, "must be made by the people and for the people." If revolution remained the monopoly of a single class and led only to the substitution of one aristocracy for another, Italy would never be able to take its rightful place among other nations. For him the intellectual had to be fully committed—*engagé* in the events of his times.

Gioberti and Mazzini agreed that Italy had had a great past and was destined to a greater future. The very title of Gioberti's most popular work *Del primato morale e civile degli italiani* [The moral and civil primacy of the Italians], published in 1843, and Mazzini's vision of a "third Rome"—that of the people—which would lead in the emergence of a better society expressed a deeply felt conviction that the Italian people were destined for leadership. All that prevented them from fulfilling their destiny was lack of independence and unity. Once these were attained, Italy would take its rightful place among the great nations. However, the ideas of Mazzini and Gioberti did not receive unqualified acceptance by all Italian intellectuals, for some, like Cattaneo, could not agree to such a simplistic view of Italian problems.

During 1848 and 1849 the intellectuals had their opportunity to become men of action. In Italy, as elsewhere in Europe, the upheavals of these two years truly represented the "revolution of the intellectuals." Leaving their studies, they moved into positions of leadership. Capponi became prime minister of Tuscany. Cattaneo assumed direction of the insurrection in Milan. The historian Cesare Balbo and Gioberti were successively called to the premiership in Piedmont. Tommaseo participated in the Venetian revolt. The Neapolitan literary critic Francesco De Sanctis served Ferdinand II in a short-lived ministry. Hastening to Italy from his English exile, Mazzini became triumvir of the Roman Republic. By 1850 these various popular and constitutional governments had collapsed. Their brief hour as political leaders ended, Italian intellectuals returned to their customary role as men of letters and ideas.

Among the states of the peninsula, Piedmont alone preserved the constitution granted in 1848. Another intellectual, the painter and novelist Massimo D'Azeglio, headed the ministry after 1849, to be succeeded by Cavour in 1852. Cavour, who was to assume control of the national movement, appreciated the importance of winning over that sector of public opinion represented by the intellectuals. Accordingly, he welcomed and helped many whose involvement in the 1848 and 1849 revolts had made them persona non grata in their own state. As a result, an influential number of intellectuals rallied to the support of the Savoy monarchy.

Thus, through this decisive period in the emergence of modern Italy, intellectuals created an idealized and glorified past for their country, influenced and sometimes participated in shaping the course of events in their own times, and formulated an Italian future that had little reality or substance. Yet without their dreams, faith, fervor, sacrifices, and support, the Italian peoples would not have been joined into a state.[4]

After 1860 the cumbersome task of uniting twenty-odd million people at different levels of economic development, political sophistication, and literacy revealed the hollowness of claims to potential leadership and primacy. Disillusionment was widespread, though not all would go as far as Mazzini in condemning the new Italy. Mazzini's republicanism colored his profound distrust for unity achieved under monarchical leadership. In 1870 he summed up his life's work in these bitter words: "I thought to evoke the soul of Italy and I see only its corpse." Increasingly, intellectuals became critical of a state flawed by bureaucratic pettiness, financial stringency, and political weakness. Giosuè Carducci, Italy's leading poet, echoed the feelings of many when he warned to walk softly so as not to wake those sleeping in Rome.

Part of this disillusion and disenchantment stemmed from the fact that Italy had been united on the bases of certain liberal principles prevalent in nineteenth-century European thought which were being abandoned at the time Italy came into existence as a nation. Social Darwinism, Marxian socialism, imperialism, Bismarckian politics influenced Europe's thinking and acting after 1870. The ideals of the Risorgimento were obsolete, but Italy's leaders failed to make the transition to a position from which to deal effectively with a rapidly changing European scene.[5] Thus, many intellectuals turned from supporters into bitter critics. In a sense, they remained true to their vocation as intellectuals—if to be an intellectual is to be the critic and conscience of society. During the Risorgimento they had opposed the status quo. In the dialectics of historical change the Italian nation-state now represented the status quo to be viewed critically.

The thrust of their criticism was directed against the parliamentary system as a corruption of higher values and a betrayal of the ideals of the Risorgimento. In 1877 De Sanctis, a veteran of the 1848 Neapolitan revolution and one of Italy's leading literary critics, aired his views. He accused parliament of perverting representative government and pointed out that lacking national parties, Italy was governed by groups drawing support from regional clienteles. As transformism became the established practice of government, criticism increased. The 1880s witnessed a growing dissatisfaction, widespread throughout the country but articulated particularly by the intellectuals, with the institution of parliament as it functioned in Italy.

One of the first to sense the changed intellectual and cultural *Weltanschauung* in Europe, Pasquale Turiello applied Darwinian terminology to politics and referred to the "struggle for life" between nations and among groups within a nation. From his analysis of the growing breach between government and governed in Italy, he concluded that parliament ignored national interests. Parties lacked ideological context, fragmented as they were into factions and clienteles. Elections were farces. The national conscience was fading into the personal and immediate goals of individuals. Bitterly, Turiello noted that Italy's political parties fought *in* the country and not *for* the country.[6]

A more analytical criticism of the parliamentary system came from Gaetano Mosca, then a young scholar in his mid-twenties, just beginning a long and distinguished career. He accused the government of betraying the Risorgimento and denounced the very character of parliamentary institutions. According to Mosca, the commonly accepted premise that deputies were elected by the people was false, for voters did not elect the deputy; the latter had himself elected by the voters.[7]

Some years later Vilfredo Pareto elaborated upon the same theme in his study of political leadership. Also a journalist, Pareto commented on Italian life for the *Giornale degli economisti* and discussed current problems. When Enrico Corradini started the nationalist journal *Il Regno* in 1903, Pareto contributed to it. With the early nationalists he shared an impatience at the incompetence of the Italian ruling class, but he differed from them on imperialism, which he did not view as the solution to Italy's problems.[8] Undoubtedly, both Mosca and Pareto contributed not a little to the disenchantment with Italian parliamentary institutions. After Benito

Mussolini came to power, he claimed them as intellectual godfathers.[9] The extent to which Mussolini had read either may be questioned. However, he did grasp the essence of their criticism of the parliamentary system and used it for his own ends.

After 1870, in contrast to Italian weakness, inefficiency, and poverty, the newly unified German state assumed a leading position in Europe, not only politically and economically, but also intellectually. A long-lasting admiration for German thought and culture on the part of Italian intellectuals resulted. More short-lived were the attempts to find an explanation for the difference between the two countries. Inspired by positivism and particularly by social Darwinism, a number of pseudosociological and anthropological studies proclaimed the superiority of the Anglo-Saxon peoples and the decadence of the Latins. These theories offered a seemingly rational, scientific explanation of the problems besetting Italy and justified German advances. No real blame could be fixed on anyone, since degeneracy was the result of biological phenomena and not of willful malfeasance. The events of the 1890s, when Italy faced revolt and corruption at home and defeat in Africa, merely strengthened the conviction of those intellectuals who believed in the inevitable decadence of the Latin races.

The book that perhaps more than any other aroused polemics, enthusiasm, and general interest was Alfredo Niceforo's *Italia barbara contemporanea*. It appeared in 1898 and applied the then prevalent scientific-anthropological theories to Italian society. To contrast this book with Gioberti's *Primato* is to understand the fundamental change that had occurred in the self-image of Italians. Niceforo used the expression "contemporary barbaric Italy" to describe southern and insular Italy. According to him, Italy was inhabited by two races, physically and psychologically dissimilar. He argued that while Italy might be politically united, sociologically it was "a vast mosaic with a thousand colors and shadings . . . a shimmering canvas on which a mad painter had mixed the most diverse and strident colors." Anthropologically, Italy was divided into two peoples, "diverse as to degree of civilization, social life, [and] morality . . . [completely modern] northern Italy and [socially backward] southern Italy." [10]

But Niceforo refused to accept Latin decadence as an excuse for bad government, and the last chapter of his book indicted Italy's political leadership. In its pursuit of false political goals, the ruling class had lost that sense of patriotism which had characterized the men of the Risorgimento. Prompted by self-glory, it had saddled Italy with a bloated, inefficient bureaucracy and high military expenditures. These placed a heavy burden on the country, impoverished the masses, and resulted in widespread malnutrition—the real cause of the physical and moral decadence of the Italians.

Meanwhile, by the end of the century a new generation was coming of age, the first to have been born and educated under the new Italian state. Eclectic in its intellectual interests, enthusiastic, and hopeful, even when discouraged by the inertia of its elders who held the power, it demanded the right to be heard. Like their counterparts elsewhere, young Italian intellectuals were conscious of belonging to a new century. Their activities and interests led them to scrutinize all aspects of Italian life and to embrace many ideologies.[11] During the 1890s a large number among them had been attracted to Marxism, whose principal exponent in Italy was Antonio Labriola. In his lectures at the University of Rome and in his writings Labriola presented the ideas of Marx and Engels, and in these same years the Socialist party was founded.

In the pages of the party's journal *La Critica Sociale* Socialist intellectuals discussed both theoretical and practical questions. In 1897 Gaetano Salvemini, who perhaps more than any other intellectual of his generation believed that the intellectual should be as much a man of action as of ideas, began his collaboration with *La Critica Sociale*. As a Socialist, Salvemini, later to emerge as one of the leading opponents of Fascism, fought his first battles for change and reform, but in 1911 he broke with the party, disillusioned by its failure to understand the problems of the peasantry in southern Italy and by its delay in condemning Italian imperialism in north Africa.

In a frame of reference quite different from that guiding Italian socialist intellectuals before the First World War, the philosopher and historian Benedetto Croce and the poet-dramatist Gabriele D'Annunzio pursued opposing paths in their efforts to infuse new vitality into Italian life and letters. Croce advocated a return to the traditions of the past, to a genuine patriotism that would inspire sacrifice and hard work for the benefit of Italy. For Croce, intellectuals could best serve by being good writers and good thinkers, and he rejected political activism.

D'Annunzio held to a diametrically opposed view. He saw the intellectual as a Nietzschean superman, above traditional morality, the member of an elite who would guide the masses, for "the masses would always be slaves, since they had a natural impulse to be chained. Never would they have a sense of liberty." [12] He called for military strength, since "Italy will either be a great naval power, or it will be nothing." [13] D'Annunzio's hour of leadership came with the First World War, when he acted out his vision of the intellectual deeply involved in action.

Quietly and methodically, Croce worked to educate his fellow Italians and to improve his country's intellectual and moral fiber. From Naples,

Croce's influence spread throughout Italy, and it lasted over half a century. He acquired his preeminent position as cultural leader in the decade before 1914, during which he forged his bimonthly *La Critica* into an authoritative journal of opinion and criticism. The first issue appeared on January 20, 1903, and in the opening note to his readers Croce explained that its specific purpose would be to fill lacunae left by specialized journals on the one hand and popular ones on the other.

At the beginning *La Critica* aroused no great hostility or attention. Croce later remembered that it had counted about two hundred readers. Italy, in those years, was accustomed to the birth and early demise of many periodicals. Since 1890 there had been numerous "little magazines." Most led ephemeral lives of one or two years, but their combined efforts aired new ideas, introduced foreign writers and artists to their readers, fought complacency, aridity, ignorance, and dishonesty in public and academic life. But the unity and coherence of *La Critica* set it apart from these other more lively and vivacious journals. With the help of the philosopher Giovanni Gentile, his friend and collaborator, Croce prepared most of the articles, reviews, and notes that filled the pages of *La Critica*.

Forty years later Croce reminisced that when *La Critica* began to appear it had followed

> a program suited to those years of peace, work, and progress in every sphere of life. . . . It abstained from politics as such, not only because it saw other men, better disposed and prepared . . . involved in it, but also because it recalled the warning of a teacher, Francesco De Sanctis, that each citizen should cultivate the field best suited to him. . . . It chose "to carry out good politics" by contributing to the healthy life of its own country and of society in general.[14]

This insistence that "politics as such" should be left to the politicians characterized the outlook of many intellectuals during these years. Such an apolitical attitude was shared, for example, by Luigi Russo, critic and writer, who many years later wrote that in his youth he had felt completely alien to politics.

Despite Croce's desire to ignore politics, he could not avoid involvement in political life. As the self-appointed reformer of Italy's cultural and academic life he was inevitably drawn into polemics whose ramifications transcended intellectual bounds. His experiences during and after the First World War revealed the weaknesses of his idealized position as an ivory tower intellectual and eventually brought him to an active political role.

To assess Croce's activity and his influence from 1903 to 1914 in the physical sense is not difficult. There is an imposing body of writings. We cannot help but be struck by his knowledge, his wit, his awareness of so many issues and problems, and also by his blindness to many of the new forces that were being set in motion and to political problems in general. To assess his spiritual influence is more difficult. True, he forced many to think critically, either with him or against him. Hardly any young intellectual during these years failed to go through a Crocean period at some time or other—either of assent or of violent dissent. But Croce formed no real group of disciples and remained a rather solitary figure.

During these same years, two young men in their early twenties, Giovanni Papini and Giuseppe Prezzolini, led a group in Florence. Working as hard, if not as methodically, as Croce to rid Italy of the incrustations of the past, their activity found expression in many journals, which were often bizarre and always thought-provoking. Those who collaborated with them came from all parts of Italy. Differing in their interests and points of view, they often fought bitterly among themselves and agreed only that change and progress were needed if Italy were to become a truly modern nation. Some followed Croce, some D'Annunzio, others rejected both. Their journals spoke for youth. They lacked a common goal, except to rid Italy of prejudice and bourgeois values. They aired the ideas of William James, Henri Bergson, and Miguel de Unamuno. They reported on new art movements in Paris. They were constantly embroiled in polemics among themselves and with the intellectual "establishment." In the pages of their journals appeared almost every name that was later to achieve some recognition or play some part in Italian life. Their focus of interest shifted rapidly; their membership varied; but by 1914 they had indeed introduced a great deal of fresh air into the musty atmosphere of Italian intellectual life.

Futurism, basically an antiintellectual movement of intellectuals, issued its first manifesto from Paris in 1909, but sought adherents in Italy. Among its leaders were the poet Filippo Tommaso Marinetti, the painters Umberto Boccioni and Carlo Carrà. Futurism represented the rebellion of the young against the old and supported the mystique of the machine in a society that clung to humanistic values. To diffuse their ideas, the futurists sought to shock the complacent bourgeoisie. They repudiated all that was traditional; museums and libraries they considered graveyards. War was to be the purifier of society. Nihilists, the futurists wanted to shatter the pattern of the past and to create a new society in which the machine, for them the symbol of the new century, would dominate. Futurist poetry, architecture, art, theatre, music, and politics were developed. Nothing and no one were immune from their ridicule and attack. Considered a lunatic fringe by their contemporaries, they contributed to the disintegration of the world that had existed before 1914 by attacking and ridiculing its basic values.[15]

Despite all their concern for Italian life and letters, however, Italy's intellectuals had not succeeded in bringing about any fundamental changes in the outlook of the average Italian bourgeois by 1914. The latter remained wedded to his prejudices, jealous of his prerogatives, and suspicious of change. It was this essentially static society that had to face the shock of war and the postwar socioeconomic dislocations and mass agitation.

With 1914 came the outbreak of the First World War and the agitation of the nationalists and of D'Annunzio, whose influence in Italy during the prewar years had probably been greater than that of anyone else. It has been said that Croce educated the prewar generation but that D'Annunzio dominated them. Always a controversial figure, for some two decades he strutted on the Italian scene, even when living in France. While Croce spoke to the mind, D'Annunzio appealed to the senses through his poetry and his prose, which was closer to poetry than to prose. D'Annunzio enchanted young Italians with his rhetoric and stimulated their machismo, and the D'Annunzian hero was the model for many of them.[16] In the *Canzoni della gesta d'oltremare*, written to celebrate Italy's victory over Turkey in 1912, he proclaimed: "Africa is the whetstone on which we Italians shall sharpen our swords for a supreme conquest in the unknown future." The future seemed within reach in 1914, and on his return to Italy D'Annunzio found allies among the nationalists and futurists, both of whom chafed at Italy's role as a bystander in a conflict that, they felt, could open the way to a complete change in Italian life.

Though he realized that Italian entry into the war was inevitable, Croce favored nonintervention and refused to be swept by the wave of anti-German feeling. In 1915 he wrote in *La Critica* that the world was facing the "beginning of a long period of wars and profound revolutions . . . one of those leaps ahead that humanity makes with gigantic upheavals." [17] He would not confuse culture with politics, two activities that he felt should be kept separate. While he did not approve of Germany's war conduct, he would not condemn its culture. This position alienated many, who labeled him a Germanophile, and especially after Italy's entry into the war, Croce became increasingly isolated. D'Annunzio, on the other hand, emerged a war hero, while many futurists and nationalists died in the trenches.

Croce had not been alone in his attempt to distinguish between German culture and German militarism. Numerous other Italian intellectuals joined him in this effort, but their attempts met with suspicion and distrust. A deep cleavage developed between them and those who supported Italy's entry into the war, and the results of this breach were perhaps disastrous for Italy after 1918.

With the end of the war came the problems of peace. The political scene grew more turbulent as the old ruling class, so often indicted and criticized, proved incapable of meeting the demands of a changed European society which Italian events reflected. When Italy's political leaders faltered at Versailles and then vacillated at home, D'Annunzio enjoyed his final hour of glory in the occupation of Fiume, from September 1919 to December 1920.

More than a flamboyant gesture of a would-be superman, the Fiume incident represented the active involvement of the intellectual in political affairs.[18] For a while D'Annunzio seemed to be destined to control the future of his country. At least so thought Francesco Saverio Nitti, the historian, economist, and prime minister of Italy in 1920. On the eve of the Fascist take-over Nitti wrote asking him to act "against the violence and brutality" that threatened Italy. "Perhaps never had an artist had a greater duty towards his people," concluded Nitti.[19]

But D'Annunzio stood aside and let the Fascists proceed with their brutal attacks on those men and institutions they considered obstacles to their achievement of power. After the murder of the Socialist deputy Giacomo Matteotti in 1924, D'Annunzio withdrew from active political life into his secluded villa. Honored as the national poet of the regime, he was increasingly ignored while Mussolini consolidated his position; then he was kept under surveillance and well paid until his death in 1938.

As the *squadristi* purged, rioted, and burned, Italians realized that Fascism was no transitory outburst of postwar violence and lawlessness. Rather it represented a new force that basically rejected traditional Italian values, while claiming to defend them from "bolshevism." Perhaps never in the history of modern Italy had intellectuals been as divided as they were in their attitude toward Fascism. Some made a choice almost immediately; others, after considerable doubt, soul-searching, and reappraisal of their role and position as citizens and intellectuals. Many saw a conflict between their responsibilities as citizens, to which they owed a political commitment, and what they considered to be their obligations as intellectuals who should rise above the passing conflicts and passions of political life. They tried to escape into the proverbial ivory tower. Prezzolini proposed the creation of a Society of Apoti, whose members would withdraw from public life to devote themselves to their work and to educating a new generation of elite.

Intellectuals thus assumed a variety of political postures during the next two decades.[20] A number among them elected opposition and continued it until Fascism was overthrown. Their efforts almost always brought exile, imprisonment, and occasionally death. Among these were Piero Gobetti, Giovanni Amendola, and Antonio Gramsci, all of whom died as a result of Fascist persecution, as did Carlo Rosselli. They exemplify the intellectual *engagé* to his utmost, making no distinction between his intellectual and political activities.

Amendola had participated in various intellectual movements before the First World War. A journalist and a member of the Chamber of Deputies when the Fascists came to power, he played a leading role in organizing parliamentary opposition to Mussolini after 1924 and 1925. Leader of the dissident Liberal group in the Aventine secession from parliament, he was severely beaten by the Fascists and died in France of his injuries.

The liberal Gobetti and the Communist Gramsci had belonged to a group of university students at Turin, where economic growth had led to an early awareness of the problems posed by a modern, industrial society. Here developed the intellectual leadership of the Italian Communist party: Gramsci, Palmiro Togliatti, and Angelo Tasca, all three active in the immediate postwar years in *L'Ordine Nuovo*, "the only example of revolutionary Marxist journalism . . . in Italy before Fascism." [21]

Between 1919 and 1922 Gobetti evolved a political philosophy that was to become the foundation of the *Giustizia e Libertà* movement against Fascism, led by Carlo Rosselli from Paris. In 1922 he launched *La Rivoluzione Liberale*, one of the first openly anti-Fascist journals. His aim in founding it was not only to attack Fascism, but also to help educate a "political class that would have a clear idea of its historical traditions and of the Social exigencies arising out of the participation by the masses in the life of the state." [22] Like Amendola, Gobetti was physically punished for his efforts and died from a Fascist beating. Rosselli, who used Gobetti's sociopolitical ideas as a basis for his opposition to Fascism, was shot down in 1937 by Fascist gunmen.

Arrested in 1928, when the Fascists first succeeded in routing the Communist underground, Gramsci was sentenced to twenty years' imprisonment. Despite frail health, Gramsci, who died in 1937, produced a mass of writing in prison which has had a far-reaching influence on Italian thought after the Second World War. Like Gobetti, Gramsci subjected the Italian past to a penetrating revaluation, in the course of which traditional shibboleths were exposed. Both men saw the Risorgimento as an incomplete movement in which social and economic reforms had failed to materialize.[23] Mazzini's dictum that a revolution must be by the people and not merely for them found echoes in both Gobetti and Gramsci, for whom the Risorgimento had failed to modernize Italy and had perpetuated the exclusion of the masses from political life.

Gaetano Salvemini also had no hesitation in opposing Fascism. After twenty years of exile, he survived to return to Italy after the Second World War. Always the educator and reformer, for him opposition to Fascism had required no inner struggle. To Salvemini, heir to the Mazzinian tradition of thought and action, meaningful intellectual activity had to be concerned with practical matters. The intellectual had a responsibility to society, and he was indeed part of its actions and problems.

These men initiated, led, and spoke for the active intellectual opposition to Fascism—not only as a dictatorship, but as a perversion of human and humanistic values. Inspired by their intransigence, many intellectuals both within Italy and outside the country continued their struggle to overthrow the regime throughout its twenty years in power.

At first Croce had considered Fascism "a simple revival of flagging patriotism, a bold entry into . . . politics by the younger generation who had fought war . . . a disorderly, but generous impulse to renew Italy." [24] After 1925 he became increasingly disenchanted. Unable to speak out publicly, yet allowed to continue publishing *La Critica*, which became the bond among anti-Fascists in Italy, Croce used it as an instrument of intellectual criticism. During these years he also published a series of historical and political studies on liberty and liberalism in which he sought to determine why liberalism had been undermined. Had liberalism, Croce asked, been superseded by materialistic postwar political ideologies?

But to Croce these new forces, with their strong-arm methods and suppression of all opposition, did not represent progress. Rather, they symbolized "mental impoverishment, moral weakness . . . desperation" and a social order that crushed individuals. As he was to say in 1930 at the International Congress of Philosophy at Oxford, they idolized a future without a past. They adored force for its own sake, the new because it was new, and believed in a rootless existence. History had witnessed other such authoritarian regimes based on violence, but "liberty . . . had always risen again . . . drawing strength for its continued existence from its apparent defeats." Fighting against Fascism, Croce held fast to the belief that the words and deeds of men who suppressed liberty could not permanently alter the basic law of history, that culture and civilization could flourish only where liberty prevailed. Croce's conviction that man would inevitably return to the path of liberty and liberalism sustained him and the readers of *La Critica* through the years of Fascist dictatorship, during which Croce became for many the symbol of unbending intellectual independence against coercion and control.

Meanwhile Fascism had strengthened its hold over Italy, and the regimentation of culture proceeded.[25] Writers, journalists, university professors, artists, teachers—all had to accept Fascist directives. Few of those who had not joined the anti-Fascist opposition failed to conform at least outwardly. "The intellectuals of Italy," commented one observer, "were cautiously and politely indifferent to Fascism. . . . Italian thought and art have a tradition of fleeing from extreme positions." [26] By the early 1930s many writers had retreated within the confines of their own artistic world. Hermeticism in poetry, the "prosa d'arte," described as a "frigid exercise in descriptive bravura," and the provincial focus of many novelists may be viewed as an escape from the rhetoric and bombast of official culture.

A degree of sincerity must be recognized in some of those intellectuals who espoused Fascism. Many doing so saw a postwar society beset by political and economic instability, unable to function. Fascism seemed to offer a solution in which order would be restored. In the process, they believed that culture would also revive, and they accepted Fascism on the basis of this assumption. The two most outstanding examples are the neo-Hegelian philosopher and university professor Giovanni Gentile and the jurist and nationalist Alfredo Rocco. To Gentile, who could write that the illegality of Fascism between 1919 and 1922 was necessary to bring about a new, regenerated Italy, Fascism came to personify the "ethical state." For Rocco, Fascism presaged "the powerful state." The rank and file followed, and an "official" culture emerged.

By the 1930s a new generation of intellectuals was growing up under Fascism. Though conditioned and controlled by a regime allowing little independence of thought, they were beginning to think for themselves. (The emergence today of a group of Soviet intellectuals critical of Communism in the Soviet Union is another example of the impossibility of regimenting ideas by political force.) A growing disenchantment with Fascist leadership developed among university youth in these years. Despite—or perhaps because of—Fascist education this generation of young intellectuals became increasingly dissatisfied with the regime. For many this dissatisfaction grew out of their growing awareness that Fascist practice did not correspond to Fascist precepts and slogans. They wanted a return to the original program of Fascism—revolutionary, republican, and antiestablishment. They revolted in the name of Fascist dynamism against a Fascism grown complacent and smug in power. Involvement in the Spanish Civil War and the closer ties with Nazi Germany disillusioned others. And eventually many came to see through the slogans and to oppose the very principles of Fascism.[27]

Among older Fascists, while there might not be open disaffection, there was a variety of intellectual outlooks. United in the pursuit and maintenance of power, Fascist intellectuals differed among themselves as to what Fascism should try to achieve. Giuseppe Bottai, for instance, saw Fascism leading to the creation of a new managerial class, attuned to the needs of modern technological society. Editor of the *Critica fascista* from 1923 to 1943, he continued to support his view of Fascism as modernization of Italian society. Aware of the growing alienation of the youth, in 1940 he also began publishing the *Primato*, a conscious reference to Gioberti.

Among its contributors he tried to include many points of view and actively sought the collaboration of the young.

With the defeat of Italy in the Second World War, the fall of Mussolini, and the subsequent struggle against German occupation, the various strands of anti-Fascist dissent came together in what has been called the "second Risorgimento." Old anti-Fascists met with new converts. Disciples of Croce joined followers of the Salvemini-Gobetti-Rosselli Justice and Liberty opposition. Catholics worked with Communists. Intellectuals went back to the Italian traditions of the Risorgimento. "Italy was born from the ideas of a few intellectuals; the Risorgimento was the effort of a minority. . . . once again today Italians face all the options presented by the Risorgimento." [28] Giaime Pintor, the young intellectual who wrote these lines in his last letter before losing his life in a mission behind German lines, expressed the feelings of many of his generation. A deep sense of responsibility moved them to participate actively in the events of their time while planning a better future.

Intellectuals, young and old, became politicized. In southern Italy Croce and his contemporary, the Neapolitan jurist Enrico De Nicola, dealt with the Allies and struggled to give Italy south of Naples a modicum of government. In northern Italy workers, disbanded soldiers, peasants, and anti-Fascist intellectuals organized an underground resistance against Mussolini's puppet government at Salò and its German ally. The Communists who had been the only group to maintain a functioning clandestine organization in the twenties and thirties, despite constant police harassment, presented the most appealing program to solve Italy's social and economic problems. In the bivouacs of the Resistance, they strengthened this appeal by their bravery and patriotism in fighting for the liberation of Italy. A new political group, the Party of Action, going back to Mazzini's program of thought and action, gathered the followers of the Justice and Liberty movement. Its program for postwar reforms combined political liberalism and social reforms. Catholic principles inspired others.

In the years immediately after the end of the war in 1945, Italian intellectuals continued their political involvement. The octogenarian Croce, abandoning all his former scruples, plunged into politics and tried to revive a liberalism inspired by nineteenth-century ideals. Ferruccio Parri, hero of the Resistance, Adolfo Omodeo, professor at the University of Naples and rector after the fall of Mussolini, and others struggled to keep the Party of Action viable, but Parri's brief tenure as prime minister in 1945 ended disastrously. A few young Catholics formed the *Cronache sociali* group, which combined a social reform program with integral Catholicism and tried to influence the Christian Democratic leadership. None of these, however, could equal the appeal of Communism, which when associated with the patriotism of the Resistance seemed to provide the inspiration to action for Italian intellectuals. Many turned to it in the hope of finding a program of reform and change for Italy. In 1949 the publication of Gramsci's prison manuscripts was begun, indicating the extent to which Marxism could be integrated into the Italian intellectual heritage.

Another strong influence was that of American culture in all its forms and manifestations—good and bad. Open to new ideas, Italian intellectuals turned to American literature and culture for a new dimension of life. While many saw in these American and Communist influences a threat to Italy's cultural identity, others used them to accelerate the modernization of a cultural-intellectual tradition that persisted in clinging to its humanistic past. This humanist framework still dominates Italian education, but increasingly the demands and problems of modern society and politics are forcing new cultural orientations and leading to new conceptual formulations.

In the years since the Second World War, developments have led Italian intellectuals, like their peers elsewhere, to become increasingly involved politically. Changes in the American image, caused first by the election of John F. Kennedy to the presidency (a positive change) and then by the Vietnam war (a negative one), brought about a very different attitude toward American ideas and culture. Pope John XXIII and Vatican Council II briefly suggested a Catholic reconciliation with the modern world which many Italians found attractive. Among Communists the death of Stalin and his subsequent denunciation by Khrushchev created a crisis, sharpened by Russian suppression of revolts in Hungary and Poland and later in Czechoslovakia and by the Chinese challenge to Russia. These events forced Italian intellectuals into a reevaluation of ideological allegiances. Many became disillusioned. Others chose to explore new ways of expressing themselves. The turmoil and confusion culminated toward the end of the 1960s and early 1970s in the emergence of a new left.[29] Similar to the new left in other countries, the Italian new left broke its ties to the now old left and proclaimed a revolutionary mission for the intelligentsia. As in the days of Gramsci and Gobetti, the first center of this new alignment was Turin, where its leader Raniero Panzieri founded the journal *Quaderni rossi* and focused on the problems of the workers, who, he felt, were being co-opted by the goals of a burgeoning capitalism. But until 1967 and 1968 the *Quaderni rossi* group and other small schismatic leftist factions had little success. In that year, however, the smoldering unrest among university students erupted to demand drastic changes, and a revolutionary situation prevailed at universities throughout Italy. The new left joined the student movement and in a sense may be said to have directed its actions. Intellectuals once again turned to political activism to bring about change. In 1969 came the *autunno caldo* (hot autumn) of the workers, during which the new left emerged as an important factor. On the ideological front in this same year, the appearance of the *Manifesto* group, composed of dissidents expelled from the Communist party and including Luigi Pintor, former director of the Communist daily *L'Unità*, helped to create a variety of intellectual orientations.

Thus, almost thirty years after the end of the Second World War, Italian intellectuals, or at least the more politicized among them, are once again deeply involved in ideological and political conflicts; they are playing an active role in the revolutionary vanguard and are hoping to bring fundamental changes to Italy's political, social, economic, and intellectual life. Like Mazzini they believe that thought and action are inextricably bound and that change is brought about only by total commitment.

NOTES

1. There is no one work tracing the role and influence of intellectuals in Italian life. The following provide useful treatments of various periods: Emiliana P. Noether, *Seeds of Italian Nationalism, 1700–1815* (New York: Columbia University Press, 1951); Franco Venturi, *Settecento riformatore: Da Muratori a Beccaria* (Turin: Einaudi, 1969); Michele Sciacca, *Il pensiero italiano nell'età del Risorgimento* (Milan: Marzorati, 1963); Rodolfo Mondolfo, *Il pensiero politico del Risorgimento italiano* (Milan: Nuova Accademia, 1959); Luigi Salvatorelli, *The Risorgimento: Thought and Action*, trans. Mario Domandi (New York: Harper & Row, 1970); Antonio Gramsci, *Gli intellettuali e l'organizzazione della cultura*, 8th ed. (Turin: Einaudi, 1966) and *Letteratura e vita nazionale*, 6th ed. (Turin: Einaudi, 1966); Eugenio Garin, *Cronache di filosofia italiana, 1900/1943*, 2 vols. (Bari: Laterza, 1966); Franco Gaeta, *Nazionalismo italiano* (Naples: ESI, 1965); Giorgio Luti, *Cronache letterarie tra le due guerre, 1920/1940* (Bari: Laterza, 1966); Simonetta Piccone-Stella, *Intellettuali e capitale nella società italiana del dopoguerra* (Bari: De Donato, 1972); Giulio Cattaneo, *Letteratura e ribellione* (Milan: Rizzoli, 1972).

2. See Noether, *op. cit.*, for an elaboration of this point.

3. Sciacca, *op. cit.*, p. 247; see also E. P. Noether, "Vico in the Risorgimento," *Harvard Library Bulletin*, 18, No. 3 (July 1969), 309–319, for a discussion of the source for many of Gioberti's ideas.

4. For the best short treatment of the various currents of thought see Salvatorelli, *op. cit.*

5. For a masterly analysis of this crisis in Italian life, see Federico Chabod, *Storia della politica estera italiana dal 1870 al 1896:* Vol. I, *Le premesse* (Bari: Laterza, 1951).

6. Pasquale Turiello, *Governo e governati in Italia* (Bologna: Zanichelli, 1882) and *Politica contemporanea* (Naples: Pierro, 1894).

7. Gaetano Mosca, *Sulla teorica dei governi e sul governo rappresentativo: Studi storici e sociali* (Turin: Loescher, 1884); idem, *Partiti e sindacati nella crisi del regime parlamentare* (Bari: Laterza, 1949); idem, *Elementi di scienza politica* (Turin: Bocca, 1896).

8. See the following by Vilfredo Pareto: *Cours d'économie politique*, 2 vols. (Lausanne: F. Rouge, 1896–1897); *Systèmes socialistes*, 2 vols. (Paris: Giard & Brière, 1902–1903); *Lettere a Maffeo Pantaleoni, 1890–1923*, ed. Gabriele De Rosa, 3 vols. (Rome: Edizioni Storia e Letteratura, 1962); *Cronache italiane*, ed. Carlo Mongardini (Brescia: Morcelliana, 1965); *The Ruling Class in Italy Before 1900* (New York: Vanni [1950]).

9. See James L. Meisel, ed., *Pareto and Mosca* (Englewood Cliffs, N.J.: Prentice-Hall, 1965).

10. Alfredo Niceforo, *Italia barbara contemporanea* (Palermo: Sandron, 1898), pp. 9–10.

11. See Garin, *op. cit.*, vol. I.

12. Gabriele D'Annunzio, *Le vergini delle rocce* (Milan: Treves, 1905), p. 73.

13. Gabriele D'Annunzio, "L'armata d'Italia," *Prose di ricerca*, 3 vols. (Milan: Mondadori, 1947–50), III, 10.

14. Benedetto Croce, "Proemio," *La Critica*, 42, No. 1 (January 20, 1944), 2.

15. See Filippo Tommaso Marinetti, *Teoria e invenzione futurista* (Milan: Mondadori, 1968); Maria Drudi-Gambillo and Teresa Fiori, *Archivi del futurismo* (Rome: De Luca, 1958); Rosa Trillo Clough, *Futurism: The Story of a Modern Art Movement* (New York: Philosophical Library, 1961); Joshua C. Taylor, *Futurism* (New York: Museum of Modern Art, 1961).

16. See Philippe Jullian, *D'Annunzio*, trans. S. Hardman (New York: Viking, 1973).

17. Benedetto Croce, "Intorno a questa rivista," *La Critica*, 13, No. 4 (July 1915), 318.

18. Paolo Alatri, *Nitti, D'Annunzio e la questione sociale* (Milan: Feltrinelli, 1959); Umberto Foscanelli, *Gabriele D'Annunzio e l'ora sociale* (Milan: Carnaro, 1952).

19. Letter of August 1, 1922, quoted in Nino Valeri, *D'Annunzio davanti al fascismo, con documenti inediti* (Florence: Le Monnier, 1963), p. 70.

20. Some of these problems are discussed by P. Vita-Finzi, "Italian Fascism and the Intellectuals," *The Nature of Fascism*, ed. S. J. Woolf (New York: Vintage Books, 1969), pp. 226–244; George L. Mosse, "Fascism and the Intellectuals," *The Nature of Fascism*, pp. 205–225; and

Emiliana P. Noether, "Italian Intellectuals Under Fascism," *Journal of Modern History*, 43, No. 4 (December 1971), 630–648.

21. P. Gobetti, "Storia dei comunisti Torinesi scritta da un liberale," *La Rivoluzione Liberale*, 1, No. 7 (April 2, 1922), now in Piero Gobetti, *Scritti politici*, ed. Paolo Spriano (Turin: Einaudi, 1969), p. 283.

22. "Ai lettori," *La Rivoluzione Liberale*, 1, No. 1 (February 12, 1922), now in Piero Gobetti, *Scritti politici*, ed. Paolo Spriano (Turin: Einaudi, 1969), pp. 225–226.

23. Piero Gobetti, *Risorgimento senza eroi* (Turin: Ed. Baretti, 1926) and Antonio Gramsci, *Il Risorgimento* (Turin: Einaudi, 1966).

24. Benedetto Croce, *Pagine sparse*, 3 vols. (Naples: Ricciardi, 1943), II, 321 ff.

25. See Edward R. Tannenbaum, *The Fascist Experience: Italian Society and Culture, 1922–1945* (New York: Basic Books, 1972).

26. Vita-Finzi, *op. cit.*, p. 244.

27. See Michael A. Ledeen, "Fascism and the Generation Gap," *European Studies Review*, 1, No. 3 (July 1971), 275–283; idem, "Italian Fascism and Youth," *Journal of Contemporary History*, 4, No. 3 (July 1969), 137–154.

28. Giaime Pintor, *Il sangue d'Europa (1939–1945)*, ed. Valentino Gerratana, 2nd. ed. (Turin: Einaudi, 1966), pp. 187–188.

29. On the impact of events in the 1950s and 1960s see Valdo Spini, "The New Left in Italy," *Journal of Contemporary History*, 7, Nos. 1–2 (January-April 1972), 51–71.

CHAPTER 13

GERMANY AND ITALIAN INTELLECTUAL LIFE FROM UNIFICATION TO THE FIRST WORLD WAR

Rosario Romeo
(Translated by Emiliana P. Noether)

The influence exerted by Germany on Italian affairs during the entire period from the 1860s to the First World War reached into every sector of activity: from classical philology to economic life, from music to medicine, from military organization to foreign and domestic policy. A comprehensive attempt to trace this influence would therefore involve a reexamination of all aspects of Italian society during the first fifty years of political unity, and it would be difficult to discuss completely and meaningfully; in any case, it could not be covered within the limits of this chapter. In the following pages we shall therefore limit ourselves to indicating the moral and political importance that German cultural influence assumed in Italy and how it helped to arouse and guide a number of movements particularly characteristic of the intellectual life of the peninsula.

In April 1871, commenting on the establishment of the new German Empire, Giuseppe Civinini wrote in the widely read journal the *Nuova Antologia* that in Italy this event "revived a thousand painful memories of the past." In effect, opposition to Germanism and vindication of the battles fought throughout the Middle Ages by the Latin peoples against the Germans had constituted—as much if not more than the memory of republican and imperial Rome—the leitmotiv around which the most robust and modern cultural forces of the nation had rallied in the nineteenth century. Perhaps it had been a foreigner, the Swiss historian Léonard Simonde de Sismondi, who had stimulated thinking along these lines with his *Histoire des Républiques italiennes,* in which literary and romantic love for the Italy which was heir to great memories and ruins was united, for the first time, with hope for the rebirth of its people and for a new great and creative era in its civilization. During the Risorgimento the most popular of the Italian historiographical schools had portrayed the history of medieval Italy as a battle constantly fought by the Italian peoples against the German invaders. After the failure of the effort at assimilation by Theodoric and the Goths—the only invaders upon whom Italian historians looked with open sympathy, and whose German origins Carlo Troya persisted in denying—the Germans had crushed and held the defeated Romans in servitude throughout the Lombard period. Then, with feudalism they had built a bastion of privilege against which the Italians had moved in revolt with the great uprisings during the age of the communes.[1] These traditions had by no means died out after the foundation of the new Kingdom of Italy. Once again, in 1862, the historian Pasquale Villari went back to them in an essay on *L'Italia, la civiltà latina e la civiltà germanica.*

Until the end of the nineteenth century these themes recurred almost verbatim in a good part of Italian historiography on the Middle Ages; time and again it was maintained that "the commune represents the rebirth of the Latin peoples and tradition." In 1863 Francesco Schupfer, the leading nineteenth-century historian of Italian law, wrote that "two different principles hold forth in history—the Latin principle and the Germanic principle—which, though starting . . . from the same origin led nonetheless to opposite conclusions." [2] Furthermore, for a long time the relation between Roman and German law and the importance in the history of Italy of the respective individual German tribes and the classical Roman tradition remained a central concern for generations of scholars. Moreover, it is useless to emphasize how in the age of the Risorgimento the "Germans" were usually identified with the Austrians, without any distinctions and clarifications, since the different political and intellectual currents in the Germanic world were almost completely beyond the ken of the majority of Italians of that time.

Nevertheless, even before 1866 or 1870, medieval Germany was not the only Germany known to educated Italians, or at least to an important and growing number among them. Since 1815 some awareness of the great German philosophy and culture of the *Goethezeit* had begun to spread in Italy, even though largely through French publications. This indirect knowledge had gradually been substituted, especially after 1840, by a greater and more direct familiarity with German authors and works that now began to be read in the original, mainly in the south, but in growing numbers throughout Italy. Thus, even before unification, the philosophical thought of idealism—above all of Hegelianism—had begun to exercise a great and lasting influence on men like Francesco De Sanctis and Bertrando Spaventa, with important consequences for the future development of the literary and philosophical culture of the peninsula. German erudition—which at the time of Barthold Georg Niebuhr had already thrown into confusion the conventional outlook of Italian ancient historians by reopening the discussion not only of the Livian tradition but of all Roman archaic history—began to acquire new authority with Theodor Mommsen, who was soon to become famous also in Italy.[3] Meanwhile in all areas of literary and historical studies the requirements of German philology and criticism became more compelling. Thus the imposing image of German science rose before Italian intellectuals. Many of them, trained in Hegelianism or already open to the appeals of positivism, discovered a new historical and civic force behind German science which particularly claimed their attention after the great military and political successes of Bismarckian Prussia. Consequently, in the debate on the new Germany which developed with particular intensity vis-à-vis the war of 1870 to 1871, Italian arguments were much more varied and subtly shaded than one would have expected when looking only at the prevailing Germanophobe traditions of the Risorgimento.

The ideological solidarity of Italian democracy with that of France received a clamorous expression in the intervention of Garibaldi and his volunteers on the side of the armies of the Third Republic, and the proclamation of this new French regime brought about a sudden change in an attitude that, prompted until then by hostility to Napoleon III, had been clearly pro-Prussian. And if justification for such a change was not lacking in the Italian leftist press, pro-French sympathies among the ranks of the right were no less widespread.

The writings of one of the right's leading spokesmen, Ruggero Bonghi, against Bismarck and Bismarckism denounced the rebirth of the concept of force which for fifty years the liberal movement had tried to subordinate to the concept of law. In the *Nuova Antologia* of February 1871 Bonghi inveighed against the Prussian chancellor and against Germany with a violence and a bias explainable, to be sure, by the passions of the moment, but also expressing deep-rooted convictions formed by the constant attention that Bonghi, perhaps more than any other Italian political writer, had paid to the process of German unification and to the political figure of Bismarck. Even before 1871 Bonghi had written that the Germans had no clear idea of the boundaries that their state should have: "Many of them sincerely believe that their real frontier with Italy lies on the Mincio, and that no other frontier exists with Denmark, France, or Russia than the one that includes the last German-speaking citizen, the last German moral and material interest to be defended. . . ."[4] Along with this dangerously dynamic view of nationhood Bonghi emphasized the illiberal and authoritarian character that distinguished Bismark's policy from that of Cavour. The Prussian leader, he wrote, "understood neither the value nor the strength of liberal ideas and the place that necessarily must be given to them in modern society." And Bonghi came out against any attempt to establish a parallel between the two men and the movements that they had led to success: "How different," he continued, "were the ways by which Cavour and Bismarck each fulfilled his design."

But men of the same moderate circles objected strongly to the attitudes and judgments of the more orthodox among them and to the ideological and cultural premises on which they rested. Thus, in *Nuova Antologia*, the same journal that had published the anti-Bismarckian outbursts of Bonghi, Giuseppe Civinini, already mentioned above, undertook to dispel the fears aroused in Italy by the foundation of the German Empire by indicating—with specific reference to one of the fundamental theses of *kleindeutsche* historiography, and in particular to Heinrich von Sybel's *Die deutsche Nation und das Kaiserreich*—that the new German Empire was different from, and the opposite of, the Holy Roman Empire which for centuries had impeded the national development of Germany, no less than of Italy. Rather, the new empire was a national state and found its justification in a wholly modern principle. So far was this historical phenomenon from resembling the old Holy Roman Empire that it was its absolute negation. And the basis of the political rebirth of Germany was its intellectual revival. As Civinini wrote in the *Nuova Antologia* of May 1871:

> Literature, science, history, and philosophy have given the German people a profound sense of their own nationality . . . have taught them to consider themselves destined to a great historical mission . . . have persuaded them that to achieve it was a duty. In fact, the real character of the German movement is that it was first, so to speak, an intellectual process. When this was fully developed, it became an act of force. The idea preceded the act, and before becoming the physically strongest people of Europe, the Germans were the most intellectually advanced.

Certainly, Civinini did not deny that the empire had been achieved by force, which Bonghi and many like him deplored, but asserted that it was by "force in the service of ideas," by force that, as the most enlightened German philosophy taught, "is *ab aeterno* the necessary instrument of reason" and "the sole means given men to make Law triumph."

On the other hand, the problem of the conflict between France and Germany for European supremacy had already been faced by the Neapolitan historian Nicola Marselli from a very different point of view than the liberal moralism of Bonghi. In his book on the events of 1870, he first illustrated Germany's right to achieve the national unity that France was trying to deny it and its right, therefore, to refuse to give in to the demands and the blackmail of Parisian policy; he then portrayed the conflict as the inevitable clash between the decadent French and the new and energetic German civilizations:

> It is undisputable that the France of 1870 presented itself to Europe with all the signs of decadence and stripped of all the principal adornments of a serious and robust civilization. . . . Even the life of French, and above all Parisian, society dragged on devoid of any deep feeling, in artificial conventionality, in superficiality . . . in brutish material interests.

By contrast, Prussia furnished the example of a more serious and vital civilization, the expression of a country "ruled by freedom of thought, widespread education, sober habits, moral administration, faith in an ideal principle, and army discipline, and where all [people] had the sense of duty and that same respect for the rights of authority which authority must enjoy [to uphold] the rights of the people." Although the liberal Marselli was not unaware of the authoritarian character of Prussian society, "still weighed down by feudal institutions and an excess of militarism," he believed that the Germanization of Prussia, which he saw as an inevitable result of the unitary movement, would coincide with its inevitable liberalization. Precisely for this reason, in Marselli's judgment, those who wanted to draw reactionary consequences from the Prussian victory were wrong. Reaction and absolutism had not won with Moltke's armies, but "German thought, liberated by Luther, strengthened by science, animated by an Idea . . . defeated France on the battlefields of civilization before defeating it on those of war." [5]

Two years later these same themes were repeated by Carlo De Cesare, another exponent of the southern right, one of the best known economists during the Risorgimento, and a convinced free-trader. With pride he declared that he belonged to that Neapolitan school which had first welcomed German culture in Italy, and he briefly traced the history of Germany's intellectual life during the preceding two centuries, showing how greatly it had surpassed that of France, which had deserved defeat because of its divisions, its instability, and the anarchical doctrines it propagandized. The example of Prussia-Germany indicated to Italians the means and principles by which a people deprived of political existence until that time could reach greatness and strength. Italy and Germany therefore had a long way to go together. Italy's every interest lay in following a policy of friendship with the new power, leader of Europe. In contrast to what was asserted on the basis of an uncritically accepted traditional view of the relations between Italy and Germany, the two countries were united by a substantially identical historical destiny.[6] This was what Marselli had already believed in 1870, but he had not ignored "the dangers that Europe faces from the rise of a powerful Germany, with its hand armed, its fore-head burdened by nebulous thought, and led by a daring man." On the other hand, he had found that it was "childish to exaggerate subjectively the dangers and to provoke hatreds through jealousy." [7] In this Marselli agreed with Civinini, who also hoped that the Italians, by forging a solid alliance with the new empire, and by "following its virile example" would see "in it a friend that would help them to defend themselves, not so much against merely political dangers, but also against those deadly principles that little by little are also invading our society and threatening it. It is of deep concern to me that a close bond to Germany assure us more the example of its faith, perseverance, science, and moral dignity than of its military help and advice." [8]

It appears clear, then, that at the root of these sympathies for the new Germany lay both a cultural and political choice coinciding with a clear vision of the future of European civilization. A growing lack of faith in the fate and future of France in fact accompanied the exaltation of German strength and virtue. In the new Germany observers like Marselli saw "a nation that will give Europe an example of the coexistence of individual liberty and the authority of law, of the development of intellectual freedom and the dignity of life. . . . Europe needs liberty as much as it does order and authority." [9] In his articles on the new German Empire Civinini fought a real battle to foster sympathy and admiration for modern Germany among Italians. It is important to note that these sympathies for Germany cannot be attributed solely to conservatively inspired considerations. An authentic liberal outlook and motivation impelled these men to discover in the new empire a national and modern element linking it to the movement from which the Italian state had risen, without losing sight of what still remained illiberal and authoritarian in Germany.

Even the extollers of the German victory in the war of 1870 and 1871 did not deny that "the leaden sky of bureaucracy and militarism" still afflicted Prussia, and they remembered along with Marselli that "Germany had been the cradle of the barbarians and the great home of feudalism, where the influx of the modern spirit still finds stumbling blocks to erode and to crush." But they were persuaded that the future would give the lie to "those who hurry to draw conclusions from the German victories which could be ruinous to the cause of liberty." "The strength of Germany," continued Marselli, "does not lie in its aristocratic and absolutist elements, but in the fact that these draw vigor from the country and from culture." The future would bring about a gradual advancement of the democratic element that "represents progress and strength, because strength lies in being in harmony with the times." [10]

Germany was not regarded, in short, as a reactionary and feudal alternative to France, but rather as a liberal and modern one. So thought men of unquestionable liberal feelings such as the historian Pasquale Villari, who pointed out as models for the Italians German schools and German historiography, with its political educators, Georg Gottfried Gervinus and Johann Gustav Droysen. According to Villari, before its own unification Germany had found the solution to the fundamental problem that Italians still faced after 1861. In Germany, in fact, "a literary, scientific, industrial, and social upheaval had preceded the political revolution that had been only the necessary consequence of the first." [11] Italy, instead, had begun with the political revolution and still had to bring about the transition from the old to the new world in the most important sectors of its moral life and social reality. And the argument that Germany might also be a source of valuable guidance on how to face the growing problems of the new industrial society was vigorously upheld by knowledgeable men like Luigi Luzzatti, supporter and admirer of German academic socialism, from which he borrowed the doctrine that "the new and formidable social problems cannot be solved with liberty alone and without the participation of the state." [12]

In fact, the more the weaknesses and the problems of their new nation became evident to Italians after 1860—above all after the bitter disillusionments of 1866—the more important became the need to give life to a culture capable of bringing about that renewal of Italy's moral life which German culture had achieved in Germany. The exaltation of knowledge and science which characterized the now triumphant positivism helped increase the value of the example offered by the "learned" Germany. In the same way, the example of the great national war, fought and won with so many sacrifices by Germany, continued to inspire the expectations of Italian anti-Austrian circles, which hoped that some day a great trial would also come for Italy, not only to redeem the humiliations of 1866, but also to give the national edifice the cohesion that only great struggles and common sacrifices could furnish it.

Italian admiration for Germany was paralleled during these years by the development of admiration for Italy in German cultural circles. Its outstanding expression was the biography of Cavour by Heinrich von Treitschke in 1869. In it Treitschke held up the political action of the Italian statesman as a model to the Germans and hoped for a common future for the two countries united in a struggle against the reactionary power of the papacy and the domineering aspirations of France. During this period, in fact, a radical change occurred in the image of Italy prevalent in German culture as interest shifted from Italy's glorious past to Italy as a modern society and state.[13] This change was due above all to Treitschke but also to men of very different political opinions, like Karl Hillebrand (founder and director from 1874 to 1877 of *Italia*, a journal published in Leipzig), who had resolved to acquaint German cultural circles with the most significant aspects of contemporary Italian life and civilization.[14] Moreover, the impressive development of classical studies in Germany created a wave of interest which spread through German high schools to the middle class and achieved much wider diffusion than a merely cultural interest would have created. With the beginning of widespread tourism at the start of the twentieth century, it assumed the dimension of a true social and mass phenomenon. This atmosphere, therefore, must also be kept in mind, together with the well-known political and diplomatic motives, as background for the alliance that was signed in 1882 and lasted for more than thirty years.[15]

All this helps to explain how Italy—a country recently formed and engaged in a strenuous effort to modernize its intellectual life and to achieve political and social parity with the great countries of modern Europe—accepted German cultural influence to a greater degree than any other country outside Mitteleuropa, where German culture traditionally predominated. In history and philosophy, and in particular in classical philology and ancient history, German professors were appointed in Italian universities, where they taught for decades with lasting effects. Adolf Holm taught ancient history at Palermo; Joseph Muller taught Greek literature at Turin. From the capital Julius Beloch exercised a dominant influence on Italian students of ancient history between 1880 and the First World War, and Emanuel Loewy taught art history. Disputes raged between the supporters of the old literary-rhetorical Italian tradition and those of the new philology on questions such as the originality or lack of originality of Latin literature with respect to the Greek, or Mommsen's historical vision aiming at the "deflation" of the ancient Romans. Men (including the illustrious poet Giosuè Carducci) who were basically tied to a backward and provincial tradition fought the modern historical and critical ideas. In history and philology, however, the scientific method and the "German" method became synonymous terms in current usage, and for decades specialized study in Germany was considered indispensable training for any serious research.

In legal studies the successes of German scholarship in the theoretical interpretation of private law, culminating in the theory of the *Rechtsgeschäft*, decisively effected the triumph of the dogmatic or technico-juridical method that has continued to prevail in Italy for almost a century. The study of public law as a legal science in Italy was due above all to the work of Vittorio Emanuele Orlando, law professor, politician, and prime minister of Italy from 1917 to 1919. He recalled that an important part of his education had been his advanced training in Munich under Aloys von Brinz, who took pleasure in bringing out the affinity between German and Latin thought, and under the greatest German theorist of public law, Georg Jellinek.

German influence on economic studies was attacked violently by Francesco Ferrara, the greatest economist of the Risorgimento, because it threatened to turn Italian economic thought away from classical economics to theories that smacked, in his judgment, clearly of socialism. But German economic studies found strong defenders who showed how arbitrary it was to identify such studies with ideas advocating state intervention and who praised both academic socialism and the work of Franz Hermann Schulze-Delitzsch, the German economist and organizer of people's cooperatives. However, economics was probably the only discipline in which German ideas did not succeed in dominating; here British and French ideas remained preeminent. In the natural sciences and in medicine, as well as in engineering and technical studies, the influence of German laboratories and clinics prevailed uncontested. Italians compared the technical schools of the Second Reich favorably with their English and French counterparts and judged them clearly superior in their results, which were attributed to a wise mixture of government intervention and independence.

An analysis of the specific significance of German influence in each of these disciplines would require more space than is available here as well as very diverse kinds of expertise. Such an inquiry should be carried out by specialists in the various disciplines, who could thus shed light on important aspects, only imperfectly known, of Italian intellectual history. Here I wish to set forth a single, hypothetical observation of a general character, suggested by what is revealed in the history of a few disciplines, including the natural sciences.

It seems that from Germany Italian culture accepted technical, rather than conceptual or theoretical, guidance. Thus, for example, philological studies—whose rigorous and strict techniques of linguistic philology, prosody, and speculative criticism had been identified for decades with the Florentine school of Girolamo Vitelli—turned a deaf ear to the new theory of philology as history which Ulrich von Wilamowitz was authoritatively supporting and developing. In Italy Wilamowitz's ideas became immediately identified with positivism, thus lacking in the historical meaning and content that had prevailed in philology from 1870 to 1890.[16] The same outlook prevailed in biology where, thanks to the work of the pathologist Giulio Bizzozzero and the *Archivio italiano per le scienze mediche* founded by him in 1876, Italian biological studies mastered new techniques in the use of the microscope and again achieved European recognition and reputation. But they remained substantially indifferent to the great theoretical questions raised in Rudolf Virchow's *Archiv fur pathologische Anatomie*, even though it was the model for Bizzozzero's journal. This situation in Italian scholarship played a part in determining the violent reaction against German influence which occurred at the time of the First World War in fields like classical philology and ancient history, where the limitations of the "German method" as practiced by Italian universities were more evident. In contrast, there was no substantial opposition in related studies like those of medieval and modern history, in which German erudition enjoyed no less authority and where great scholarly collections, like the new edition of *Rerum Italicarum Scriptores,* modeled on the *Monumenta Germanica,* had been started.

Nevertheless, during the first decade of the twentieth century the influence of German studies in economic and legal history, strengthened by Marxism and the Hegelian revival carried out by Benedetto Croce, had superseded the old Risorgimento dichotomy of Latins and Germans with a more historical and factual vision of a religious and social middle ages. But it remained an Italo-German middle ages beyond which only the scantest attention was paid to the great national kingdoms of the West. It is not necessary to insist further on the importance of the Hegelian influence on philosophical studies in Italy, where for decades the University of Naples, with its philosophers Antonio Tari and Augusto Vera, was the European stronghold of latter-day Hegelianism.[17] Indeed German Hegelians looked to Naples even before the triumphant recovery of Italian Hegelianism at the beginning of the new century. All in all what Benedetto Croce said in December 1915 can hardly be denied even after more than half a century:

> For a long time German "science," "seriousness," "method," and "accurate documentation" served Italian scholars as a banner and at the same time as a weapon behind which they gathered aggressively, rejecting from their ranks the dilettantes, the idlers, the improvisers, the bunglers. To know German and through it to know and to have the example of German books, to keep abreast of changes in knowledge has been the way to "deprovincialize" Italian science, to modernize it, and to harmonize it with European culture.[18]

The philo-Germanism of the intellectuals was reinforced among other Italians by the esteem that German industry and scientific precision were gaining in every area of technological and economic life. More generally appreciated, especially in southern Italy, was the example offered by the new Germany of a strong and orderly state, founded on authentic political virtues, a spirit of discipline, and a profound sense of duty. In an Italy deprived for centuries of any real political life, these qualities held particular appeal for those people who felt most keenly their deficiency and aspired most strongly to overcome it. But German culture also contributed to some expressions of irrational revolt against the prevailing mediocrity of the positivist age. Nietzschean and Wagnerian ideas had a particularly

widespread and significant following in Italy, culminating in the decadent interpretation given to them by Gabriele D'Annunzio. Even earlier,
Italian Wagnerites had been described as "an intolerant church that willingly reestablishes the bonfires of the Inquisition" and whose devotees
announced to the world their desire for renewal through pilgrimages to
Bayreuth, intransigent polemics, and, not least, "strange behavior, bizarre
attire, long hair, cryptic language." [19]

In the *Réflexions sur la violence*, Georges Sorel had written that during
the nineteenth century Germany had been "nurtured by the sublime."
The sublime could lead, as already indicated, to D'Annunzian decadence,
but it could also stimulate a commitment to a higher intellectual and
moral life in men like Croce. In December 1914 Croce openly professed
"profound admiration" for Germany's example: "Who does not admire
. . . Germany? Even those who abhor it, or claim to abhor it, admire it;
because [their] abhorrence includes envy, jealousy, deference, as well as
respect and admiration; [their] antipathy reflects an attempt to react
violently against a spontaneous affection that would be extremely repre-
hensible for us." [20] In some cases this admiration assumed passionate and
even poetic expression, as in the works of the historian and critic Francesco Montefredini, who was devoted to the memory of the "heroic race"
of the Lombards and who cherished the vision of medieval Germany inhabited by "knights, barons, troubadours, and young dreamers, resplend-
ent in armor and avid for beauty and glory" no less than the model of
modern Germany "where so much progress, so much strength of thought
and action are in evidence." [21]

This mood converged with the more general tendency to exalt the
northern Germanic peoples in contrast with the southern Latins. In the
culture of that period this tendency was strengthened by the so-called
scientific contributions of anthropology and positivist sociology. In 1897
Gugliemo Ferrero's *Europa giovane*, significantly dedicated to Cesare
Lombroso, was a sensational example of this outlook. The book does not
lack acute and prescient observations on the limitations, for example, of
the Bismarckian edifice, built by a gigantic personality but substantially
out of tune with its time and based on a temporary equilibrium of interests not truly reconciled in the new Reich. But together with these views
appeared strange and arbitrary analyses. Ferrero labeled the governments
prevalent in Latin countries "caesarism," or governments controlled by
the "classes who do not represent productive labor." According to Ferrero, such governments were now in agony and were destined to give
way to a "society based on labor," which was typically German. Thus,
the "Latin" mentality, until now unchallenged, would have to be modified by a sense of morality expressed in the solidarity and cooperation
so characteristic of the German races.[22] This praise, combined with

similar exaltation of the Slavic race in comparison with the Latin, did not fail to arouse violent reactions, notably in the Sicilian republican deputy Napoleone Colajanni, who, in his *Razze inferiori e razze superiori: o latini e anglosassoni,* written in 1903, polemicized harshly with Ferrero and exposed the flimsy substance of his theories.

Colajanni's work also deserves to be mentioned here for other reasons. Not only does it contain a special chapter pointing out that the lesser progress made by Italy in contrast with Germany depended on nonracial factors, but it also constitutes one of the most noteworthy intellectual expressions of the anti-Germanism that was spreading among the ranks of the republican and radical left, especially after the signing of the Triple Alliance. According to Colajanni, Germany had achieved greater progress than Italy in every field except politics; in this last, it remained inferior because of the lesser degree of popular participation in the achievement of German unity, the authoritarian structure of the state, the remaining privileges of the nobility, the racial and imperialistic doctrine, and the exaltation of force which inspired so many segments of its cultural and political life. Colajanni continued:

> The Germans, who had exalted the cult of force and blood with Hegel, Hellwald, and Mommsen (who had paved the way for Nietzsche), who with Ranke had found in men's bloody battles the struggle of moral energies, called more honestly by Nietzsche brutal energies . . . who with Treitschke had acquired a modern scientific veneer using Darwinism to justify their conquering brutality had felt no restraint after their victories in 1864 to 1866 and 1870 to 1871 in berating the Latins. . . ." [23]

These arguments were to reappear with unexpected virulence in the polemic of 1914 and 1915 and the subsequent war years.

It must be emphasized, however, that the aversion of the Italian left for official Germany was counterbalanced by the influence that German social democracy had begun to exert both through the contacts between its theoreticians and Italian socialist intellectuals and through the importance, especially after 1875, that the German party and its affairs began to assume in the eyes of Italians. The importance of Marx's thought had first been pointed out in 1875 by Vito Cusumano, who was convinced that "the modern age of revolutionary socialism" had begun with the thinker from Trier, who "in the history of socialism occupies the same place as Adam Smith in political economy or Kant in philosophy." Friedrich Engels corresponded for a long time with the leaders of Italian socialism, beginning with Antonio Labriola and Filippo Turati, who were vitally interested in Eduard Bernstein's debate on revisionism and who until 1914 continued to consider Karl Kautsky the major intellectual authority in international socialism. But even among the socialist rank and file the German model exerted an authority comparable to its influence on other and opposing sectors in Italy's social and political spectrum. In 1894 the young Mario Novaro, who had studied for some years in Berlin, wrote: "Modern socialism is essentially international, but Germany, in line with its general cultural predominance, leads other nations also in socialism, the harbinger of the real culture of the future." [24] And Guglielmo Ferrero had listed the German Social Democratic party among the great creations of the young races for whom he reserved the future of civilization. That party was characterized, in his judgment, by an ethical intransigence that made it more a religious than a political organization and that aimed at the total overthrow of the existing order rather than at partial successes in trade-union battles and particular questions.[25] In the very important contacts between the two parties and the trade unions of the two countries, there are records of repeated financial contributions by the powerful German organizations in support of their Italian comrades in their struggles.

Something, nevertheless, was changing in this Italian philo-Germanism in the first ten or fifteen years of the twentieth century. In part, the new orientation of Italian foreign policy which followed the fervid adherence to the Triple Alliance by Francesco Crispi contributed to it. But, in part, some revision or cautious criticism was also beginning to appear in the judgments of those circles of high culture in which admiration for Germany was strongest. The most significant evidence is the book *La nuova Germania* by the writer and journalist Giuseppe Antonio Borgese, which appeared in 1909 and was the result of his extensive, firsthand knowledge of the country as well as his special competence in German culture. The book was full of enthusiasm for German seriousness, discipline, method, and strength and revealed aversion for "all the stenches that rise from the sacred bed of the Seine." It underlined the widespread sympathy felt for Italy by all Germans because they "love our country with a noble passion that is unique in history"; and it declared that "more than . . . the Latin peoples the Germans are the Romans of today, if to be Roman means to be strong, patient, and persistent—to quote the lyrics of Giosuè Carducci." For Borgese, as for all educated Italians of that time, the German people remained "one of the poles, as we were the other, between which modern Christian civilization developed." But he also noted the dangers and the errors of recent German policy, whose imperialistic designs mortgaged the nation's economic development and whose commitment to a naval program weighed heavily on the country without any concrete evidence that its goal of overcoming England's navy was attainable. Even Germany's cultural life, after the great victories of 1870, had entered into an age of spiritual impoverishment and diminished creativity, while growing wealth had marked the end of the former simplicity of life. Acutely, Borgese prophesied a great political future for German Catholicism, and even that early, he labeled German social democracy an unwitting agent of Hohenzollern imperialism. He came to the extremely significant conclusion that the Germany hailed by its admirers in 1870 and 1871 as the heir of the Reformation and the initiator, with Luther, of modern freedom was more comparable to the Spain of Philip II.

None of this means that German supremacy and, generally speaking, German cultural influence did not remain entrenched in Italy until 1914. Their destruction required the great historical crisis opened by the First World War, which demolished the world of Mommsen and Croce, of Kautsky and Labriola, and so many other things. A veritable crusade against Germanism was launched in the press and in cultural circles, banding together two types of men: those who were impatient with material positivism—with which for decades the German method had been identified more or less correctly—and those supporters of a mediocre and provincial Italian cultural nationalism in whose hands the vindication of "Latinity" became a battle against everything that German cultural influence on the peninsula had represented in a seriously modern and progressive way. A veritable rebellion against German pedantry occurred in the name of the originality and brilliance of the Latin mind, especially in fields like classical philology, where conflict had been most explicit between the supporters of the "German method" and the rhetorical traditions of humanism. In 1917 this polemic reached its peak in the highly successful *Minerva e lo scimmione*, an extremely violent attack by the Hellenist Ettore Romagnoli against German science and above all against its Italian representatives, beginning with Girolamo Vitelli, the classical philologist at the Istituto di studi superiori of Florence.

But the struggle for the so-called emancipation of the Italian and Latin mind from the enslavement of many decades flared up in other areas also. Historians like Corrado Barbagallo, defender at one time of the merits of Guglielmo Ferrero for his work in ancient history (against the extremes put forth by the followers of the "German method"), scholars like Arturo Farinelli, and many others entered the fray, which even had its Italo-French journal in the *Rivista delle nazioni latine*, published for a few years during the war. Also at the roots of this anti-German revolt were legitimate demands and an impatience with the deafness of certain intellectual circles to the desire for a less extrinsic and richer culture, which had been permeating Italian society after the rebirth of idealism. But in most cases Croce's harsh judgment appears justified. He saw among the champions of this anti-German revolt "too many known faces from the intellectual rabble and the scientific and literary demimonde, too many people who would be only too happy to go their own way while at the same time gaining plaudits from . . . patriotic fervor without too much effort." The Neapolitan philosopher added: "Faced with them I raise high the banner and bear the arms of the 'German method.' " [26]

It is not possible here to follow adequately the events of the very grave crisis of those years, which seemed, after so long, to overthrow German cultural, as well as political and economic, influence on Italy. The position of the intellectuals who sympathized with Germany was immediately rendered difficult by Germany's alliance with Austria-Hungary. Since this alliance made every Germanophile a supporter of the hereditary enemy, the position to which they had to retreat—best represented in the newspaper *Italia nostra*, directed by the critic and writer Cesare De Lollis—was one favoring neutrality. This defensive position was further weakened by the virulence of the campaign waged by the supporters of the Triple Entente, a campaign which mixed national and ideological motives with appeals for the defense of democracy and territorial claims. Many of these Germanophiles were men of conservative tendencies, united by an old distrust for democratic ideas of French origin. But their conservatism was much more modern and richer in serious cultural content than the rhetorical nationalism that pitted many of the promoters of the anticipated Latin resurgence against the culture that had restored to Italy an intellectual life suited to the breadth and needs of the modern world.

During the decades preceding the First World War, the growing impatience in certain cultural circles with the malfunctioning of parliamentarianism and the ever more frequent discussions about its crisis had strengthened rather than weakened the value of the alternative for political development which the German example seemed to offer. To Croce it seemed that "the peoples of Western Europe, French, English, and Italian" had entered into "a centrifugal process that threatens the dissolution in the not-too-distant future of the idea of the state and of social unity for the transitory advantage of single individuals and single social groups." In contrast, "an inverse process, a centripetal development," had taken place in Germany "which, despite its large-scale collaboration with modern civilization, has vigorously kept up the feeling for the fatherland, the state, and the historical mission of the German people and has subordinated the individual to the state." Westerners and above all Italians could have learned much from this "stern concept that the Germans have cultivated of the state and of the fatherland." [27]

Indeed the Germanophile intellectuals also interpreted the ideological basis and significance of the war in line with the German origin of their particular mental outlook. They could, therefore, with absolute consistency desire victory for their own country at war with the admired Germany and work to achieve it. But they thought it should be a "German-style war," a "great war," as Cesare De Lollis wrote in several letters published by the *Giornale d'Italia* in September 1914, which were among the first to unleash in the intellectual world the polemic on intervention. It should be one of those wars "that elevates the victorious nation in the eyes of the entire world, but that can be won only by a perfectly organized country." [28] They thought that out of this war the political ideal to which they remained faithful would emerge strengthened, an ideal that if not exclusively German was nevertheless the one that Germany "had epitomized better than other nations in recent times." In 1916 Croce declared:

> I am persuaded that in this war the Latin nations and their democratic ally England rather than strengthening their democratic and utopian ideal are gradually destroying it in order to strengthen themselves, and that once the war is ended they will find themselves spiritually changed. They will be much less democratic and idealistic than they were and believe they can remain, much more "militaristic," or more warlike, than they had been for a long time; [in this way they too will fulfill the] historical and fighting ideal of life.[29]

This line of thought was repeated literally by Borgese, who, unlike Croce, had gone through an interventionist conversion and now came to the defense of the liberation of the Latin mind from German domination. Nevertheless, he proclaimed that this position put him "on the great path of German and European thought . . . in the great line of classic German poetry and prose, of Goethe and his contemporaries" and declared that "the liberal states, if they succeed in winning, will have other things to do than to celebrate democracy and disarmament: they will have to learn from the hard lessons [of war] to rearm, to discipline themselves morally and militarily against new threats of tyranny and dangers of vengeful *revanches*." [30]

Thus, these men thought they would be able to regenerate Italy now that it was at war and to cure it of its ills by once again following the teaching of German thought. This was also the ideal that inspired Enrico Ruta, another southern idealist and Hegelian, who during the war translated Nietzsche and Treitschke. From Treitschke's concept of the "state understood as strength," Ruta drew the teaching that the Italians had the right to assert themselves in a world fighting a war that would be won by those nations in which serious, moral men predominated—men able to combine their daily activities with an awareness of a common ideal.

These ideals and intentions were destined to be swept away in the last phase of the conflict, when the Wilsonian program and the ideological struggle for democracy provided the definitive slogans of the Allied war effort. Basically, the Italian Germanophiles committed an error analogous to that of the German ruling class with which they shared identical cultural and political premises: to a large extent, each group underestimated the damage that their support of the ideal of force—so easily open to moral accusations—did to their cause. They also underestimated the propaganda value of idealistic crusades proclaimed in the name of democracy in an age dominated by the masses. The world that emerged from the war was very different from the one they had hoped for. However, this disappointment did not persuade those Italians who had been brought up on German thought to deny ideals born of a deeply felt intellectual experience and now largely identified with the national culture of the new Italy. If anything, the vacuity of the claims for the superiority of the Latin spirit and the Italian and Mediterranean "genius" was exposed after the intoxication of the war years. Certainly, the "pious credulity and wide-eyed trust that everything the Germans continued to write had a seriousness and a profundity not found in books of other languages" [31] gradually lost ground. But not until the Second World War and the break it marked with the preceding history of united Italy can one speak of a replacement of Germany's cultural influence by other countries—primarily the United States.

NOTES

1. On these themes in Italian historical writings during the Risorgimento, see Benedetto Croce, *Storia della storiografia italiana nel secolo decimonono*, 4th ed., 2 vols. (Bari: Laterza, 1964), I, 96–158.

2. Francesco Schupfer, *Delle istituzioni politiche longobardiche* (Florence: Le Monnier, 1863).

3. Paolo Treves, *L'idea di Roma e la cultura italiana del secolo XIX* (Milan: Ricciardi, 1962), pp. 49–53, 81–89.

4. Quoted in M. Sandirocco, Preface to Ruggero Bonghi, *Nove anni di storia d'Europa nel commento di un italiano, 1866–1874*, 3 vols. (Florence: Le Monnier, 1938–1958), I, xvii.

5. Nicola Marselli, *Gli avvenimenti del 1870* (Turin: Loescher, 1871), pp. 12–13, 16, 17, 85.

6. Carlo De Cesare, *La Germania moderna* (Rome: Pallotta, 1872), *passim.*

7. Marselli, *op. cit.*, p. 91.

8. Giuseppe Civinini, "L'antico e il nuovo Impero in Germania," *Nuova Antologia*, 17 (May 1871), 55.

9. Marselli, *op. cit.*, p. 86.

10. *Ibid.*, pp. 76–77, 78, 84.

11. Pasquale Villari, "Was die Ausländer in Italien nicht bemerken," *Italia*, 4 (1873), 3.

12. Luigi Luzzatti, "L'economia politica e le scuole germaniche," *Nuova Antologia*, 27 (September 1874), 174–192. On Villari's analogous sympathy for academic socialism see I. Cervelli, "Cultura e politica nella storiografia italiana ed Europea fra Otto e Novecento," *Belfagor*, 23 (September 1968), 603.

13. Theodor Schieder, "Das Italienbild der deutschen Einheitsbewegung," *Studien zur deutsch-italienischen Geistesgeschichte* (Köln: Böhlau, 1959), pp. 141–162.

14. On Hillebrand and the journal *Italia* see brief references in Ernesto Ragionieri, *Socialdemocrazia tedesca e socialisti italiani, 1875–1895* (Milan: Feltrinelli, 1961), p. 30; see also W. Mauser, "Incontri italiani di Karl Hillebrand," *Nuova Antologia*, 469 (April 1957), 541–550.

15. See Ernesto Ragionieri, *Italia giudicata, 1861–1945* (Bari: Laterza, 1968), pp. 170–171.

16. Treves, *op. cit.*, pp. 193–220; on Vitelli see "Lo studio dell'antichità classica nell'Ottocento," *La letteratura italiana: Storia e testi*, ed. Paolo Treves (Milan: Ricciardi, 1962), vol. 72.

17. The most recent bibliography on Neapolitan Hegelianism can be found in Cervelli, *Belfagor*, 24 (January 1969), 68, n. 69.

18. Benedetto Croce, *Pagine sulla guerra*, 2nd ed. (Bari: Laterza, 1928), p. 87.

19. F. D'Arcais, "Riccardo Wagner," *Nuova Antologia*, 38 (March 1, 1883), 1–32.

20. Croce, *Pagine sulla guerra*, p. 22.

21. Quoted in Benedetto Croce, *Letteratura della nuova Italia*, 4th ed., 6 vols. (Bari: Laterza, 1943), III, 362, 364.

22. G. Ferrero, *Europa giovane* (Milan: Treves, 1897), *passim*.

23. N. Colajanni, *Razze inferiori e razze superiori: o latini e anglosassoni*, 2nd ed. (Naples: Pansini, 1906), p. 53.

24. Quoted in Ragionieri, *Socialdemocrazia tedesca . . .* , p. 294. Besides providing rich and precise data on the relations between German and Italian socialism from 1875 to 1895, Ragionieri's work also serves as an introduction to the years between 1895 and the First World War; see especially pp. 36–41.

25. Ferrero, *op. cit.*, pp. 60–120.

26. Croce, *Pagine sulla guerra*, p. 87.

27. *Ibid.*, pp. 73–74.

28. On these letters by De Lollis and the debate to which they belong see Brunello Vigezzi, *L'Italia di fronte alla prima guerra mondiale:* Vol. I, *L'Italia neutrale* (Milan: Ricciardi, 1966), pp. 613 ff.

29. Croce, *Pagine sulla guerra*, p. 129.

30. Giuseppe A. Borgese, *Italia e Germania* (Milan: Treves, 1915), pp. x ff., xliii, 74.

31. Benedetto Croce, *Pagine sparse* (Bari: Laterza, 1960), II, 518.

PART IV

FOREIGN POLICY AND
DIPLOMACY SINCE UNIFICATION

After 1870, to compensate for its domestic weakness and backwardness, Italy tried to follow a foreign policy that would give it prestige and the standing of a first-rate power. Its efforts to achieve these ends met with a marked lack of success. Thwarted by France in its ambition to control Tunisia, Italy attempted to establish an empire in Ethiopia, an attempt that ended disastrously at Aduwa in 1896. Social imperialism undoubtedly played an important role in driving Italy to Africa at this time, as it did in 1911 when Giovanni Giolitti ordered Italian troops to attack Turkey in Tripolitania and Cyrenaica. Between 1900 and 1914, however, as the situation at home became more stable and prosperous and a balance of power began to emerge in Europe, Italy was able to insert itself in the European state system. It retained its formal membership in the Triple Alliance with Germany and Austria. At the same time it developed close ties with the members of the Triple Entente: France, Russia, and Great Britain. With the outbreak of the First World War, Italy had three choices: to remain neutral, which it did from August 1914 to May 1915, to enter the war on the side of the Central Powers, or to join the Entente forces. The majority of Italians, led by Giolitti and the Socialists, preferred neutrality, but a vociferous and determined minority—among whom were King Victor Emmanuel III, the nationalists, the conservatives Salandra and Sonnino, and the poet D'Annunzio—opted for the third alternative and imposed their will on the nation. The fruits of victory were, however, disappointing in the eyes of Italians, who blamed the inept diplomacy of their leaders at Versailles.

Under Fascism, Italy followed its most aggressive foreign policy and diplomacy with some success, as the results in Corfu and Ethiopia indicate. But the close alliance with Nazi Germany revealed Italy's weaknesses and reduced it once again to the status of a junior partner. After the Second World War, Italy abandoned its imperial ambitions and delusions of greatness and became a strong supporter of European integration and common action. Accepting the reality of small-power status in a Europe where empires have disappeared, Italy has developed a sane foreign policy that corresponds to its resources and world position.

The two chapters in this section survey Italian foreign policy since 1870. William C. Askew discusses its course before the First World War and considers the first decade of this century, when sanity and moderation prevailed, as the high point in the diplomacy of liberal Italy. René Albrecht-Carrié surveys Italian involvement abroad during the Fascist years. He writes that during the 1920s Italy seemed to have accepted its role in the European power structure. But in the 1930s Italy embarked upon a disastrous series of adventures, first in Ethiopia (which, however, brought success and an "empire"), then in Spain, and finally as a satellite of Nazi Germany in the Second World War. Carrié concludes that since the end of the Second World War Italian foreign policy has been once again marked by moderation within the context of European cooperation.

CHAPTER 14

ITALY AND THE GREAT POWERS
BEFORE THE FIRST WORLD WAR

William C. Askew

In 1870 the new, united Italy was thrust into the world of the great powers, a world in which nationalism set nation against nation and threatened the disintegration of whole empires; a world in which naked power wielded by the sovereign state was the supreme arbiter.[1] Italy's role in this age of realpolitik was strangely ambiguous—too weak to be a great power except by courtesy and yet too strong and proud to accept a lesser role. Pressing internal problems—poverty, illiteracy, railroad building and industrial development, the Southern Question, the breach between church and state, the gap between the government and the people —demanded the undivided attention of the Italian nation. Foreign affairs, the definition of vital national interests and the choice of the best means to defend these interests, seemed a cruel diversion of attention and effort from the paramount task of developing inner strength and cohesion.[2] Indeed foreign policy became a divisive issue in the new state.

After centuries during which the small Italian states had been the pawns of the great powers, there were perhaps only four alternatives dictated by past traditions which Italy could follow. First, the tradition of ancient Rome demanded greatness. Italy should live dangerously and compensate for domestic weakness through imperial expansion. But to many Italians this tradition seemed singularly out of place in the real world of the late nineteenth century. From the Kingdom of Sardinia came the second tradition, that of exploiting Italy's strategic position, allying first with France for conquest and then with Austria for defense of the status quo.[3] To reach its objectives Italy should use the only two weapons readily available—its geographic position and skillful diplomacy—but to many Italians Austria was the eternal enemy, and militaristic, autocratic Germany was almost equally repugnant. Many Italians preferred friendship with France, the cultural model and the home of liberty, equality, and fraternity. A third tradition, perhaps less clearly defined, was to turn inward, to place faith in neutrality, to abjure military power, and to admit that a poor country could not afford the burden of modern war—to live humbly but to live well. Those who supported this alternative believed that the principles of nationality and liberty had such great moral force that they were bound to triumph, even without the backing of great material force. The fourth tradition—friendship with England—derived from common sense and history. Most Italians agreed that a country with some four thousand miles of coast must be on friendly terms with England, the greatest naval power.

Torn among these traditional approaches to foreign policy, the Italian people have never presented a united front to the world. This unfortunate situation explains in large part the oscillations in foreign policy and the exaggerated role played by individual premiers and foreign ministers in changing the style and direction of Italian diplomacy. It perhaps also helps to explain the enormous impact of domestic issues and crises on the conduct of Italian foreign policy.

Since 1870, Italian foreign policy appears to have gone through five major stages or phases. A careful examination of developments in each of these periods will reveal deviations that make generalizations very difficult, if not impossible. First, from 1870 to 1887 the new nation followed a policy of extreme caution, of evading risks and obligations, of looking inward, of consolidating the status quo. Deeply conscious of its poverty, weakness, and divisions, the Italian nation sought conciliation, carefully weighed the relationship between means and ends, and postponed any daring action until it could gather inner strength and passions could cool. Second, from 1887 to 1896, under the leadership of Francesco Crispi, Italian foreign policy threw caution and restraint to the winds and no longer balanced means and ends. This path led to the military defeat at Aduwa, Ethiopia, and the ensuing shame and frustration may have played a major role in the unrest that seemed to shake the very foundations of the nation. Third, the zenith of Italian diplomacy probably was reached between Aduwa and the outbreak of the First World War. In this period Italy achieved prestige and influence among the great powers. Fourth, war and Fascism found Italian diplomacy at its worst. Entry into two world wars and unsteady and inept diplomacy between these wars brought Italy close to disaster. In some respects Benito Mussolini's conduct in foreign affairs resembled that of Crispi, but his errors were more pronounced, the course of Italian diplomacy less steady, and the price of failure even greater. Fifth, since 1945 Italy has returned to a sane and sensible course in foreign policy which is in harmony with its finest traditions and the means at its disposal.

This chapter will deal primarily with the aims, methods, and style of Italian diplomacy from 1896 to 1915 and will discuss Italian foreign policy before 1896 only briefly. Between 1870 and 1887 Italy's leaders pursued a cautious diplomacy that brought safety but no glory and left the Italian people unusually sensitive to foreign slights and insults and unusually hungry for some dramatic success. In 1878 Italy left the Congress of Berlin (called to settle the Russo-Turkish conflict in the Balkans) empty-handed. In 1881 Tunisia passed under effective French control. And in 1882 Italy refused a British invitation to join in the occupation of Egypt. These were heavy blows to the nation's pride.[4] In retrospect, however, this was realpolitik at its best, for, having no real alternatives, Italy's leaders did as much as they could under the circumstances.

After the defeat of France by Prussia in 1871, perhaps the greatest danger for Italy was that the clerical, monarchist, and conservative elements in control of the new French national assembly might join forces with the pope and perhaps other Catholic countries to correct the "mistake" made by Napoleon III in encouraging the unification of Italy. How serious this danger was may never be determined with certainty. Marquis Emilio Visconti Venosta, Italy's able foreign minister from 1869 to 1876,[5] was the ideal man to calm the French and placate Austria, with whom there may have been a tacit understanding whereby Italy refused to encourage irredentism in Trieste and the Trentino and Vienna took a negative stand on the Roman Question.[6] The shift of France to an anticlerical stance after the triumph of the republicans in 1877 probably ended any danger of a French crusade on behalf of the pope. But it was the Triple Alliance of 1882 which dispelled any possible threat to restore the temporal power, while at the same time giving a powerful boost to the monarchy.

When the Triple Alliance was first signed, Italy had little bargaining power. Germany and Austria-Hungary gave no support to Italy's colonial and Balkan aspirations. But by 1887 the Bulgarian crisis and the political rise of General Georges Boulanger in France had enhanced Italy's bargaining position. The Italian foreign minister, Count Carlo di Robilant, then forged an additional protocol with Austria which obligated the two nations to make no change in the Balkan status quo without prior agreement based upon reciprocal compensation. He also won Germany's promise of assistance if France threatened Morocco or Tripoli and Italy opposed France. To defend the Mediterranean status quo, England joined Italy and Austria in the First and Second Mediterranean Agreements of 1887, as did Spain through a separate agreement with Italy to which Germany and Austria acceded.[7]

At the death of Prime Minister Agostino Depretis in July 1887, Francesco Crispi succeeded him in office. The policy of patience and caution ended, and a period of living dangerously began. Crispi undoubtedly appealed greatly to a country starved for glory and success. He still remains a controversial figure and has admirers and severe critics. Perhaps the strongest indictments that can be made against him are that he failed to keep means and ends in harmony and that he tended to identify his own personal pride and ambition with the good of Italy. Moreover, he talked too much. During his years in office, Franco-Italian relations deteriorated and trade suffered as a full-scale tariff war developed. Crispi antagonized Russia and irritated England and to some extent his own allies by his alarmist attitude toward France and French colonial ambition. While assuming far-reaching obligations to send five army corps and three cavalry divisions to Germany, he neglected adequate defenses against King Menelik of Ethiopia during Italy's first attempt to conquer that East African land. In 1896 the defeat at Aduwa brought Italy's greatest humiliation since unification and ended Crispi's political life.

"All is saved except honor" exclaimed the *Tribuna* on March 14, 1896. Rent by internal disorder and social unrest, without effective friends, its foreign policy apparently bankrupt, its institutions tottering, Italy seemed to face a dark and impossible future. The Triple Alliance had failed except in the most negative way. Russia and France had intrigued with the Ethiopian enemy and now seemed ready to gather in the spoils. England had been at best a lukewarm friend, generous with advice but slow to come forward with help. Public confidence was at a low ebb. The zest for empire had momentarily disappeared.

Beneath the surface, however, the nation had much vitality. The economy was ready to begin a decided leap forward, and the first years of the twentieth century witnessed substantial industrial progress. For many Italians the struggle to earn a living became a little easier. The ruling elite now took a hard look at social problems and made minor adjustments and reforms. Giovanni Giolitti, henceforth the dominant political leader until the First World War, at least had some sympathy and appreciation for the problems of the proletariat.

A new era began in Italian diplomacy which was to give the country greater weight in the councils of Europe and which finally allowed Italy to play the role of a great power. The new leaders in control of Italian foreign policy had learned the lessons of the past quarter century quickly and well. Their policy was highly sophisticated, extremely complex, completely selfish, and for a time remarkably successful. Made possible by the changing power relationship in Europe this new orientation was designed to take full advantage of it. Visconti Venosta's somewhat contradictory precept "Always independent, never isolated" was now realized for the first time. Italian policy between Aduwa and the First World War was basically honest, and Italy was as loyal to its commitments as any European great power. The legend that the Italian ruling class was essentially dishonest and that Italian agreements were only made to be broken collapses when the evidence is minutely examined. Likewise, the legend that there was no stability in Italian objectives and no rational basis behind these objectives will not hold up under critical examination. Shrewd calculation rather than opportunism dictated Italian policy. Reason rather than impulse or emotion guided Italian diplomats in the period under survey.

Several new factors influenced Italian foreign policy in the years just before and just after Aduwa. France had recovered strength, if not unity, had found a major ally in Russia, and was on the brink of a momentous change in its relationship with Great Britain. Second, the Triple Alliance was not designed to give positive support to Italy's Mediterranean and colonial objectives; its advantages were in protecting Italy from a French attack or attempt to restore the pope's temporal power and in preventing an Austro-Italian confrontation over Italia Irredenta (Italy's "unredeemed lands" in the Trentino and the Trieste area). Third, the new Anglo-German antagonism threatened to push Italy into a future war with England. If there was one firm axiom in Italian policy until the time of Mussolini, it was that Italy must never expose its long coastline to attacks by the British navy. Fourth, the situation in southeastern Europe was changing radically as Russia turned its attention to the Far East, as nationalism increased in the Balkans, and as Austrian ambition in this region mounted. Finally, the Roman Question was virtually extinct, and an uneasy modus vivendi had already been created between the Vatican and Italy. Thus, all of the bases on which, according to Salvemini, the Triple Alliance had once rested had ceased or were ceasing to be valid.[8]

The Italian press of the turn of the century contains thousands of articles praising the Triple Alliance and thousands of condemnations. Obviously the alliance elicited much interest, and the small group of Italians which made up the reading public was hopelessly divided on the issue of Italian membership. It is my conclusion that the makers of Italian foreign policy were sincere in their desire to maintain the alliance and in their professions of loyalty to it. But they were convinced that the Triple Alliance, strictly interpreted, was not enough to safeguard Italian interests. They made it abundantly clear to Austria-Hungary and Germany that they were loyal to the alliance only as long as Germany and Austria-Hungary did not encroach upon Italy's vital national interests and did not prevent Italian friendship and collaboration with the other great powers.

With Germany, Italy maintained close, generally friendly, and at times intimate, relations. The German government had no great faith in Italian military support, especially after the Moroccan crisis of 1905 and 1906, but wished to keep Italy in the alliance in order to protect Austria's rear and to prevent Italy from upsetting the European equilibrium by joining France. The German foreign office remembered only too well Bismarck's pronouncement that one corporal with an Italian flag and a drummer on the French frontier rather than on the Austrian frontier would make him content if war came. At home the connection with conservative Germany gave Italy a safeguard against republicanism. But the most useful function Germany served, as countless documents in both Italian and German archives indicate, was as mediator between Italy and the Hapsburg Monarchy. Without this German mediation relations between Italy and Austria-Hungary would have become impossible.

Having dealt with the Austro-Italian antagonism in some detail elsewhere, the author will limit himself here to a few brief comments.[9] In the late nineteenth century, relations between Austria and Italy had been surprisingly satisfactory, except for an occasional incident involving Italian claims on the Trentino and Trieste. This situation changed after 1900, for by then one of Italy's main foreign policy objectives was to achieve absolute parity with Russia and Austria in all Balkan questions. Consequently, Italian diplomats followed events in that area carefully. While they wanted a strong Austria-Hungary as a barrier to Russian domination of the Balkans and Adriatic, they feared Austria's expansionist tendencies in Albania and elsewhere in the Balkans. By 1901 full agreement had been reached that neither state would seize political control of Albania and that the ultimate solution for this troubled area should be autonomy. Nevertheless, a veiled struggle for influence and concessions continued, and even an agreement on absolute parity did not end this rivalry. By 1914 the Albanian question had created extremely tense relations between Italy and the Hapsburg Monarchy, and Italy and Austria had been strengthening the defenses on their common frontier in the previous decade as if they had been enemies rather than allies. It was rather on the French frontier that Italy relaxed preparations. In this contest over Albania the Italians appear not only to have held their own but also to have bested their Austrian rivals. Elsewhere in the Balkans the Italians held firmly to the principle of nationality as a basis for reordering the area. Having no clear, consistent policy towards its weak neighbors, Austria-Hungary oscillated between brute force and harsh treatment and kindness and justice. By 1908 certainly Austria had turned firmly against any solution based on the principle of nationality.

Another area of possible disagreement between the two countries was Macedonia. When the Mürzsteg agreement of 1903 indicated clearly that Austria and Russia would assume the leading roles in Macedonian reform, the Italians began a desperate drive to have equal participation by all of the major European powers. In 1904 and 1905, during the Russo-

Japanese conflict, Italy's main fear was that Austria would take advantage of Russia's involvement in Asia to gain hegemony in Macedonia. Italian diplomacy worked with considerable success to have Macedonian reform entrusted to all of the great powers before the Young Turk revolution of 1908 ended any talk of reform by Europe.

The Bosnian annexation crisis of 1908 and 1909 further strained relations between Italy and Austria, almost beyond repair. Italy's foreign minister, Tommaso Tittoni, correctly judged that Austria lost more than it gained from the annexation of the former Turkish province of Bosnia-Herzegovina (which it had occupied since 1878) by agreeing to give up all rights to garrison the Sanjak of Novibazar and all supervision of Montenegran use of the port of Antivari. Unfortunately, Italian public opinion did not agree with the minister, and an enraged parliament and public were sharply critical of his policy. Tittoni sought desperately and unsuccessfully to persuade Austria to make some slight concession with regard to the creation of an Italian university in the empire or with regard to the disputed boundary at Aquileia, near Trieste. He survived the crisis and soon became Italian ambassador to France, but his influence and reputation had been impaired. Having failed to forge an Italo-Austro-Russian agreement for parity of influence in the Balkans, Italy achieved the same result by separate and somewhat contradictory agreements with Russia at Racconigi in October 1909 and with Austria-Hungary in December 1909.

Italy's attack on Turkey in September 1911 was in part an effort to restore the Mediterranean equilibrium that France was in process of destroying in the Agadir Crisis and to forestall any possible future French threat to Libya. In part Italy moved because of pressure from the Banco di Roma, which, unable to meet growing Turkish obstruction, was threatening to sell its Libyan interests to German and Austrian banks and was arousing Italian public opinion against Turkey. But Italy's leaders also wanted to liquidate the Libyan problem before the Balkan issue came to a head. Otherwise Italy's allies might consider Libya as compensation for Austrian gains in the Balkans and disregard Italian claims on Ottoman territory in southeastern Europe. The war with Turkey over Libya caused considerable friction between Italy and its allies, especially Austria, and Italy feared that Austria might move in the Balkans while Italy was busy in Libya. But the long-range result was probably to bring Italy a little closer to its allies.[10]

During the Balkan wars in 1912 and 1913 Italy worked quite loyally with Austria to block Serbia from the sea by the creation of an independent Albania. But relations became strained as Austria tried to increase its role in the Balkans. Italy firmly vetoed a separate Austrian action when Montenegro seized Scutari and strongly opposed Austrian threats to side with Bulgaria against Serbia in July 1913. Foreign Minister Marquis Antonino di San Giuliano complained to Austria for not consulting with its allies when Austria sent Serbia an eight-day ultimatum to evacuate Albanian territory in October 1913.

Italy followed a cautious and friendly policy in dealing with the small Balkan states, and they reciprocated with a large measure of friendship for and confidence in Italy. These contacts enabled Italy always to be well-informed about political developments in the region. On countless occasions Italy urged caution, calm, and prudence on its small Balkan neighbors. Between 1896 and 1898, during the Greek-inspired Cretan insurrection against Turkey, Italy had sympathized with Greece, but the Italian government supported the other European powers in blocking the union of Crete with Greece. The only other question that caused serious friction arose over Greek claims to southern Albania, which Italy opposed. After Tittoni became foreign minister in 1903, Italian policy supported a union of the Balkan states. It also supported plans for a Danube-Adriatic railway as a counterweight to the Austrian project for a railroad across the southern Balkans and ultimately to Salonika. Agreements in 1908 provided that Italy would supply 35 percent of the capital for the Danube-Adriatic railway and 55 percent of the capital to develop its terminus on the Adriatic, but Italian capitalists were cool toward this investment.

From 1888 to 1898 the tariff war between Italy and France had caused serious damage to the Italian economy, but after 1896 the two countries embarked on new courses in their dealings with one another. France ceased insisting that Italy desert the Triple Alliance or even reveal its terms. Rather, the French began to weaken the alliance by removing all Italian grievances against France. Between 1896 and 1902 the hostile atmosphere changed into a warm friendship. Théophile Delcassé, the French foreign minister, and Camille Barrère, the French ambassador at Rome from 1898, played the leading roles for France. On the Italian side Visconti Venosta and Giulio Prinetti deserve most of the credit. The first step toward a detente occurred on September 29, 1896, when conventions were signed which safeguarded the rights of Italians in Tunisia and which gave Italy all that could be expected at that time. More important was the new commercial treaty of November 21, 1898, which established most-favored-nation treatment except for wine and silk and certain other fabrics. Thus ended the long tariff war between the two nations.

The Italians were still concerned about French intentions in Tripolitania and Cyrenaica, and the Anglo-French delimitation of March 21, 1899, only increased their fears of French encroachment on the hinterland of these Libyan dependencies of the Ottoman Empire. The exchange of notes (dated December 14 and 16, 1900) between France and Italy on January 4, 1901, provided for French disinterest in Libya and Italian disinterest in Morocco; Italy was left a free hand to act in Libya only after

France acted to change the status of Morocco. On January 24, 1900, France accepted Italy's proposal for delimiting Eritrea and French Somaliland. Then followed the Prinetti-Barrère exchange of letters on June 30, 1902, whereby Italy obtained freedom to move in Libya before France took Morocco. Both states also pledged neutrality if either one should be the object of direct or indirect aggression or went to war as a result of direct provocation.

These agreements placed Franco-Italian relations on a new plane, ending the long antagonism. At the same time, Italy's new commitment to France was in harmony with the text of the Triple Alliance. In 1902 Prinetti informed Germany that France had disinterested itself in Libya and that Italy had done the same for Morocco. Although the 1902 agreements were secret, Tittoni and Giolitti did inform Germany in March 1905 that Prinetti had declared Italy not obligated to depart from neutrality in case of aggression or provocation directed toward France. The German chancellor, Bernhard von Bülow, advised the Kaiser that Germany should have no illusions about the active cooperation of Italy in war but should not underestimate the value of Italian neutrality. There was a growing awareness that Italy had become a major arbiter of the peace of Europe and that war was inevitable if the Triple Alliance disintegrated.

In 1905 the First Moroccan Crisis placed Italy in a difficult and delicate situation between the conflicting interests of France and Germany in Morocco. Barrère opposed the projected conference at Algeciras, and Monts, the German ambassador, asked for Italian support. Replying evasively to both ambassadors Tittoni asked what position England would take. Representing Italy at the conference, Visconti Venosta maintained close contact with his Austrian colleague and practiced a policy of "conciliatory impartiality." The harsh German reaction to Italy's conduct at Algeciras was not deserved. Even Bülow had to admit that Italy's official conduct had been correct, but the chancellor still deplored the language of the Italian press during the conference.

On the whole Franco-Italian relations remained good from 1902 to 1912. By giving up its monopoly on the protection of Roman Catholics in the Near East in August 1905, France removed another source of friction. But four grievances still remained concerning the treatment of Italian residents in Tunisia: the creation of new private schools was not allowed; France favored its own citizens in awarding work contracts; harsh conditions existed for Italian fishermen; and there was no labor legislation. However in 1910 France relented on the opening of new schools and on the teaching of Italian in French schools. With the Anglo-Italian-French agreement on spheres of influence in 1906 Ethiopia had largely ceased to be a bone of contention, and by 1910 France actually regarded Italian membership in the Triple Alliance as useful to the cause of peace and thus to France.

Lingering fears still remained in Italy about French intentions in the hinterland of Libya and French hegemony in the Mediterranean. In 1911 one of the arguments Foreign Minister San Giuliano used in persuading Giolitti and the king to prepare for an expedition to Libya was that France was about to upset the Mediterranean equilibrium by gaining a protectorate over most of Morocco. After the "Tunisification" of Morocco, France would have less interest in living up to the agreement of 1902. Contraband from Tunisia into Libya and the Italian seizure of French ships suspected of carrying contraband early in 1912 placed a severe strain on Franco-Italian relations from which recovery was slow.

Of all the great powers, France offered the firmest opposition to Italy's retention of the Dodecanese Islands, occupied during the Turko-Italian war. Perhaps the major reason that Italy was reluctant to surrender the Dodecanese Islands, while admitting in principle that they should be relinquished, was the growing fear that Asiatic Turkey could not long survive the Balkan wars and that the eastern Mediterranean might become an Anglo-French lake. This fear also explains the enormous Italian drive in 1913 and 1914 to carve out a sphere of influence around Adalia, on the southern coast of Turkey. Angered and perplexed by difficulties with Austria in Albania and by Austria's favoring Slavs over Italians along the Dalmatian coast, San Giuliano frankly declared that Italy could never afford to fight a diplomatic duel with both Austria and France at the same time. He sought permission from his German and Austrian allies to reach an agreement with France on the future of Asia Minor, but they refused.

The Italo-French friendship had given Italy an independence of action previously lacking, a voice in European affairs far greater than its physical power warranted, and a real choice in diplomatic alternatives. One immediate result was that Italy acquired a new importance in English eyes, even though the Anglo-French entente of 1904 may have lessened the need for Italian support in the Mediterranean. In April 1896 Foreign Minister Onorato Caetani made it only too clear to Germany and Austria that Italy could never participate in a struggle against the two strongest naval powers, and countless reaffirmations of the intention never to confront British naval power continued to be made. Crispi's foreign minister, Alberto Blanc, had already told Bülow, the German ambassador, on January 15, 1896, that a lasting estrangement between England and Germany must drive Italy to the side of France and Russia. Rarely did Italy side against England on any question of foreign policy, and Italy was the only European great power to show disinterested sympathy for England during the Boer War.

Britain was not unappreciative of Italy's sympathy and above all of Italy's strategic position. In a sense the reconquest of the Sudan was a British effort to strengthen Italy's sagging colonial position in the Red Sea area. In 1898 a French challenge to this reconquest brought on the Fashoda crisis, causing alarm in Italy and some preliminary naval preparations. Italy clearly sympathized with England, and its greatest fear was that France might be provoked by the Fashoda defeat to redeem its prestige by making some demand upon Italy. These fears proved to be groundless, but Italy suspected that the Anglo-French agreement of March 21, 1899, compensated France at the expense of Libya's hinterland for its capitulation at Fashoda. The British took a long step toward ending Italian anxiety over Libya and toward the consolidation of the traditional Anglo-Italian friendship with an exchange of notes in 1902 and with a highly secret agreement on the delimitation of the frontier between Cyrenaica and Egypt in 1907. Many Italians also welcomed the new Anglo-French friendship, symbolized by the Entente Cordiale in 1904. And the Italian government tried to encourage better relations between England and Germany. Between 1912 and 1914 there were many discussions of some kind of agreement among Italy, France, and Great Britain to assure the security of their respective Mediterranean possessions. These discussions led to no practical result, but they indicated Italy's close attachment to Britain and Britain's new respect for Italy's position and potential in the Mediterranean region.[11]

Italian diplomats worked as hard to bring about an improvement in Italo-Russian relations between 1896 and 1914 as they did to keep on close and friendly terms with France and England. After Aduwa, Italy feared that Russia was seeking to establish a protectorate over Ethiopia. How serious this Russian activity at the court of King Menelik really was is difficult to evaluate. In any event, Italy countered it by a careful effort to make peace quickly with the Ethiopian sovereign and by treating him with great fairness and respect. Visconti Venosta also began a drive to improve Italo-Russian relations and in August 1896 sought to arrange a visit of Tsar Nicholas II to Italy. This visit did not take place, but two years later the Russian foreign ministry disavowed its secret agent in Ethiopia. Still, the Italians suspected that both France and Russia aimed at a protectorate there. In the fall of 1903 the tsar postponed a scheduled visit to Italy because of Italian socialist agitation. Italian expressions of sympathy with Japan at the time of the Russo-Japanese conflict did not improve relations.

In 1903 close collaboration between Russia and Austria in Macedonia also strained Russo-Italian relations. Foreign Minister Tittoni feared new agreements between Austria and Russia which would set up spheres of influence in the Balkans and eventually lead to a partition of Turkish territory there. On February 21, 1905, the Russian daily *Novoe Vremia* also expressed fear of Austrian intentions and called for Italo-Russian joint efforts to stop the Austrian advance and to prevent an Italo-Austrian war. By July 12, 1906, this influential newspaper was advocating a union of Slavs and Latins to stop Pan-Germanism. Giulio Melegari, the Italian ambassador in St. Petersburg, praised Foreign Minister Alexander P. Izvolsky, concluded that Russian and Italian intentions in the Balkans were in harmony, and urged that their two countries reach a clear agreement.

In 1908 both Tittoni and Izvolsky emerged humiliated and enraged from the Bosnian crisis resulting from Austria's unilateral annexation of the former Turkish provinces of Bosnia and Herzegovina. In December of that year Izvolsky announced to the Duma that Italo-Russian relations were excellent, thus setting the stage for the visit of Nicholas II to Racconigi in the following October and for Izvolsky and Tittoni to reach full agreement for cooperation on Balkan questions. They agreed on the principle of nationality as a basis for settling these questions if the status quo could not be maintained. Italy left Russia a free hand in opening the Straits to its warships, and Izvolsky left Italy a free hand to take Libya. Russia was to prove more friendly to Italy than any other great power during the Turko-Italian War in 1911. Thus, Italy had found another strong friend and increased its alternatives in foreign policy.

With great skill Italy's three important foreign ministers in these years—Visconti Venosta, Tittoni, and San Giuliano—had steered Italy through a dangerous period and had safeguarded its interests and security. Visconti Venosta and San Giuliano, along with Robilant, rank as perhaps Italy's greatest foreign ministers up to the end of the Second World War. There was only one basic flaw in the delicate system that they constructed: it was geared to the existence of peace between the great powers and was designed to aid in maintaining this peace. War between any two of the great powers would destroy the delicate balance and would impair Italy's influential position in Europe.

In July 1914 the Italians stood to lose no matter what they did if war came. The thought of an arrogant France on one border and a great surge of Slavic power over the ruins of the Austro-Hungarian Empire on the other was just as distasteful as the prospect of victory by Germany and the Hapsburg Monarchy. San Giuliano played a desperate game to keep the peace. He sought to convince his allies that England would not stand aside. He urged Russia and Rumania to restrain Austria. He pressed caution and restraint on Serbia and Montenegro but advised military measures to prevent an Austrian seizure of Mount Lovčen. He sought to persuade Austria through Germany to recognize the correct interpretation of Article 7 of the Triple Alliance—that Austria must reach prior agreement with Italy before disturbing the Balkan status quo, and he made an almost impossible demand for compensation when he asked for the Trentino. San Giuliano was really trying to make it impossible for Austria to punish Serbia for the assassination of Archduke Francis Ferdinand at Sarajevo. He proposed that Serbia accept the entire Austrian ultimatum but envisioned great-power supervision of its implementation. He was trying to restrain Austria and at the same time to bring about a great diplomatic victory that would restore Austrian prestige and prolong the life of the Hapsburg Monarchy. That Russia and Serbia were willing to accept his proposal for peace and that Austria was beginning to waver is generally admitted. Had Sergei D. Sazonov, the Russian foreign minister, not lost his head over a fairly minor Austrian bombardment of Belgrade and persuaded his sovereign to order general mobilization, San Giuliano might have won the desperate game he was playing to keep the peace. It was his and Italy's greatest failure.[12]

The outbreak of war in Europe opened a complex period of stress and strain for the Italian people which lasted almost ten months and resulted in the fateful decision to enter the war on May 23, 1915. Some notable studies of this mighty contest between neutrality and intervention have appeared,[13] but even now all of the diplomatic documents have not been published, and what promises to be the definitive study is still in progress.[14] Viewed from the vantage point of almost sixty years, Italy's decision to fight appears to have been a tragic error by three men: the king, Prime Minister Antonio Salandra, and Foreign Minister Baron Sidney Sonnino. Aided and abetted by Colonial Minister Ferdinando Martini and by a small but noisy minority, these men defied the will of the great passive majority and threw Italy into a long struggle of titanic proportions for which neither the army nor the country was prepared. Here the seeds were sown for Fascism and the even greater suffering of a longer and more devastating war between 1940 and 1945.

In theory Italy had three choices: to fight on the side of Germany and Austria-Hungary; to join France, England, and Russia; to remain neutral. In reality, hostility and mistrust of the Austrians made support of the Central Powers unthinkable except to a few conservatives, the Italian ambassadors at Berlin and Vienna, and the nationalists, who were ready for war—any war. The proclamation of neutrality was popular with most Italians and was in harmony with the obligations of their alliance and with their liberal traditions. On this program, socialists, most Catholics, and most liberals could agree. It left Italy's future among the great powers uncertain but seemed to be the sanest and safest way through a situation fraught with great peril, no matter what course was adopted. The interventionists included democrats, freemasons, republicans, radicals, reformist socialists, futurists, nationalists, revolutionaries, irredentists, and some liberals. They were joined by Benito Mussolini, who began to shift position in October and come out for intervention on the side of the Allies in November 1914. The neutralists were on the whole passive; the interventionists were vocal and active. The majority in the Chamber of Deputies was still loyal to Giovanni Giolitti, who was for neutrality, but Denis Mack Smith argues that representative institutions had become irrelevant and that Luigi Albertini's *Corriere della Sera*, which urged intervention, was more of a political force than the Chamber.

There were really three acts in the tragedy: first, a period of cautious probing and watchful waiting, ended by the death of San Giuliano in October 1914; second, an unsuccessful search by his successor, Sidney Sonnino, to obtain compensations from Austria under Article 7 of the Triple Alliance from early December 1914 to late February 1915; third, serious and successful negotiations in London from March 4 to the signing of the Treaty of London on April 26, 1915.

The Italian historian Gabriele de Rosa, in a preface to Ferdinando Martini's *Diario*, concludes that both Salandra and Sonnino were convinced that Italy could fight a *piccola guerra* limited to its own frontiers, of short duration, and involving only the opposing armies. They did not foresee a total war or a war of long duration. This "little war" would complete the work of the Risorgimento and reinforce the power of the liberal party without disturbing the internal structure of the country. We know that Salandra ceased being a neutralist and became an interventionist in early September, shortly after the First Battle of the Marne. Certainly this transformation was complete by September 17, when Salandra met Martini and revealed his plans to negotiate with the Triple Entente in London and indicated that his goals were the Trentino, Trieste, and Dalmatia.

The Italian diplomatic documents, now published up to the death of Foreign Minister San Giuliano, reveal that he was following precisely the policy of arranging the suitable moment for a small war with limited risks and of short duration. In fact the Italian policy of intervention in its main outlines had already been formulated before San Giuliano died, except that Italy's demands for territory were increased after Sonnino became foreign minister. The outlines of this policy are worth describing. San Giuliano constantly pressed Austria-Hungary to agree to the German and Italian interpretation of Article 7 of the Triple Alliance: there must be prior consultation before Austria acted to disturb the status quo in the Balkans, and there must be compensation to Italy if Austria disturbed the Balkan status quo.[15] Meanwhile, Italy should bring its army and navy to a state of efficiency and take defensive measures on the Austrian border. The best solution for Italy would be an indecisive war.

By August 9, 1914, San Giuliano admitted the possibility of an Italian attack against Austria and suggested to Salandra that an agreement between Italy and the Triple Entente provide for joint cooperation of the English and French fleets to destroy the Austrian fleet. He was ready at this time to restore the Dodecanese Islands to Turkey, provided that some Italian officials were employed and Italy was assured of economic concessions in the zone of Adalia. At war's end, he wanted Italy to have at least the Trentino and possibly other parts of the "unredeemed Italian lands" in Austria and a defensive agreement among the four powers to maintain the peace settlement. To the king, San Giuliano recommended a policy of prudent reserve, rapid military preparation, and good relations with all the belligerents. He urged Salandra to influence the *Tribuna* and other papers not to publish anti-Austrian articles.

Unfavorably impressed on August 11 by Austria's rejection of an exchange of ideas on compensation, San Giuliano on the same day instructed Ambassador Guglielmo Imperiali in London to speak personally and under a pledge of absolute secrecy to Foreign Secretary Sir Edward Grey concerning the conditions for Italian entry into the war against Austria. These included the following: England must consent to export coal to Italy; there was to be no separate peace; from the first day French and British squadrons should join the Italian fleet in the Adriatic against the Austrian navy; Italy should have Trieste and the Trentino to the main watershed of the Alps. Greece and Serbia could have most of Albania, but the coast was to be neutralized and Valona and its vicinity made autonomous and internationalized. If Turkish integrity was maintained, Italy would return the Dodecanese Islands, provided that some Italian officials continued to be employed. If Turkey crumbled, Italy should have a part of the provinces on the Mediterranean. In any case, Italy should be assured of economic concessions in the Adalia zone. Italy should share in any war indemnity corresponding to its efforts and sacrifices. The peace settlement should be guaranteed by a defensive alliance of the four allies. San Giuliano suggested that an Anglo-French attack on the Austrian fleet would provoke demonstrations of joy in Italy which the government could not suppress and which would give Austria an excuse for remonstrances unacceptable to Italy.

There are several reasons why the negotiations in London did not advance much until the spring of 1915, even though Grey and his allies were ready to meet virtually all the Italian demands. In the first place, Italy could not abandon neutrality until its military preparations were more complete. Second, Germany and Austria-Hungary, after a first brief moment of irritation, went out of their way to avoid friction with Italy, except on the key matter of a cession of Austrian territory, and Austria denied that military measures had been taken on the Italian frontier. Third, San Giuliano thought it dangerous to depart from neutrality until he could predict the outcome of the war. There was a probability that Germany and Austria would win. He was not certain as to how much aid Italy would receive from the French and British fleets and how much pressure the Russian army would be able to exert on Austria. In short, could Italy have a *piccola guerra?* In addition, San Giuliano was impressed by the large majority of Italians favoring neutrality. There was also some thought that Italy might serve as a mediator to bring peace between the belligerents. The restoration of peace would further San Giuliano's desire to see a moderately strong Austria maintained, for Italy must not trade off an Austrian for a Slavic threat. On the other hand, there was always the danger that Italy might wait too long and fail to realize its national aspirations once its aid was no longer needed. Ambassador Imperiali in London had this fear, but it was not shared by Ambassador Riccardo Bollati in Berlin, who continued to believe that Germany and Austria would be disposed to take account of Italy's desires even in victory.

To the end, San Giuliano held that Italy could not face a long war. Before committing Italy, he wanted certain guarantees: a loan from England, assurance that Russia would prevent Austria from concentrating its strength against Italy, safeguards for the future. He insisted that Italy's enemy was Austria-Hungary and not Germany, and he complained that the Triple Entente was mainly interested in defeating Germany, whereas for Italy the greatest interest and the greatest threat lay in the Adriatic. Therefore a decisive operation by the Anglo-French fleet against Austria in the Adriatic would justify Italy's entry into the war. San Giuliano now added a new requirement for Italian participation in the war: England and France must give assurances of effective action against an Ethiopian threat to Eritrea. By September 25, shifting from his earlier position, he was insisting that Italy must be sovereign over Valona but might agree to internationalize it with an Italian garrison.

San Giuliano's death on October 16, 1914, robbed Italy of an extremely cautious and astute foreign minister. Italian diplomacy, first under the interim direction of Salandra and then in the hands of Sonnino, became more daring and impatient. While much probing still remains to be done in the archives in Rome and other European capitals, the general outline of the negotiations that Sonnino, a supporter of the Triple Alliance, conducted with Austria has long been known. As is indicated by both the *Austro-Hungarian Red Book* and the *Italian Green Book,* there was diplomatic fencing rather than honest negotiation between the two countries. Italy initiated negotiations on December 9, 1914, but only on March 9, 1915, did Foreign Minister Count Stefan Burián reply indicating willingness to discuss the surrender of Austrian territory, at the same time advancing counterclaims because of Italy's continued occupation of the Dodecanese and its occupation of Valona in December. Italy rejected Burián's claims. In fact, by March 4, Sonnino had already concluded that nothing could be expected from discussions with Burián regarding territorial compensation under Article 7 of the Triple Alliance and had resumed negotiations with England. Germany pressured Austria to surrender the Trentino, and finally on March 27 Burián offered part of it to Italy. Only on April 8 did Sonnino formulate his demands on Austria. He asked for the Trentino with its frontiers of 1811 and the Isonzo river area to include Gradisca and Gorizia. Trieste should become an autonomous state with a free port completely independent of Austria-Hungary. Austria should cede the Curzolari Islands. Occupation of ceded territory should be immediate, and Austria should grant a complete amnesty to natives of the ceded territories. In addition, Austria-Hungary must recognize Italian sovereignty over Valona and renounce its interests in Albania. In return, Italy offered neutrality and 200 million lire for state rights in the ceded territories. No further claims under Article 7 would be made for the duration of the war, and Austria should end its opposition to Italy's occupation of the Dodecanese.

Germany, at times working in close cooperation with the Vatican, spared no efforts to maintain Italian neutrality and to persuade Austria-Hungary to make prompt and adequate territorial concessions to Italy. The full story based on the German archives has now been told in a study by Alberto Monticone, and Friedrich Engel-Janosi has thrown additional light on Vatican diplomacy.[16] Space limitations do not allow even an adequate summary of these efforts. They all foundered on Austrian reluctance to make a prompt and generous settlement and on Italian lack of faith that a victorious Austria would live up to its pledges.

Monticone reveals that the Bulow-Macchio note of May 10 which offered large Austrian concessions for Italian neutrality was really drawn up by Bülow and Center Deputy Matthias Erzberger in a last desperate effort, desired by Pope Benedict XV, to bring Giovanni Giolitti or a neutralist to power and to halt Italy's mad rush toward war, now that the Treaty of London had been signed. Giolitti received the note on May 10 and the Italian government received it on May 11.[17] Vienna was thus presented with a virtual fait accompli. Had this note been presented a month earlier, Italy might have avoided war, for Austria offered the following: the entire Italian-speaking area of the Tyrol, the western bank of the Isonzo (including Gradisca), autonomy and an Italian university at Trieste, Valona, Austrian disinterest in Albania, examination of other

Italian demands for Adriatic islands and Gorizia, guarantees for Italians remaining in Austria-Hungary. Following Italy's renunciation of the Triple Alliance on May 4 and Gabriele D'Annunzio's impassioned call to arms at the Garibaldi commemoration at Quarto, near Genoa, on May 5, the currents of hatred against Austria mounted daily, and popular passion and violence soon came to dominate the streets and piazzas. Again a noisy minority was making history. Giolitti's contention that a considerable amount could be gained from Austria without war was no longer enough to stem the tide and turn Italy from that course, especially since Burián refused to make the promised concessions immediately.

The negotiations that culminated in the Treaty of London had been initiated, as noted above, by San Giuliano on August 11, 1914. All three Entente powers were involved. In August Russia had pressed hardest for Italian entry into war and had been willing to grant Italian dominance in the Adriatic. But as the war progressed, Russia came to care less and less about Italian intervention and to press more and more for Serbian and Montenegran interests on the eastern shore of the Adriatic. England and France now urgently wanted Italian intervention and successfully brought pressure to bear on Russia for a compromise division of disputed territory in Dalmatia and the islands offshore. The Entente could be generous, for it was bargaining away enemy territory. Russian resistance to Sonnino's claims, the uncertainty about the course of the war, and continued Italian unreadiness to enter the war delayed formal agreement until April 26.

The terms of the Treaty of London as finally negotiated by Sonnino are common knowledge, but a brief summary will complete the account of Italy's entry into the war. Drafted in the form of a memorandum, the Treaty of London provided for the conclusion of a military and naval convention and for Italy to make war on all the enemies of Britain, France, and Russia. In the peace treaty Italy should obtain the Trentino and the Brenner frontier, Trieste, Gorizia, Gradisca, Istria, a number of Adriatic islands, a substantial part of Dalmatia, Valona, and Saseno. The rest of Albania, except for an autonomous state in the center, could go to Serbia, Greece, and Montenegro. The Dodecanese Islands should be kept by Italy. In the event of the partition of Turkey, Italy should receive an equitable zone bordering Adalia. If France and Britain made colonial gains in Africa, Italy should receive compensation by rectification of the borders of its African colonies. Italy pledged to enter the war within a month and was promised a share in any war indemnity and that a loan of 50 million pounds would be arranged in Great Britain.

Thus did three men—the king, Salandra, and Sonnino—against the will of a clear majority of the Italian people and without their knowledge make a secret agreement to go to war against former allies. Just as Italy in 1866 could have gained Venetia without war, so in 1915 it could have had a substantial part of its national aspirations at least pledged by Germany and Austria without firing a shot. The thirteen-day period between the substantial Austrian offer of May 10 and the declaration of war on May 23, 1915, has left many complex questions that even today cannot be answered with certainty. They all revolve around the conduct of Giovanni Giolitti, the man who still commanded the loyalty of a majority of the Italian parliament, and his relations with Salandra. Giolitti was clearly in favor of neutrality and convinced that Italy could gain substantial concessions from Austria. He had argued strongly for neutrality on December 4, 1914, and had revealed Italy's efforts to prevent an Austrian attack on Serbia in July 1913. His letter of January 24, 1915, to his friend Camillo Peano was published with small modifications in the *Tribuna* on February 1. In this letter Giolitti defended himself from charges of intriguing with the German ambassador, denied that he was for neutrality at all costs, and expressed the view that *parecchio* [18] (*molto* in the original) could be obtained without going to war.[19]

Giolitti was clearly the central figure in the drama which began to unfold after he arrived in Rome on May 9. His loyal followers demonstrated their support by leaving their calling cards at his Rome residence on May 9 and 10. Giolitti judged the Austrian offer of May 10 as the indispensable minimum necessary to keep Italy at peace, and it was at his suggestion that the note was transmitted to the Italian government on May 11. Giolitti suggested that the government could free itself from its pledges to the Entente by submitting the matter to a vote of the Chamber of Deputies. Instead the Salandra cabinet resigned on May 13. The German and Vatican plans to bring Giolitti back to power seemed to be working. But Giolitti, Giuseppe Marcora, president of the Chamber of Deputies, and Paolo Carcano, minister of the treasury, refused to head a new cabinet; and Paolo Boselli, *doyen* of the Chamber, spoke in favor of the retention of Salandra when the king asked him to form a cabinet. Whereupon, the king brought the Salandra government back to power on May 16, and Giolitti left Rome on May 17. To his friends Luigi Facta, Camillo Peano, and Giacomo Rattazzi, who made one last desperate effort to persuade him to assume power on May 15, Giolitti replied that this would mean civil war and that he could not assume the responsibility. The king also told Raffaele Cappelli, vice president of the Chamber, that the monarchy faced either war or revolution and that neutrality could end the dynasty.[20] The Chamber granted exceptional powers to the government by an overwhelming vote on May 20 and the Senate made it unanimous next day. Italy's declaration of war on Austria-Hungary on May 23 became effective as of May 24.

Was Giolitti's greatest political mistake to trust Salandra too long and to believe that Salandra planned to keep Italy out of war? How much information did the king, Salandra, and Carcano give Giolitti about the Treaty of London? (Giolitti denied that he was given any knowledge of the treaty.) Did Giolitti really fear civil war if he resumed power? Was he seeking to prevent the abdication of a king who was ready to leave the throne if the London pledges were not honored? Was Giolitti's answer to Olindo Malagodi, editor of the *Tribuna*, that he was too compromised as opposed to war to be able to negotiate successfully with Austria any nearer the truth? [21] Was Giolitti frightened and intimidated by the repeated insults and threats against him, or was this merely a part of his nature to retire to his home when controversial matters were before the Italian nation? The final answers may never be known, but the results of Giolitti's great retreat certainly changed the course of Italian history.

Once more a policy of reckless adventure had triumphed over the cautious policy of the years after 1896. The ghost of Crispi had returned. Italy would not again weigh means and ends carefully and consistently in its foreign policy until the country had suffered immeasurable damage to life and property in two long wars and the surrender of its freedom and parliamentary government to the most notorious interventionist of them all, Benito Mussolini. Salandra's timing for Italy's entry into war could not have been worse. Had Salandra foreseen Russia's defeats on the eastern front in May 1915, even he might have listened to the voice of Giolitti and reason.[22]

NOTES

1. For background see Friedrich Engel-Janosi, *Geschichte auf dem Ballhausplatz* (Graz: Verlag Styria, 1963), pp. 143–205; *idem.*, *Österreich und der Vatikan, 1846–1918*, 2 vols. (Graz: Verlag Styria, 1958–1960), I, 143–180; S. William Halperin, *Diplomat Under Stress: Visconti-Venosta and the Crisis of July, 1870* (Chicago: University of Chicago Press, 1963); *idem.*, *Italy and the Vatican at War* (Chicago: University of Chicago Press, 1939), pp. 28–65; Lillian Parker Wallace, *The Papacy and European Diplomacy, 1869–1878* (Chapel Hill: University of North Carolina Press, 1948), pp. 116–150.

2. For the best statement of Italy's new problems in foreign policy see Federico Chabod, *Storia della politica estera italiana dal 1870 and 1896: Le premesse* (Bari: Laterza, 1951), vol. I. For a helpful analysis of the formulation of Italian policy see Norman Kogan, *The Politics of Italian Foreign Policy* (New York: Praeger, 1963). Also most useful is Carlo Morandi, *La politica estera dell'Italia*, ed. F. Manzotti (Florence: Le Monnier, 1968).

3. Augusto Torre, *La politica estera dell'Italia dal 1870 al 1896* (Bologna: Pàtron, 1959), p. 16. Torre, a leading specialist on Italian diplomatic history and editor of the two volumes of *I documenti diplomatici italiani* which have appeared for 1914, is the author of numerous important studies. Many valuable insights are offered in two other works by Torre: *La politica estera dell'Italia dal 1896 al 1914* (Bologna: Pàtron, 1960) and his "L'Italie et l'Europe" in *L'Europe du xixᵉ et du xxᵉ siècle (1870–1914)* (Milan: Marzorati, 1962), II, 665–697.

4. For this period see Gaetano Salvemini, *La politica estera dell'Italia dal 1871 al 1915*, 2nd ed. (Florence: Barbèra, 1950), pp. 15–82; Wallace, *The Papacy and European Diplomacy*, pp. 261–325; Halperin, *Italy and the Vatican at War*, pp. 167–278, 312–473; Engel-Janosi, *Österreich und der Vatican*, I, 181–197; Christopher Seton-Watson, *Italy from Liberalism to Fascism, 1870–1925* (London: Methuen, 1967); F. Salata, *Per la storia diplomatica della questione romana* (Milan: Treves, 1929); Francesco Cognasso, "I problemi di politica estera del Regno d'Italia, 1861–1940" in E. Rota, ed., *Questioni di storia del Risorgimento e dell'unità d'Italia* (Milan: Marzorati, 1951), pp. 483–544; A. Sandona, *L'irredentismo nelle lotte politiche e nelle contese diplomatiche italo-austriache*, 3 vols. (Bologna: Zanichelli, 1932–1933), vols. I and II; K. R. Greenfield, "The Italian Nationality Problem of the Austrian Empire" in R. J. Rath, ed., *Austrian History Yearbook* (Houston: Rice University, 1967), III, pt. 2, 491–531, with comments by Raymond Grew; W. L. Langer, "The European Powers and the French Occupation of Tunis, 1878–1881," *American Historical Review*, 31 (October 1925, January 1926), 55–79, 251–265; idem, *European Alliances and Alignments, 1871–1890*, 2nd ed. (New York: Vintage, 1964), pp. 121–166.

5. For perhaps the finest description of the man and his style see Chabod, *Storia della politica estera italiana*, I, 563–599.

6. John A. Thayer, *Italy and the Great War: Politics and Culture, 1870–1915* (Madison: University of Wisconsin Press, 1964), p. 154.

7. Luigi Salvatorelli, *La triplice alleanza: storia diplomatica, 1877–1912* (Milan: Istituto per gli studi di politica internazionale, 1939), pp. 21–132; William L. Langer, *European Alliances and Alignments*, pp. 217–247, 365–407; W. N. Medlicott, "The Mediterranean Agreements of 1887," *Slavonic Review*, 5 (June 1926), 60–88; Federico Curato, *La questione marocchina e gli accordi mediterranei italo-spagnoli del 1887 e del 1891*, 2 vols. (Milan: Edizioni di Comunità, 1961–1964), I; G. Volpe, *L'Italia nella triplice alleanza, 1882–1915*, 2nd ed. (Milan: Istituto per gli studi di politica internazionale, 1941), pp. 29–121; L. Chiala, *Pagine di storia contemporanea*, 3 vols. (Turin: Roux, 1892–1898).

8. Salvemini, *Politica estera dell'Italia*, p. 80. Studies of fundamental

importance on Italy's changing relationship with the European powers are the following by Enrico Serra: *Camille Barrère e l'intesa italo-francese* (Milan: Giuffrè, 1960); *La questione tunisina da Crispi a Rudinì ed il "colpo di timone" alla politica estera dell'Italia* (Milan: Giuffrè, 1967); see also J. L. Glanville, *Italy's Relations with England, 1896–1905* (Baltimore: Johns Hopkins, 1934) and Enrico Decleva, *Da Adua a Sarajevo: La politica estera italiana el la Francia, 1896–1914* (Bari: Laterza, 1971).

9. "The Austro-Italian Antagonism, 1896–1914" in L. P. Wallace and W. C. Askew, eds., *Power, Public Opinion, and Diplomacy* (Durham: Duke University Press, 1959), pp. 172–221.

10. New materials from the Italian archives add many fresh details but leave fundamentally unaltered my findings in *Europe and Italy's Acquisition of Libya, 1911–1912* (Durham: Duke University Press, 1942). Space limitations, however, allow only a very partial citing of documents used in this study.

11. Gianluca Andrè, *L'Italia e il Mediterraneo alla vigilia della prima guerra mondiale: I tentativi di intesa Mediterranea (1911–1914)* (Milan: Giuffrè, 1967).

12. See especially Mario Toscano, "L'Italia e la crisi europea del luglio 1914" in his *Pagine di storia diplomatica contemporanea* (Milan: Giuffrè, 1963), I, 125–165; Luigi Albertini, *The Origins of the War of 1914*, 3 vols. (Oxford: Oxford University Press, 1952–1957), I, II, III; *I documenti diplomatici italiani* (4) XII (5) I; Roy Price, "Italy and the Outbreak of the First World War," *The Cambridge Historical Journal*, 11, No. 2 (1954), 219–227; Augusto Torre, "Ricordi di Antonio di San Giuliano," *Nuova Antologia*, 463 (January 1955), 29–42; *idem*, "Il marchese di San Giuliano fra la neutralità e l'intervento," *Nova Historia*, Nos. 22–25 (June 1954), pp. 104–119. My larger study, not yet published but based on the documents of all of the great powers, leads me to conclusions that are far different from those of Albertini about Italy's role in the coming of the First World War.

13. For Italy's entry into the war see Seton-Watson, *Italy from Liberalism to Fascism*, pp. 413–450; Thayer, *Italy and the Great War*, pp. 271–370; Augusto Torre, *Imperialismi in conflitto nell'Europa dal 1870 al 1918* (Milan: Vallardi, 1970), pp. 337–350; Augusto Torre, "Dimostrazioni anti-austriache del Maggio 1914 in un carteggio di San Giuliano-Salandra" in *Studi storici in memoria di Leopoldo Marchetti* (Milan: Direzione dei musei del Risorgimento e di storia contemporanea, 1969), pp. 363–375; Augusto Torre, "La posizione dell'Italia fra gli alleati nella prima guerra mondiale," *Rassegna storica del Risorgimento*, 56 (October-December 1969), 535–545; Pietro Quaroni, "L'Italie et l'Europe" in *L'Europe du xixᵉ et du xxᵉ siècle (1914–aujourd'hui)*, II, 995–999; W. W. Gottlieb, *Studies in Secret Diplomacy during the First World War* (London: Allen

& Unwin, 1957), pp. 135–401; A. Salandra, *La neutralità italiana 1914* (Milan: Mondadori, 1928) and *L'intervento 1915* (Milan: Mondadori, 1930); Mario Toscano, *Il patto di Londra* (Bologna: Zanichelli, 1934); Ferdinano Martini, *Diario, 1914–1918*, ed. G. de Rosa (Milan: Mondadori, 1966); Luigi Albertini, *Venti anni di vita politica*, 5 vols. (Bologna: Zanichelli, 1950–1953), pt. 2, vol. I; O. Malagodi, *Conversazioni della guerra 1914–1919*, ed. B. Vigezzi (Milan: Ricciardi, 1960), vol. I; B. Vigezzi, *I problemi della neutralità e della guerra nel carteggio Salandra-Sonnino 1914–1917* (Milan: S. E. Dante Alighieri, 1962); V. E. Orlando, *Memorie, 1915–1919*, ed. R. Mosca (Milan: Rizzoli, 1960); L. Aldrovandi Marescotti, *Guerra diplomatica 1914–1919* (Milan: Mondadori, 1937); G. Giolitti, *Memoirs of My Life* (London: Chapman, 1923); Denis Mack Smith, *Italy* (Ann Arbor: University of Michigan Press, 1959), pp. 289–305; Arthur J. May, *The Passing of the Hapsburg Monarchy, 1914–1918*, 2 vols. (Philadelphia: University of Pennsylvania Press, 1966), I, 170–202; Carlo Avarna di Gualtieri, ed., *Il carteggio Avarna-Bollati* (Naples: Edizioni Scientifiche Italiane, 1953).

14. Overwhelming in detail is the first volume of Brunello Vigezzi, *L'Italia di fronte alla prima guerra mondiale: L'Italia neutrale* (Milan: Ricciardi, 1966), which will take the story to May 1915 in four volumes.

15. Austria disclaimed any intention to take territory but would be ready to talk about compensation if these plans changed. For San Giuliano's policy see Vigezzi, *L'Italia di fronte alla prima guerra mondiale*, I, 40–140. For earlier studies see G. Tadini, *Il marchese di San Giuliano nella tragica estate del 1914* (Bergamo: Istituto italiano d'arti grafiche, 1945) and R. Longhitano, *Antonino di San Giuliano* (Rome: Bocca, 1954).

16. See Engel-Janosi, *Österreich und der Vatikan, 1846–1918*, II, 190–247. Alberto Monticone's *La Germania e la neutralità italiana: 1914–1915* (Bologna: Il Mulino, 1971) is a work of major importance. Monticone has skillfully integrated a vast number of unpublished German documents with such published works as Matthias Erzberger, *Erlebnisse, im Weltkrieg* (Stuttgart: Deutsche Verlags-Anstalt, 1920), Leo Valiani, *La dissoluzione dell'Austria-Ungheria* (Milan: Il Saggiatore, 1966), Klaus Epstein, *Matthias Erzberger und das Dilemma der deutschen Demokratie* (Berlin: Verlag Annedore Leber, 1962), Karl von Macchio, *Wahrheit! Fürst Bülow und Ich in Rom, 1914–1915* (Vienna: Jung Österreich Verlag, 1931), C. Pavone, ed., *Dalle carte di Giovanni Giolitti: Quarant'anni di politica italiana*, 3 vols. (Milan: Feltrinelli, 1962), vol. III, and many others to throw fresh light on the efforts of Germany and Austria to keep Italy from joining the Entente. Germany attached vital importance to Italian neutrality; constantly pressed Austria to satisfy Italy; and was even willing to make territorial concessions to Austria to promote adequate

Austrian concessions to Italy. Monticone dwells at length on the difficult question of Austrian and German sincerity and comes up with a mixed answer. He supports the findings of Leo Valiani (*La dissoluzione dell'Austria-Ungheria*, p. 118) that France had broken the German code and turned over to Italy in April evidence that Austria planned to take back ceded territory after victory (pp. 551–553).

17. Monticone, *La Germania e la neutralità italiana*, pp. 561–573.

18. Acting through Senator Alfredo Frassati, editor of *La Stampa*, and Roberto Prezioso of *Il Piccolo* of Trieste, Giolitti in April pressed for a speedy Austrian offer of the Trentino and Friuli, with Trieste and Fiume as free cities under Austrian sovereignty but with absolute guarantees for the *italianità* of these cities, see Leo Valiani, *La dissoluzione dell'Austria-Ungheria*, pp. 120–123.

19. The published version of this letter is toned down by the substitution of *parecchio* (a considerable amount) for the original *molto* (much).

20. Monticone, *La Germania e la neutralità italiana*, pp. 583, 584.

21. Malagodi, *Conversazioni della guerra*, I, 61, 62.

22. Salandra said as much; see Mack Smith, *Italy*, p. 308.

CHAPTER 15

FOREIGN POLICY SINCE
THE FIRST WORLD WAR

RENÉ ALBRECHT-CARRIÉ

When Italy declared war on Austria-Hungary on May 24, 1915, it did not proceed vigorously against its former ally. Furthermore, Italy had no immediate plans to declare war on Germany, as the Entente powers expected it to. Indeed, Italy did not declare war on Germany until August 28, 1916. Since Austria was fully occupied on the Russian front, no major action on the Austro-Italian front occurred for over two years. At home the initial division between interventionists and neutralists persisted. The majority of the Socialists adopted the slogan, "neither support nor sabotage" the war. On August 1, 1917, in a peace note to all belligerents, Pope Benedict XV—widely suspected of pro-Austrian sympathies and of opposition to the war—called for a "just and lasting peace" and an end to the "useless struggle."

In this same year the Bolshevik Revolution in Russia and the American entry into the war created a new balance among the Western allies. In Italy, the immediate effect of the October Revolution was to increase the influence of the extremists within the Socialist party. They began to speak openly of bringing about "revolution by defeat," as in Russia. Meanwhile the military collapse of Russia enabled the Austro-German forces to launch a major attack on the Italian front and to drive back the Italians. The ensuing military debacle at Caporetto rallied the majority of the Italian people to Vittorio Orlando's new government of national unity. Although French and British units bolstered Italian military resistance, the Italian army itself finally stopped the Austrian advance in December 1917 after two months of fighting. This Italian revival, plus the prospect of imminent military reinforcements on the western front from the United States, effectively counteracted both the Russian withdrawal from the war and any threat of revolution at home.

By January 1918 President Wilson's statement of American war aims, the Fourteen Points, put Italy's territorial ambitions in jeopardy. The Allies, who had not originally contemplated the dismemberment of Austria-Hungary, now committed themselves to the principle of national self-determination. Moreover, Wilson's Point 9 spoke of redrawing the frontiers of Italy "along clearly recognizable lines of nationality," putting in question Italy's claim to the Tyrol and Dalmatia. At the April 1918 Congress of Oppressed Nationalities in Rome certain prominent Italians also endorsed the principle of national self-determination for all peoples. Foreign Minister Sonnino ignored the congress and its statement and continued to insist on the strict fulfillment of the Treaty of London.

In October 1918, during the discussion of the reply to the German request for an end of hostilities on the basis of the Wilsonian program, Orlando and Sonnino raised the issue of the discrepancy between Point 9 and the Treaty of London. Wilson's representative, Colonel House, pointed out that the problem did not concern Germany and evaded a clear-cut answer. Thus an ambiguity was created, the German armistice was concluded, and preparations for the coming peace began. Meanwhile, with the Italian victory at Vittorio Veneto, the war on the Italian front came to an end on November 4, 1918.[1]

At the Paris Peace Conference, Orlando, the weakest personality, represented the weakest power. In addition, he suffered from the disadvantage that for his colleagues Germany was the chief concern. There was also the question of language. Clemenceau's command of English led to discussion among the Big Four being largely conducted in that language. Orlando, who knew no English, was thus further isolated. Italy's weakness was also compounded by Orlando's failure to exercise even what influence Italy's power warranted, for he generally let Wilson, Lloyd George, and Clemenceau make decisions save in matters of purely Italian concern.

The Adriatic question arose early in the proceedings, in February 1919, when the South Slavs presented their case to the conference as a whole. This move embarrassed the Italian delegation, which sought to reserve the issue of Italy's demands for consideration by the five big powers (United States, Great Britain, France, Italy, Japan). Supported by victorious Serbia, the Yugoslavs insisted on an open discussion of their claims. In addition, they skillfully endeavored to make the most of Wilson's known sympathy for small nationalities and were quite willing to accept his arbitral decision.

At the beginning of January 1919 Wilson had visited Italy. That visit had unfortunate results. The American president left Italy confirmed in his feelings that he was a more authentic representative of the wishes of the Italian masses than their own government, especially as the Italian government endeavored to confine him to official contacts. Moreover, he met Leonida Bissolati, who supported self-determination and had resigned from the government on December 28, 1918. To add to the confusion, it was then that Wilson seems to have committed himself to the Brenner frontier for Italy, clearly a violation of the principle of nationality. By doing this he created dismay among some of his own advisers and at the same time weakened his case vis-à-vis the Italians when he proceeded to uphold national self-determination for the South Slavs.

In Paris Orlando and Sonnino mishandled their case. Sonnino, with the greater consistency, would have rested Italy's claims on the Treaty of London—no more and no less. The more flexible Orlando, with an eye to a possible bargain, entered a plea for the application of this treaty and at the same time claimed Fiume, basing this claim on the fact that the city contained a narrow majority of Italians. In contrast, the population in Fiume's hinterland was almost exclusively Slavic. Orlando's hope was the not unreasonable one of effecting a compromise: exchanging Fiume for the northern half of Dalmatia might have been a solution acceptable to the Italian parliament, but he could hardly have taken a worse position. To Wilson, tired and irritated by this time, Orlando's claims were disingenuous. Thus developed the one open and unresolved clash of the 1919 peacemaking. It was an Italo-American clash, for the British and French were quite willing to let the two antagonists fight it out, even if they did offer some suggestions for compromise.

Moved in part by his sympathy for small nations—of which the South Slavs made good use—and supported by a number of his indignant advisers, Wilson yielded to the temptation to issue a public statement of his case, the manifesto of April 23. As he put it:

> The war was ended, moreover, by proposing to Germany an armistice and peace which should be founded on certain clearly defined principles which should set up a new order of right and justice. . . . We cannot ask the great body of powers to propose and effect peace with the succession states of Austria-Hungary on principles of another kind. . . . These, and these only, are the principles for which America has fought. . . . Only upon these principles, she hopes and believes, will the people of Italy ask her to make peace.[2]

In his own terms Wilson's case was unanswerable, but he had also shifted the grounds of the debate, for he was in effect appealing to the Italian people over the heads of their own representatives in Paris.

It was too easy an opening, and on the next day Orlando replied:

The step of making a direct appeal to the different peoples certainly is an innovation in international intercourse. . . . To oppose, so to speak, the Italian government and people would be to admit that this great free nation could submit to the yoke of a will other than its own, and I shall be forced to protest vigorously against such suppositions, unjustly offensive to my country.[3]

On April 24 Orlando and Sonnino left the conference in high dudgeon and returned to Italy. Their gesture elicited widespread popular support at home and a resounding parliamentary endorsement. But it was also an empty victory, for Wilson could not be coerced into changing his mind. Orlando's ministry fell on June 19, 1919, nine days before the final signing of the Treaty of Versailles. The Italo-Yugoslav dispute over Fiume remained unresolved and was not settled until the two countries reached direct agreement in the Treaty of Rapallo on November 12, 1920, negotiated for Italy by the new foreign minister, Count Carlo Sforza.

Meanwhile, Gabriele D'Annunzio had occupied Fiume, which served him for over a year as a stage for constitution making and even for a declaration of war against Italy. He created considerable embarrassment for the government in Rome, but finally yielded to a show of Italian force. In the troubled Italy of the postwar years the incident confirmed the widespread feeling that the national government was ineffectual.

From the peace settlement Italy secured the Brenner frontier, roughly what it had been promised in Istria, but had to yield northern Dalmatia, except for Zara and some islands. Fiume became a free state. But Italy was frustrated in its imperial claims. In Asia Minor the Allies backed a Greek landing at Smyrna (Izmir), and in southern Anatolia it was Sforza again who came to terms with the resurgent Turkish government of Kemal Ataturk in 1921, abandoning any claims on the mainland of Anatolia and retaining only the Dodecanese Islands. In fulfillment of Article 13 of the Treaty of London the frontier between Egypt and Libya was adjusted, Jubaland was transferred by Britain to Italian Somaliland, and France ceded some territory adjacent to Libya, but Italy consistently denied that this constituted adequate implementation of Article 13. Thus, the peace settlement at Paris became for Italy the "lost victory" and the "mutilated peace."

Because of the limited extent of Italy's resources the war had proved a greater strain for it than for richer countries that had contributed more in absolute terms. After the war socioeconomic problems combined with the frustration of an unsatisfactory peace to find expression in general unrest and dissatisfaction, with which the government proved itself incapable of dealing. Even old Giovanni Giolitti misjudged when he diagnosed the condition as a passing fever; after a year he too gave up the attempt to govern. In October 1922 the Fascists came to power.

As events would show, the aggressive nationalistic content of Fascism was not idle talk. The Corfu incident in 1923 was the first example. The demands made on Greece when General Tellini was murdered in Albania bring to mind the Austrian reaction to Sarajevo. But the crisis was overcome, and thereafter the prevalent impression of Italian foreign policy was one of apparent moderation. Winston Churchill was far from being alone in thinking Fascism suited to Italian conditions and in taking a generally favorable view of its leader. Austen Chamberlain was also on very good terms with Mussolini.

Some fundamental characteristics—of a national rather than of a peculiarly Fascist character—remained in Italy's foreign policy. Sforza's resignation as ambassador to France soon after the Fascist take-over was an isolated gesture. In October 1922 Mussolini became not only prime minister but also minister of foreign affairs. Continuity in Italy's foreign policy, however, persisted, as career diplomat Salvatore Contarini retained his post as secretary-general of the foreign office after the advent of the new régime. Even after Contarini's resignation and his replacement by Dino Grandi in 1925, it was not long before this formerly militant Fascist became the representative of the peaceful face of Fascism. Four years later, in September 1929, Grandi took full charge of the foreign office and remained at his post until Mussolini again assumed control of the foreign ministry in July 1932.

Italy's hope that its influence could penetrate into central Europe was frustrated by France. This was inevitable, for the succession states of the defunct Austrian monarchy shared with France a desire to maintain the status quo. Poland and the members of the Little Entente (Czechoslovakia, Romania, and Yugoslavia) were tied to France in a system of alliances which excluded Italy. As a result, Italy was bound to be a revisionist power and strove to diminish France's preponderant position in Europe in favor of a more balanced distribution of power. This policy strengthened Italy's affinity with the traditional British view that no one state should dominate the continent. A restoration, therefore, of Germany and of Russia as well was desirable to reestablish the balance of Europe. Yet Italy wanted this to be done only within certain limits, for there would be little merit in merely replacing one dominant power by another. Italy, after all, even if frustrated in the peace, had derived considerable benefits from the war, and it did not want its new northern and eastern frontiers called into question. On the independence of Austria it could agree with France, but the issue of naval parity remained an unresolved source of contention between the two countries. At the Washington Naval Disarmament Conference in February 1922, Italy gained parity with France in capital ship tonnage. France consented to this reluctantly, and subsequent attempts to extend the Washington agreements to other categories of vessels failed.

In the context of Fascist ideology it was logical that Mussolini should set little store by the League of Nations. For that reason, among others, Italy was not particularly enthusiastic about the Locarno Treaty, stabilizing Germany's frontiers with France and Belgium in October 1925, even though Italy's prestige was enhanced by the fact that it, along with Great Britain, was one of the guarantors of this treaty. Its relations with France continued to fluctuate, generally not informed by cordiality, in part for ideological reasons. One source of irritation was the fact that many anti-Fascists sought a haven in France.

The replacement of Contarini by Grandi at the Italian foreign office coincided with the inauguration of a more active policy in the Balkans. Instead of promoting good relations with Yugoslavia, which the Treaty of Friendship in 1924 had initiated, Italy began to cultivate Yugoslavia's neighbors. It continued to be actively involved in Albanian affairs, especially in the upheavals that occurred in that country in 1924 and 1925. The Yugoslav response to the intensification of Italian influence in Albania was the alliance with France in 1927.

Bulgaria and Hungary also found favor in Rome, as did Romania. But this revealed an ambiguity on Italy's part, for Romania was a status quo power, allied with France, whereas Hungary was definitely a revisionist power. By way of countering French influence in central Europe, Italy was trying to assume leadership of a league of the dissatisfied states, not a very rewarding or promising position, for among themselves the malcontents commanded little power.

On the whole, Italy's activities in the Mediterranean during the 1920s amounted to little. Friendly relations with Primo de Rivera's Spain, the status of Italians in Tunisia, the problem of Tangiers, toying with intervention in the Riff rebellion, expressions of interest in the Near East which caused Turkish suspicions—none of these produced either crises or significant results. On August 28, 1928, it was a quiescent world that put its signature to the Kellogg-Briand Pact to outlaw war.

In that same year, in a speech before the Italian Senate which achieved considerable notoriety, Mussolini openly espoused the cause of revisionism. As he put it, "grave complications will be avoided if a revision of the treaties of peace, where that revision is warranted, gives a new and freer breath to peace." [4] Naturally, the speech was not well received by the status quo powers. A comparison between this statement and the one he had made six years earlier in the Chamber of Deputies on November 16,

1922, is enlightening, for it brings out the factor of continuity as well as the measure of change which had taken place in Mussolini's thought and in Fascist foreign policy in this period. On the earlier occasion Mussolini had said:

> The fundamental orientations of our policy are as follows: the peace treaties, good or bad as they may be, once they have been signed and ratified, are to be executed. A state which respects itself can have no other doctrine. But treaties are not eternal and irreparable. They are chapters in, and not epilogues to, history. To execute them means to test them. If in the course of execution their absurdity becomes manifest, it may contribute a new fact that opens up the possibility of a further examination of the respective positions.[5]

By the early 1930s the illusory stability of the late 1920s disappeared. The world depression affected the economic and political stability of all countries. As world trade declined, each country sought individual solutions to its problems. Despite the fact that the lira, partly for reasons of prestige, had been stabilized at a higher rate than the French franc (nineteen instead of twenty-five to the dollar), Italy did not follow the British example of abandoning the gold standard in 1931. The Hoover moratorium in the same year was the prelude to the virtual cancellation of German reparations, sanctioned at Lausanne in 1932. Meanwhile, the occupied Rhineland had been totally evacuated in 1930, five years ahead of schedule. But these obvious relaxations of the peace terms did not satisfy Germany. Developments in Germany after Hitler's accession to power in January 1933 resembled those in Italy after October 1922, with the qualification that the process of *Gleichschaltung* was far more rapid, thorough, and brutal. Germany left the League of Nations in 1933 and two years later denounced the disarmament provisions of the Treaty of Versailles.

The advent of Nazism to power in Germany confronted Italy with a major decision. Fascism may not have been initially an article for export, as Mussolini himself had declared, but he was undoubtedly flattered by the compliment of imitation, and Hitler's admiration of Mussolini at this time was authentic. In cruder and more realistic terms of power a major problem was raised. Could a revitalized Germany be used to further Italy's ambitions, or did it contain the threat of a more oppressive hegemony than that of France? Actually, both things happened, and in the process Italy failed to make proper use of its opportunities.

France might have been expected to have reacted vigorously to the incipient German threat to the European status quo, but for a variety of reasons, in considerable part domestic, the impact of Nazism had a divisive effect on France. The legislature in power from 1932 to 1936 presided over what can only be described as the abdication of French power. Within conditions of increasing economic difficulty and governmental instability, Louis Barthou in 1934 and then Pierre Laval in 1935 tried unsuccessfully to put new life into a policy of collective security against the German threat.

The Italian role in the shifting European balance of power is important. The disarmament discussions sponsored by the League of Nations during the 1920s had elicited only passive cooperation on the part of Italy. The full-scale disarmament conference that finally convened in 1932 produced nothing but futile discussions and proposals. At this moment, Mussolini, ever proud of his realistic approach, thought the time ripe for a different sort of initiative. This was his proposal of a four-power pact. Its conception was simple. Essentially, it revived the nineteenth-century concert of Europe. The four major European powers—Great Britain, France, Italy, and Germany (Russia was not included)—were to maintain order and peace. This they could do by undertaking "to follow such course of action as to induce, if necessary, third parties, as far as Europe is concerned, to adopt the same policy of peace" (Article 1), and by confirming "the principle of the revision of treaties" (Article 2).

The proposal for a four-power pact could remove at one stroke the German grievance of discrimination, while it insured an automatic coalition of three against undue pretensions or aggressive designs by a fourth. Clearly, it furnished opportunities for exploitation, one of its most desirable aspects in Italian eyes. In England, Ramsay MacDonald—the almost renegade Labour prime minister presiding over a National, but in effect essentially Conservative, government—also favored the proposal. More surprisingly, perhaps, the French did not at first seriously object, though clearly the new combination meant the replacement of France's dominant role in Europe by an alliance of equals. No less clearly, it further diminished the authority of the League of Nations.

There was a loud outcry from the smaller countries, particularly those in the Little Entente, and to French diplomacy fell the task, successfully accomplished, of emasculating Mussolini's proposal. The pact was signed in Rome on July 15, 1933, but even in its diluted form it never became effective. Yet, for all the justifiable criticism that could be directed against Mussolini's proposed four-power pact, the fact remains that neither the subsequent ineffectual fumblings of the French nor the even more incompetent bunglings of the British provided an adequate answer to the problem of how to preserve peace and order in Europe. Hitler, of course, had an answer, and the disintegration of the French system of alliances in central Europe began. On January 26, 1934, Poland weakened it by signing a nonaggression pact with Nazi Germany.

For Italy the problem was how to profit from a rapidly changing but still fluid situation. But in attempting to do this, it began to follow a dangerous course and to pursue a policy that contained elements of irresponsible gambling. Had Germany remained weak, Italy might have consolidated its influence in central Europe, but German power under Hitler presented a formidable obstacle to Italian ambitions in that area. Events in Austria illustrate the changing Italian position. Since the end of the war, the independence of Austria had been a cardinal tenet of Italian foreign policy. In 1931 Italy had voted with France at The Hague against the proposed Austro-German customs union. But in February 1934 the suppression of the Social Democrats by the Austrian Chancellor Engelbert Dollfuss—an action strongly urged upon him by Mussolini—removed from Austria one of the most dependable anti-Nazi elements, even while it increased Austria's dependence on Italy. The Rome Protocols, which bound both Austria and Hungary more closely to Italy, were signed on March 17, 1934.

On June 14, 1934 occurred the first meeting between Mussolini and Hitler in Italy. Two weeks later, in commenting on the Nazi's great blood purge, the Fascist press expressed nothing but contempt for the northern barbarians. When in July an attempted Nazi coup in Vienna resulted in the murder of Chancellor Dollfuss, Italy reacted immediately. It dispatched troops to the Brenner Pass, a gesture Hitler understood; but the fundamental weakness in Italian policy was that in the long run Italy alone could never match Germany's power.

We have already discussed the obstacles to Franco-Italian cooperation during the 1920s. A further setback to improved relations between the two countries resulted from Italy's part in abetting, and even arming, the Croatian terrorists who killed King Alexander of Yugoslavia and Foreign Minister Barthou of France in Marseilles on October 9, 1934. At that time a potential crisis was overcome, in part at least because of French reluctance to press matters—a decision for which Pierre Laval, who succeeded Barthou at the French foreign office, deserves credit or blame. In January 1935 Laval met Mussolini in Rome. The encounter was successful beyond expectations, and the world was informed on January 7 that all outstanding differences between France and Italy had been resolved. Austrian independence undoubtedly was an authentic point of agreement, but there is no evidence that France recognized Danubian Europe as an exclusively Italian preserve. In any case, for Italy to have aligned itself with France against Germany at this time would have weakened its bargaining position. So, for the moment, Mussolini found the answer in imperial expansion and declared himself satisfied, especially since he assumed that he had French approval for his aggression against Ethiopia.[6] This alleged approval later proved to be the source of contradictory claims by both countries. The difference lay in Laval's insistence that he had only consented to France's economic disinterest in Ethiopia, whereas the Italians contended that no such qualifications had been made by him.

In March 1935 Germany's announcement of its intention to rearm prompted France, Italy, and Great Britain to meet at a conference in Stresa a month later. By limiting their talks to the situation in Europe, the three powers succeeded in leaving Ethiopia out of the discussions. As it turned out, the Stresa front never materialized because Italy's invasion of Ethiopia in October of the same year strained relations among the three powers.

Actually, Mussolini had made up his mind in the early 1930s to return to the Crispian imperial vision and to erase the shame of the 1896 defeat of Aduwa in the process. Provoking Ethiopia, as was done at Wal Wal in 1934, was easy. In terms of realpolitik and diplomatic preparations it was sound to make sure that France would look the other way. However, Ethiopia took its case to the League of Nations. The League at this time was dominated by Great Britain and France, and both of them, mainly concerned with Europe, hoped to avoid conflict with Italy over Ethiopia. After a series of behind-the-scenes maneuvers, the French and British foreign ministers, Laval and Sir Samuel Hoare, contrived a scheme that by giving Italy large territorial concessions in Ethiopia and a privileged position in what would be left of the country would have effectively established Italian control there. The premature disclosure of their proposal in the French press led to a storm of indignation in England. As a result, the Hoare-Laval scheme of December 1935 had to be abandoned.

Meanwhile the League had tried to postpone taking a stand by recourse to investigating and mediating procedures. But when the Italians invaded Ethiopia, the League had no choice but to find Italy the aggressor and impose sanctions against it. However, the limitation of these sanctions rendered them ineffectual, and far from stopping Italian aggression, they increased the popularity of Mussolini at home. By May 1936 Italian forces entered Addis Ababa and formally proclaimed the annexation of Ethiopia; the king of Italy assumed the imperial title. On July 4 the League council voted to discontinue sanctions.

For a brief moment, with the League effectively dead and the crude politics of power once again dictating the course of diplomacy, Italy found itself in a position to exert influence on international developments out of proportion to its military capabilities. The Ethiopian War, coinciding as it did with Germany's reoccupation of the Rhineland in March 1936, had brought Italy and Germany closer together. Yet this was a dangerous development, and in February 1936 Fulvio Suvich, Italian undersecretary for foreign affairs, warned Mussolini that such a rapprochement should be limited and that the other countries should be made aware that it did not have broader significance. The problem of East Africa should not, Suvich continued, induce Italy to burn its bridges with the Western powers. But power and success are corrupters, and perhaps the temptation was too strong. Mussolini's Italy went on irresponsibly to exploit its new position in a rapidly changing Europe and must bear a large share of the responsibility for the outbreak of the Second World War.

After Italy's success in Ethiopia, Mussolini had stated that Italy had no further territorial ambitions. He might have been expected to move Italy diplomatically closer to Great Britain and France and to make the Stresa front an effective instrument in the containment of German ambitions. But the civil war in Spain presented Mussolini with the possibility of enhancing Italy's Mediterranean position at little risk or cost. Italian interest in Spanish affairs went back to 1934, when the possibility of a military coup in Spain had been discussed on March 31 between Mussolini and a group of Spanish monarchists visiting Rome. The actual rising of the Spanish generals on July 17, 1936, in Morocco does not seem to have involved Italian connivance, but Italy immediately despatched airplanes, some of which were forced to land in French North Africa. After the first week of fighting, the quick victory that the generals had hoped for failed to materialize. Republican forces rallied and what had been expected to be a rapid take-over degenerated into a three-year civil war. How to deal with it when the Western powers and the Soviet Union did not want war and Germany was not yet ready for it? The farce of nonintervention was the answer for the moment.

Behind the screen of the Nonintervention Committee sitting in London, intervention in Spain continued. It came from various quarters, but Italy made by far the heaviest contribution to the insurgents. Eventually, it sent regular army formations, still dubbed "volunteers," to Franco's assistance. By mid-1937, it has been estimated that some fifty thousand Italians were supporting the Franco forces. England meanwhile sought to isolate the Spanish conflict and to prevent it from leading to a general war. Its solution was a continued policy of nonintervention which was to lead from equivocation to hypocrisy and to humiliation.

Thus the Spanish Civil War [7] furnished Italy with further opportunities to exploit the weakness and confusion of the Western powers. British attempts to prevent an Italo-German combination failed, and Neville

Chamberlain's overtures to Mussolini from 1937 to 1939 only confirmed
Mussolini's image of a weak and vacillating England. The tacit cooperation between Italy and Germany continued and finally culminated in
the Pact of Steel, a military alliance signed on May 22, 1939. The basis
for this Italo-German cooperation had been laid in October 1936 on the
occasion of Mussolini's visit to Germany, during which the Rome-Berlin
Axis had been created. On November 6, 1937, Italy moved closer to
Germany by joining the Anti-Comintern Pact. After this it was clear
that the Anschluss between Germany and Austria was but a matter of
time. "Nazi insincerity and Fascist acquiescence and superficiality" is
the apt characterization used by the Italian diplomatic historian Mario
Toscano for this period. German power was greater than that of Italy,
and just as France after the remilitarization of the Rhineland abjectly
surrendered to inept British leadership, so Italy became, instead of an
equal partner, a prisoner of the Axis association, the leadership of which
was neither inept nor indecisive.[8]

Mussolini had burned his bridges, or perhaps thought he had. Echoing
Hitler, he mercilessly berated Czechoslovakia during the September 1938
crisis, but earned the gratitude of his own people—and of others—for
"saving" the peace at Munich. Here was a perfect application of his
four-power-pact concept, though perhaps not quite in the manner originally intended.

As German power grew, so did German disregard for Italy. However
loyal Hitler personally may have been to Mussolini, there was in Germany little respect for Italian power, and Hitler's reassurances that the
Mediterranean remained Italy's preserve had no more solidity than his
repeated public reassurances each time he removed his "last" grievance.
Shortly after the conclusion of the Pact of Steel in May 1939, Hitler
showed clearly the unimportant role he assigned to his Italian ally when
he did not see fit to consult Italy during the negotiations that culminated
in the Nazi-Soviet Pact on August 23, 1939.

When Hitler moved against Poland, Mussolini did not save the peace
as he supposedly had done at Munich, but he did elect to stay out of
the conflict, claiming nonbelligerency rather than neutrality for Italy.
But the argument of unpreparedness and the exorbitant Italian requests
for goods and equipment were not exploited with the same skill used
by Italian diplomats a quarter of a century earlier. Given the nature of
the German leadership and aims, it is doubtful that Italy could have done
so. In any case, when France collapsed in June 1940, it was not an unreasonable judgment that German victory, or perhaps some accommodation with Great Britain, would shortly be forthcoming. Precipitous
Italian entry into the war and the "stab in the back" of falling France

may have been logical steps, but were certainly not popular or honorable ones. Mussolini, however, reasoned that he must be a belligerent before the war ended and that he needed a few thousand dead to give him the right to sit at the peace table with Germany. The decision to enter the war was his own—in the face of the contrary advice of his military chiefs, who stressed the unpreparedness of the country.

This fact and the unpopularity of the war among the Italian people may account for Italy's inglorious performance. In addition, there was no steady direction of the war, Italian interest alternating between the Balkans and North Africa, with consequent failure in both areas. After some initial progress, the offensive against Egypt, launched from Libya, was repulsed. Instead of Mussolini riding into Alexandria, the British reached Benghazi, and the German Afrika Korps had to be sent to bolster sagging Italian defenses.

In the Balkans Italian and German interests clashed. On April 7, 1939, Albania had been taken over by the Italians, partly as a show of independence after the German occupation of Prague. As Germany extended its control over the Balkans, Mussolini became increasingly irritated. On September 28, 1940, he presented General Metaxas of Greece with an ultimatum. When it was rejected a few days later, Italy launched an inadequately prepared attack on Greece without prior consultation with Germany. Hitler in turn was annoyed, and the subsequent Italian failure in Greece, after the North Africa fiasco, ended any possibility for independent action by Italy. Mussolini meekly acquiesced to Hitler's hardly veiled demand in a communication of April 5, 1941, that he should henceforth take orders from him.

Thus, despite Italian claims to primacy in the Mediterranean, allied Italy, in Hitler's calculations, did not carry any more weight than defeated France or shrewdly neutral Spain. Italy had sunk to the status of Germany's number one satellite, and Hitler did not share with it his plans for the Barbarossa operation against Russia, started on June 22, 1941.

Japan's entrance into the war on December 7, 1941, had initially seemed to open new possibilities for the Axis, whose members declared war on the United States. The year 1942 witnessed the nadir of Allied fortunes, but at its end the tide began to turn at Stalingrad in Russia and El Alamein in Africa, while Anglo-American troops were landing in French North Africa. Mussolini thought that terms could and should be made with Russia, but he did not vigorously press the point in his meetings and communications with Hitler. By this time Mussolini was once again in charge of the foreign office, having removed his son-in-law Galeazzo Ciano, foreign minister since 1936, who was becoming ever more critical of the German alliance.

Following the complete defeat of the Axis in North Africa in May

1943, Sicily was invaded on June 10 and shortly overrun. Defeat in Sicily brought to a head the crisis that had been long developing in the Italian government. Anti-Mussolini sentiment at the royal court found support among dissident Fascists who were disenchanted with Mussolini's leadership. The fact that the Italian monarchy had been preserved in 1922 served a useful purpose at this point. At a meeting of the Fascist Grand Council on the night of July 24/25, 1943, a majority demanded Mussolini's resignation. The following day he was dismissed by King Victor Emmanuel III and arrested upon leaving from his interview with the monarch. The king appointed Marshal Pietro Badoglio prime minister in his place. Thus, by a stroke of the pen Mussolini's twenty-year rule ended.

But Italy could not extricate itself quite so easily from the war. While Ambassador Raffaele Guariglia was uncomfortably explaining to the Germans that Italy was still their ally, Badoglio's emissaries were awkwardly negotiating an armistice with the Allies on the basis of Italy's unconditional surrender. It was signed on September 3, 1943, at Cassibile.[9] In the ensuing confusion the Germans seized control of Italy north of Rome, and for another two years Italy was a hard-contested battleground. Mussolini was rescued by the Germans, and headed the puppet Italian Social Republic of Salò under German control.[10] On April 27, 1945, Mussolini was captured by Italian partisans while trying to escape to Switzerland. He was executed, and his body, together with that of his mistress Clara Petacci, was gruesomely displayed in Milan. In the south, after the conclusion of the armistice, the government of the king had sought to reinsert Italy in the war on the side of the Allies. It achieved the ambiguous status of co-belligerency, but its freedom to maneuver diplomatically remained understandably minimal.

At the end of the Second World War the victors, reversing the 1919 peacemaking procedure, elected to deal first with the problem of restoring peace with the secondary powers, Germany's satellites, among which Italy was included. In 1947 the task was concluded at another peace conference in Paris. Italy lost its empire. The disposition of its former colonies was eventually settled by the United Nations. Libya achieved complete independence on January 1, 1952. Eritrea, with some guarantees of autonomy, was joined to Abyssinia. Italy was given a ten-year trusteeship over its part of Somaliland, after which time it was merged with British Somaliland to form an independent state. In Europe, apart from some minuscule cessions of territory to France in the west, Italy's principal losses were its northeastern border regions peopled predominantly by Slavs. The result was a political boundary that almost coincided with ethnic lines. The one unsolved problem remained the final disposition of the city of Trieste. Like Fiume after the First World War, Trieste was

now a bone of contention between Italy and Yugoslavia. Giving Trieste—
which had become the meeting point of the rival influences of east and
west—the status of Free Territory did not prove to be a viable solution.
After much wrangling, the issue was finally settled in October 1954 by
dividing the Free Territory between Italy and Yugoslavia, Italy retaining
the city itself and Yugoslavia getting the rest.

With the passing of Fascism, Italian foreign policy returned to the
moderation that had characterized it in the past. This judgment, however,
needs some qualification. In a Europe where all the former great powers
were demoted to second rank and had or were about to lose their empires,
traditional national rivalries had become outmoded. Even the possible rewards of exploiting the balance of power seemed minimal. Such a policy
could only be effective if adopted by a united Europe capable of playing
a role commensurate with that of the two superpowers. Italy's policy reflected the general orientation of Europe as a whole.

Quite early, Italy emerged as a strong supporter of European unity.
The 1948 constitution contained the provision that "in conditions of
parity with other states" Italy would consent "to the limitations of sovereignty necessary for a system that would secure peace and justice among
nations." But the initial enthusiasm for a united Europe received many
setbacks as the postwar international situation deteriorated into a struggle between the Soviet Union and the United States. In Italy the Communists, capitalizing on their Resistance record, commanded nearly a
third of the electorate. As in France, they were evicted from the governmental coalition in May 1947. Adhering to the Soviet line, they opposed
Italian participation in the American-sponsored Marshall Plan after 1947
and were supported in this position by the Socialists. Like other recipients
of American aid, Italy benefited greatly from it. This, in combination
with its own efforts, laid the bases for the Italian economic "miracle," in
some respects even more striking than the postwar German recovery.

Sforza, who had returned to Italy from his exile shortly after Mussolini's dismissal, once again directed the foreign office. Long a convinced
Europeanist, he unsuccessfully endeavored to expand economic cooperation among the countries of Western Europe into some form of political
union. Meanwhile, in 1949, the United States proposed the military North
Atlantic Treaty Organization. There was strong opposition (not only
from Communists and their allies, but from many other Italians) to the
crystallization of military blocs. In that same year, however, Italy did
support the French effort to give substance to the power of the assembly
of the Council of Europe, a first step towards a possible future European
union. Sforza's resignation from the foreign office in June 1951, when
Prime Minister Alcide De Gasperi himself took the post, did not alter the

line of Italy's European policy. In the European Defense Community
Italy likewise perceived hope of a further contribution to integration,
and the French rejection of the proposal in 1954 dismayed Italy.

Although Italy was a staunch supporter of European integration, the
first postwar steps toward closer ties among the Western European states
did not originate with Italy. However, as Italy recovered from Fascism
and the war and regained its self-confidence, it began to show greater
initiative. Nowhere more than in Italy was there authentic enthusiasm
for the aims of such men as Jean Monnet and Robert Schuman, for whom
the Coal and Steel Community established in 1952 was but a step on the
road to political integration. In 1955 at a conference called by the Italians
at Messina, the beginnings of the more ambitious undertaking that was to
develop into the European Economic Community were outlined.

In March 1957 the Treaty of Rome gave life to the "Europe of the
Six"—Italy, France, Germany, Belgium, Luxembourg, and the Nether-
lands—and started the free flow of goods among the participants at the
beginning of 1958. The negotiations leading to it had not always been
easy, for in all the countries involved existing interests were fearful of
the impact of competition. But the judgment of those who had great expectations of its possibilities proved wholly correct. In taking advantage
of the opportunities it offered, Italian industry showed an impressive
adaptability, a large infusion of young blood at the managerial level being
a contributing factor. For Italy it meant a reorientation of its foreign
trade, and in fact, during the period from 1956 to 1968 its imports from
its partners within the European Economic Community increased more
than fivefold. Thus the tables were turned.

> In 1958 the politicians had attempted to convince the industrialists
> that economic union was needed for political reasons; in 1968, the
> industrialists were urging the politicians that political union was
> necessary for economic reasons.[11]

During these years there has been some realignment of political forces
within Italy. The close bonds between the Communist and Socialist
parties have been weakened, and the Socialists have swung over to support
a leftist-oriented cabinet led by Christian Democrats. These conditions
have given rise to a measure of uncertainty as to the future course of
Italian foreign policy, especially with respect to its position in the North
Atlantic Treaty Organization and the Western alliance. But, taking a
broad view, the Italian position has been to further European unity as
much as possible.

Thus, it is probably fair to say by way of general summation that since the Second World War Italy has adopted a foreign policy that Giuseppe Mazzini could approve, undoubtedly the most promising both for itself and for others within the wider sphere of European cooperation.

NOTES

1. On Italian foreign policy after the First World War see: René Albrecht-Carrié, *Italy at the Paris Peace Conference* (New York: Columbia University Press, 1938); Alan Cassels, *Mussolini's Early Diplomacy* (Princeton: Princeton University Press, 1970); Giampero Carocci, *La politica estera dell'impero fascista, 1925/1928* (Bari: Laterza, 1969); Ennio di Nolfo, *Mussolini e la politica estera italiana, 1919–1933* (Padova: Cedam, 1960); Mario Donosti (pseud. Mario Luciolli), *Mussolini e l'Europa: La politica estera fascista* (Rome: Leonardo, 1945); Raffaele Guariglia, *Ricordi, 1922–1946* (Naples: E.S.I., 1950); Georgio Rumi, *Alle origini della politica estera fascista* (Bari: Laterza, 1968); Gaetano Salvemini, *Mussolini diplomatico, 1922–1932* (Bari: Laterza, 1952); *idem, Preludio alla seconda guerra mondiale,* ed. A. Torre (Milan: Feltrinelli, 1967); A. Torre et al., *La politica estera italiana dal 1914 al 1943* (Turin: E.R.I., 1963); Mario Toscano, *Storia dei trattati e politica internazionale,* 2 vols. (Turin: Giappichelli, 1963); *idem,* "Gli studi di storia delle relazioni internazionali in Italia," in *La storiografia italiana negli ultimi vent'anni,* 2 vols. (Milan: Marzorati, 1970), II, 823–855. The most important single documentary source for the present discussion is the *Documenti diplomatici italiani,* the publication of which is proceeding apace. Series V to IX cover the period from August 3, 1914 to August 9, 1943. Other documentary collections, American, British, French, German, Vatican, for example, are also relevant.

2. Albrecht-Carrié, *op. cit.,* Document 42, pp. 498–500.

3. *Ibid.,* Document 43, pp. 501–504.

4. Benito Mussolini, "L'Italia nel mondo," speech delivered in the Senate on June 5, 1928, *Opera omnia,* ed. Eduardo and Duilio Susmel, 36 vols. (Florence: La Fenice, 1951–1963), XXIII, 158–197, especially p. 177.

5. Benito Mussolini, speech of November 16, 1922 in the Chamber of Deputies, *Opera omnia,* XIX 15–23, especially p. 18.

6. George W. Baer, *The Coming of the Italian-Ethiopian War* (Cambridge: Harvard University Press, 1967); Emilio de Bono, *La conquista dell'impero: La preparazione e le prime operazioni* (Rome: Istituto Nazionale Fascista di Cultura, 1937); Luigi Villari, *Storia diplomatica del conflitto italo-etiopico* (Bologna: Zanichelli, 1943).

7. Roberto Cantalupo, *Fu la Spagna: Ambasciata presso Franco, febbraio-aprile 1937* (Milan: Mondadori, 1948); Dante A. Puzzo, *Spain and*

the Great Powers, 1936–1941 (New York: Columbia University Press, 1962); Hugh Thomas, *The Spanish Civil War* (New York: Harper, 1961).

8. Dino Alfieri, *Due dittatori di fronte: Roma-Berlino, 1939–1943* (Milan: Rizzoli, 1948); Frederick W. Deakin, *The Brutal Friendship* (London: Weidenfeld & Nicolson, 1962); *Hitler e Mussolini: lettere e documenti* (Milan: Rizzoli, 1946); Massimo Magistrati, *L'Italia e Berlino, 1937–1939* (Milan: Mondadori, 1956); Mario Toscano, *Le origini del Patto d'Acciaio* (Florence: Sansoni, 1966); Elizabeth Wiskemann, *The Rome-Berlin Axis: A History of the Relations between Hitler and Mussolini* (London: Oxford University Press, 1949).

9. Mario Toscano, *Dal 25 luglio all'8 settembre: Nuove rivelazioni sugli armistizi fra l'Italia e le Nazioni Unite* (Florence: Le Monnier, 1966).

10. Filippo Anfuso, *Da Palazzo Venezia al lago di Garda*, 3rd. ed. (Bologna: Cappelli, 1957); Ivone Kirkpatrick, *Mussolini: A Study in Power* (New York: Hawthorn, 1964); B. Mussolini, *Gli ultimi discorsi* (Rome: Danesi, 1948); *idem, Storia di un anno: il tempo del bastone e della carota* (Milan: Mondadori, 1944).

11. F. Roy Willis, *Italy Chooses Europe* (New York: Oxford University Press, 1971), p. 77.

CHAPTER 16

A CLOSING COMMENTARY
PROBLEMS OF DEMOCRACY AND
THE QUEST FOR IDENTITY

ALBERTO AQUARONE

This commentary will concentrate on a few selected themes and interpretative problems of Italian history since unification. These themes and problems have generated much controversy during the past twenty-five years or so, and the way they will be presented here will itself be controversial because of the need for brevity in dealing with such a broad topic. I will have to strive for clarity by avoiding all those nuances and sophisticated qualifications which in other circumstances I would have deemed necessary; instead I will underline a few rather simple ideas. Indeed, in several instances, grains of salt aplenty will be needed to grasp without distortion my true meaning.

First let us consider the now commonplace way of looking at the history of united Italy as if the main and most significant problem were to explain why and how the new state failed to become a true and working liberal democracy and to develop its full economic and cultural potential. Inevitably this approach has often degenerated into a tendency to view the entire period before 1922 *sub specie fascismi*, that is, in the light of the single problem of the origins of Fascism. Although there is not unanimous agreement in this direction, this approach has certainly become the most widespread since the Second World War, among Italians even more than among foreign scholars. As a reaction against the narrow-mindedness and eulogistic lack of subtlety of most of the traditional historiography of the Risorgimento and the post-Risorgimento, and as a symptom of a new, more perceptive awareness of certain fundamental problems of Italian society and its development both in the past and in the present, this tendency has performed a useful and healthy function, even in those cases where it has been pushed to the borders of absurdity. But it has lost much of its effectiveness and fruitfulness once it has been allowed to crystallize in a definite, rigid frame of reference.

In my view, what is really puzzling and deserving of our main attention in the history of Italy after unification is not the whole set of deficiencies, malfunctionings, and breakdowns which beset liberal institutions and the democratic process, but rather the astonishing extent to which the latter did survive during the dramatic early years of the new kingdom and then continued to work, although clumsily and more or less curtailed in its functioning, down to the advent of Fascism. Indeed, the democratic process finally revived and went on, again clumsily, but curtailed to a far lesser degree, after more than twenty years of a tragically grotesque dictatorship that had ended in military defeat, wholesale humiliation, and widespread material destruction. I have always been inclined to find all this puzzling and even surprising, considering what the starting point was, what the economic and social potential of the country has always been, and, finally, what the historical development of other states and nations—often more advantageously placed and equipped—has been in approximately the same span of time. This is not a Panglossian view of the last hundred years of Italian history: I do not claim that throughout this period the ruling classes were without blemish, that they always acted for the better either in their intentions or in their actual achievements. Mistakes were obviously made, crimes committed, resources wasted, corruption fostered or allowed. But a mere catalog of errors and horrors would not be very meaningful historically.

What I wish to point out here is that on the morrow of unification the cards were heavily stacked against a working constitutional system based on parliamentary and liberal institutions. We all know, of course, the overall picture. Unfortunately, however, many people, looking back in disillusioned anger at all the turns that Italian history took contrary to their retrospective wishes, tend to forget how dismal this picture was, or at least to dismiss as trifles its darkest points. Italy was just emerging from a long period of political division and subjugation, of general cultural backwardness (notwithstanding the achievements of many scientists, artists, and men of letters), of moral staleness that could not be overcome by a handful of great souls acting in a void. With the exception of a very few and limited areas and sectors of production, the economy of the country was at a standstill; natural resources were lacking; mismanagement of agriculture was rampant in perhaps nine-tenths of the peninsula; technical knowledge and skills were virtually nonexistent. Among the dominant classes there was no deep-rooted tradition of self-government; in most cases there was no such tradition at all. Even in Piedmont representative government was in its infancy, and the machinery of the state was still to a considerable extent in the hands of a nobility only partly and lukewarmly reconciled to the new system. The majority of the people was either indifferent or downright hostile to unity, representative institutions, and the separation of church and state. Unity itself was not only far from being completed, but, to the extent that it had been achieved, was also threatened from the outside. These outside dangers included the military possibility of an Austrian comeback and the devious and unpredictable diplomacy of Napoleon III, who had never wanted Italy's full unification and who as late as 1863 was scheming with the Austrian government for a new settlement that would have left the peninsula divided into three states. The new kingdom was also threatened by a vociferous and influential Catholic international which was putting pressure on the various governments to intervene in the pope's support.

While these circumstances at home were compounded by what was perhaps the main source of weakness of the state born in 1861—the constantly looming threat of financial collapse—what were the foreign models available to the new and unexperienced rulers of Italy? It is well known that imitation has always played an important function in the history of political and administrative institutions. For the members of the new Italian ruling class, well aware of their own shortcomings and of the backwardness in many essential fields of their now united country, with a deep-rooted tradition to look beyond the Alps for models in the fields of politics, of law, of economics, of science and technology, the temptation to conform to what had been done or was being done in the more advanced countries of Europe was bound to be great. Yet, looking around, what could they see? On the continent the norms were plebiscitary dictatorship in France and absolutism in most other countries, aside from a few narrow constitutional regimes that for all practical purposes left the essentials of power to the monarchs and to the extremely restricted traditional ruling circles, with popular participation in public affairs either absent or effectively circumscribed. Even England, the great source of inspiration and admiration for all liberals, was more aristocratic than democratic before the second electoral reform. When the Kingdom of Italy was born, only one in seven of the adult males in Great Britain had the vote. This proportion was not strikingly different from the one existing in Italy under the electoral law implemented in 1861, especially considering the wide difference between the two countries in literacy and political maturity. As for that precious jewel of democracy, local self-government, surely it was an old and revered tradition in England, but it was far from a general rule there during the nineteenth century. Furthermore, the great municipal reform had come only one generation before Italian unification, and only in 1888 were elective county councils finally set up.

When one looks at the European political landscape of the 1860s, one cannot fail to be amazed when one realizes that Italy, this newcomer among the nation-states, weakened by centuries of backwardness and now beset by great problems, was after all one of the few countries where representative government and liberal institutions existed and were not a mere sham, every allowance being made for the many short-comings and deficiencies of their actual working. The fact that the new kingdom was born as a parliamentary regime under the leadership of men who did believe in the principle of political freedom (though not necessarily in its thorough implementation) is perhaps not so surprising, given the close relationship established during the Risorgimento between national independence and unity on the one hand and constitutional liberalism on the other. But that united Italy went through the decades of its infancy and adolescence without disowning its liberal origins is a feat that deserves, I think, some recognition.

What are the main explanations of this feat, which was far from natural or predictable? For me, they were essentially two: centralization and the lack of a wide, true participation of the majority of the people in the political process for a long time after unification.

Active participation in public affairs during the first decades of the new kingdom was restricted in two ways: by the limited suffrage and by the voluntary withdrawal from political life and responsibilities on the part of the die-hard supporters of the old regimes and, most impor-tant, of the great mass of intransigent Catholics. Under normal circum-stances, one might well have frowned upon the exclusion of these people from the levers of power; but the beginnings of united Italy did not take place under normal circumstances, and that exclusion gave the new regime just the respite it badly needed in order to survive and consoli-date itself. Of course, a price had to be paid for all this, and a pretty high price it was: not so much the disaffection of the democratic fringe of the national movement, a disaffection that was not of great conse-quence because of the limited influence of the disaffected and of their readiness, with a few exceptions, to rally around the liberal institutions of the monarchy in case of a real emergency, but rather the unavail-ability of the great reservoir of economic influence, social prestige, ad-ministrative experience, and intellectual capabilities of the intransigent Catholics in the upper and middle classes.

It has been argued that the absence of the Catholics from political life during the first decades that followed unification was one of the main sources of the weakness of the liberal state, preventing as it did, among other things, the formation and working of a healthy two-party system. Yet, it is very likely that an immediate participation of the Catholic bourgeoisie, especially if strengthened by a partly enfranchised peasan-try, would have led to the disruption, if not of unity itself, certainly of representative government and liberal institutions—in sum, of political freedom. After all, the papal *Syllabus of Errors* came just three years after the foundation of the unified Kingdom of Italy. The failure of the new regime to gain the support of such an important segment of the upper and middle classes of the country and to establish the basis of a healthy two-party system can be blamed only to a very limited degree on the liberal ruling class that had led the national movement. Instead, it must be considered primarily as one of the many significant cases in which the predominant influence of the Catholic church played a negative role in the history of Italy.

Surely, in the years immediately following unification, the liberal elite did at times express its own kind of intransigence toward the church and Catholic opinion, but this reaction was understandable and even necessary, not only as an act of self-defense against the encroachments of the Holy See and of a great part of the clergy, but also and even more so as an expression of that quest for identity which was but one aspect of the very problem of survival of the new constitutional state and of its young ruling class. It was not only a matter of building up and stabilizing political union in a country that had been divided since the fall of Rome, of reconciling regional differences in all fields of social and economic life; certainly, this task alone would have been tremendous. But Italy differed from all other European nation-states because the centuries-old special connection between Italian society and the Catholic church was bound to provoke a permanent, if only latent, crisis of identity in the most politically conscious Italians, an emotional strain that could even upset nonbelievers. This crisis of identity came to a head dramatically with unification. Given the historical impact of Catholic tradition on all aspects of Italian life, it appeared quite possible indeed that the Vatican, notwithstanding its recent period of political and even spiritual decline, might in the end dwarf the new secular state. It would have been an ironic twist of history if unification had ended up in a surreptitious triumph of the papacy, in an amazing and unforeseen sort of enlargement of temporal power, covering the whole peninsula. In order to forestall this eventuality the Italian kingdom and its ruling class had to stay aloof from the church and its hierarchy, to underline the distinction between Catholicism as a religion and the papacy as a political organization, and to demonstrate once and for all that Italy as a united nation had a moral and cultural identity of its own which could stand on an equal footing with the values of the Catholic church.

Centralization was but one of the various means through which the liberal ruling class tried to meet its own and the more general identity crisis of the nation, a crisis that was closely intertwined with unification and the process of its consolidation. Needless to say, the choice of a centralized state cannot be explained only in such terms. But all the selfish, shortsighted, and even sordid motives that led the Cavourian right to make this fateful choice have been so often listed, especially in Italy during recent years, that it would be superfluous to dwell on it further. Nevertheless, one thing needs to be said. All the debate that has raged over centralization and the causes and consequences of the lack of a true and viable system of local self-government in the new state that emerged from the Risorgimento has been vitiated, in my view, on two accounts. First, because the whole issue has been seen and discussed much too often in the light of present-day political problems and polemics rather than in the proper historical perspective. Second, because I find myself obliged to quarrel with the tendency, nowadays very widespread indeed, to see in decentralization and in local self-government stretched to its fullest possible extent a positive value in itself, something inherently good, irrespective of time and place, of particular circumstances. The so-called politics of participation, which has become such a popular catchword, and the constant longing for a "true" form of grass-roots democracy can have a meaning and a purpose in the context of our own society—for instance, as one of the most efficient means of putting up a successful fight against the authoritarian and technocratic pressures of industrial mass civilization and all its evils. But they can hardly be considered as an eternal and ubiquitous panacea. Decentralization and local self-government can assume different shapes, degrees, and consequences; they are means and not ends, and as such have a neutral political value. Everybody is familiar with all the praise that has been bestowed upon local self-government as the cradle of liberty, government by consent of the governed, *real* democracy, and so forth. Granted; but this praise could easily become debased into a dangerous myth if not accompanied by an awareness that local self-government can also mean social conformism, political oppression of minorities, free rein to religious bigotry and intolerance, racial discrimination, and cultural staleness.

Of course, it may well have been more propitious for the fate of Italian liberal democracy if—once the process of unification and of consolidation of the new state had been completed and the most immediate and threatening dangers had been pushed into the background—courageous measures aiming at implementing a wider degree of decentralization and local self-government had been taken. Why this did not happen is a question meriting investigation more than the reasons for the trend toward centralization during the *first* years that followed unity, which have been emphasized up until now. It is here, probably, that we are confronted with a political failure, with a lack of vision, of remarkable consequences and magnitude. But it is a failure that belongs to that hollow, unimaginative bumbling period of Italian history which extends more or less from the capture of Rome to the beginning of the Giolittian era, a period when the Italian ruling class and the Italian bourgeoisie in general were at their worst (with the exception of the years just preceding Fascism) and when the labor movement was in its infancy.

It has often been asserted that centralization stifled public life at the local level and sapped many burgeoning energies that were essential to the good working of the liberal state. This was sometimes true, but certainly not always. Indeed, one tends to forget that in most communes, and not only in the south, there was nothing whatsoever to be stifled because of the very lack of public life and of vital social and economic energies. Civil society, as it were, lagged panting behind the state, and in many parts of the country the few energies and initiatives available for the improvement of public life and for the solution of local problems came from or were stimulated by the central government and its representatives.

Centralization is generally associated with "Piedmontization," with Piedmontese intrusion, arrogance, and self-righteousness. If this is true, it is also true that at the beginning (and later as well) regionalism found even more supporters in Piedmont than elsewhere and that the Farini-Minghetti proposals did not fail primarily because of Piedmontese opposition. Two things must be borne in mind: on one hand, many Piedmontese—whose ties with their native lands and traditions were generally stronger or at least more manfully felt than in most other places—hated the very idea of losing their identity and of being absorbed into a huge, shapeless centralized state, where people whom they often despised would sooner or later be in positions of preeminence. On the other hand, in many of the ancient states regionalism was vigorously opposed by most segments of public opinion in the provinces and especially in the major towns because it was viewed as mainly a justification for preserving the traditional hegemony of the old, parasitic capitals.

It is generally agreed that a political and administrative system based on decentralization and local self-government might have been viable, or at least considered viable by the liberal ruling class, had it not been for the annexation of the south and the momentous problems that this posed. The social, economic, and cultural balance of the new state was utterly upset by this annexation; a new, common identity had to be found, and it was hard indeed to find. What was good for the north and for Tuscany could not be immediately good for the south. To a certain extent, the general level of public life—the forms, quality, and working of the institutions that supported it—tended to conform to the conditions of the most backward areas of the new kingdom.

Since the main issues of the debate on the Southern Question are well known, only some random observations will be given here. The northern ruling class has often been charged with having grossly neglected the south or even with having ruthlessly exploited it. Certainly, as has been repeated time and again, the northern bourgeoisie, either as a matter of interest or out of ignorance and apathy, did nothing serious to improve the social and economic conditions of the Mezzogiorno. But among other things, one tends to forget that most northern liberals had not intended unification to extend immediately to the Bourbon kingdom and that in 1860 they found themselves saddled against their will, or at least without any exertion on their part, with the south and its pressing problems. It is quite understandable that the Mezzogiorno, which was for most northerners terra incognita, should not have been among their main preoccupations and that the northern liberals hardly felt inclined to pay what seemed to them too high a price for Garibaldi's irrepressible insistence on freeing the southern provinces in 1860.

But the Southern Question leads us at once to another connected problem. It has been said repeatedly that the national-liberal Italian bourgeoisie, after having wanted and achieved the independence and unification of the country, refused to pay the full price involved and that this refusal was one of the main causes of the social and economic weakness of the new state. Here two points are in order. First, such a contention may not be completely accurate. For instance, there is no proof that during the first decades after unification Italy was really a fiscal paradise for the rich and the middle classes in general, or at least—and this is what really counts historically—that it was much more of a fiscal paradise than the other, and in many cases wealthier, European states. If it is certainly true that the tax system in Italy was so conceived and implemented as to make the poor pay proportionately more than the well-to-do, it is also without question that this was the rule of the time practically everywhere, even in more advanced countries. Fiscal justice, or something approaching it, is a quite recent phenomenon. In any case, the immediate consequence of unification was a considerable increase in the tax burden for all classes.

But even if we take for granted that the national-liberal bourgeoisie did try to avoid as much as possible being saddled with the burdens of unification, what should be our proper conclusion? The argument that such an attitude was after all understandable and human is beside the point for our purpose. The real question is: if the main cost of unification and of the setting up of the machinery of representative government had really been paid at the start by those who had wanted and established them, how many of the supporters of the new state would have been left soon thereafter? When one is creating a new system of government, a system that runs against the interests, habits, and ingrained traditions of many powerful social groups, one's policies cannot afford to curtail and disregard the interests of the very people who are supporting or would be ready to support this new system. The stronger the opposition of the traditional conservative forces, the greater must be the opportunities of benefit for the innovators. This is what Alexander Hamilton understood so well when he established the basis of his economic policy; and I think there was a touch of sound "Hamiltonianism" in the economic policy of the first generation of Italy's national-liberal ruling class. If the new state were to survive, a privileged position had to be secured for those men and social groups that had built it and were defending it against so many odds. This consideration must not blind us to the dangers implied in all this or to the many negative consequences that such a situation had upon the future development of Italian society and political institutions. I only wish to draw attention also to this aspect of the question, which is far from irrelevant.

To be sure, the national movement, led by the liberal gentry and urban middle classes, was in the first place neither an association for the improvement and welfare of the common people nor a dark conspiracy for the more efficient and ruthless exploitation of the lower classes, although the liberal leaders were far from timid in pursuing their own interests. As for the common charge that the south, with the connivance of its own big absentee landowners, was exploited as a colonial market by the north and therefore doomed to economic and social backwardness in the long run, there are some points to be made.

First, the degree of this colonial exploitation has never been measured, even approximately, and it is quite likely that it never will be. As a rule, at least for the period up to the Second World War, we lack reliable figures about the extent to which the industrial output of the north was absorbed by the southern provinces rather than by the rest of Italy or foreign markets. More accurate studies in this field may show one day that the southern market was far less essential to the Italian industrial takeoff than is commonly believed. Second, even taking for granted that the south was indeed exploited as a colonial market to a degree that was essential to the economic and, more precisely, industrial development of the north, it is far from demonstrated that this would not have been the case without unification and centralization. Informal economic imperialism, as we well know, can be much more profitable than annexation and downright colonialism. Insofar as the south did become a colonial market for northern products and an object of economic exploitation, it was probably doomed to this fate anyhow, since there is nothing in the economic, social, and political trends of the Kingdom of the Two Sicilies to indicate that it might have followed with greater success the path of economic growth and modernization if left to its own resources as an autonomous entity. We all know, of course, that there were several aspects of southern economy which did suffer immediate damage from annexation by the north. But even several of those writers who have stressed the unfair treatment meted out to the Mezzogiorno have often done so in terms conveying the impression that the real fault of the national ruling class and of the northern economic interests was less a conscious determination to exploit the south than a failure to grasp intellectually the right techniques for rapid economic development. But it is really unfair to take to task an individual, government, class, or generation belonging to the nineteenth century or even to the first decade of the twentieth for not having utilized the works of John Maynard Keynes or Paul Samuelson.

If we are to follow some major trends of contemporary economic and political thinking and in this context consider the alleged colonial exploitation of the south by northern Italy, we should be prepared to ask ourselves how much truth is in the contention of people like Paul Baran and Andre Gunder Frank that in a capitalist system economic growth depends on the exploitation by certain privileged areas (the so-called metropolises) of their underprivileged satellites in a relentless dialectic of development and underdevelopment. If this contention were correct—if it were true that in *any* viable capitalist system a metropolis-satellite relationship exists in which underdevelopment is a necessary condition for development—then obviously the problem of the Mezzogiorno vanishes, at least as it has been generally posited and studied. Better still, it ceases to be a specific Italian historical problem and becomes instead a further demonstration of the inherent contradictions of capitalism. Since Italy had no satellite in the form of colonies or of countries subjected to its economic imperialism, Italian capitalism had to produce its unavoidable quota of underdevelopment at home rather than abroad and to establish the necessary metropolis-satellite relationship between north and south. Consequently the only viable alternative would have been not a different economic policy, not a different political strategy based on different alliances, aiming at that total dissolution of the so-called feudal remnants of the southern social structure, but rather the downright rejection of capitalism and all the political, social, and economic institutions that supported it. But should we come to the conclusion that the persisting and even constantly growing imbalance between north and south was something inherent in the capitalist system, we should be prepared to draw the further inference that this imbalance was something going beyond the responsibility of the liberal ruling class and the burgeoning industrial bourgeoisie of the north, since it would be quite nonsensical to pretend that they should have moved out of the capitalist system and into a socialist one of their own free will.

But let us not be led astray. *That* liberal ruling class and *that* industrial bourgeoisie must undoubtedly bear the burden of responsibility for the shortsightedness, the incompetence, the excess of narrow-minded greed, which in so many instances were the basis of their policy toward the south and to which not a few of the evils that plagued the Mezzogiorno after unification can be related. Yet it is neither possible nor right to strike a kind of balance sheet of the profits and losses which both north and south derived from their connection in strictly economic terms only. If we look at things from a different, less unilateral, vantage point, we shall see that, all things considered, the south gained more than it lost, whereas the opposite is true for the north. Despite all its negative aspects, their union did release in the Mezzogiorno many cultural, social, political, and even economic energies that otherwise would most likely have remained stifled for a much longer time. Of course, the north did take advantage of the happy consequences of such a release, but it paid a pretty high overall price in new hardships in establishing and implementing a healthy representative form of government and a working democratic process.

At the moment of unification, northern Italy, including Tuscany and possibly Umbria and the Marches, was a fairly balanced society: although regional differences were great, there was still a sufficient degree of homogeneity in the general texture of cultural, political, and social values, traditions and modes of life. To a certain extent a fruitful network of promising contacts and exchanges had been set up—although at different levels of intensity—with the more advanced societies beyond the Alps. The general conditions of the northern half of the country pointed toward a reasonably swift and successful integration of the state with the civil society. There were certainly many great difficulties in all fields to be overcome at home, and threats from the outside had not disappeared. Yet one can say realistically that all the main premises existed for the establishment of an open, pluralistic society based on slow but steady economic progress and social responsibility coupled with individual enterprise. Political maturity was neither widespread nor without flaws, but it was probably capable of sustaining the strain of liberal institutions and responsible representative government while gradually taking firmer and deeper roots. All this balance, precarious perhaps, but real and rich in potential, was disrupted by the annexation of the south and was never recovered again. It would be quite pointless at this stage to say "Serves them right!" Nor does it help to berate the allegedly inherent incapacity of the people of the south for self-government under the rule of law. Even so, it would be difficult to deny some specific traits of their character which have hampered their adaptation to a modern industrial society based on working representative institutions—particularly that social frame of reference which Edward Banfield has called "amoral familism." It would simply be futile to pretend that the annexation of the south, at that particular time and in that particular way, with the consequent deep, fundamental heterogeneity it imposed upon the new state, was not one of the chief sources of the basic weakness of the democratic process in Italy thereafter. Without looking for a single scapegoat, we must try to detect the main historical forces at work, disregarding the usual charges of self-righteousness, smugness, or even of racial bias.

Another source of the weakness of Italian democracy should be traced back to the general failure of the Italian intellectual as a political man. Insofar as any political movement, whatever its social and economic roots, can be constructive in the long run only to the degree to which it finds and expresses an adequate intellectual leadership, there can be little doubt that the backwardness and lack of breadth of the whole of Italian intellectual life aggravated considerably the constant predicament of the democratic process in Italy. It would be quite meaningless at this point to list all the possible exceptions. As Francesco De Sanctis put it in his essay "La coltura politica": "A country is not cultivated (*colto*) just because there are many cultivated individuals. What is necessary is the propagation of culture among all strata, or at least among the upper strata of society. For politics to be possible there must be a political class with a deep faith in certain ideas and willing to support them manfully and to spread them. Without such a basis, politics operates in a void, remains without echo, and rots at once" (from *Scritti politici di Francesco De Sanctis raccolti da Giuseppe Ferrarelli* [Naples, 1890], p. 73).

In very general terms, Italian intellectuals failed in their role of national leadership mainly because they lacked moral and political passion, because they did not view politics as a part of their intellectual pursuits, because as a whole they did not believe in intellect as a means of participation in the political process. All this was just one aspect of a broader characteristic of the typical Italian intellectual which has been often emphasized: a kind of gap between him and reality, his inability to grasp the real terms of an objective situation and then to adjust his ideological program and his action to them. Far too often the Italian intellectual, floating in a void, drifts between trivial opportunism and stale utopia, without being able to cast anchor on cultural programs and achievements belonging also to the realm of concrete politics. All this has been particularly true of that crucial period between the conquest of Rome and the political crisis at the turn of the century, when once the basis of survival for the new state had been secured, mainly under the spur of circumstances, it was of essential importance to start looking at the problems of the country not in terms of sheer survival, but of the quality of that existence, giving free rein to political imagination. It was roughly during the lifespan of those two generations that one of the chief weaknesses of modern Italy as a democratic society became apparent: the incapacity to reach stability within the framework of a constantly creative political process. Instead, instability and immobilism became the two dialectical poles of Italian politics; in a sense they always remained so, though set against different backgrounds.

This instability and immobilism were also the source and the expression of a weak bourgeoisie. This timid and vacillating ruling class viewed political power chiefly as a means of coercion used by the government for ad hoc day-to-day purposes dictated by narrowly interpreted class interests rather than as the impersonal authority of the state which would be not only the source of law and order but also of social and economic change within a stable framework. It was a weak and apprehensive bourgeoisie. Fearful of the emergence of reactionary trends and trying to check what it considered exceedingly illiberal methods of government, the best way it saw to tackle and solve the problem was by weakening of the executive. A healthier approach would have been to counterbalance the latter through new or strengthened sources of power, tapped from the very texture of civil society.

When a political leader showed the unusual trait of having a clear and not too absurd idea of the ends to pursue and of the means of accomplishing them—a vision of politics that was neither sheer opportunism nor a theatrical quest for the total regeneration of the country—the intellectuals, as a rule, turned their backs on him. Giolitti's "New Deal" thus lacked those qualities of moral tension, of cultural and political adventure, of conquest of a new identity for the nation, which were in part at least to characterize Roosevelt's New Deal. Instead, it got stranded in the marshes of bureaucratic routine and parliamentary vacuity. (There were of course other reasons for the dark sides of the Giolittian system.)

This reference to the New Deal has been made not only because of the many general parallels that one can draw between the historical significance of those two periods of Italian and American history but also because of some peculiar similarities between the political strategies of Giolitti and Roosevelt and because of the analogies that one can detect in the main weak points of those two experiences. Notwithstanding the radical differences in the historical setting, we find in both cases a rational attempt to create a system based on a creative confrontation between big business and big labor, with big government as a broker. Although neither system worked smoothly, to the extent that they worked at all each one helped to solve with remarkable success some of the more pressing problems that the two countries had to deal with at the moment. And in both cases the primary aim and the final result of the policy adopted was more to reinforce the existing organized pressure groups than to extend to the most unprivileged sections of society the benefits of political and economic democracy. Even in this last respect, however, the progress made should not be underestimated.

One of the fiercest critics of the Giolittian system was the historian-publicist Gaetano Salvemini. In his later years, after having witnessed all the evils of the Fascist experience, his judgment of Giolitti and his policies mellowed. Yet, as A. William Salomone has noted in his book *Italian Democracy in the Making*, Salvemini insisted to the very end that to whatever extent economic, political, and moral democratization for the period before the First World War had been achieved, it had come from below, not from above, against Italy's ruling political class and not by it or through its leadership. By means of resistance against "reactionary policies," through immense sacrifices, and collective determination the Italian working-class movement, organized or not, succeeded in "bending" Giolitti to the liberal cause. Frankly, it is difficult to see much more that one could have asked from Giolitti in the particular circumstances of the Italy of his day. To have allowed reactionary policies to be thwarted from below, to have at least adjusted his aims and strategy along some of the lines indicated by the working-class representatives, to have established conditions under which for the first time in Italian history the nation's politics and economics were not shaped exclusively according to the wishes and interests of the upper and middle classes—all this was not a small contribution to liberal democracy, even making allowance for all the well-known shortcomings of what has been called, as a derogatory term, *Giolittismo*. And insofar as the more progressive aspects of Italian public life during the Giolittian era owed more to pressure from below than to action from above, this might well be considered an asset rather than a liability for the implementation of a democratic system. There is a strange notion, more or less explicitly at work among several historians, that the chief historical role of the privileged classes or groups is, and ought to be, the meek surrender of their privileges at the first opportunity. But neither history nor the democratic process in a free society works in this way. Democracy in a free society does not entail the elimination of conflict between opposed interests but rather the containment of this conflict within the bounds of a sane and bloodless competition that is never allowed to degenerate into the forceful oppression of the weakest. Surely there was still much economic and social oppression in Giolitti's Italy, but there was less of it than at any other time before or than in several other countries at the same level of economic development; more important, the objective possibilities for oppression were diminishing.

One of the main forces at work against the Giolittian system was nationalism, which emerged more and more from its primarily cultural and emotional frame of reference into an organized political movement with a precise economic and social program. Customarily, discussions of Italian nationalism before the First World War tend to underline either its cultural poverty, the superficial and often grotesque equality of all its rhetorical paraphernalia, its plainly reactionary character, and its obvious links with some of the biggest monopolistic interests of the country, or all these aspects. Indeed, nationalism can be understood only as an ideological process springing from both culture and material interest, the one stimulating the other and vice versa. It would be a mistake, however, to identify that material interest exclusively with some particular economic group and to deny or dismiss as irrelevant the fact that at the basis of the nationalist ideology there was *also* the historical predicament of Italy's struggle for economic growth and social modernization against real and grave obstacles. In view of the undeniable structural weaknesses of the Italian economy and Italian capitalism, there might be something to Enrico Corradini's argument that just because of Italy's industrial backwardness, a policy of mere economic expansion was doomed to failure and that only a type of colonial imperialism based on military conquest could have solved the country's economic problems. On the one hand, it seemed clear that Italian industry was unable and would be unable for a long time to compete on equal terms with that of the far more advanced countries. On the other hand, historical examples were not lacking to show that a major military effort could itself be one of the best ways to foster industrial and technological development. (Of course, Italy was also unable to compete with the great powers in the military field, but such basic weakness could in part at least be overcome through shrewd diplomacy.)

We should also remember that Italian nationalism in its more aggressive and plainly imperialistic aspects was to a remarkable degree an imitation of the kind of imperialism that had been thriving everywhere since the last decades of the nineteenth century and whose best fruits had already been picked by practically all the major world powers. It is of course easy to smile rather contemptuously at the itch for grandeur besetting a country as poor and weak as Italy, a feeling on which the nationalists were to bank with amazing results even among people who were poles apart from them on domestic issues. But it would have been difficult for Italians to accept willingly the role of a minor power in keeping with their effective strength, not only because acceptance and success in the club of the great powers was an essential element of that quest for identity which continued to be one of the guiding, if unspoken, forces of Italian national life after unification, but also because Italians were bound to be prisoners of their past. Even leaving aside the myth of Rome (which in its more extreme forms was the monopoly of some exalted and restricted minorities only), the inescapable facts were that Italians had played too vital a role in the history of Europe since the twelfth-century renaissance, with its great communal blossoming, and that Italian art, culture, and science had had too great an influence in molding European civilization to allow even the more sober and realistic members of the intelligentsia and the bourgeoisie to easily reconcile themselves to a policy of retrenchment and petty bargains right in the middle of the great power struggles of the age of imperialism. The impossibility of recreating the old glories compounded the frustrations of the present, and the new frustrations were additional fuel for nationalism in its basest forms.

But that was not all. One can recognize the rather low quality of the cultural background of the nationalists, the intellectual shortcomings of most of them as individuals, the triviality of the material interests that were often at the root of their ideology. Yet the fact remains that the nationalists were, in a certain sense, the most modern among Italian politicians, the ones who, despite their superficial, fumbling, and vociferous manner, were more in touch with the main historical trends in the world around them. It was certainly unfortunate that among all the political forces the nationalists often seemed to be the most sensitive to the great pressing problems posed by industrialization, by the monopolistic tendencies of finance capital, by the new type of class relations that was developing in an industrial society, by the emergence of mass democracy, by worldwide power politics and economic imperialism. Or, if the nationalists were not the most sensitive to these new trends, they surely proved to be the ablest in adjusting their ideology and their political action to them. One cannot explain convincingly the great influence of the Italian nationalists—an influence far out of proportion to their number, intellectual level, electoral following, or political tradition and prestige—unless one agrees that it was to a considerable extent through them that the country, for good or evil, was uprooted from the obsolete (though well-sheltered) world of the Risorgimento and ushered into the tempestuous ocean of contemporary reality.

As for the alleged futility of the nationalist program, aiming at solving the nation's domestic problems through imperialist expansion, more than the usual caution may be needed on this point. It is one thing to note that in the specific conditions of Italian and world politics at the time the premises for the successful implementation of such a program were lacking and that in any case the nationalists themselves failed to give the necessary leadership, both on the theoretical and practical levels; it is quite another thing to deny outright that there could be some basis of truth in their argument. The Italian Marxist historian Renato Zangheri has recently remarked that the primary accumulation of capital—an indispensable prerequisite of industrial takeoff—is bound to create and foster internal imbalances; the less feasible it is to tap the needed capital from international trade and/or colonial exploitation, the greater the internal imbalances will be. In other words, the delay in Italy's industrial takeoff, coupled with the original gap between north and south, led inescapably to the need to saddle the most backward regions of the country with the burden of the economic cost of the takeoff, a burden that in other cases was paid by subjected or colonial countries. We can accept such an assumption or not, but we cannot dismiss it too easily as absurd or irrelevant. Taking it into account, we find that the argument of the nationalists in favor of colonialism and in general of an active imperialist policy aiming at overseas expansion loses some of that quality often attributed to it of silly megalomania, of bombastic literary exercise woven by frustrated second-rate intellectuals. We can question the soundness of their argument, the nature of the means they advocated, the loftiness of their basic, true motives; but the problem itself was real and not insignificant.

The connection between the imperialist brand of Italian nationalism and the problem of the imbalance between north and south (the connection, as opposed to an explanation of Italian imperialism merely in terms of the Southern Question) is reinforced by the fact that in both pre-Fascist and Fascist imperialism we can detect a pretty strong and persistent rural, antiindustrial tone. In many quarters colonial expansion was seen as a revenge of country over city, of the peasant world against the urban-industrial one. It was seen as a means of sidetracking the problem of the diminishing social, economic, and political importance of the land in a growing industrial economy. Instead of dealing with agricultural inefficiency and the demographic exuberance of the countryside by means of further modernization and by thrusting the available rural manpower into the urban industrial areas, the colonial expansionists sought to channel this manpower into imperialist adventures. In this sense, imperialism was a last attempt to prolong the hegemony of land over factory, of the landowner over the businessman and the manufacturer. The fact that in practice it was industrial capital and not the traditional forms of landed wealth which harvested the tastier fruits of imperialist policy simply indicated that the growth of the former was irreversible and that its dominant influence was bound to become irremovable and to provide the permanent guidelines for the development of modern Italian society.

The position of Italy as a latecomer on the stage of world politics and its deep-rooted economic weakness of which its endemic shortage of capital was but one facet—greatly limited its chances to embark successfully on a full-fledged policy of colonial imperialism. Insofar as this was true, the organized nationalist movement could not fail to become more and more reactionary at home; it was in effect the kernel of a preventive counterrevolution willed by a fragile bourgeoisie in order to stem the tide of a rising and ever more demanding working class. This class was organized by powerful labor unions and increasingly gave allegiance to a Socialist party that was seen by the majority of a timid, shortsighted middle class preoccupied with petty greed as a fearful menace to be suppressed at all costs, rather than as an appropriate agency for channeling those newly emerging forces into the existing framework of liberal institutions.

In the rise of Fascism, however, there was more than this streak of preventive bourgeois counterrevolution. So far, the widespread tendency to see Fascism as something built in, as it were, to the very process of development of the liberal state born from unification has not amounted to much more than the rather banal recognition that all the present is somehow built into all the past. The main flaw in such an interpretation stems from a rather common feature of modern historiography: the search for historical explanations too much in terms of the past at the expense of the present. This search magnifies the importance of the vertical, diachronic processes and minimizes the influence of the horizontal, synchronic ones. In trying to probe to the roots of events, to the *real* and deep reasons for what happened, historians too often tend to disregard the impact of short-range, casual and at times almost trivial factors, of individual decisions and actions; they fail, in other words, to relate in a meaningful pattern the pressure of history from below to the pressure of politics from aside, the solidified past to the ebullient present. The rise of Fascism, for instance, was related to some of the well-known deficiencies of the liberal state that emerged from centuries of decay and backwardness in Italy to no greater extent than to the Bolshevik Revolution and the intricacies of the new political and socioeconomic problems that grew directly out of the First World War. The forces at work in the origins and advent of Fascism were many and various, and by now they have been studied fairly thoroughly, with different degrees of emphasis in the search of the main causes, by historians of all cultural and political persuasions. Here only a few that are generally perhaps too much overlooked will be mentioned.

During the immediate postwar years some leaders of the traditional liberal ruling class were attracted to the Fascist movement by the belief that it could provide a convenient instrument for bridging that gulf between themselves and the masses which in the past they had been unable, or simply unwilling, to eliminate. Under the converging pressure of the two powerful, newly organized political movements that were challenging the whole set of narrow power bases that had dominated, though precariously enough, the public life of the country in the post-

Risorgimento era, the old liberal ruling class saw in the rise of Fascism the only means to accept the challenge and fight both Socialists and Catholics on their own ground—the one that was the chief source of their menacing strength and impact—the mobilization of the masses. The result was typical of the situation in which a declining ruling class resolves to make use of hirelings to try and preserve its shaky power: the hirelings take over. In this instance the take-over was not complete, nor did it stem from or result in a complete breach between the two groups. Instead, a fairly successful though in no way smooth process of fusion ensued, a process in which the traditional ruling class managed more and more to regain the upper hand, albeit in a far different political setting.

The relative ease with which Fascism came to power was due, among other things, to the fact that very few people—Fascists, anti-Fascists, and noncommitted alike—had any clear idea of what Fascism was or what it was really up to in the long run. Another factor that greatly helped Mussolini to make the utmost of the general situation and of the many mistakes of his opponents was that underlying theme of all Italian history since unification: the quest for identity through some kind of dimly conceived and childishly pursued process of total regeneration of the country. Even many of those Italians who saw in Fascism—in its methods and in the values it stood for more or less vaguely—just the opposite of the sort of regeneration they sought were inclined to consider the supposedly temporary victory of that movement as a step forward along the right path, as a useful and perhaps necessary means (though hardly the best one) of sweeping aside for good all the rot, the meanness, the inefficiency, the petty materialism, and the generally oppressive character of prewar Italy as they saw it. Some comments along this line of reasoning of men like Salvemini after the March on Rome are very significant and revealing in this sense; and he was not alone among Italy's intellectual elite in his views.

The old liberal ruling class had not been mistaken when in 1921 and 1922 it had seen in the rising Fascist movement a great potential for mass mobilization and manipulation. Unfortunately, one cannot fail to recognize that the traditional gulf between the masses and the state, which had characterized Italian history since unification, was partially bridged during the Fascist era. If it is true that the only significant opposition to the dictatorship in those dark years came mainly from the more conscious and responsible segments of the working class as well as from certain groups of bourgeois intellectuals—especially of the younger generation—it is also true that it was under Fascism that the bulk of the masses began to identify, although dimly and waveringly, with the national state. It is difficult to gauge the degree to which this change was due to the charismatic figure of the Duce, the bombastic plebeian, to the shrewd and consistent use of propaganda through those modern mass media that had not been available to the old ruling class of the post-Risorgimento, to some highly advertised and at times even effective policies of social welfare, to a foreign policy of power and prestige with the many forms of vicarious satisfaction it offered to large sections of the underprivileged, or to a certain sense of belonging—without the burdens of personal responsibilities—which a one-party regime could at times induce. All these factors helped create a situation in which for the first time the majority of the Italian people did not feel completely alien to the national state.

The fact that the partial integration of the Italian people into the national state occurred under the very regime that led the country into total political, military, and moral bankruptcy makes it particularly significant and even astonishing that the nation emerged from that bankruptcy as a liberal democracy and that this liberal democracy survived through all the dramatic strains of reconstruction and the painful transformation of the nation's economy and society by industrial and technological modernization.

Of course, the events of the Second World War and the nature of the postwar European settlement, both of which led Italy into the Anglo-American sphere of influence, had something to do with all this. One may also wonder whether the fall of Mussolini would have been a sufficient condition in itself for the establishment and maintenance of a democratic system in Italy if that fall had not been followed by the German invasion and occupation, with their disastrous effects on the daily lives of about two-thirds of the population. Without the Armed Resistance that sprang directly from the shock of Nazi occupation and brutality, much of the old edifice would probably have remained intact—much more, at least, than actually survived.

For many people, now as in the postwar years, the Armed Resistance is another case, like the Risorgimento, of a revolution that failed: Italy was not morally and spiritually regenerated, and the political setting and the social structure of the country were not transformed root and branch. But the Resistance did not fail as a social revolution for the simple reason that from the beginning it was not primarily a social revolutionary movement; it was always much more of a national movement of liberation. It was in the first place a struggle against the invader, not a struggle against bourgeois society or capitalism. Of course, social aims were far from absent; for some people they even took precedence over any other consideration, but as a whole, they were mainly an outgrowth of a national movement that was in its essence a fight against foreign oppression. This was the reason for the basic unity that was reached during the period of the Resistance, unity not in the sense of unanimity (the Resistance after all also involved a tragic civil war) but in the sense that the struggle was characterized by the active participation of all classes, of all segments of the nation. Furthermore, Italians did what they had never done before—not even during the Risorgimento: they fought with rage, the rage that creates a common bond leading to deep, meaningful, and at times even lasting, political and social solidarities.

Despite the limitations of the Resistance movement, its disruptive social potential was sufficient to put Italian politics in the postwar period on an entirely new basis and to pave the way for quite significant socio-economic transformations within a democratic political framework. To be sure, this democratic framework was not sustained by the unqualified allegiance of the bulk of Italian public opinion but rather by the persistent stalemate between the two main political forces in the country, neither of which had a flawless pedigree in matters of freedom and democracy: Communists and Catholics. Over the years this apparently shaky foundation proved to be more solid than it might have seemed at the beginning, thanks also to a characteristic trait of most Italian politicians: their capacity to play with perfect ease and with unbecoming (though in this case blessed) alacrity a role in which they do not believe.

Looking back to the last twenty-five years or so of their national experience, Italians can take some pride in having built and preserved—starting from scratch, and making their way through a jungle of deep-rooted inefficiency and corruption—what is nowadays one of the rare examples of a humane and decent liberal democracy. Surely, economic and social inequalities are often jarring even now, and many areas of the country still lag behind in conditions of great backwardness; but this is probably the price that had to be paid for a kind of economic growth pursued without forsaking representative government and individual freedom.

Although such pride would be largely justified, there is little room for complacency; the system is far from vigorous, and prospects for the future are not too bright. In my view, there is one chief reason for qualified pessimism: the connection between the interests and the aspirations of the working class on one hand and the struggle for freedom and democracy on the other—a connection that had been a most significant feature of Italian history under Fascism, and to a certain extent even before Fascism—has ceased to exist. Although today's workers can be militantly disruptive in fighting for economic and social advantages, these advantages are not necessarily linked with the preservation of political freedom. Even the gradual withering away of the old traditional forms of working-class subculture, a process that at first sight would be welcomed as a further step in the direction of national unity and stability, is loaded with a dangerous potential. The proletariat is becoming increasingly integrated into the bourgeois system, tending to ape more and more uncritically the modes of life of the middle class and to absorb from the latter its present widespread contempt or indifference for the loftier cultural and political values. This trend is the more worrisome in view of the traditional ineptitude of the Italian intellectuals to give adequate moral leadership to the country. And gloomy indeed will be the day when the proletarian and the bourgeois visions of the world will have blended into a single, shapeless, plebeian conformism.

CONTRIBUTORS

René Albrecht-Carrié is Professor Emeritus of History at Barnard College and the School of International Affairs of Columbia University. His publications include *Italy at the Paris Peace Conference* (1938), awarded the George Louis Beer Prize of the American Historical Association, *Italy from Napoleon to Mussolini* (1950), *A Diplomatic History of Europe since the Congress of Vienna* (1958), *France, Europe and the Two World Wars* (1960), *The Meaning of the First World War* (1965), *Britain and France* (1970), and numerous articles. He has received a Rockefeller Grant, and has been Fulbright Lecturer in Italy and a Guggenheim Fellow. He is currently working on an interpretation of international relations in the twentieth century.

Alberto Aquarone is Professor of History at the University of Pisa. He has also been visiting fellow at All Souls College, Oxford University, and visiting lecturer at several American universities. His publications include *L'organizzazione dello Stato totalitario* (1965), *Alla ricerca dell'Italia liberale* (1972), *Le origini dell'imperialismo americano* (1973), and numerous articles.

William C. Askew is Professor of History at Colgate University. He has also taught at the University of Arkansas, the University of Texas, the University of Kentucky, and Duke University. He is the author of *Europe and Italy's Acquisition of Libya, 1911–1912* (1942), coeditor and contributor to *Power, Public Opinion and Diplomacy* (1959), and author of several scholarly articles. His research in Rome, Vienna, and London has been supported by a John Simon Guggenheim Memorial Fellowship and an extended Fulbright grant.

Elisa Carrillo is Professor of History at Marymount College, Tarrytown, New York. She is the author of *Alcide De Gasperi: The Long Apprenticeship* (1965) and has contributed articles on various aspects of Italian and Mediterranean history to scholarly journals. She has served as President of The New York State Association of European Historians, Chairperson of the Columbia University Seminar on Modern Italy, and member of the Advisory Council of the Society for Italian Historical Studies.

Jon S. Cohen is Associate Professor of Economics at the University of Toronto. He has also taught at Yale University. He has published articles in various scholarly journals and edited collections on the economic history of Italy.

Raymond Grew is Professor of History and has been Director of the Center for Western European Studies at the University of Michigan. He has also taught at Brandeis and Princeton Universities. He is the author of *A Sterner Plan for Italian Unity: The Italian National Society in the Risorgimento* (1963), which was awarded the Unità d'Italia Prize of the Italian Government. He has also received the Society for Italian Historical Studies Prize and the Chester Higby Prize of the American Historical Association, and has been a Fulbright and Guggenheim Fellow. He has held a number of positions in the Society for Italian Historical Studies, the Society for French Historical Studies, the American Historical Association, and the Council for European Studies. Currently Director of the Sarah Lawrence–University of Michigan Summer Program in Florence, he also serves on the editorial board of *Comparative Studies in Society and History* and as Secretary of the Modern European Section of the American Historical Association.

Norman Kogan is Professor of Political Science and Director of the Center for Italian Studies at The University of Connecticut. Among his publications are *Italy and the Allies* (1956), *The Politics of Italian Foreign Policy* (1963), *A Political History of Postwar Italy* (1966)—all three of which have been translated into Italian—*The Government of Italy* (1962), and numerous articles. His research has been supported by several Social Science Research Council grants and a fellowship from the Italian Foreign Office. He has been Fulbright Research Professor in Italy and is a Knight in the Order of Merit, Republic of Italy. Currently Executive Secretary-Treasurer of the Society for Italian Historical Studies, he is also on the board of editors of *Comparative Politics* and on the board of directors of the America-Italy Society.

Denis Mack Smith is Senior Research Fellow and Dean of Visiting Fellows at All Souls College, Oxford University. He has also been University

Lecturer at Cambridge University. His publications include *Cavour and Garibaldi* (1954), *British Interests in the Mediterranean and Middle East* (1958), *Italy: A Modern History* (1959, 1969), *Medieval Sicily* (1968), *Modern Sicily* (1968), and *Victor Emmanuel, Cavour and the Risorgimento* (1971), and he has edited *The Making of Modern Italy* (1968), *Garibaldi* (1969), and E. Quinet, *Le Rivoluzioni d'Italia* (1970). He is also joint editor of *A History of England* (Nelson, 1960) and a regular contributor to the *Corriere della Sera*.

Leonard W. Moss is Professor of Anthropology, Wayne State University. Since 1970, he has been Professor of Italian Ethnography in the Trinity College/Rome Campus Summer Program. His field work in Italy has been sponsored by the Fulbright-Hays Program, American Council of Learned Societies, and the Wenner-Gren Foundation. He was a founding member of the Italian Center for Cultural Anthropology (Università di Roma and Museo Nazionale delle Tradizione e Arti Popolari). He has served on the executive board of the American Italian Historical Association and was granted a Knighthood in the Order of Merit, Republic of Italy. Although his primary concentration has been on contemporary peasantry, he has also worked in pre-Roman archaeology.

Emiliana P. Noether is Professor of History and Associate of the Center for Italian Studies at The University of Connecticut. She has also taught at New York University, Rutgers University, Regis College, and Simmons College and has been Research Associate at the Center for International Studies, Massachusetts Institute of Technology. She has been a Senior Fulbright Scholar in Italy, a Fellow of the Radcliffe Institute and the American Association of University Women, and received a research grant from the American Philosophical Society. Under a grant from the National Endowment for the Humanities, she was coproducer of the film *Man in the Renaissance*. She has contributed numerous articles to scholarly journals and is the author of *Seeds of Italian Nationalism, 1700–1815* (1951), and of a forthcoming biography of Victor Emmanuel II. She has been Chairperson of the Columbia University Seminar on Modern Italy, and since 1958 has been Italian Section Editor of the *American Historical Review*.

Nunzio Pernicone is an Assistant Professor of History at Columbia University. He was a Fulbright Fellow in Italy from 1967 to 1969. He is presently completing a book on the Italian anarchist movement.

Rosario Romeo holds the Chair in Modern History at the University of Rome. He has also taught at the University of Messina, been Editor of the Istituto of the Enciclopedia Treccani and Secretary of the Istituto italiano di studi storici. His publications include *Il Risorgimento in Sicilia* (1950), *Le scoperte americane del Cinquecento* (1954), *Risorgimento e capitalismo* (1959), *Breve storia della grande industria in Italia* (1961), *Dal Piemonte sabaudo all'Italia liberale* (1963), *Cavour e il suo tempo*, vol. I (1969), and numerous articles and monographs.

Salvatore Saladino is Professor of History at Queens College, CUNY. He is the author of *Italy from Unification to 1919* (1970), co-author with Shepard B. Clough of *A History of Modern Italy* (1968), and contributor to *The European Right, a Historical Profile*, Hans Rogger and Eugen Weber, eds. (1965). In 1949 he received a Fulbright Award for research in Italy, where he returned in 1956 on a Fulbright Teaching Award.

A. William Salomone is Wilson Professor of History at the University of Rochester. He has also taught at Haverford College, the University of Pennsylvania, New York University and Columbia University. His publications include *Italian Democracy in the Making* (1945), *L'Età giolittiana* (1949), *Italy in the Giolittian Era* (1960), *Italy from Risorgimento to Fascism* (1970), and numerous articles and monographs. He has served as President of the Society for Italian Historical Studies, member of the editorial board of *The Journal of Modern History*, member and consultant of Fulbright and Italian Government Fellowship Committees, and President of the Association of European Historians. He has received the Adams Prize of the American Historical Association, the Award of Merit of the Italian Republic, Citation for Distinguished Achievement from the Society for Italian Historical Studies, and fellowships from the Guggenheim Foundation and the National Foundation on the Arts and the Humanities.

Roland Sarti is Associate Professor of History at the University of Massachusetts in Amherst. He has also taught at Ohio State University and has held a Fulbright Fellowship to Italy. His publications include *Fascism and the Industrial Leadership in Italy, 1919–1940* (1971), several articles in scholarly journals, and a forthcoming anthology, *The Ax Within: Italian Fascism in Action*. He has served as Chairman of the Columbia University Seminar on Modern Italy.

Edward R. Tannenbaum is Professor of History at New York University. He has also taught at Colorado State University and Rutgers University. His publications include *The New France* (1961), *The Action Française* (1962), *European Civilization since the Middle Ages* (1965, 1972), *The Fascist Experience: Italian Society and Culture, 1922–1945* (1972), *A*

History of World Civilizations (1973), and numerous articles on French and Italian history. He has received research grants from the Ford Foundation and the American Philosophical Society and has held posts in the Society for French Historical Studies and the Society for Italian Historical Studies. He is currently writing a book on European society and culture in the period 1890 to 1914.

INDEX

EDWARD R. TANNENBAUM is Professor of History at New York University. He has a Ph.D. Degree from the University of Chicago and has studied at the Universities of Wisconsin and Paris. Among his many publications are four books: THE NEW FRANCE (1961), THE ACTION FRANCAIS (1962), EUROPEAN CIVILIZATION (1965, 1971), and THE FASCIST EXPERIENCE: ITALIAN SOCIETY AND CULTURE, 1922–1945 (1972).

EMILIANA P. NOETHER, who is Professor of History at the University of Connecticut, is a graduate (Ph.D.) from Columbia University. She specializes in Italian History and European Intellectual History, has written extensively for numerous journals on these subjects, and is the author of SEEDS OF ITALIAN NATIONALISM, 1700–1815 (2nd edition, 1969).